REINVENTING THE ENEMY'S LANGUAGE

CONTEMPORARY NATIVE

WOMEN'S WRITINGS OF NORTH AMERICA

Also by Joy Harjo

The Last Song (chapbook)

What Moon Drove Me to This?

She Had Some Horses

Secrets from the Center of the World

In Mad Love and War

Fishing (chapbook)

A Map to the Next World

Reinventing the Enemy's Language

CONTEMPORARY NATIVE WOMEN'S WRITINGS OF NORTH AMERICA

EDITED BY

Joy Harjo and Gloria Bird

WITH

Patricia Blanco, Beth Cuthand, and Valerie Martínez

W. W. NORTON & COMPANY ▪ NEW YORK ▪ LONDON

The text of this book is composed in Minion with the display set in Birch.
Composition by PennSet, Inc.
Manufacturing by Quebecor Printing, Fairfield.
Book design by BTD/Robin Bentz.

LIBRARY OF CONGRESS CATALOGING-IN-PUBLICATION DATA
Reinventing the enemy's language : contemporary native women's writings
    of North America / edited by Joy Harjo . . . [et al.].
        p.   cm.
    Includes index.
    ISBN 0-393-04029-1
    1. American literature—Indian authors.   2. Indian women—Literary
collections.   3. American literature—Women authors.   4. American
literature—20th century.   5. Indians—Literary collections.
    I. Harjo, Joy.
    PS508.I5R38   1997
    810.8'09287'08997—dc20   96-36547
                                                              CIP

ISBN 0-393-31828-1   pbk.

W. W. Norton & Company, Inc.
500 Fifth Avenue, New York, N.Y. 10110
www.wwnorton.com

W. W. Norton & Company Ltd.
Castle House, 75/76 Wells Street, London W1T 3QT

                    8   9   0

Acknowledgments

This project could not have been accomplished without the support and hard work of so many who shared our vision and generously helped. We especially wish to acknowledge the grant we received from the Columbus Quincentenary Program funded by the Office of the Vice President for Research at the University of Arizona. This grant gave us funds and moral support to initiate the first phase of the anthology. We also wish to thank the Sun Tracks series at the University of Arizona Press, especially Larry Evers and Ofelia Zepeda, who gave their wholehearted support from the genesis of the project to the conclusion.

We could not be here to speak without the gift of our mothers' and grandmothers' dreams, hopes, tears, and laughter. We honor Marie Grant, Alice Abrahamson, Louise She-she-tay, Wynema Jewell Baker, Leona May Bradshaw, Lena Mae Bradshaw Christian, Naomi Harjo Foster, and Katie Monahwee Harjo.

We could not have completed our work without the assistance of those who typed, edited, and otherwise aided this anthology. They include Anastasia McCrae, Patrick Houlihan, Jefferson Voorhees, Debra Haaland Toya, Rebecca Aronson, Gwen Ebert, Deanna Darral, Valerie Martínez, Rainy Ortiz, and Roseanne Willink.

We also wish to thank all of those who gave advice and moral support along the way. They include Laura Coltelli, Jeannette Armstrong, Lee Maracle, Susan Williams, Viola Thomas, Guy Lopez, Susan Lobo, Peggy Berryhill, Greg McNamee, Cecilia Vicuña, Jimmie Durham, Winn Starr, Miriam Laughlin, Margaret Randall, Joel Huerta, Michelle Saint Germain, Tom Miller, Charles D. Kleymeyer, the *Bloomsbury Review*, Tom Auer, Rosalinda Romero, Sandra Cisneros, Beth Brant, Norma Alarcon, Robin Morgan, the Feminist Bookstore News and Carol Seajay, Richard Z. Kristin, Gay American Indians, Annette Kolodny, the English Department of the University of Arizona, the English Department of the University of New Mexico, the Institute of American Indian Arts Creative Writing Program, Adrienne Rich, Luis Morato, Geary Hobson, Jeffrey Brooks, Charlotte Bunch, Roxanne Carrillo, Lois Olsrud, Dee Hershberger, Andy Robinson, Barney Bush, William Yellow Robe, Jr., the Penticton Gang, and all the others unnamed and yet to come.

We also wish to acknowledge the many other native women writers who should be included in this collection: Jean Starr; Jacki Marunycz; Pauline Brunette Danforth; Geri Gutwien; Andrea Lockett; Anita McLemore; Kate Berne Miller; Monica Mojica; Spiderwoman's Theatre: Lisa Mayo, Muriel Miguel, and Gloria Miguel; Linda St. Claire-Hawpetoss; Cheryl Savageau; Jo-Ann Thom; Kateri Damm; Regina Quinn; Kim Wensaut; Marty Will; Carole Yazzie-Shaw; Marta Aida Yoshimura; Nancy Johnson; Doris Seale; Petrina Bigman; Diane Glancy; Lenore Keeshig-Tobias; Miryam Yataco; Annette Arkeketa; Lise Erdrich; Elvira Colorado; Hortensia Colorado; Susan Clements; Melanie Ellis; Virginia Driving Hawk Sneve; Jeanetta Calhoun; Rosemary Diaz; Serena Mis. Ta-Nash; Rosemary Gonzales; Anne Acco; Guyneth Cardwell; Minerva Allen; Linda Anfuso; Elise Arviso; Marie Annharte Baker; Katherine Bell; T. M. Baker; Anne Burke; María González Sánchez; Petrona de la Cruz Cruz; Isabel Juarez Espinosa, and Kate Shanley, and many unnamed.

We must also acknowledge Rayna Green and Beth Brant, who began this task when there were no such collections in the world.

We also thank Jill Bialosky and Charlotte Sheedy for their dedication and assistance.

And most of all, we thank the spirit that feeds us, inspires us, ensures that we continue beautifully.

Contents

IV. DREAMWALKERS: THE RETURNING

Introduction

Reinventing the Enemy's Language was conceived during a lively discussion of native women meeting around a kitchen table. Many revolutions, ideas, songs, and stories have been born around the table of our talk made from grief, joy, sorrow, and happiness. We learn the world and test it through interaction and dialogue with each other, beginning as we actively listen through the membrane of the womb wall to the drama of our families' lives. When Gloria Bird and I began this introduction we decided to continue with dialogue. It is a dialogue we began some years ago and have continued through various stages of our lives: from high school, through the births of our children and grandchildren, through many stories and songs. Some of this dialogue has been excerpted from letters, from notes drafted on yellow pads, typed carefully on a typewriter or a computer after reading manuscripts or cooking dinner. No matter, the kitchen table is everpresent in its place at the center of being. It has often been the desk after the dishes are cleared, the children put to bed. We see this anthology as a continuing dialogue between the writers who speak to us here, between the writers and the readers, and within the field of meaning this book generates. We welcome you here.

JH: This anthology is a journey that began in 1986 when I accepted an invitation to present my work as part of an international conference on aboriginal education in Vancouver, British Columbia. The gathering brought together aboriginal peoples from the Arctic Circle, including the Saami people from as far away as Norway and the Maori from the southern Pacific. Many tribal peoples gathered to speak regarding the future of the children in a world apparently governed by the greed of multinational corporations and to share ideas in presentations of speeches, songs, and stories as well as a rich array of food. (I especially remember baked salmon and fry bread.)

It was during this gathering that I first met an exciting group of Canadian native* writers, publishers, and activists who had taken up the task of making sure literature was represented at the conference. To write is often still suspect in our tribal communities, and understandably so. It is through writing in the colonizers' languages that our lands have been stolen, children taken away. We have often been betrayed by those who first learned to write and to speak the language of the occupier of our lands. Yet to speak well in our communities in whatever form is still respected. This is a dichotomy we will always deal with as long as our cultures are predominately expressed in oral literatures.

This dynamic group of Canadian native writers included Jeannette Armstrong, Okanogan, the author of the first published novel by a Canadian native writer, *Slash*; Lee Maracle, whose book *I Am Woman* was the first book of political essays by a native woman published anywhere in the Americas; and Viola Thomas, a cultural worker on behalf of the tribes in Canada. We all knew of each other through the published word.

We met in Lee Maracle's kitchen with her two daughters Columpa and Tanya, her then partner Dennis, and neighbors who

*Note regarding the use of the terms "Indian," "native," and "Native American": *Native American* is a term invented in academe and is the term of the moment. It was invented to replace the term *American Indian*. This is a serious misnomer. In our communities we first name ourselves by tribe, but the general term commonly used is *Indian* in the United States and *native* in Canada. Canadian tribes also use the term *First Nations* with which to address their peoples.

joined us in shifts, fortified with bannock and coffee as we made plans for the kind of world we wished to see for the future. It was here the anthology was born. We wished the collection to be as solid as a kitchen table and imagined creating that kind of space within the pages of a book, a place where we could speak across the world intimately to each other. We wanted to know about the lives of women throughout the hemisphere who were writing, creating, as we were in the north. The Columbian Quincentennial celebrating the American myth of Christopher Columbus's "discovery" in 1492 was approaching, as were, in 1993, The Year of Indigenous Peoples and the anniversary of the overthrow of the traditional Hawaiian government by that of the United States. We wanted the anthology to be a collective voice from the women of the continual indigenous presence here. To understand the direction of a society one must look toward the women who are birthing and intimately raising the next generations. We wanted to see how well we had survived the onslaught of destruction.

We are still dealing with a holocaust of outrageous proportion in these lands. Not very long ago, native peoples were 100 percent of the population of this hemisphere. In the United States we are now one-half of one percent, and growing. All of the ills of colonization have visited us in its many forms of hatred, including self-doubt, poverty, alcoholism, depression, and violence against women, among others. We are coming out of one or two centuries of war, a war that hasn't ended. Many of us at the end of the century are using the "enemy language" with which to tell our truths, to sing, to remember ourselves during these troubled times. Some of us speak our native languages as well as English, and/or Spanish or French. Some speak only English, Spanish, or French because the use of our tribal languages was prohibited in schools and in adoptive homes, or these languages were suppressed to near extinction by some other casualty of culture and selfhood. Shame outlines the losses.

But to speak, at whatever the cost, is to become empowered rather than victimized by destruction. In our tribal cultures the power of language to heal, to regenerate, and to create is understood. These colonizers' languages, which often usurped our own tribal languages or diminished them, now hand back emblems of our cultures, our own designs: beadwork, quills if you will. We've transformed these enemy languages.

GB: Too, the very nature of the politics of publishing for native women from the beginning has remained hidden beneath the more obvious issues that all native people face. For native women writers in particular, to write and to be published, we work within a system that mimics a larger publication industry where our words are edited and legitimized still by an overwhelmingly male majority who are perceived as the authorities. Empowering ourselves, as in this long journey of compiling this anthology, needs to include looking toward other ways of filling the gaps in native women's experience in literature. That this is a native women's anthology edited by native women is a remarkable step.

As with colonization, the moment we are able to identify the source of pain, we are free of its power over us. As women writers, we should note how native women's "voice" has been shaped by the people who have control over the narrative production, and have functioned as editors. Often, the voice of tribal, land-based women writers with ties to community, history, and language has been marginalized and silenced by those who control what is published. Native writers have not been well served by this process.

There are many interlocking dynamics that come into play. The lack of female editorships, which are few and far between, says more about control of the publishing end, and privileging of the native male voice. Though there certainly have been, and continue to be, many non-native editors as well, the concerns about the control of native literary production impact not only upon native women but upon all native writers. This anthology is only a beginning. "Reinventing" in the colonizer's tongue and turning those images around to mirror an image of the colonized to the colonizers as a process of decolonization indicates that something is happening, something is emerging and coming into focus that will politicize as well as transform literary expression.

JH: As we read stories and poems to each other, talked into the night in Lee's kitchen, we were excited to discover the many similarities in our work. Native women in the Americas share similar concerns based on community. We also share the questions of any artist doing her work within any culture. That work demands truth-telling, for any poet, writer, or artist in any tribal community must certainly measure herself against the truth. We, too, appreciated the differences between us, and recognized that though the differences may sometimes be difficult (which can include old tribal enmities and divergent customs) these were to be appreciated, for our differences add dimension to any knowledge. We wondered about other native women who were in the kitchens and streets throughout the hemisphere. What were they singing, speaking, and writing?

The editorial board of this anthology includes Valerie Martínez, Spanish from Santa Fe, New Mexico; Patricia Blanco, Hispanic from Phoenix, Arizona; Beth Cuthand of the Cree Nation; Gloria Bird of the Spokane Tribe; and myself of the Muscogee people. We are all poets.

This collection of contemporary native women's writings includes eighty-seven writers from many and varied tribes and backgrounds, from the Tohono O'odham people born at the southern border of the United States to the Athabascan near the Arctic Circle. They represent approximately fifty tribal nations and come from traditional rural homelands as well as from the cities that sprang up around these original lands. The writing includes poetry, fiction, personal narrative, prayer, and testimonials. Some of the writers are recognizable names in literary circles; many are publishing here for the first time.

We have much in common, particularly that we have come to life in an age in which we are aware of ourselves as native women (in all the various constructs) in a language that we have chosen to name our own. When our lands were colonized the language of the colonizer was forced on us. We had to use it for commerce in the new world, a world that evolved through the creation and use of language. It was when we began to create with this new language that we named it ours, made it usefully tough and beautiful. There-fore, we decided to name the anthology *Reinventing the Enemy's Language*.

GB: "Reinventing" is a good word. The "enemy" was deter-mined to control the language of real life and in that process ma-nipulated how we, as native people, perceived ourselves in relation to the world. Often our ancestors were successfully conditioned to perceive native language as inferior or defective in comparison to the English. A direct response, as it often happened, was that the previous generation did not teach tribal languages to our genera-tion. My relationship to the English language is not as dramatic or transparent as with those earlier generations. English is the only language I have ever spoken. In the shift to reclaim native lan-guages, it is the people of my generation and of our children's who perceive ourselves as impoverished because we do not have access to that mode of production. We represent two generations upon which colonization successfully severed the link between native lan-guage and the production of culture.

In the long process of colonization, what has survived in spite of the disruption of native language is a particular way of perceiving the world. For example, my aunt once, when we were looking at what was left of Mt. St. Helen's, commented in English, "Poor thing." Later, I realized that she spoke of the mountain as a person. In our stories about the mountain range that runs from the Olym-pic Peninsula to the border between southern Oregon and northern California our relationship to the mountains as characters in the stories is one of human-to-human. What was contained in her sim-ple comment on Mt. St. Helen's, Loowit, was sympathy and con-cern for the well-being of another human being—none of which she had to explain.

It is at this site where "reinventing" can occur to undo some of the damage that colonization has wrought. In becoming attentive to the nuances of the English language and its ability to "capture" us, we can eliminate from our vocabulary terms of domination such as speaking of ourselves as a "minority" in relationship to a "dom-inant" culture, which will only serve to keep the power structure in place, unchallenged and unchanged. It is possible to recognize other forms of mental bondage that reflect themselves in literary production as well—for instance, the way in which we have internalized the stereotypes and romanticisms of "Indian," stereotypes such as the drunken Indian, the inferiority of native languages and religion, and the speaking of "red English." The subtle forms of domination that require a white heroine or savior follow from the American literary tradition, from writers such as James Fenimore Cooper, Henry Wordsworth Longfellow, or many of the captive narratives. In addition, the focus on what is being "lost" reinforces what we are told about ourselves, that we are dying, that our cultures are dying. Yet all around me I see evidence of the opposite.

I do not believe that English is a new native language in spite of its predominant use as a vehicle for native literary production. What we have is a native literature produced in English that is written for an English-speaking audience and that incorporates a native perception of the world in limited ways. Within the written literary traditions of native people, we have *one* volume of poetry, by Diné poet Rex Lee Jim, written totally in a native language with no English translation. There are a number of writers in this anthology who incorporate native language in their work, some of whom feel the need to include a glossary of terms in order for the work to be accessible to a larger audience. In many ways, we have a long way to go. Other nationalist literary movements from other colonized peoples have recognized the need for a literature to be produced in native language for native language speakers. Along the way, there is hope that in "reinventing" the English language we will turn the process of colonization around, and that our literature will be viewed and read as a process of *de*colonization. To that end, native women in particular, who are the caregivers of the next generation, play an important role as mothers, leaders, and writers.

JH: When we began collecting this anthology we were influenced by the urgency of the impending quincentenary celebration on behalf of Christopher Columbus, the interloper onto our lands. We decided the theme should center around survival, how native women continue to survive. But the anthology gradually became a book about the process of writing and speaking as well as the interwoven issues of being Indian and female in these particular times.

We decided that the work should be arranged by theme, rather than by false political boundaries (or any other arbitrary category). This was important. As native peoples we were now restricted by national and political boundaries that did not exist before colonization. There was no Canada, United States, or Mexico, for example. And nations such as the Yaqui, Okanogan, and Mohawk weren't falsely divided by these boundaries as they are now, their lands separated by two international borders.

Our relationship with these intruder nations, as members of independent sovereign nations, has also been one tempered with deceit and mistrust on the part of the interloper nations. Therefore, we did not wish to acknowledge their borders.

For this anthology we did not require previous publication, but the contributors were asked specifically that they be "tribally identified"—that is, that they be culturally part of a particular tribal nation. We wanted the anthology to be made of the voices of those who have directly experienced being Indian in their everyday lives. It seemed such an obvious request, but it was not to be this easy. We thought specifying "tribally identified" would make the distinction clear. We were wrong, and it was to become a very charged issue.

We believe, as do many, that the tribes reserve the right to define their membership. And tribes define differently. The Cherokee enrollment, for instance, is based on Cherokee ancestry. This means that certified Cherokee tribal members can have as little as ¹⁄₂₀₀th Cherokee blood. For most tribes the cutoff is one-quarter blood. Some have other restrictions; for instance, to be identified as a Hopi tribal member the individual's mother must be Hopi. To point to blood quantum is inherently racist, but how do you define your members via culture? Some tribes have attempted to define culture as having one parent raised on the reservation.

GB: I would add that in the United States, and because of the legal implications of doing so, we are obligated to leave member-ship issues to the tribal groups as their sovereign right. There are cases where descendants of full-bloods have fallen through the cracks because historically there have been native peoples who re-fused to be listed on tribal rolls for political reasons. For others in this country, it became a social imperative to sever all claims to Indian descent. Nevertheless, asking that contributors be enrolled in Indian tribes was definitely a difficult parameter to set, but nec-essary to ensure the integrity of the anthology, even though blood-quantum issues leave much to be desired. In academia, if one argues for any type of distinction, or uses any means to determine who is Indian, the argument is often dismissed as "essentialist," a convenient term that is used to undermine native people's unique legal and political position to determine for themselves who are their members.

JH: In Canada there is an additional problem. Many non-status Indians were created through massive adoption and baby stealing that took place in the earlier years of this century. This happened in the United States, too, and has begun to recur with new gov-ernment policies. These policies invoke the years of termination, when the U.S. government attempted to disband tribal groups. Bill C31 was enacted in Canada and as a result many, many native women were dispossessed of their status when they married non-Indians. When the law was amended in 1982 to reinstate these dispossessed Indian women, two and three generations of women came back to their reserves. Many of their children are now re-turning. If they can trace their ancestry through parents and grand-parents, they are given full rights.

And what of the mestiza and Chicana in the United States, many of whom know their tribes? We did not address the presence of the Indian in the mestiza or Chicana in this anthology, though it is certainly due exploration and attention. Gloria Anzaldua in her groundbreaking *Borderlands* addresses this connection of Indian blood and land, as does Ana Castillo.

Editing this anthology was a difficult and complicated process. It brought up many different issues and questions.

GB: This process of editing has brought many issues into focus: audience/readership; questioning my own integrity or right to say what writing is acceptable; questioning by whose standards I was reading; and acknowledging my own biases in making those decisions. In reading the manuscript submissions, I had to learn to read differently, or to unlearn the critical aspect of reading that I have been taught in creative-writing workshops and in university literary courses. Basically, I had to confront my own internalized views on what constituted literature and recognize the learned preference of written over oral literatures in academia. I had to acknowledge the oral nature of the submissions and value the literal testimony of the women's voices that came through their writing.

Most published writers in North America are educated in the university system, which guarantees a "site of privilege" from which to speak. I am not questioning the integrity of educated native women writers, who have in many ways broken the ground for all of us, but we often reject other authentic stories and voices every time we judge their worth through conventional Euro-American standards of what constitutes good literature. Native women living on the reservation often write in the first person. They appear to have no need to construct or reinvent themselves to accommodate a literary form outside themselves. There is no pretension, no mediation between their art and their readers. Within Euro-American educational systems we learn literary strategies, grammars, and techniques that mostly differ from tribal constructs that are culture bound. We then become more self-conscious in our literary inventions, mediating between literal and metaphorical place and time. Reading the submissions for this anthology, it occurred to me that they were a long testimony, more in the way of journal writing.

I thought about the women who were not included in our anthology. I began to question my right to silence them. I don't believe it ever becomes easy to reject a piece, and I don't think this issue was ever totally resolved in my mind. Fortunately, we were able to accept a large amount of work, but we also had to comply with space considerations.

Reading my responses to manuscripts, I began to see a pattern of biases. I had to confront my own intolerance for romanticism, an aversion to "explaining ourselves," and my own prejudice against rhyme (Hallmarkese). I know everyone has their own definition of what constitutes poetry, and that we all come to our own conclusions about the underlying motives of a piece of fiction, but it became important for me to qualify my biases as I recognized them.

I spent more time on something that initially triggered a negative response. In spite of my first reactions, I re-read, and asked myself whether the piece was still a good piece of writing, and if it would contribute something to this anthology. In order to learn tolerance, I had to first acknowledge and identify my own intolerance. In retrospect, this experience wasn't just about reading manuscripts, but creating a narrative. Each piece has gone into the creation of a narrative that is also part of an even larger narrative.

JH: We soon saw that through our efforts we would be defining native women's literature by what we included as well as by what we omitted. Questions came up: How do we know what a good poem is, a good story? By whose definition, the community's or the university's? How much have we been manipulated by our educations? Will our efforts be useful or harmful? If we are inventing a truly native literary criticism, and central to that is the usefulness to the community, then what are other aspects of this criticism? Are there new paradigms here other than patriarchal and hierarchical? Are we inadvertently feeding negative stereotypes in our work? *What are we creating together?*

We imagined the women behind the work and could see the dedication it took to make those efforts to write a poem or a story, the commitment of time and energy especially when one has heavy family and community obligations, as do many of the women.

We began to see within the internal structure of the anthology the cycle underlying each process of creation, a cycle that is characterized by the phases of (1) genesis, (2) struggle, (3) transformation, and (4) the returning. We realized that we are involved in this process together, as individual humans struggling toward knowledge, as persons born into our families, tribes, nations, as literary artists involved in the creative act. This form appeared to be the most natural structure for the shape of the anthology.

Survival suggests itself, again as the final unifying theme, but even more than that, beautiful survival.

GB: We are still involved with survival struggles, such as the overthrowing of the Hawaiian government and the Oka rebellion. Since the passing of the NAFTA agreement large corporations are displacing indigenous peoples, once again, with the purpose of wresting their lands from them. The native Chiapas women participated in a protest walk. I saw an incredible photograph of these women dressed in traditional dress coming out of the mountains, and the line of people seemed endless.

As women, we have confronted institutionalized attacks on our gender—for instance, forced sterilizations. As caretakers, tradition bearers, we are aware of the growing impress of Aryan nations, of neo-Nazi, race-hating movements disguised as sportsmen (and religious) organizations, and of the potential physical danger they pose to our children as well as their insidious tactics to undermine the U.S. government's obligations to tribes as sovereign nations.

So there are these continued struggles for survival, but, more important it seems, there is continuity, a native tenacity *to persist through* . . . That we are still here as native women in itself is a political statement. Our physical presence denies the American myth of the vanishing red man. The stories and songs are subversive. Where white women struggle to assert their voice in a patriarchal, hierarchical system and have had to pit themselves against men, Indian women were heard, relied upon, and in some cases have controlled the politics of a tribal group. Contact denied the voice of women—I am thinking of the Creeks, Cherokees, Haudenosaunees, and those people whose women were the political force behind them—and fabricated the image of the "squaw" as a beast of burden, taking a native word and turning its meaning into a pejorative term. Native women are undoing those damaging layers of stereotypes of native people in general and native women in particular.

Reinventing the Enemy's Language represents a tone in the universe that has been silenced for far too long. It is the harmony of diverse native women's intellectual, creative, and emotional genius that has always been alive, only our access to it has been limited (by America's mythology of itself) or diffused (by male privilege and Eurocentrism). It is a tribute to the Indian mothers who raised these women, and, in turn, their mothers back to antiquity; and from this moment on, it is for the daughters to come who will carry on in a world where, as I have been told, "Indian work" is the hardest.

JH: We are still here, still telling stories, still singing whether it be in our native languages or in the "enemy" tongue.

The literature of the aboriginal people of North America defines America. It is not exotic. The concerns are particular, yet often universal. Anyone of these lands shares in the making of this literature, this history, these connections, these songs. It is a connection taken in with our mother's blood and milk, constructed of the very earth on which we stand.

This collection is a promise that will bring together the collective voice of nations. The sound of our collective voices in poetry, in story, will strengthen the link between Tierra del Fuego and the Arctic Circle, for it is certainly there, beneath the swell of destruction.

This anthology is a celebration, in honor of this ongoing journey.

JOY HARJO AND GLORIA BIRD

Grace Boyne

N A V A J O

I was coached by my mom years and years ago about how to pray. When I go out for my morning walk, I usually do my talking to the deities at that time. One of the interesting things about prayer is the use of the words in Navajo; it is very difficult to translate Navajo into English. It loses a lot in the translation. You must have a good command of both languages to be able to go back and forth.

In Navajo, the primary method of relating to other Navajos is the clan system, which still remains strong today. Because I was taught that one always introduced oneself by mentioning the clan affiliation, I am going to tell you my clan. I belong to Hanaagháanii; my father's clan is Kinyaaa'áanii. My maternal grandfather is of the clan Táḫạhá and my fraternal grandfather is of the Tsi'naajinii clan.

Although my original means of expression was oral (as Navajo was not a written language until recently), I understand the necessity of the written expression. There is another aspect of the spoken word; it is the belief of the Navajos that oral expression can have a significant impact—that is, spoken words have power. Thus, it is more meaningful to speak rather than to place the words on paper.

But I also understand the propensity of written expression in Western society. Thus I do it because it is required. The written word is considered more valid than the oral expression. I expect that I will do more writing in the upcoming years.

Invocation: Navajo Prayer

Talking God, Speaking God
Dawn, Dark Wind
First Man, First Woman
Changing Woman,
The four Sacred Mountains,
We ask for your blessings on this act
of creating beautiful words
We ask for your assistance in creating words
which bring enlightenment

At the hogan made with dawn,
The dawn goes out along the pollen path
The hogan where words originate
The words originate in beauty

With corn pollen, I will create
Create the words that beautify
Create the words that bridge misunderstanding
Create the words that enlighten
Create the words that bring harmony

Through the words we shall journey
along the corn pollen trail with beauty
Surrounding us and in that we shall live beautifully
Through words, we shall journey
along the corn pollen trail with harmony
Surrounding us and in that we shall live beautifully

Through the sacred words we shall create the beauty
Through the sacred words we shall create harmony
Through the sacred words we shall create enlightenment
Through the sacred words we shall create understanding

Around me, there will be beauty
Ahead of me, there will be beauty
Behind me, there will be beauty
Underneath me, there will be beauty
Above me, there will be beauty

Hózhǫ náhásdlį́į́
Hózhǫ náhásdlį́į́
Hózhǫ náhásdlį́į́
Hózhǫ náhásdlį́į́

REINVENTING THE ENEMY'S LANGUAGE

CONTEMPORARY NATIVE
WOMEN'S WRITINGS OF NORTH AMERICA

I.

THE BEGINNING OF THE WORLD

Gloria Bird

S P O K A N E

As soon as I learned to read and write, I started writing, making "books" and forcing my younger sister to read them. When I began writing seriously —that is, when I recognized that I needed to find a way of incorporating my need and love of writing into a profession— I lived way out in the boonies on the reservation. Outside of my family, I saw few people. I chopped wood to heat our house while eight months pregnant. Out of that isolation came some of the first poems that mark, for me, a beginning. I knew there had to be another Indian woman somewhere who was living like I was, who might hear me and identify.

Why I write now is complicated and yet simple. I write because I have to, and because the more I learn the more I believe in the power of the word. I hear people say that poetry won't make any difference, but I know that isn't true. In 1988 the Nicaraguan poet Ernesto Cardenal was denied a visa to tour the United States to read poetry. To read poetry! Cardenal is a Catholic priest and poet, and the threat he poses, I think, is representative of the threat Native American writers pose in this country.

I've been educated in the English language, and this is my tool. I know that I can take what I know and turn it around. I think what we need are our speakers: storytellers, linguists, writers, historians, as well as poets. One of the functions of language is to construct our world. We are the producers of this world who create ourselves as well as our social reality, and we do this through language. The possibilities are unlimited. I write for many reasons; these are some of them.

In Chimayo

The one-room adobe skeleton sat on a hill overlooking a field that would not grow anything but adobe brick. We packed holes around the vigas in winter, built a fire to "sweat" the walls insulating us for moving in.

Sr. Lujan sold the land as dried and Mexican as he, would sell what lay on the land: the rusted equipment of his father, the cellar dug into the dirt, and the bridge we crossed to reach the land he's sold.

His fat lawyer spoke with hands as coarse and brown as burnt fish asking for the price of the bridge belonging to Sr. Lujan, one hundred dollars to not be bothered any longer, Sr. Lujan whispering "*es verdad*" next to him.

In Chimayo a crucifix is planted higher up on a ridge watching over what sacrifices made of Chimayo all year. From my knees, I watched brighter stars journey the path of sky the cross did not fill through the night of my labor, rocking for comfort not found through an open window.

Early morning I lay on the floor to give birth, a veil of rain falling. *Hina-tee-yea* is what he called it in his elemental language. Four days later, named our daughter also, fine rain, child of the desert mesas, yucca, and chamisal.

Across the arroyo, the news would remind Manuelita of her grief, *y su hijito* lost the month we moved in. That spring, centipedes sprinkled sand from the warming vigas where they were hidden.

Laura Tohe

NAVAJO

The way to learn stories is to listen. As a young child I grew up hearing my relatives tell stories about their daily lives, about long-ago events, gossip, listening to the radio because we didn't have TV, and listening to my mother tell us stories in the car on the way to Gallup to shop. Then there were the other sounds that are particular to growing up on the Diné rez: crickets chirping on summer nights, the sewing machine clattering, Navajo Hour on the radio, dogs barking, my brother chopping wood, a lonely wind blowing in early March, the rustle of sheep in the corral, crows cawing from tall pine trees, and my grandmother tamping the wool down on the loom.

All these stories and sounds are what I remember growing up. From being immersed in the oral tradition, language came easily to me. When I was twelve or thirteen, I wanted to become a writer. I liked how words came echoing back to me on the page. Echoing words, echoing images. Though I fantasized about becoming a writer, I had no role models. I knew writers put words on paper but didn't know the process a writer went through to get there. So I gave up on that idea and besides I didn't have confidence in myself to write. Then I read Leslie Marmon Silko's Ceremony. Silko validated the oral tradition and enabled me to write what I know. Consequently, the voices of my grandmothers and ancestors are part of that oral tradition from which I write. They are all there helping me create; I never do it alone. The act of writing is claiming voice and taking power.

She Was Telling It This Way

Shimá Shił hoolne'
My mother, she was telling it this way,
    as we looked in the stores up and down Highway 66.
We examine basket design and weaving.

       The four points represent sacred mountains of the Diné.
       My grandmother told me that when First Woman,
                                  'Ałtsé' Asdzáán
             was making the first basket
                              she came to the end
          and wondered how she should finish it
       Haaléit' éego 'ałtso ádiishlííl, jiniizį́į.

We look over the stacks, turning individual ones over,
    earthy smells of sand, roots, plants, and water.

       Aádóó 'áádę́ę́' bitó iin gad hwił yah ayíiłhan jiní
       Ako' ní'jidiitą jiní, gad.

We count each of the points and decide which
are the most authentic,
    the best quality,
        tracing finger over the ridges,
feeling the peaks of mountains and earth in basket form.

       'Aádóó jinił'į.
          Nt' ę́ę́ baa' a' hwizhniizį́į.
       Díigii át' áogo doola, dooleeł
       díigii át' áogo ałtso 'ádoolníił.
       'Eii béíjiidlaa'jin.
          'eiigii át'aogo nizhnítl'ǫ' jiní.
       When you hang it, the opening should be placed upward.

My eye glides down the vertical opening,
   descends into the belly,
      into the womb of the earth.

   That way good things will pass through the doorway,
   that way you'll not enclose yourself, your thoughts,
         your feelings.
   Ch' é' étiin hwii'hólǫ́ǫ́łeh.
   One should always have a doorway leading from their
                                                heart
   You see, we cannot permit ourselves to be perfect,
      to lock up perfection in anything that we create,
   in weaving, making pottery, or even in making bread.
   We must allow for our imperfections
      We must have a doorway

A doorway, ch'é'étiin,
to bring forth in colors or red, black, and yellow,
   health, happiness, prosperity, life.

The Diné woman behind the counter nods.
We leave the store,
into the afternoon light,
   brilliant.
A basket securely at my breast.

Katsi Cook

MOHAWK

I was born at home in my grandmother's bedroom in 1952 on the reservation at Akwesasne. My grandmother Elizabeth Kanatires Herne Cook delivered me and many of the babies in my generation there. When I was born, my grandmother bundled me up and put me aside in a basket while she cared for my mother who needed her attention. Later, my grandmother noticed my blankets were bloody and that I was bleeding from the cord stump. Today, we know that a baby in this condition needs a shot of vitamin K. Then, my grandmother took a needle and thread and sewed up my belly button. As I grew close to my grandmother in my childhood, my sister and brothers and cousins used to tease me, "You'd better not make Grandma mad or she'll take her thread back!" I used to search my belly button looking for that thread, and when I started practicing midwifery myself in 1977, it was as though I finally found it.

One word which has been used since colonial times to denigrate Indian women is the word "squaw." It wasn't until I was having children myself and began practicing midwifery that I began to ask the old people about Mohawk words used to describe female anatomy and physiology. It was then that I learned that the word "squaw" comes from the Mohawk word otsiskwah (oh-gee-squaw), which means "it's slippery," describing the vagina. Being called a squaw is like being called a cunt. However, otsiskwah is an excellent and empowering word to describe the clear, abundant, thready mucus the cervix *produces when a woman is fertile! So when I teach the young Indian women about their bodies, I always tell them about this. Instead of using the German term* spinnbarkeit *for this characteristic of mid-cycle ovulation, let's call it* otsiskwah.

The Coming of Anontaks

That time, we were living in the Adirondack Mountains in Mohawk territory. We lived on top of a steep hill in a cabin overlooking a wide, long valley and we were surrounded by wilderness for miles and miles. We had no running water or electricity. We used kerosene lamps and burned wood for cooking and heat and we hauled our water with a shoulder yoke in two five-gallon buckets from the stream down the hill. We lived in that place throughout my pregnancy and a cycle of seasons. In the fall, we cut wood. In the winter, the old logging road to our house got blocked by heavy snows and three, four times a week we walked the nearly two miles of deep snow with our two children to the country road below where our friends Sotsitsowah and Carol lived. In the spring and summer, fruits and berries were plentiful. Fresh mountain air and clean water nourished us.

We all felt privileged to live in a place which was a constant reminder of the spirit and power of the natural world. The demands of a lifestyle in harmony with the land were directly opposed to the demands made on our families to produce the oldest and largest international journal for native and natural peoples, *Akwesasne Notes*. There was a temperamental generator to maintain, mail runs to make, and we were entrenched in the continuing struggle of the Mohawk people of Akwesasne against the jurisdiction of New York State on our lands. Our men were always making trips to Akwesasne to participate in meetings and negotiations. Every issue of *Notes* carried the latest developments in a nation's struggle for sovereignty, which in the spring and early summer of 1980 was particularly tense. State police seemed to be everywhere, arresting Mohawk warriors. But by June 8, despite the political pressures and military threat our nation was enduring, my son, the porcupine, began to let me know he wanted to be born.

On June 8, it was a bright, clear day. All morning I had been outside chopping wood and turning the compost heap. By afternoon, I could feel a heavy, constant pressure through my abdomen and back. I was "ripe" and I felt as if I were carrying the baby between my knees. When I would sit down to rest, the pressure subsided. I watched my mucus when I went to the outhouse and I had seen two tiny spots of blood. Although "bloody show" is one of the signs of impending labor, I didn't get too excited because with my second child, Tsiorasa, I saw the same thing and he wasn't born until a week later.

In spite of the heavy pressure, I felt energetic. The moon was new. I decided I must be in the early stage of labor when I saw how hard my husband Jose was working. He was behaving like a bird making its nest. He was bringing up his fourth load of water when the sweat really broke out on him. It was a steep hill; "cardiac hill" we called it. He put the pails down and asked, "What do you think?"

"I'm losing my mucus plug."

"I had a feeling today was it," he said. "Take it easy."

"I feel full of energy, I can't sit still. Besides, it's hard to say. It could be three hours or three days. By the way, the porcupine was back last night. He chewed up a rug on the line and a chair on the porch. We'd better get a salt lick for him before he eats us out of house and home."

That evening, Sotsitsowah, Carol, and their two children, Charlene and Forrest, came up the hill for a visit. Luz and Mary, two friends, had also shown up that day to help me with the kids and the house while I gave birth. They were staying in the small cabin behind ours. We all sat at the table and laughed and joked and ate the big spinach salad I had made. Forrest wanted to know about the porcupine. We all started to talk about animals, about these woods that were their home, too. Pretty soon a big story developed about a giant porcupine.

The Adirondack Mountains are one of the areas of North America most affected by what is called "acid rain." This deadly rain is caused by the industrial pollution coming out of the smokestacks of the Midwest. The rains are carried by the westerly winds and fall on the Adirondacks. As a result, many of the lakes are being destroyed; fish are dying out. As with many other catastrophes plaguing modern existence, the fact of acid rain is something that we can contemplate seriously only by making humor of it.

That evening we evolved a tall tale. The acid rains were now discovered to be responsible for gene mutation among porcupines. Porcupines were growing into giants, with quills ten feet long. They were eating up the woods, impaling humans who got in their way and eating their way south to New York City. They were huge, with voracious appetites. Bark would not suffice them anymore . . . now they craved concrete. It was horrible!

"Forrest," Sotsitsowah said to his ten-year-old boy, "I hear one outside!"

Forrest looked up, his eyes wide. Then he covered his ears. "Cut it out! Stop this stupid story!"

We all cracked up.

I was laughing when I felt it—a small wave beginning in my pelvis and gripping around toward my lower back. Everyone at the table noticed the change in my face and, finally, the grip melted away as suddenly as it had come. One thing I knew: this was for real.

After everyone left, we made a fire and put the kids to sleep. I sat in my rocking chair. A steady pattern of contractions swept my abdomen. They were still light. We timed them and they were six minutes apart.

In bed, two hours later, I woke my husband. I couldn't sleep. The contractions were getting stronger and stronger. Jose fixed me a warm bath and an enema and stirred the fire. He went after the women in the other cabin.

It was a dark night and very still. There was a little path through the trees to the bunkhouse cabin. My husband walked slowly and then he heard him—the porcupine. He was chewing up a piece of wood by the door to the cabin. Jose turned off the flashlight and stood in the dark. If you've ever seen a porcupine up close, you know that you don't argue with them. They are slow, but they have long, sharp quills that can be very painful. Jose would tell me later that he could hear him chewing. He thought to get his gun, but then it didn't seem right, not that night with a birth coming.

"Porcupine!" Jose had called out, flashing his light on him.

Porcupine looked up, quills bristling.

"My wife is in labor and she needs those women to help her. Let me through!"

Porcupine backed off, slowly, then he turned and waddled off into the woods.

At the house, I was walking around in my robe. I had called my aunt on the reservation and asked her to send my sister Saka and my cousin Beverly up to help me. I tried to lie down but suddenly my body was overtaken by a chill and I couldn't get warm. I stood by the fire. The kerosene lamp threw a warm glow on the dark wood walls which soon became a mural of shadows of people moving, fixing tea and coffee, making preparations for the birth; a sense of expectancy loomed over everything.

I went back to bed to rest and stay warm. I felt good, and full. We had been waiting for our new little one for a long time. He would be our third child, and we knew exactly how we wanted things to be. We had prepared ourselves. We took care of our home; kept it clean physically, emotionally, and spiritually. Friends and family who would matter to our child and play a part in his upbringing would be there to welcome him into the world.

During my pregnancy, an awareness of natural world ways was especially important to us. It was an integral part of my prenatal care. In the woods, you learn to pace yourself and hold on to your strength. You work hard and feel good and can't complain. You keep the senses and heart open and you learn the natural laws.

For example, unless you know the feeling of walking through pine to a clear, cold mountain stream for water to prepare your family's food and wash your children with, it might be difficult to appreciate the spirit and life water is. We did what we had been told by the Ottawa elder who had hand-carved our ash water yoke: "When you get the water, dip your bucket in the stream in the same direction as the water is flowing; out of respect for the spirit of the water, don't go against it."

Lying there, I thought of the waters of birth which had swelled inside me during pregnancy and now cushioned my little one in his passage. Even our daily activity of going for water had provided a truth which would assist me in the delivery of this baby. As wave after wave of contraction swept my back, abdomen, and pelvis, I worked to relax, to yield to the current, and let my cervix open. The worst thing a woman in labor can do is to tense up, to fight against the very muscles that exist to contract and expel the child.

An hour later, everyone arrived: my sister Saka, who attended the births of my other two children; her husband Ray; my nephew Rasennes; and Beverly, our cousin and a midwife. I could feel the arrival of the two women as they walked through the house and into the bedroom. It was like a caravan of two and all the spare energy of the house seemed to follow them in.

My labor intensified. Beverly checked me inside for dilation so I would have an idea of the progress I was making.

"You're eight centimeters, Kats," she announced. "The membranes are bulging."

My legs were trembling and I felt cold. Saka put warm socks on my feet and bundled me in her old housecoat. My six-year old daughter, Wahiahawi, who was also born at home and had participated in other births, walked into the room. She was rubbing her eyes and took my hand and said in a sweet voice, "Mommy, is the baby coming? Can I hold the flashlight when the head comes out?"

Outside my window, I could hear the porcupine chewing and pacing on the front porch. So he came back. I was thinking about the porcupine when the trembling in my legs spread to my whole body and I felt I needed to stretch. I got up and sat on the chamber pot near my bed. It felt good to squat through the contractions.

For several hours I labored, alternating walking, lying down, and squatting on the pot. The pains were incredibly strong, and for a while, Saka helped me breathe through a few. I remembered her at Hawi's birth, kneeling next to me, tears in her eyes. She didn't know how to help. Since then, she had become a good labor coach. Now, her eyes commanded me to endure.

Beverly checked the baby's heartbeat and dilation of the cervix. "You're fully, Kats," she said.

Jose sat on the bed in front of me and I knelt on the floor with my arms folded in his lap. Behind me, through the window facing east over the mist and mountains, you could see the sun coming up. Sotsitsowah had come and was outside burning Indian tobacco. With every contraction, I grasped my husband's firm shoulders and put the energy coming from my uterus into massaging him there. (His shoulders ached for days afterward.)

The contractions were powerful now and very painful. But they were also very, very short. As soon as I felt I couldn't bear it anymore, they would dissipate. This went on for a while until I caught myself and realized I was holding the baby up inside me. I was dreading the baby's passage through the bones. I felt like I would explode. So I talked to myself, "Let the baby move down, Katsi. Relax. Let go. Let the baby come down."

I said, "I'm going to break the waters."

For the first time, I pushed hard, and in the next contraction, the bag ruptured and clear water with bits of milky vernix made a pool in the blankets and pillow below me.

"All right!" Beverly said.

"I'm going to push the baby out!" I told myself out loud.

"Go ahead and push," Beverly said.

I had wanted to work the head out slowly, carefully, and guide it with my hands. But one huge contraction came and *whoosh!* I could feel the baby slide out of me into the pile below.

Beverly caught the dark round bundle.

"You got a boy, Kats," she said. "He's beautiful!"

I wept with joy and relief as I reached down through my legs to receive my new son. He was still connected to me through the umbilical cord. I got up on the bed and laid back and put him to my breast.

It was three hours after the birth. I had fallen asleep with my new son in my arms. I awoke to the phone ringing. It was one of our people from the Racquette Point Encampment on the St. Lawrence River. Her voice sounded very serious.

"The state police are building up again," she said. "They beat up some more people. They've also been working up that vigilante goon squad. We think they're trying to lay the groundwork for another attack. We need you to come down here right away."

The people were really in trouble that time. A siege against our traditional government by New York State troopers, one that lasted for nearly three years, was reaching a crisis. There was no doubt in my mind that I would follow my family to the reservation and settle in at my sister's house. I couldn't stay in the mountains wondering, worrying what would become of that day that had begun so preciously. We buried the placenta in the rich brown earth beneath a large cherry tree with the prayer that everything would go the right way on the reservation and that no life would be lost.

We gathered our family and made the trip out to the road and then the reservation.

In my community, I work as a midwife. So it is natural that occasionally people ask me, what happens when a complication arises at a birth? At those times, I can't help but smile to myself. Lots of people have been conditioned to fear birth and imagine the worst of all possible complications. My birthing at Hilltop had met only one: the state of New York.

Janice Gould

I feel that writing is an act of survival. But there is more than my own survival that is at stake. These days I feel a kind of urgency to reconstruct memory, annihilate the slow amnesia of the dominant culture, and reclaim the past as a viable, if painful entity. I think of writing as a way to make questions, ponder, meditate, dream, and locate powerful truths that may enrich the imagination and deepen our desire to affirm life.

Coyotismo

My mother lay on her side to birth me.
This was millennia ago
when the earth was still fresh
with the energy of being.

I was her first.
If any came before me
they were lies and unwanted.

We are poor, I was hungry.
You can't imagine the places I've begged:
beaches, city streets, conference tables.
I will eat garbage,
but not from anyone's hand.

We were poor, I was cold.
Mama made me a coat, but no trousers.
People laughed at me.
I was always angry.

They joked about my sex,
said nasty things about my genitalia.
I became vengeful.

Once I heard the moon whisper behind my back.
I scooped hot coals
and threw them in her fat face. *female planet*
Sure, it burned my hands—
but she is marked with permanent surprise.

Another time the night began a rumor
that I'd hump anything that moved.
What did she know? When she opened her mouth to laugh
I pulled her tongue real hard.
She vomited a trail of stars no one can clean up.

I know more than I can say!
No poetry exists which wasn't first on my lips.
I was a live seed planted by a woman
in another woman's womb.
All things insatiable belong to me.

Joy Harjo

MUSCOGEE

Poetry came to me through my need for a language of truth and revelation. Through my early years I was practically mute in my everyday interactions outside the home, particularly school and church. I was terrified. Perhaps to speak meant opening the possibility for truth to spill out—and to acknowledge truth meant to face the terrible destruction deep within, as an Indian, female, and child within my family and culture of the late twentieth century.

At Indian boarding school nearly everyone wrote poetry or read it. One high school English class teacher forced us to read aloud out of fourth-grade readers. I remember the flat orange covers of those boring texts whose characters lived in the same white middle-class neighborhood of Dick and Jane. There was no magic, mystery, or paradox of the kind we dealt with everyday in the strange worlds we navigated in the postcolonial tale. We wrote poetry to speak of these things. We instinctually loved the rhythmic, undulant language that was called poetry, whether it was in the constant storytelling and laughter or the songs we sang, both traditional and contemporary, that shaped our consciousness.

When I was in my early twenties, an art student at the University of New Mexico, poetry once again found me, as I took part in the revolution of pride in our nations that swept North America. Within the shape of poetry I found a sacred language within the English language. The interior landscape within me was breaking down and many nights I held on to *my pen to keep from drowning in the undertow of emotional chaos. Poetry then saved me, turned into a force of beauty all its own, beyond me, beyond anything I could imagine on my own.*

Warrior Road

It was still dark when I awakened in the stuffed back room of my mother-in-law's small rented house with what felt like hard cramps. At seventeen years of age I had read everything I could from the Tahlequah Public Library about pregnancy and giving birth. But nothing prepared me for what was coming. I awakened my child's father and then ironed him a shirt before we walked the four blocks to the Indian hospital because we had no car and no money for a taxi. He had been working with another Cherokee artist silk-screening signs for specials at the supermarket and making $5 a day, and had to leave me alone at the hospital because he had to go to work. We didn't awaken his mother. She had to get up soon enough to fix breakfast for her daughter and granddaughter before leaving for her job at the nursing home. I knew my life was balanced at the edge of great, precarious change and I felt alone and cheated. Where was the circle of women to acknowledge and honor this birth?

It was still dark as we walked through the cold morning, under oaks that symbolized the stubbornness and endurance of the Cherokee people who had made Tahlequah their capital in the new lands. I looked for handholds in the misty gray sky, for a voice announcing this impending miracle. I wanted to change everything; I wanted to go back to a place before childhood, before our tribe's removal to Oklahoma. What kind of life was I bringing this child into? I was a poor, mixed-blood woman heavy with a child who would suffer the struggle of poverty, the legacy of loss. For the second time in my life I felt the sharp tug of my own birth cord, still connected to my mother. I believe it never pulls away, until death, and even then it becomes a streak in the sky symbolizing that most important warrior road. In my teens I had fought my mother's weaknesses with all my might, and here I was at seventeen, becoming my mother, who was in Tulsa, cooking breakfasts and preparing for the lunch shift at a factory cafeteria as I walked to the hospital to give birth. I should be with her. Instead, I was far from her house, in the house of a mother-in-law who later would try to use witchcraft to destroy me.

After my son's father left me I was prepped for birth. This meant my pubic area was shaved completely and then I endured the humiliation of an enema, all at the hands of strangers. I was left alone in a room painted government green. An overwhelming antiseptic smell emphasized the sterility of the hospital built because of the U.S. government's treaty and responsibility to provide health care to Indian people.

I intellectually understood the stages of labor, the place of transition, of birth—but it was difficult to bear the actuality of it, and bear it alone. Yet in some ways I wasn't alone, for history surrounded me. It is with the birth of children that history is given form and voice. Birth is one of the most sacred acts we take part in and witness in our lives. But sacredness seemed to be far from my lonely labor room in the Indian hospital. I heard a woman screaming in the next room with her pain, and I wanted to comfort her. The nurse used her as a bad example to the rest of us who were struggling to keep our suffering silent.

The doctor was a military man who had signed on this watch not for the love of healing or of awe at the miracle of birth, but to fulfill a contract for medical school payments. I was another statistic to him; he touched me as if he were moving equipment from one place to another. During my last visit I was given the option of being sterilized. He explained to me that the moment of birth was the best time to do it. I was handed the form but chose not to sign it, and am amazed that I didn't think too much of it at the time. Later, I would learn that many Indian women who weren't fluent in English signed, thinking it was a form giving consent for the doctor to deliver their babies. Others were sterilized without even the formality of signing. My light skin had probably saved me from such a fate. It wouldn't be the first time in my life.

When my son was finally born I had been deadened with a needle in my spine. He was shown to me—then taken from me in the name of medical progress. I fell asleep with the weight of chemicals and awoke yearning for the child I had suffered for, had anticipated in the months proceeding from his unexpected genesis when I was still sixteen and a student at Indian school. I was not allowed to sit up or walk because of the possibility of paralysis (one of the drug's side effects), and when I finally got to hold him, the nurse stood guard as if I would hurt him. I felt enmeshed in a system in which the wisdom that had carried my people from generation to generation was ignored. In that place I felt ashamed I was an Indian woman. But I was also proud of what my body had accomplished despite the rape by the bureaucracy's machinery, and I got us out of there as soon as possible. My son would flourish on beans and fry bread, and on the dreams and stories we fed him.

My daughter was born four years later, while I was an art student at the University of New Mexico. Since my son's birth I had waitressed, cleaned hospital rooms, filled cars with gas (while wearing a miniskirt), worked as a nursing assistant, and led dance classes at a health spa. I knew I didn't want to cook and waitress all my life, as my mother had done. I had watched the varicose veins grow branches on her legs, and as they grew, her zest for dancing and sports dissolved into utter tiredness. She had been born with a caul over her face, the sign of a gifted visionary.

My earliest memories are of my mother writing songs on an ancient Underwood typewriter after she had washed and waxed the kitchen floor on her hands and knees. She too had wanted something different for her life. She had left an impoverished existence at age seventeen, bound for the big city of Tulsa. She was shamed in a time in which to be even part Indian was to be an outcast in the great U.S. system. Half her relatives were Cherokee full-bloods from near Jay, Oklahoma, who for the most part had nothing to do with white people. The other half were musically inclined "white trash" addicted to country-western music and Holy Roller fervor. She thought she could disappear in the city; no one would know her family, where she came from. She had dreams of singing and had once been offered a job singing on the radio but turned it down because she was shy. Later, before she could copyright it, one of her songs would be stolen and make someone else rich. She would quit writing songs. She and my father would divorce and she would be forced to work for money to feed and clothe four children, all born within two years of each other.

As a child growing up in Oklahoma, I liked to be told the story of my birth. I would beg for it while my mother cleaned and ironed. "You almost killed me," she would say. "We almost died." That I could kill my mother filled me with remorse and shame. And I imagined the push-pull of my life, which was a legacy I deal with even now when I am twice as old as my mother was at my birth. I loved to hear the story of my warrior fight for my breath. The way it was told, it had been my decision to live. When I got older, I realized we were both nearly casualties of the system, the same system flourishing in the Indian hospital where later my son Phil would be born.

My parents felt lucky to have insurance, to be able to have their children in the hospital. My father came from a fairly prominent Muscogee Creek family. His mother was a full-blood who in the early 1920s got her degree in art. She was a painter. She gave birth to him in a private hospital in Oklahoma City; at least that's what I think he told me before he died at age fifty-three. It was something of which they were proud.

This experience was much different from my mother's own birth. She and five of her six brothers were born at home, with no medical assistance. The only time a doctor was called was when someone was dying. When she was born her mother named her Wynema, a Cherokee name my mother says means Beautiful Women, and Jewell, for a can of shortening stored in the room where she was born.

I wanted something different for my life, for my son, and for my daughter, who later was born in a university hospital in Albuquerque. It was a bright summer morning when she was ready to begin her journey. I still had no car, but I had enough money saved for a taxi for a ride to the hospital. She was born "naturally," without drugs. I could look out of the hospital window while I was in labor at the bluest sky in the world. I had support. Her father was present in the delivery room—though after her birth he disappeared on a drinking binge. I understood his despair, but did not agree with the painful means to describe it. A few days later, Rainy Dawn was presented to the sun at her father's pueblo and given a name so that she will always be recognized as a part of the people, as a child of the sun.

That's not to say that my experience in the hospital reached perfection. The clang of metal against metal in the delivery room had the effect of a tuning fork reverberating fear in my pelvis. After giving birth I held my daughter, but they took her from me for "processing." I refused to lie down to be wheeled to my room after giving birth; I wanted to walk out of there to find my daughter. We reached a compromise and I rode in a wheelchair. When we reached the room I stood up and walked to the nursery and demanded my daughter. I knew she needed me. That began my war with the nursery staff, who deemed me unknowledgeable because I was Indian and poor. Once again I felt the brushfire of shame, but I'd learned to put it out much more quickly, and I demanded early release so I could take care of my baby without the judgment of strangers.

I wanted something different for Rainy, and as she grew up I worked hard to prove that I could make "something" of my life. I obtained two degrees as a single mother. I wrote poetry, screenplays, became a professor, and tried to live a life that would be a positive influence for both of my children. My work in this life has to do with reclaiming the memory stolen from our peoples when we were dispossessed from our lands east of the Mississippi; it has to do with restoring us. I am proud of our history, a history so powerful that it both destroyed my father and guarded him. It's a history that claims my mother as she lives not far from the place where her mother was born, names her as she cooks in the cafeteria of a small college in Oklahoma.

When my daughter told me she was pregnant, I wasn't surprised. I had known it before she did, or at least before she would admit it to me. I felt despair, as if nothing had changed or ever would. She had run away from Indian school with her boyfriend and they had been living in the streets of Gallup, a border town notorious for the suicides and deaths of Indian people. I brought her and her boyfriend with me because it was the only way I could bring her home. At age sixteen, she was fighting me just as I had so fiercely fought my mother. Yet I felt strangely empowered, too, at this repetition of history, this continuance, by a new possibility of life and love, and I steadfastly stood by my daughter. It was during this time that Rainy wrote her first poems, much as I did when I was pregnant with her. This poem became a touchstone for me during our difficult years.

Every Day It Is Always There

Every day it is always there
Whether in mind or body
Whether I want it to be or not—
Sometimes it's like being haunted
By a constant presence
Of sometimes happiness
Sometimes anger—
But it is always filled with love.
That love is my protector.
That protector is my mother.

RAINY ORTIZ

I had a university job, so I had insurance that covered my daughter. She saw an obstetrician in town who was reputed to be one of the best. She had the choice of a birthing room. She had the finest care. Despite this, I once again battled with a system in which physicians are taught the art of healing by dissecting cadavers. My daughter went into labor a month early. We both knew intuitively the baby was ready, but how to explain that to a system in which numbers and statistics provide the base of understanding? My daughter would have her labor interrupted; her blood pressure would rise because of the drug given to her to stop the labor. She would be given an unneeded amniocentesis and would have her labor induced—after having it artificially stopped! I was warned that if I took her out of the hospital so her labor could occur naturally, my insurance would cover nothing.

My daughter's induced labor was unnatural and difficult, monitored by machines, not by touch. I was shocked. I felt as if I'd come full circle, as if I were watching my mother's labor and the struggle of my own birth. But I was there in the hospital room with her, as neither my mother had been for me nor her mother for her. My daughter and I went through the labor and birth together.

And when Krista Rae was born she was born to her family. Her father was there for her, as were both her grandmothers and my friend who had flown in to be with us. Her paternal great-grandparents and aunts and uncles had also arrived from the Navajo Reservation to honor her. Something *had* changed.

Four days later, I took my granddaughter to the saguaro forest before dawn and gave her the name I had dreamed for her just before her birth. Her name looks like clouds of mist settling around a sacred mountain as it begins to speak. A female ancestor approaches on a horse. We are all together.

Wilma Elizabeth McDaniel

CHEROKEE

Poetry was always a force within me, long before I could possibly understand what it was that affected me so deeply. I couldn't write at the age of four, but I thought a poem about minnows in the rock bottom of a small creek. The tiny silvery fish had such grace and beauty that I could barely live without expressing how I felt about them.

I was almost seven when I got the most vivid impression for a poem. I had to walk over the grave of a Creek Indian child. The county had built a new road over the tribal burial ground and covered all traces of the site. An old settler recalled the dead child was a seven-year-old girl. That bonded her to me forever. She had been a child like me. I gave her the name Lily Jane Skiatook. Many, many years later I would write her poem and see it published in Blue Cloud Quarterly.

Eavesdropping

Papa had company that November afternoon when I came home from school.

I knew from the visitor's dirty high-peaked Stetson that it was Orval Potts. He had worn that same old hat as long as I could remember. Neighbors had jokingly offered to take up a collection and buy him a new hat, but he didn't want that. His reasoning was, "This hat is set to my head."

He and Papa were squatted down on the south side of the barn out of the wind. That meant they were in deep conversation, Papa's favorite pastime, right above horsebreaking and racing some donated greyhounds.

The two had not seen my approach, which pleased me very much. I ardently wished to hear some of their conversation, knowing full well that Papa never allowed me to listen to "men's" talk. They spoke a peculiar language, just as women do. Papa wanted to keep their worlds and tongues separate.

He and Orval were utterly engrossed in their conversation. They had not heard my stealthy approach and never looked around.

I gathered all my courage and slipped in through the half door of the barn, tiptoeing through its stalls, past the harness hanging on pegs. The clean fragrance of hay delighted my sense of smell. I only prayed it wouldn't cause me to sneeze and announce my presence. I sat down on a bale of hay, almost directly behind Papa and Orval, hoping they could not hear my rapid breathing.

Orval coughed his cigarette cough. It was almost like being in the same room with him, without the smoke rings he liked to blow for us kids.

Clearing his throat, he said in his slow voice, "Like I told you some time ago, I'm gettin' real worried about Uncle Newt. He *still* don't realize that he has to get off his land, that it don't belong to him anymore. It now belongs to First National Bank, but no one can get that through his head."

Papa answered kindly, "Poor old fellow, he will find out soon enough when the bank sends the sheriff and moves him out bodily." He paused a few seconds. I knew he was thinking the matter over seriously.

He went on. "It's not right. No way in God's world. It's been an abomination from the very start. First, the U.S. government took all his people's land in North Carolina, then they drove them out here to Indian Territory. Finally, the government doled them back a few acres of their own country. Now the rotten system has caved in and the bank is gonna foreclose and take that land back."

Orval said, emotionally, "Don't it beat the hell out of you?"

Automatically, I covered my ears. *This* was the type of men-talk that Papa tried to protect me from. I wondered what I should do if the conversation grew more unacceptable to my young ears. For the present, I would just hang around and listen.

Papa spoke again. "Orval, your Uncle Newt is more attached to the land than most men are. It isn't just a piece of land to him, if you know what I mean."

"I do know what you mean, Bernie. Land ain't just land to Uncle Newt. *He loves it more like you love a woman.*"

These words tingled through my nine-year-old being. It dawned on me that Papa was smarter than I had imagined. More amazingly, I saw that Orval was smarter then *he* appeared to be.

Papa spoke in a consoling voice. "You have to see things from Uncle Newt's viewpoint; remember he is alone now. It was a hard blow for him to lose his wife of so many years. Then, to have to vacate the only home they ever had lived in is too much for him."

Orval cleared his throat again, confiding slowly, "To tell the truth, Uncle Newt showed more feeling for the land than he ever showed for Aunt Permelia." He paused, as if he might be half ashamed of what he'd just said. "I don't mean that he didn't love her. He just couldn't seem to express it freely like he does about the land."

"It comes real hard for some people to express their deepest feelings, Orval," Papa said. He thought of something else. "I remember when your Uncle Newt lost a little girl with the flu in 1918. Is she in the old Creek Cemetery?"

"That's the other thing," Orval sighed. "Uncle Newt don't want to leave that old place with his own burying ground up on the ridge. Aunt Permelia is there and the little girl you remember. The burying ground would be part of the farm."

Papa was silent for quite a while, thinking about that. "I see more and more why Uncle Newt is upset. Once the place belongs to someone else, they can do exactly as they please with it."

Orval sounded as if he might break down and cry. "Why, someone could go up there and yank up all the wooden crosses and stakes and burn 'em, easy as not. They could gather up them glass fruit jars with the paper flowers in 'em, *clean it all away*. There wouldn't be a trace of Uncle Newt's loved ones."

"That's the truth, Orval. Some people have no respect for the dead and the places where they are buried. I think they are worse than pagans, and we are supposed to be a Christian country. You sure couldn't tell it, the way things are going right now."

Poor Orval sounded more upset than ever. "I can't help myself, but I'm getting more worried about Uncle Newt every day that passes. When it finally soaks into his mind that he has lost his farm to the bank, he may do something desperate, I mean real desperate."

There fell a total silence on the other side of the wall for several seconds. My heart was thumping. I knew that "desperate" was a big word and meant serious trouble.

Orval went on. "When the sheriff comes out with the eviction papers, Uncle Newt might just take a gun and shoot him point-blank." He paused only a second, adding, "When he reaches that stage, he will sure enough mean to kill him. He won't be trying to scare him."

Papa's words came solemnly. "Yes, Uncle Newt would figure that he had nothing to lose. A cornered man is like a cornered animal: very, very dangerous."

At that point, a car honked on the county road behind the tool shed.

"Oh, there's my old lady," Orval said. "She said she'd pick me up on her way back from Drumright."

I knew that Orval was rising from his squatting position when he said, "My goldarned legs have went to sleep on me. I'll have to stomp around and get the circulation goin' again."

I knew Papa would be rising too. It was odd that he could squat like that for ages and never complain that his legs had gone to sleep.

I heard him say, "Glad you stopped by to see me, Orval," and I knew that he would shake hands as he always did when a visitor arrived or departed.

It was high time for me to exit. I stooped under the barn's half door and, swinging my books, went around the cowpen to the back of our sharecrop house.

The story I had overheard burned into my mind, but I couldn't share it and give myself away. I was beginning to feel that it shouldn't be shared anyway. What other silly kid would hide in the barn to overhear grown-ups talk? Maybe other kids didn't really *care* what grown-ups talked about. *I cared.*

Entering the house by the back door, I put my books on the kitchen table. The cool air and the walk from school had left me very hungry. I pulled down the warming oven of the wood range and found some biscuits. Three slices of breakfast bacon had congealed there in their cold grease. These made a hearty sandwich and I sat down to enjoy it.

Mama had just returned from a neighbor's house. She and Papa entered the front door together. Neither was aware that I was in the kitchen. I kept perfectly quiet.

With a deep sigh of relief, Mama said, "This was the hardest confinement case I've ever been on. I was so relieved when the doctor finally arrived, but it was all over by then." She smiled, and added, "He said I did a better job than he could have."

I stopped chewing, to catch every word. Measles and mumps and chickenpox and typhoid fever I'd heard of all my life, had lived through most of them. But a case of confinement in our own community had to be really serious if it meant having to call Doc Casswell out into the country.

I heard Papa ask, with great delicacy, "What was it?"

With pleasure in her voice, Mama answered, "A big boy, ten pounds. Wendell was fit to be tied. You'd think he was the only man who ever fathered a child. Anyway, the baby is perfect and Flora is doing alright. Her sister will stay with her for a few weeks."

"You look tuckered. I'll kindle the fire and make some coffee."

The two had forced my hand. Taking a huge bite of my sandwich, I yelled brightly, "Hey, I'm home and starving!"

I didn't want to talk to anyone just now. I needed time to sort things out in my mind. One thing had become instantly clear:

Mama was a very smart woman, maybe even smarter than Papa. That was probably why women had their own talk and their own world.

I liked it.

June McGlashan

ALEUT

I used to think that my poetry was inadequate to other writers. Abstract readers would label my work "pigeon talk." It isn't. People actually talk as I write. The formation of the Aleut-language sentences is sometimes backwards to English.

I still write about the Aleutians as a captivating place. The paradise of this place is simple. Each year I watch the grasses turn green, then a darker green. In the fall, the grasses switch to a shade closer to yellow, all the while hugging the mountains. . . . The effect is smooth and sharp at the same time, as if nature could not decide whether the Aleutians should look wild or timid. The ocean is always blue, moving and alive. Many fishermen risk their lives fishing the Bering Sea . . . they know they cannot tame the ocean; the ocean is an unpredictable body that makes the rules.

I have read Mary Tall Mountain's poetry for years. I would lie to myself if I stated I would never want to write like her. She is my idol. I met her in Unalaska/Dutch Harbor, Alaska, during one of her poetry readings. When meeting her she only said one word to me, "Finally!" I will never forget that event. She has a wonderful attitude.

Jerah Chadwick, poet of Unalaska, has been an inspiration to me. He has always believed in me, and for that I am thankful. There are many people who influence my poetry: the people who live in Akutan, our ancestors who left legendary stories to write about, and my mother and family who were always the backbone of my writings.

The Island of Women

In the mid-1800s.
Aleutian Island.

Our culture honors women as
well as men.
A survival technique.
For a woman can be a shaman,
as well as a man.

We are the species of the descendants
of the great sea-dwellers.
We have crossed the great ocean,
and sought a land suitable to
our livelihood.

The men were enslaved by the
great evil Russians.
It was but the women who
took over the survival of
the village.

There were no woman movements.
No public announcements.
Life had to go on.

They had waited.
For their spouse to return.
Only to find they never will.
The men were killed.
Or drowned hunting sea-otter
in high seas.

One ambitous young woman
tired watching the elders
starve and die.
She formed a group of hunters.

They waited in the winter storm.
With the seas within reach of
their lives.

They waited for the sea-cows
to pass islands.
They prayed the sea-cows would
venture on the rich kelp on the coves.

It was days.
They ate barnacales.
They ate kelp.
Sucked their fingers to
keep hunger pains out of the
bottoms of their stomach.

Finally they held their heads up
to the sky and sang a sad song of
death to the Mighty God.
And they ate snow for thirst.

In between the bardarkis,
just in reach of their paddles,
a sea-cow emerged.

The brave girl,
not yet sixteen,
reached for her spear,
which had a poison mixed with
the blood of a deceased one on
it.

The spear caught the sea-cow.
The string held tight and secure.
The sea-cow swam in one direction and
then the other.
The other bardarkis chased and
stuck sharp long spear heads into
weak flesh under the flippers
of the cow.
The cow struggled, fought, and
bled.

The young woman ordered others
to attach more strings to the cow,
spear and tighten the lines.
Two bardarkis had successfully
latched onto the monster cow.

They waited the listliness of the
cow.
Finally it no longer struggled.
It allowed the Aleut women to
take its life.

The group of women would be fed
for several months.
And clothed for the duration of
winter.

They reached home.
The young girl isolated herself
in a hut.
She was purifying her soul.
And asking forgiveness from the
Great Spirit for using human
blood.

After three days and three nights,
they feasted and danced.
They sang of the young girl,
whose life they prayed will
be good.
May many years of happiness
come your way,
they sang.
They feasted.
They ate until their stomachs ached.

Eventually they moved to another island
where there were Russians holding their
men as slaves.
They were married properly in Russian
custom, in the Russian Orthodox Church.

They learned to be civilized.
They were raped, their husbands
were killed. They married again.

They had children.
They protected the children.
And knew that the children
will one day be the only living
species left of the
great sea-dwellers.

Emma Lee Warrior

BLACKFOOT

It was not so long ago that everyone I knew spoke Blackfoot. That has changed. Yet though the sounds I hear back home are more English than Blackfoot, I find the stories told more from a Blackfoot-language perspective, be they legends, customs, or accounts of everyday happenings—they have a rich combination of awe for the power of our natural surroundings, a laughing at absurdity, and the pain of oppression.

Ours is not a written history. We have not immigrated. Our minute land bases are vestiges of our expansive past.

My grandmother was a medicine woman; she put up the Sun Dance. She cured people through prayer and herbs. My grandfather held the Beaver Bundle, the sacred bundle that ties us with our animal brothers. They observed sacred feasts and dancing in their home. My grandfather regularly sweated with his friends. As an attendant at the purification ceremony I was both an observer and participant. The main thing I learned from them was to be good to people and animals and to look toward the summer. Animals are our relations. People, animals, and nature were given to us by the Giver of Life.

That's the good side of my life. The not-so-good side includes ten years of boarding school and alcoholism as a single parent. I guess I try to find salvation through my connection to my childhood. I've been advised to "look to the future," but my head keeps turning around to the wisdom back there, away from 7-Elevens and twenty-four-hour video stores.

How I Came to Have a Man's Name

Before a January dawn, under a moondog sky,
Yellow Dust hitched up a team to a straw-filled sleigh.
Snow squeaked against the runners
in reply to the crisp crackling cottonwoods.
They bundled up bravely in buffalo robes,
their figures pronounced by the white of night;
the still distance of the Wolf Trail greeted them,
and Ipisowahs, the boy child of Natosi
and Kokomiikiisom, watched their hurry.
My momma's body was bent with pain.
Otohkostskaksin sensed the Morning Star's
presence and so he beseeched him:

"Aayo, Ipisowahs, you see us now,
pitiful creatures.
We are thankful there is no wind.
We are thankful for your light.
Guide us safely to our destination.
May my daughter give birth in a warm place.
May her baby be a boy; may he have your name.
May he be fortunate because of your name.
May he live long and be happy.
Bestow your name upon him, Ipisowahs.
His name will be Ipisowahs.
Aayo, help us, we are pitiful."

and Ipisowahs led them that icy night
through the Old Man River Valley
and out onto the frozen prairie.
They made it to the hospital
where my mother pushed me into the world
and nobody bothered to change my name.

Betty Louise Bell

CHEROKEE

When my mother spoke of her family, especially her mother, her face relaxed, a gentleness crept over her rough features, and I could see how she was once beautiful. And loved. Her stories always began or returned to her mother, always introduced her—as if we had forgot— as a "full-blooded" Cherokee, and always circled around the manners and behavior of Indians. Who was Indian and who wasn't Indian was determined, for her and then for us, by the way a person behaved. She was interested in the heart and the spirit of a person and when she entered memories of her mother and family, blood claimed her and, for that short time, she spoke with conviction and connection. All other times— working in the university cafeteria or cleaning other people's houses—she moved awkwardly and apologetically. She listened to the troubles of her rich employers and made those troubles her own. But she never spoke of her life to them. Compassion, my mother seemed to understand, belonged to those who could purchase it.

On the surface, my mother's lesson to me was the separation of public and private lives. I could be anything I wanted to be: I could marry a man who despised the poor and knew color to be the mark of inferiority. Of course, my mother knew differently, knew before I began to speak, "you don't have to explain." She held this silence until I broke through divorce into a wholeness she had never known. Like so many women writers, especially Native American women writers, I write be-

cause my mother could not, but also I write because it is there that I speak with conviction and connection. And it is there that I hope to recover the gentleness of my mother's face.

Beat the Drum Slowly

"Your grandma was a full-blooded Cherokee," my mother said again and again, as far as I can remember. It was the beginning of a story, the beginning of a confidence, and I lean forward, knowing that in the next few minutes no cheek will be pinched, no broom handle swung, no screams or tears wasted. I listen and watch, grateful to be part of the circle. Her words come slow, a chant filling her sunken face and smoothing her wrinkles. Across the kitchen table, I never take my eyes off her.

I did not hate her, then. It was easy to believe in the photograph on Lizzie's bureau: a dark-eyed beauty with olive skin and black hair to her waist, shapely in a cotton housedress and holding a newborn baby. She stood forward in a new field, the baby close to her cheek, the woods far behind her. As a child I called the woman "Momma," slipping close to the photograph and tracing her outline with my fingers whenever I passed through Lizzie's parlor. After my great-aunt's death, it was harder and harder to put the pretty girl with the child together with the fat, beat-up woman who cursed and drank, pushed into her only threat, "Maybe I'll just run away and leave y'all to yourself."

Some tension had given, some spirit snapped in the space of ten years, and the pretty girl had swollen into fatigue and repetition. In her last years a big cozy mother appeared, in short housedresses with snaps down the fronts and letters sticking out of her pockets, letters written to me on scraps of paper, backs of envelopes, and carried around for weeks, even months, before she dropped them in the mail. Her running scrawl refused time, pushing ahead of it the events of her day and health, always confessing her secret love and pride in me, and arriving months after the fact.

But long before the letters began to arrive, long before she knew she had something to say, she had already lost me to her stories. And there, I loved and forgave her.

"You was always her favorite. She was crazy 'bout you. I never seen her take to nobody the way she took to you. Ain't that right, Rozella? She was always too good for the likes a us. Uppity Indian. Her nose so turned up, her own shit don't stink."

"What did she look like?" I ask.

"Don't y'all 'member Lizzie?"

I shrug, my palm turned wide and open. I remember but I'm not supposed to remember. And I want to hear it again. I listen for Lizzie's name, watching as she moves before me in a calico apron and a tight face. She never smiles. Even as Momma and Auney move from laughter to tears, Lizzie stands silent and unamused.

"She was an Indian," Momma says. "She looked a lot like our momma, the same black hair and black eyes."

"Like us?"

"Y'all carry the Indian blood, that's for sure. Your black hair and Rozella's quiet ways, ain't no mistaking y'all. I ended up with the Scotch blood. Don't look like there were a drip left for y'all. Member that woman ask me if I'm Irish? Black Irish, she says. I'm a thinkin' she means nigger, and I almost give her a beating right in front of the chicken shack. I just look her in the eye and say, as cool as you please, 'There ain't no nigger in my woodpile.' But Lizzie and Momma, they looked Indian."

"Indian," Auney says with a nod and blow of smoke.

She was my now-spinster aunt, a survivor of four marriages, and my mother's chorus since birth. When one of her marriages broke up or she was looking for a new start, she came to us. And there, she was my mother's constant companion and an angel to me: silent and placid, she told no tales and didn't hit. And she gave me everything, except her bingo money. She drank and married hard-drinking no-good men. They almost killed her, more than once, but the closest she came to fighting back was to refuse to forget.

"I can forgive," she explained, "but I can't forget."

When she had had enough she came to us, put on her hairnet, and went to work in the cafeteria with my mother, giving her slow attention to portions of corn and mashed potatoes. She never bothered with divorce, she simply lived in one married name until the opportunity for another came along. And like my mother, she just as easily switched from married to maiden name without consistency or legal considerations.

They were Evers, sometimes more, sometimes less, but always Evers. The daughters of Helen Evers and some no-account Scot preacher who never married their mother, turning up only to impregnate her a second time, and leaving them, finally, on the side of the road. The young Indian mother walked, carrying one baby and coaxing the other, until she came to a junkyard. There, she made a home for them in an abandoned car. There, until the rent money was saved, she left Gracie in the back seat to look after the baby, Rozella, while she walked into town and looked for work.

"You remember, Rozella," my mother's mind fluttering from one story to the next, "the time I locked you in the outhouse?"

"I 'member."

Momma lit her cigarette from Auney's and spoke to me. "Your grandma used to have to go to work in town. Five miles there and back, she walked. Ever' day, even Sundays. She was afraid someone would steal us, so she always locked us up in the house." Her eyes darted across mine, and she blushed with shame. "It was just an old shack, tar paper and cold in the winter."

"Cold."

"We was always up to no good." Her face lit up. "Still are, eh Rozella?"

"Yep. Sure was. Your momma was always the ringleader."

My mother took the compliment with a laugh.

"As soon as your grandma was down the road, we scrambled right out the window and back 'fore she got home that night. More coffee, Rozella?"

Auney was a strong coffee drinker. She'd been waiting for the offer for some time but instead of saying "yes," she looked down into her empty cup, took a drag on her cigarette, and came as close as she allowed herself to expressing want. "I believe so," she said in a slow and uncommitted drawl. She lived with us, on and off, for most of her life, but she never asked or took without multiple invitations and assurances of plenty. That, my mother said, was the Indian in her.

Momma brought a new cup and the coffeepot to the table. She filled their cups and poured me half a cup. I wanted to smoke too but knew better than to ask.

"One day, you 'member, Rozella?"

"I 'member."

"You went to the bathroom and I locked the door from the outside." Momma laughed, Auney blushed. "You didn't so much as raise a yell. I heard you try to open the door. But then you got real quiet."

"How did Auney get out?" I was the audience, and I held the story's cues.

"She did the durnest thing. I'm waiting out front, wondering when she's gonna start yelling, and here she comes around the corner of that outhouse. What a sight you was, Rozella. I thought I was seeing things when you come around that corner." Momma turned to me. "She was covered with shit and piss from head to toe. She crawled right out of that damn hole! And she stunk! Lord have mercy."

"Amen."

"Momma came home that night and whupped the living daylights out of me. She whupped Rozella too."

"She did. Yes, she did."

"She said the county'd come and get us if we didn't behave. They woulda too. A young Indian woman with two little girls and no man around."

"No man."

"But she kept us together. I wander how she did it, Rozella?" The kitchen curtain flapped. Momma went to close the window and found it shut tight. "Witches, Rozella. You 'member them witches down there in old man Jeeter's river?"

"Sh-h-h," Auney said. "Y'all gotta watch who y'all call up."

Momma laughed and turned to me. "Your Auney were always afeared a them witches. Long afore our momma died, she'd a shiver and shake anytime she come near that water."

"Now, Grace, I weren't the onliest one afeared."

"That's true," Momma admitted, "true enough. Momma used to say only fools don't know what to be afeared of. And the good Lord save us from them. Eh, Rozella?"

"Ain't nothing scarier'n a fool. The God's truth."

In the dream I'm being chased. Through city streets, down alleys, only a few slippery feet ahead of the monster behind me. I feel his reaching darkness, gaining and gaining, almost in grabbing distance. I watch the horror of running without moving, screaming without noise, the terror striking and missing, striking and missing, and I pull myself treading to the surface. Sweating and shaking, I lie still in my corner of the room. "Shoo," I whisper. "Go on."

"Those was tough times," Momma said. "The depression and the wind blowing the topsoil clean outta Oklahoma. Times was rough all over. There was no welfare, no nothing for an Indian woman with two little girls to feed. Even if'n there was, she had that Indian pride, don't take nothing from nobody."

" 'Member she beat me for askin' Miz Wilkins for that apple?"

"I thought she was gonna kill you."

"Almost did."

"Why'd Grandma do that? It was just a apple." The words slipped out of my mouth. I knew better. "I mean," I tried to explain as I watched the humor drain from Momma's face, "why'd she have to be so mean?"

"What ya know 'bout it? It ain't ever just a apple. Things ain't never that simple. 'Cept you, sometime." Auney dropped her laughing eyes, and Momma commenced shaking her finger at me. "Missy, ya ain't but ten years old and you think ya know it all. Y'all don't know donkey shit."

"I know something," I mumbled and pushed my shoulders back.

"Horse manure."

Auney laughed and gagged on her smoke. Through a fit of coughing, she tried to say, "Grace . . . we . . . was . . . the same way."

"At her age Momma was dead and we was on our own with that old devil Jeeter. We had to grow up fast, it ain't the same."

I considered the distance from my mother across the table and gambled. "I can take care of myself."

"I wisht I believed it. I'd a take the first Greyhound bus and leave youse to yourself. The trouble with you, Missy, is you ain't never knowed hard times. Ya don't know what it means to spend just as much time *not* looking hungry as being hungry." She was wrong, but I knew better than to gamble again. "I wisht I'd a had a mother to look after me. Maybe things a been different for me."

"Ya did your best, Grace."

"Lord knows I tried. I'd tried and tried till I'm a plumb tired out from trying."

"Plumb tired out."

"I tried to forget an' go on living. But those was hard times. Don't seem like there's a way a forgetting 'em. I 'member Momma like it was yesterday. I see her as clear as I see myself. I 'member her taking off down that road ever' morning, walking those five miles to town to clean the Wilkins house and the Davis house. . . ."

"And that one with the big white porch. The Johnson house."

"Yep. Those white women worked her to death, and the white men was always touching her up. Sometimes she'd come home crying. You 'member, Rozella?"

"I 'member."

"You 'member how we used to sit on old man Jeeter's back porch and watch for her in the moon?"

"I 'member."

"The day she died she said she'd be watching for us from the moon. You 'member?"

"I 'member."

"Used to be we'd see her. Most every night. All's we had to do was sit on old man Jeeter's back porch and watch for her. Soon those eyes a hers would be looking at us."

"Yep. Plain as day."

"We sit right there and talk to her like she could hear us. About old man Jeeter and the hard life we had without her." Momma laughed and shrugged. "Those eyes a hers would change. Look like she were going to kill somebody."

"You 'member, Grace, what she used to tell us?" Momma and Auney laughed, and I saw Lizzie turn from her work at the sink, and almost smile.

"I sure do." Momma leaned toward me, as if I hadn't heard it a hundred times before, and said slowly, "Don't mess with Indian women."

" 'Less you're a fool."

"Even a fool got more sense'n that."

"Grace, you ever see Momma after ya left old man Jeeter's place?"

"Used to be when I ran away with that old man Baptist preacher, I'd see her. Now and again. You see her, Rozella?"

"Now and again."

Momma waited for Auney's words to clear the room. We waited for what Auney would not say. Then Momma laughed and said, "Used to be we believed Indians went to the moon when they passed on." The joke passed through Momma's face before she spoke. "What y'all think? We gonna make it to the moon?"

"I can't see why not."

"Me too?"

Momma lit a cigarette. Auney said low and careful, "I believe so."

"You just tell them you're Helen Evers' grandbaby. She ain't gonna let them turn ya away. They'd have a fight on their hands, sure enough. Wouldn't knowed what hit 'em. Ya 'member, Rozella?"

"I 'member."

"I remember."

Momma laughs, Auney stops mid-draw on her cigarette. "You weren't even born. How can you 'member?"

"I do remember."

My mother looks at me. The kitchen curtain flaps above my head. Finally she says, "You musta dreamt it."

"Dreamt it."

Carol Lee Sanchez

LAGUNA

My childhood, girlhood, and early adulthood experiences were multicultural and multilingual because of my mixed-race heritage and place of my birth. my father's people were middle-eastern immigrants who settled in a spanish land grant town bordering the laguna reservation (in new mexico)—almost a hundred years ago. my dad was born in seboyeta and my mom was born in old laguna. my mom's mom, and her mom, and her mom, and her mom . . . were born in old laguna. i grew into self-consciousness in paguate village. my earliest memories originate in this place— my first home. i continued to grow in the country, living in the very small rural community of cubero till i was almost ten. at that time, my two younger sisters and i were sent to a catholic girls' boarding school to "learn to speak properly" (without accent); to "read and write well" in the dominant language (enemy's language) because that's what my folks decided for us. i married at eighteen. i remained in the laguna, cubero, grants (new mexico) area until i was thirty in 1964. i went to san francisco. over the years, i made a lot of paintings, wrote lots of poetry, raised 3 children, and became a college instructor—"country girl made good." i now live on a farm in missouri with my husband thomas allen.

Tribal Chant

yo soy india
    pero no soy

nacio mi abuela
on the reservation, a
laguna indian—but her daddy
was a scotsman.
un gringo, tambien, un anglo y
you soy anglo
    pero no soy

yo soy arabe
    pero no soy
nacio mi papa
en un land grant town
se llama seboyeta
en un canyon de los
caboletta mountains on the
east slope of mt taylor
en nuevo mexico
su papa
nacio en lebanon
across an ocean
in another continent
embraced by those *gentes coloniales*
de mejico
spoke spanish, arabic, and
finally english
pero sin facilidad
mi papa is a *seboyetano*
heir to the grant
raised with mexican/spanish customs
y yo soy chicana
    pero no soy

este llanto plays in my head
weaves in and out
through the fabric
of my days.

yo soy india I am Indian
pero no soy But I am not a woman
yo soy anglo I am English
pero no soy

yo soy arabe
pero no soy
yo soy chicana
pero no soy

Elise Paschen

O S A G E

I am proud to be one-quarter Osage, but as "Two Standards" suggests I did not grow up in a Native American community. My Osage grandfather, Alexander Tallchief, died before I turned one. My grandmother, Ruth Tallchief, was Scots Irish, and I loved visiting her in Fairfax, Oklahoma, until her death in 1981. I was raised in Chicago by my mother, Maria Tallchief, and father, Henry Paschen, and began writing poems when I was eight years old. As a writer I aspire to learn more about my Osage heritage while I continue to open my eyes, ears, heart, and mind by reading and hearing the work of Native American writers whom I greatly admire.

Two Standards

AT A NATIVE WRITERS' CONFERENCE
IN NORMAN, OKLAHOMA

Joan's one-eighth. I'm a quarter.
When we walk into Billy's
I want to look like her,
full Osage. "You wouldn't find
an Indian here," she tells me,
"if not for the conference."

And the cigar-chewing driver
shuttling in from the Will
Rogers Airport confides:
"I never seen so many
Indians all in one spot."
The bar's packed like a bar

should be. Joan shows me off,
introducing her friends
to a light-haired, East Coast-
educated outsider
whose mother, Betty Tallchief,
is Oklahoma's pride.

"At that table are some
Osages you should meet."
They know my relatives
in Fairfax, though they come
from Pawhuska, Pawnee.
Angela says the Tallchiefs,

the keepers of the drum,
will host the Osage dances
next June. "Will you join us?

You'll be given your Osage
name." Even though my grandmother
Tallchief's daughters became

famous as ballet dancers,
she displayed photographs
of my mother and aunt
when they were twelve, eleven
in Osage ceremonial dress,
performing at a powwow.

My mother said her father's
mother taught her those dances.
I say, when asked, I never wanted
to dance, but here, in Billy's
with the jukebox repeating
the Beatles' "Twist and Shout,"

all I want is to dance
and to adopt my mother's
Osage name "Wa-Xthe-thon-ba":
"Two Standards." All I want
is to return to Oklahoma
and answer Angela "*Yes*,"

though New York City's half
a continent away.
I am my mother's daughter,
"Two Standards," and tonight,
forgetting my given name,
I will take that ancestral one.

Scott Kayla Morrison
"Kela Humma" (Red Hawk)

CHOCTAW

I've always been different. I remember being told at a young age that my family didn't know what to do with me except love me. I remember thinking that gypsies had kidnapped me and left me in Daisy, Oklahoma. That was the only explanation I had for being so different from the rest of the family.

In my early twenties, I started writing. My family heaved a collective sigh of relief, I think. "Oh, she's a writer, THAT explains it, no wonder she's so different," seems to be the consensus of the family.

An early speech impediment influenced me and my writing a great deal. I have a deformed bone in the roof of my mouth, and I stuttered until my twenties—about the same time I started writing. I did not realize until much later how lonely and isolated I was as a child because I could not communicate with others. I was cut off from human contact, so I lived in my own world in my head. This isolation was bridged with writing since no verbal communication is necessary, and writing can be a lonely business. It can also break the isolation by inviting others into your world.

Now there is just so much to say about my worldview. It is an exciting time to be an Indian with so much happening in Indian country, and the environment. As an organizer of Indian communities on environmental issues, I see Indians at *the cutting edge of a larger environmental, social-justice movement. The "browning" of the green movement, if you will. It is very exciting to be a part of that and, hopefully, to help shape it.*

An Apokni* by Any Other Name Is Still a Kakoo†

My grandson calls me Apokni. My daughter calls me Mother. My dad calls me Sweet Pea. My mother calls me Baby Girl. My aunts call me Little Droopy because I am so much like Aunt Virgie, whose nickname is Droopy. My great-aunt Doll called me Meshaya, "the future" in my Choctaw dialect. My Indian friends call me Scottie. My enemies call me many things.

I was born Phyllis Ann Isom in 1951; I had no choice in my name. I chose to become Mrs. Roger Morrison in 1970. In 1985, I chose to become Scott Kayla Morrison by court order. I adopted Kela Humma (Red Hawk) as my warrior name when I graduated from the University of Iowa College of Law in 1990. Now, I am considering another change to Scott Kayla Meshayatubbee, my ancestral family name modified.

Names for American Indian people can be adopted, discarded, changed, modified, personalized, and forgotten, over the course of a person's life. The name on a birth certificate may not be the same name on the marriage license or on the death certificate. The name on the birth certificate may not be the name you are known by throughout your life. The name your family calls you may not be the name your non-Indian friends and co-workers call you. Names are often changed throughout the cycles of a person's life. And that is how it should be. Your relationship with the universe changes over time as you grow and mature. These steps must be recognized somehow, and a change of name is one visible way. A voluntary name change signifies the choices a person has over his or her own life.

*"Grandmother" in Choctaw.
†"Grandmother" in Comanche.

My father was born Monroe Thomas Isom, son of Anganora Billy Page Isom, a full-blood Choctaw, and Charles Henry Isom, a Dutchman. Dad has never been know as Monroe his entire life. When he was small, he did a typically child-like act and cut his own hair. To even his lopsided haircut, his head had to practically be shaved. Dad looked like Jay Thompson, a bald neighbor, so he became "Jay" Isom. Dad is still called Jay by everyone, not his given name of Monroe. Sometimes Dad is called One Feather, signifying the loss of his leg twenty-three years ago.

Nicknames are very common in my rural Choctaw community of Daisy, Oklahoma. In fact, anyone who is not given a nickname by the community is suspect. A person known by their given name means that they are not trusted or liked by the community. A few people are not given a nickname out of great respect. My Irish mother, Noreen Latimer Isom, falls into this category. She used to feel excluded from the community because she had no nickname. Yet after forty-two years of marriage to Dad (and hence the community), and the mother of five little Choctaws, she came to realize that having no nickname was a sign that the community honored and respected her.

Nicknames are given in early life and can be changed over time. Often the younger generation will not know a person's given name. My uncle was always Uncle Nub to me and my generation. His wife called him Copus. His friends who lived outside of Daisy called him Charlie. Dad would call him High Pockets, and names he wouldn't translate to me when Dad was mad at him. What was his real name? I finally asked Mother. My uncle was born Charles Henry Isom, Jr. Where did "Nub" come from? She did not know; he had been called Nub for so long. Why did Aunt Nadine call him Copus? When Uncle Nub was still single, he used to dress like a country-western music star, Cowboy Copus. Oh, I guess you had to have been there, huh, Maw?

The names of places also go through transformations as years progress. When my family, the Billys, came to Indian Territory from Mississippi over the Trail of Tears in the early 1830s, they settled in Kulli Lawa, at the foot of Jack's Fork Mountain, on the north side of Jack's Fork Creek. With the passage of time, when a larger population of non–Choctaw-speaking people came into the Choctaw Nation, Kulli Lawa became known by its English translation, Many Springs. It became the county seat of Jack's Fork County, Choctaw Nation. In 1883, the first Butterfield stage line came near Kulli Lawa, and the United States Post Office was established. The name was changed to Etna. Naturally, the name became a point of dissension among the native Choctaws, so the name was changed in 1888 to Daisy, after local beauty Daisy Mae. At statehood, Jack's Fork County was redistricted and became Atoka County, part of Pushmataha and Pittsburg Counties. Indian Territory became Oklahoma.*

Chahta sia hoke: I am Choctaw. The name of the people has changed over the years. The name we call ourselves is Okla Chahta, the people of Chahta, a great prophet who led our people on a long migration at some point in our ancient past. Chahta became bastardized by non–Choctaw-speaking people to the current usage of Choctaw. After I learned to read and went to college, I discovered non-Indian anthropologists and ethnohistorians had written down two origin stories for the Choctaw. One was an emergence myth of how the Chahta came into being. We emerged from the earth at Ninah Waya (Bending Mountain), the holy place of our birth. The other legend was a migration story. We migrated to Ninah Waya in what is now central Mississippi. The purpose of story is to show how we accept others into our society and treat them as family, in much the same way my non-Indian mother was treated as family. I told my aunts about these two stories, which some of the "experts" said could not be reconciled and other "experts" said

*"Okla" in Choctaw means people, and "homa" or "humma" means red. The Treaty of Dancing Rabbit Creek of 1830 referred to the Choctaw Nation as the Chahta okla homa (the Choctaw Nation of red people). The name of Oklahoma was adopted during the territorial congressional debate. The state seal of Oklahoma is the Choctaw Nation seal, and can be seen today on the Oklahoma state flag, and license plates.

were fiction created to mask some evil deed in our past. These words worried me. Variations of the two stories were combined in my oral history. I went to my aunts, my dad's sisters, with these two stories for guidance.

"White people are so funny," my aunts told me. "You can't expect too much from them, they aren't Choctaw. Remember that. You are Choctaw, you know. And you are Billy, granddaughter of Anganora Billy, great-granddaughter of Judge Issac Billy, great-great-granddaughter of Alexander Billy. You are not to shame your family by believing nahola lies." *Nahola* means *white* in Choctaw. I know this. This lesson had been repeated so often since birth that it has become part of my consciousness.

Silence.

The silence stretched. Two of my aunts' only motion was a heel-toe foot movement which propelled their rockers. Another aunt rocked herself in her rockerless chair to the same rhythm. The youngest aunt merely stroked the arm of her chair. She was always out of sync with the other aunts. She was, after all, the youngest, and was still in the process of moving from "child" to "elder," even with forty-five years of living under her belt. Her name signified her position in the circle of women—Little Alice. Her namesake, Big Alice, Grandma's sister, was long since dead, but Little Alice was still her name. Her presence was part of her training, training that would continue until all knew she was ready to be part of the ancient rhythm which kept the community alive. Her stroking of the chair arm had at least replaced the fidgeting of her youth; she was on the right road. The aunts were in no hurry.

After everyone present had an opportunity to chew over my problem in silence, the leader, not the oldest, of my aunts began. "When you were a child," Aunt Virgie said, "you did something you saw white children do. Do you remember that?"

Yes, vividly, I said, although I did not remember what I did in the first grade. I only remembered her reaction. She sharply called me into the house from the yard where I was playing. I was bewildered. I had been a favorite, just as all of my generation were favorites. Using harsh words with me was reserved for my dad, who seldom used them except when he was drinkin' and out of his mind. My aunt's tone went beyond disapproval, and bordered on anger. What had I done, I thought. The thought of fleeing my aunt's realm to my own home entered my mind. I dismissed this in a heartbeat. My aunt's realm included my home. My dad and non-Indian mother did not have the power to save me from my aunt's disapproval or anger. Facing it was my only option. I answered her before my insolence annoyed her further.

"Why were you doing that?" she asked. Her stern tone was tempered by my transparent fright. I was on safer ground when I saw love in her eyes. But I also knew I could not evade her or whatever was to happen next. Loving me included disciplining me.

"I saw Henry's kids doing it," I answered honestly. She sighed. I knew being honest with her helped my situation. At least lying would not be included in whatever sin I had committed, but being honest did not mitigate it.

"You are not white." Silence followed the statement of this fact while she searched my eyes for understanding. I know, I've always known. These four words must have more meaning than that obvious fact. If I waited without elaboration, she would explain, and she did.

"Henry's children are allowed to go to school with you because Henry has learned his place. His family came to clear our land as sharecroppers. They were allowed to stay because they learned to keep their habits to themselves. His grandfather was a Confederate scout for the Choctaw regiment. The family earned a place in our community, but they are not Choctaw. They are not our equals. Henry knows this. His family knew this. He must teach his children this.

"You are Billy. You cannot defame your family by acting white." I was dismissed with this, confused but trusting my aunt's lesson to become clear with time. Even at a young age, I knew being Choctaw was a lifelong training, and being Choctaw was being born with the memories which made the training finally become understandable.

Aunt Virgie had been silent while I replayed that scene in my mind. The other aunts continued their rocking and stroking. "You are still not white. You are still Choctaw. You are still Billy."

Aunt Audrey stopped rocking and straightened in her chair. She was the oldest, and the strongest, but seldom exercised her strength. There was no need. Truly strong people just are without having to have their strength validated by an audience. "We worried about you going to college," she said. "We could have lost you. We are all educated. Your grandmother was educated. Your great-aunt Big Alice was a schoolteacher, just as her mother and father were, and her grandmother and grandfather. We have a history of education. But the education was in our own schools.

"Our generation was different. We were sent away to a boarding school. Me, Virgie, and your dad went when your dad was seven. You know the story of me and your dad running away and walking sixty miles back home."

Tears welled up in my eyes. I knew the words of the story, how it took two weeks for two frightened little children of age seven and eleven to walk by night and hide by day, how they had to steal what little they ate, how their fear of being discovered equaled their fear of what would happen to the ones in Daisy when their return was discovered. I knew the words, it was in my oral history. But I also knew the emotions, it was in my collective memory. The fear, hunger, and pain were more than just words to a family story, they had a force to make me cry.

"You have always been different, you know that." Aunt Audrey was referring to a speech impediment. I was born with a genetically enlarged bone in my mouth. Few people, my mother being one, could understand me. I was always frustrated with everyone because they could not understand me. This, in some ways, made me withdrawn. That lonely, isolated place within me is where the writer in me still lives. I can communicate on paper what I could not communicate in person. I was spared the lesson that being different was bad. And I learned to be obstinate about communicating. I kept repeating until someone heard me. I knew I was "heard" when my family said they did not know what to do with me except love me. Love was a universal communicator. I finally overcame, for the most part, my speech impediment in my early twenties.

"You needed to stay in our little one-room schoolhouse with all your relatives. We could have sent you to some special school, but you would have learned to be a cripple. Here, no one made fun of you or treated you as a cripple. Here, your mother and your teacher did their best to teach you to talk like the rest of us. Here, our only concern for you was Henry's white children."

Silence again. My aunts allowed me time to digest this new important information. I had simply lived my life, I had not thought about it, or my aunt's part in it. After a respectful length, Aunt Little Al asked, "What were you called during the years you were in Goss School?"

Everything but Phyllis, my given name, I responded. My aunts nodded, and set their rockers in motion to match the rhythm of their bobbing heads. Once their entire bodies were in unison again, we sat in silence, contemplating the importance of this revelation.

"I was always so proud of you," Aunt Virgie beamed. "I was happy when people said you were like me, and called you Little Droopy. The day I scolded you for acting white hurt me. I was scolding myself but I had to. What you do with your life, since we are connected, is done to me. If you bring shame to yourself, you bring shame to me."

"And to the rest of us," Aunt Opal added. Aunt Opal was seldom a part of these discussions. The alcohol that ran in her veins diluted the Choctaw blood almost beyond recognition. You cannot trust alcohol, or rather you trust alcohol to be deceitful. She was included because the white interpretation of our origin stories was too important to exclude her and her pickled memories from the discussion.

Aunt Little Al's raised eyebrow at Aunt Opal's remark was the only indication of surprise. Aunt Opal was still able to be coherent, as this rare moment of sharpness indicated. The aunts exchanged bare glances, not at Aunt Opal, but at Little Al for showing surprise. She was still not ready to be called plain "Alice," and a helluva long way from being called "Big Al." Children seeking counsel from elders called for certain decorum, decorum which comes from internal control over individual emotions. This solemn discussion concerned the collective interest of the community. It did not relate to the individual concern of Aunt Opal being sober. "Big Al" would have known that. Even plain "Alice" may have suspected that. But Little Al did not, and thus had acted on her impulse. She had a long way to go, but the aunts were in no hurry. The rocking continued, while Little Al stroked the arm of her chair.

"Times have changed," Aunt Virgie started. "When Maw was a girl, Choctaws were the majority. Now, the numbers are changing. We will soon be a minority if whites keep moving into our land. We can't stop it. We have to be careful. Whites are waiting for any excuse to say we are just dirty Indians, and to treat us like dirty Injuns. It will just be worse when you are sitting here talking to your children."

The old women recognized this when Aunt Virgie said, "We are becoming dinosaurs. Our bones are displayed in the big cities just like the extinct animals we are becoming. White men put flesh on dinosaur bones to reconstruct the entire animal, to show they are smarter than the animal they construct out of their own egos. They do the same thing with us by rewriting our history. They do not have to be right, they only have to do the act itself."

Talking of our past drew my eyes to Aunt Opal's claw-like fingernails to join with the gaze of the aunts. I felt the same sensation they felt—the collective memory connected us all in the room, even Little Al. The smoke of a memory transported us to a primitive place, the reality of which would shock the "educated" academic who miswrote our origin legend. To me, it was home.

I stood with all those who went before. The bonepicker with his long claws ascended the scaffold to tend to his sacred duty. He prepared the bones for burial while each apokni, long dead, breathed through the flimsy body I occupied, leaving behind their essence to take back with me to the other reality I lived at college. The memory still lived in me. I belonged. I was Choctaw. I was

Billy. I could speak clearly. I did not need an individual name to be recognized for what I was.

"At this college," Aunt Virgie said, "you are outnumbered in this place. White men will clothe our bones in whatever fashion they desire. They have no history so they must manipulate ours to make them feel superior. We can do nothing. We cannot teach them because they do not have the memory of their race's birth. They have not seen the entire animal so they do not know how to reconstruct it out of its bones. Nahola is to be pitied. Remember that."

The discussion was over. The leaving of the place did not un-thread the needle that beaded the patterns of our lives. For an afternoon, every family member since the emergence from Ninah Waya united to teach me, to comfort me, to name me in a way that required no name. I was accepted as a whole, not as the breed I am.

During my college years, my family was careful to name me when I came home for visits. I was always called by my childhood names. I belonged. My aunts knew, after that afternoon, they had no reason to worry about me in that white college. I was born Choctaw, I would die Choctaw. But more important, I would live Choctaw. They turned their attention to the other needs of the community. I was not a rootless, nameless, speechless child after that afternoon. I was a whole.

Law school was a horse of a different color altogether. My great-grandfather was a judge in our Choctaw National Court system, but I was to be the first lawyer in the Anglo-American legal system. Going to an Anglo-American law school raised the old fears, but not to the same level as my undergraduate years, I don't think, even though I was going to another state—Iowa. The weekend visits would end. The connection to my home would be strained, maybe broken. Raising children among foreigners was fearful. As usual though, my aunts met the occasion.

Aunt Virgie came to my house as I was packing the car. She hugged me close. "We love you and are proud of you." I could have left then, and been happy. But my aunt continued, "This is your home. It will always be your home. If it gets too tough out there, come home. You will never be a failure to us. When you get into this car to leave, you will be a success. It takes strength to leave your home and go live out there. And I know it can get bad. When it does, come home.

"And remember you are a Billy. You have no reason to bow to anyone. Do you hear me?" Yes, I have always listened to every word this woman said, without question. This innocence would change after three years in Iowa at that damned school.

During law school, I found a larger "family," a national Indian community. This family taught me that I was a warrior on the law path. I decided I needed a warrior name.

Indians were still at war, only the weapons changed. The last lines of Joy Harjo's poem "I Am a Dangerous Woman" sum up, for me, modern Indian warfare. "I am a dangerous woman/but the weapon is not visible/security will never find it/they can't hear the clicking of the gun/inside my head." We fight with our heads. We string our bows with treaties, court cases, and laws. We still face the same foes as our ancestors. Paula Gunn Allen summed up our enemies in *The Sacred Hoop*:

Consciously or unconsciously, deliberately, as a matter of national policy, or accidentally as a matter of "fate", *every single government*, right, left, or centrist, in the western hemisphere is consciously or subconsciously dedicated to the extinction of those tribal people who live within its borders.

Within this geopolitical charnel house, American Indian women struggle on every front for the survival of our children, our people, our self-respect, our value systems, and our way of life. The past five hundred years testify to our skill at waging this struggle: for all the varied weapons of extinction pointed at our heads, we endure.

We survive war and conquest; we survive colonization, acculturation, assimilation; we survive beating, rape, starvation, mutilation, sterilization, abandonment, neglect, death of our children, our loved ones, destruction of our land, our homes, our past, and our future. We survive, and we do more than just survive. We bond, we care, we fight, we teach, we nurse, we bear, we feed, we learn, we laugh, we love, we hang in there, no matter what.

The avenue to change the powerlessness my aunts described on that afternoon was the law, I believed. Law would legitimize my anger, and I could make a living doing what I have always done—fighting for my survival. I had made a sensible marriage in my choice of careers. I hoped I had overcome the lack of judgment I exercised in picking my DNA donor, long since named my ex-husband. Maybe my mate selection in the marriage to law had improved.

The war waged with our minds transcends gender. Being a woman would not be an impediment. In fact, I believed it would be an asset. Women with communal values always balance all interest in a situation. We are also more creative in using all weapons at our disposal to achieve the results we want. I discovered when I began practicing law that I would spend extra time thinking of creative uses of laws and cases to arrive at a desired result—uses that my male counterparts would often overlook.

At law school, I felt prepared to begin walking the red road (the Choctaw concept of going to war). I knew my weapons. Paula Gunn Allen named our enemies: colonization, assimilation, acculturation. Naming the enemy is powerful. To name the enemy allows no room for interpretation or misunderstanding.

The first enemy I named was called racism. I was introduced to this enemy during the first semester of law school. I discovered quite quickly that, to my non-Indian, non-black, non-Hispanic, non-women peers, I was a "minority," in every negative sense of the word. My presence in those hallowed halls deprived some poor white male of an opportunity to eat from the same trough in the pig-state of Iowa. I was not to forget that. I was also not to forget that I was admitted under the quota system, which equated to being dumb. My aunts were right, white people *are* funny.

My "peers" were clairvoyant: they could tell by my skin color how smart I was. They were right, my skin color does show how smart I am. I am smart enough to live in two worlds, two unrelated, unreconciled and unreconcilable worlds. I had to learn their world, but they would never, ever have to learn mine.

Racism, as it turned out, instigated a dilemma which was to launch me on another naming experience. The law school asked me to recruit other Indian students from Oklahoma. My recruiting trip would have included that Thanksgiving vacation during my first year. I would get a free trip home, but I would be asking other Indians to come to a school which had caused me pain. Could I do this?

Well, I went home and talked to my mother. Do I ask other Indians to come to this school? Mother told me honestly that she could not answer that because she had never been faced with that situation. She sent me to my aunts.

My aunts listened to my story. "Do you want to come home?" was the first question. And be run out by these funny people? No, I would stay. "We have heard of such things," Aunt Virgie told me.

"Come home," Aunt Audrey pleaded. "We can't protect you up there. Come home where you are loved and needed."

"Would you come home just because someone else wanted you to leave?" Aunt Virgie asked Aunt Audrey. We all knew the answer. Aunt Audrey conducted her life on her own timetable, not by the pointless dictates of someone else. "She said she would stay. We will help her do that.

"You want to be a lawyer. Other Choctaws deserve to be lawyers. We need lawyers, but at what costs? Your great-great-grandfather was a senator to the Choctaw National Council. He was one of those that demanded our students be returned from a missionary boarding school in Kentucky because they were unhappy and coming back uneducated. The solution was to start our own schools here.

"We can't start our own law school, and we can't make you come home. We need to make the school a better place for you to be. How do we do this?" she asked, looking at Aunt Audrey. Aunt Audrey looked back. Her glaucoma eyes stared back at Aunt Virgie, but lately, we never knew if she actually saw us or only focused toward the sound of our voices.

Aunt Audrey's lips started curling into that foxy, knowing smile I had seen before. It usually preceded a joke, or a cutting insult directed at someone who she decided deserved her stabbing wit. Choctaw humor is laced with ridicule and satire. One-plane documents, recorded by non-Indian, Christian males, successfully hide the three-dimensional Choctaw wit, and often misinterpret it for cruelty when read a century later.

"Knowledge is a powerful thing," Aunt Audrey began. "If other children know what to expect, they can make that decision. This school must know that we are watching them. This school must know that we know what they are doing and how they are treating our children. It is little we can do, but it is enough."

They sent me to talk to Assistant Chief Gregg Pyle, who was not in, but his office directed me to the Office of Higher Education, which in turn sent me to the editorial office of the *Bishinik*, our tribal newspaper. The editor wanted a written account of my treatment at this school so other Choctaws would know what to expect if they chose to attend the University of Iowa College of Law. The law school would learn what politicians in Oklahoma had learned, that they are accountable to the Choctaw people, even if the only accountability mechanism we have is our informed vote.

Naming the enemy of racism, and naming my weapons to combat this enemy of hate, was a powerful experience. The victimization mentality, which this experience could have perpetuated, was changed to an opportunity to gather my power. The problem which affected the community was solved by the community of Oklahoma Choctaws working together. The painful experience became a growth experience. This lesson of learning through pain I would remember throughout the rest of law school, and into my practice. It is a lesson that has served me well. No situation can defeat me when I turn it into an opportunity to overcome adversity.

One major event happened in law school which deeply affected me, and does still to this day. I finally decided where I would be buried. The name on the headstone is still in question, but the physical location of my final resting place is certain.

Daisy has two cemeteries. One is the Billy family cemetery next to the old Indian plantation home. It is a segregated cemetery with only non-Indian spouses allowed to be buried there. The other is a community cemetery. I made my choice between these two cemeteries based on who was also there now or who would be there. I wanted to be near my aunts.

My aunts believed our bones spoke to each other while our spirits went into the afterlife. Some people, including other Choctaws, disagree with this belief, and I am undecided if this is true. But I won't know for sure until it is too late. To cover all bases, I felt I should be near my aunts so I could spend the next five hundred years in their company.

Aunt Big Al died in 1971 and was buried in the community cemetery. I drove the stakes marking my grave site just east of her grave. It is a pleasant, peaceful spot, shaded by an old oak tree. Good drainage, no gophers. I went to my cousin who manages the cemetery and requested that the tree be replanted should it ever die. Standing under that tree, I could see us all talking in the shade, sharing conversations as we did that afternoon years before, as well as folksy gossip about the neighborhood. Yes, I could live there for five hundred years or so until my bones returned to Mother Earth.

Aunt Audrey had lost a son and he was buried west of my grave. She had decided to be buried next to him. Aunt Virgie will be buried across the road to the east of me. Aunt Opal will be buried next to her sons who are buried southwest of me. Aunt Little Alice is still young enough to think she will live forever. She has not said where she will be buried. Grandma and her parents are buried in the Billy cemetery. It is just "a spit and holler" as we say in Oklahoma, so maybe we can visit back and forth. Who knows? I certainly won't until after I die. Then it will be too late to change my mind.

I thought about buying my headstone and leaving the year of my death blank. I would, of course, leave the grave site nameless as well. I plan on living until I am 105 years old. I will need that much time to accomplish all that I have planned for my life. I joke that I want to be shot by a jealous wife at 105 with the husband in question being 22, but this is just fantasy, naturally. I do not know what my Creator has planned for me, so I do not know what names I will adopt and discard in the future. All I know for sure is that I am my aunts' child. I am Choctaw.

Elizabeth Woody

WARM SPRINGS ▪ WASCO NAVAJO

I am compelled to continue in my family's legacy, to demonstrate an obdurate sensitivity to the natural world. This sense of place is an instruction that upholds an honorable way of life. I am active in my art, by giving story, by observing and listening. My grandmother used to tell me, "If you can make something, you will never be poor." The makings of my great-grandmothers, our heirlooms, depicted deer, trees, birds, flowers, and dreams. My grandfather told of his parents' hard work, attaching a message from them to live by right action, to become proficient in our language, to prosper, share, and respect all life in my thoughts. My parents, aunties, and uncles have reinforced this, especially the need to nurture the land through love.

In the panorama of language and the land that makes the language, in my mother's Plateau-Wasco River oratory and my father's Diné movement, words heal others or bring strength. I clear away the obstacles that come from bad

*thoughts, remain autonomous, honor my ancestors' ability to
live and "make things" or make-do.*

*I have to thank my parents, Charlotte Pitt and Guy
Woody, for the body they have passed on to me, the "Dreamer
Brain" that loses car keys, as well as imagines, and for this
spirit of inspiration that never stops.*

The Girlfriends

Filled with old lovers, in the clutch of the chair,
you are a bloom of uncombed hair.

With a collection of roses, bowls of mashed petals,
I make clear cup of sky.
Fold away clouds. Roll up blankets of blue.
I am a body of empty husks.
Indian corn is in your hair, the tassels,
the pollen, fertility.

Indelible ink is tattooing our lungs.
We speak smoke.
We exchange our lunacy for reverence.
Respect tornados.
Windy Woman. Four Winds.

We have extended the edge of expectations
by merely living.

You have tallied compulsion
into currency.
I am measured by the excitement
my lips stir.

I am the bin for cast-offs and the weary.
I wear my veil.
I have no children,
but you have many.
You dream of heaven and they all run up to meet you.

Inez Petersen

QUINAULT

Questions of identity as an In-
dian woman writer are as brambled and sweet as the black-
berries that inch past fences and property lines where I grew
up in western Washington. Hacking the tendriling vines seems
only to make them more vigorous while a direct assault of
tearing out root and branch eradicates even the strongest—but
it is difficult to take away everything.

I am from a generation where children were taken away,
placed in foster care, and, in many cases, never lived with their
mothers again. For me the very act of removal prompted an
intense desire to remember, and later record. This act of writ-
ing gathers for me my family, gives me back a history, and
places me within my tribe, the Quinault Indian Nation.

Missing You

This is no confession for I have not sinned.
I invent stories.
Once there was a family. It was an ordinary one with the usual
cast of characters: one mother, five sons, six daughters, and eight

or nine fathers. This was, or this was not, a family. I am the fourth child, the first daughter.

Our mother's beauty was legendary. One man steamshipped halfway around the world to find her. He left the makings of a son in her fifteen-year-old body. So began the end of her life. She died for a very long time.

Already at fifteen, it was too late to remember the ways of her tribe, for she was born Indian. Nowadays she is called a woman of color, or a Native American; on the reservation the people say Quinault.

Only one tradition came easily to this beautiful Quinault, the tradition of running away from Indian boarding school. Her mother had run away, and so had her mother's mother before her. Way back then, dances were danced and songs were sung in a language that was not English. This language was spoken to the children who ran away, back home to Taholah.

One day, the grandmothers who had run away remembered carrying rocks in their mouths when they attended Chemawa Indian Boarding School. They pretended not to remember the other punishments for speaking their own tongue; they did not remember the welts, puffed tender on their own arms when they had run back to their mothers.

These women loved their children and wanted a better life for them, as mothers do. They imagined all the trouble their children would be facing once they left the village. Before that could happen, the mothers decided to speak only English.

It was hard. Love names cried to escape. Mother lips pulled firm. Nowadays only the very old trees in Taholah remember Quinault names and Quinault verbs.

It happened: the beautiful Quinault ran back home to Taholah from Chemawa to a mother who spoke English. She returned and learned a new modern tradition, drinking alcohol. Maybe in biology or chemistry class she might have learned of the genetic predisposition waiting in her red blood.

There was one good thing about having no education—she could pretend not to understand the sign placed in the entrance of all the bars in town: *No dogs, or Indians*. It was fun to spend time with people who had such a good sense of humor and she let them buy her drinks.

A flurry of children gusted behind, like the changeling leaves of autumn, in the wake of her stormy relations.

I remember a quiet knock-knocking on the door. William.

It was William asking to come into the hotel room. He took turns calling our names; my older brothers sat tense, unmoving. He called my name out, soft. Gently, he asked me to let him in.

"Open the door, Inez, it's me, William." I ran to obey.

Mama caught me by the shoulder, pulled me to her, begged me to stop. She told me to lie down on the floor, then dragged a mattress over me. Since I was about two years old, she must have been pregnant with William's son. Information unknown to me. All I knew was the hissed warning in my ear: William had a gun.

It seems I used to tell my playmates that he shot through the door and we found the bullets lodged in the wall over where we lay, protected by the mattress. Now I believe it was a girl's wish to make her mother's actions heroine worthy, instead of life endangering. Or maybe I'd just seen Hollywood shoot-'em-ups too many times and wanted to make my life seem more amazing to my peers. I hated it when they pitied me, poor foster child whose mother didn't care. I wanted to prove them wrong.

Mama gave me a family name, after her mother's sister: Inez.

It seems I've told myself so many times that I am the fourth child, the first girl, that it must be so. If that is true, there is an unaccounted boy between Frank and Bobby. One story I remember telling is that when Mama was in the hospital having Bobby, some church people offered to take care of her second son, the brother I don't remember. She said yes, signed some papers, and the church people moved out of Taholah, off the reservation, out of our lives. There are enough years between Frank and Bobby for this to be true.

Maybe I just mixed up which brother it was I never met. One

day, about a year ago, I visited my mother. A man I'd never seen before walked into the house without knocking, sat on a couch, smoked a cigarette, and watched TV without saying a word.

Like it was no big deal, Mama said, "That's your brother Willie."

I almost fell into the act-like-nothing-just-happened mode our family does so well. Even as I refused the code of silence, I realized I had no common ground with this lean, nervous man. Tightrope time, no net. I inhaled, leaned forward, and asked, "So who is *your* father?"

Mama answered for him. "It was William." Tatters of information I collect for my crazy-quilt family.

I never knew Willie, so it hardly counts when I say I don't care for him. Who could fault me lack of feeling for a stranger? But Bobby is my only full-blooded sibling, named after our father: Robert Henry Petersen. Bobby is the only one of us that I don't love. This is difficult to admit, even to myself. Perhaps my salvation is in remembering pieces of history and honoring the loyalties that remain. I believe that as long as we live we are given the opportunity to love.

"There goes my brother," I said to a co-worker in the restaurant.

"Who? That bum crossing the street?"

"Yeah. I haven't seen him in probably two years."

"Two years! If that were my brother, I'd chase after him."

No, you wouldn't, is what I thought, but I didn't say anything. What would this kid understand? Bobby has always been lost. Frank says Bobby is the smartest one of all of us; I believe him out of habit.

What I've always said is that Bobby got damaged more than me from being taken away from Mama. He never adjusted. Kids teased him. Once I was in the town where he lived, in a grocery store called Swanson's with my friend Barbie Vincent. I saw Bobby a few checkstands over, bagging groceries.

"That's my brother," I said.

"No, it isn't," Barbie argued.

"Yes it is. Come on. I'll show you."

I marched her over to Bobby's work station and demanded, "You're my brother, aren't you?" I waited with arms crossed for him to answer.

Bobby looked disgusted. " 'Course," he said.

"See, I told you." Smug, I turned on my heel, not waiting for Barbie to catch up.

Years later, he visited me in Sacramento. Bobby stole some paltry doodads from my place: a neck chain, a book, a pillow, other stuff. I zoomed around in my then-boyfriend's VW, me riding shotgun. We raced to different on-ramps, looking for Bobby hitching north on K-5. We found him standing with his thumb out, my pillowcase bulging at his feet.

"Give it back, Bobby." Imperious as ever, I hauled my stuff back through the passenger window. I wanted to say to him, *Quit sniveling, quit drinking, quit blaming. You can change. Look at me, I did.*

What arrogant surety we hold as eighteen-year-olds. What I now know is this: Bobby is a man who will not die, will not conform, will not trust. He's been seen on the streets for almost two decades. His pain must fill the earth.

I would like very much to be the sister who loves her brothers without reserve, without question, without doubt. I seem the biggest fraud sitting here, warm, clean, stomach full. My apartment is beautiful, I work two jobs, enjoy friendships. Bobby is probably outside tonight, a bitterly cold November. Maybe, if he's lucky, he will have been arrested for some misdemeanor, get to sleep indoors on a bed, eat some meals, and shower before he is released. I wonder if it is my duty to offer the comforts of my home to him and wonder again if this is my way of hiding indifference. We didn't begin like this. We used to care.

When the world turned upside down my big brothers, Snookums and Bobby, were dropped off by our caseworker in South Aberdeen.

They were to live with the Hayes family. In my world, our sudden disappearances had begun. That left me, aged five, the oldest one left in the car, a 1960 Dodge Dart, robin's-egg blue. I sat in the back seat with my arms full of little sisters. Violet was three and Tina almost two. They snuggled in close. All I could see was the back of Miss Wendell's bouffant hairdo. Miss Wendell was the case-worker. In the front seat, three-month-old Pierre Jon lay next to her. I'd always called her Miss Window.

She drove to another place. We stopped and Miss Wendell took Tina out of the car. Tina whimpered, so I had to be stern with her. *Go on. Don't make trouble.* Her chubby hands clung to my arm. I willed her to let go. Miss Wendell came back to the car alone.

We drove for what seemed like a very long time to Westport. It was getting dark. The intricate stitching of the seat covers faded as the light diminished around us. When Miss Wendell finally braked to a stop, I kneeled on the seat and peeked out the side window.

The house was one story with a flat roof, the color a wash of charcoals that blurred together as colors along the ocean do on a cloudy day. All around me each surface seemed gray whether it belonged to a bush, a tree, or a wall. In the carport ahead of us all I remember is shadows moving.

"Do you want to live here or over there?" Miss Wendell asked. I wasn't going one step further.

"Here," I answered, not knowing the consequences of my choice. Just like that, my sister and I parted. Violet had to cross the pasture to the other house, a two-story frame silhouetted against a darkening sky.

There wasn't any reason to hang around Miss Wendell's car, but I dragged my feet anyway. The worn toes of my favorite pair of Keds pulled through the sandy soil you find in seaport towns. As we approached, an outside light came on and the door opened.

A tall woman greeted us. Charlene Hubbard was not beautiful and there was a lot of her. She carried herself carefully, as if her feet hurt, or maybe so she wouldn't scare kids.

"Hi! Come on in; we were just sitting down for supper."

"This will only take a minute," said Miss Wendell. "This is Inez, and this is Pierre Jon." She spoke rapidly while handing over my sleeping brother.

Sure enough, about one minute later Miss Window left us. All at once the blue car was backing out of the driveway, crunching over gravel. The headlights came on and swept over the patchy front lawn. We were caught momentarily in the brightness: Charlene holding Pear-pear, and me alongside her. I could see the goosebumps on her fleshy arms. The cotton shift she wore hung to mid-calf, not much protection from the cold.

She looked down. I saw dark circles under gray eyes.

"Come on in, honey," she said.

"You are not my mama. Only my mama can call me that." I held my head high, resisted her kindness.

"I know. You can call me Mom. Come inside and have some fried trout."

That was a smart thing to say. I loved fried fish even more than candy. Fish would taste like home, like the reservation.

The light inside glowed warm against the wood paneling in the living room. A worn couch and an easy chair were turned toward a console TV. Beyond, in the dining area, sat Richard Hubbard, Jr.

"C-c-c-come on, d-d-dinner's guh-getting c-c-cold." His florid complexion contrasted with the tight curls of his cropped hair. His eyes were nearly black and they sparkled from deep inside. He wore jeans and a white T-shirt with a pack of Marlboros rolled in the right sleeve. He looked like a cross between Elvis Presley and Fred Flintstone. A father at the dinner table—a new thing in the world.

Then it happened. Richard Hubbard reached over one of the three children already at the table—little Hubbards I supposed; he grabbed a bottle of Heinz ketchup, unscrewed the cap, and chugged sauce out. As he held it over his plate, great blotches of red smothered the beautiful fried trout.

It was too much for one day.

"You don't *do* that," I whispered and started weeping.

I had to protect us now that Frank and Bobby were gone. And now we lived with aliens.

The second batch of kids came after the first were made wards of the court, placed in foster care forever. Mama gave birth to three more: Almeta, Jule, and Edna.

Jule is between the two girls in age, the last son. His daddy appears to have been white, or maybe a light-skinned Quinault. Almeta and Edna were fathered by black men. I used to say they were half black until I realized how stupid that notion is. I don't know if they share the same father. When I introduce Edna as my baby sister, both of us tilt our jaws, daring anyone to point out the obvious.

I look for similarity in my brothers and sisters and me. We all have soft voices, soft gestures. We all carried my father's last name, until Edna chose her adopted parents. We all carry our mother's genetic makeup. Eventually, we all grew up alone.

For a time, I was allowed one brother to live with, to love. Jonny and I lived with Don and Ruth Tuttle. These people *loved*. They loved each other and they loved us.

We lived outside Malone, a wide spot in the road some miles outside of Elma, Washington. The Moxie Chehalis River ran the property line behind Granpa and Granma's house. We called Don and Ruth that because our previous home had been with their daughter. We lived on seven acres: enough for pastureland, an orchard, a berry patch, a flower garden, an herb and vegetable garden.

The first two rows in the vegetable garden were for green onions and it was the kids' job to keep that section weeded. Our other main garden job was to salt slugs. Every night in the summer we'd stalk the slime-makers, protecting our garden perimeter. We watched as clear liquid oozed out of them when salted. By morning, the slugs resembled petrified dog turds and we would poke at their shriveled bodies with long sticks.

I remember once when I tricked my little brother into eating half a slug. He'd done something to bug me and his punishment was to eat one whole slug. His chin trembled and so I pretended to relent. *Okay, you only have to eat half of it,* I told him—as if that were a lot better. He didn't realize that what I really wanted was for him to *bite* the creature. His water-dark eyes looked into mine, full of thanks.

I wonder what he'll remember.

In the rows after the green onions, Granpa's discerning hands weeded out feathery look-alikes in the carrots, radishes, dill weed, and all the rest. He, of course, did all the rototilling. Mostly Granma picked things when they were ready to cook or can. Neighbors throughout the valley would find themselves in our living room snapping beans or husking corn. Later, gathered with us around the table at dinnertime, they'd dig in to another Ruth Tuttle meal. Her bluelake green beans won prizes at the county fair; her generosity gathered souls wanting to be fed.

With so much love around Jonny and me, I released Violet the unknown, unafraid. With supreme assurance, I'd always thought Violet and I would meet again. She was my sister and I loved her. What more does it take?

We even looked like sisters: same brown hair, same light skin, same hazel eyes. When Violet visited me one last time before she was to be adopted, I tried to bribe her into remembering me. In my Cecil & Beanie ceramic bank lay a couple of one-dollar bills, softened from rolling between my fingers. I unplugged the rubber stopper and snagged them with a crooked pinky. I wished I had more to offer. I saw a dopey stuffed chicken left over from Easter on my bed and I snatched it up. She held the chicken and two dollars. I wrapped my hands over hers. *Promise me you'll never forget.* I said it in my I'm-the-big-sister-and-you'd-better-do-what-I-say voice. She nodded and I let go.

I didn't know better. Violet died in a car wreck.

You'd think I could love all my brothers and sisters equally, having lost each one equally, but I don't. From the first batch, I love Frank, Violet, and Jonny. Fiercely and without regard to absence, I love these three beyond death, beyond reason.

Kimberly Blaeser

ANISHNABE

We travel to our place in the world by the grace of others' words. The shape of every experience known only by its nestling in among the soft folds of our history. And so we write with an ink formed of our Auntie's laugh, that old plum tree's fruit.

No matter what subject we turn to, the past is there within us. I try each time I write to listen honestly to those voices that inhabit me. Sometimes one echo rises up and gives shape to a whole poem. Sometimes the memories softly shade the background like a painter's wash. But prominent or invisible, the stories I carry, the past I remember, provide the relational depth and balance that I hope ground my work in a truth larger than my own small vision.

For me a compulsion and an ecstasy, writing seems like the finest Trickster invention. It allows me the satisfaction of working to serve and honor my community all the while doing exactly what pleases me most. And as if that weren't enough, the very process of seeking appropriate words and forms rewards us by making us focus and fine-tune our understanding. Whatever mystery we are exploring, we tell our way, and in the telling find our way. That search called writing leads us home.

In my own seeking as a writer I am drawn to represent the power and integrity of the natural world, and to claim and protect the beauty of native people's lives. I picture the simple small motions of life in my work because I believe they bear with great force upon the fate of our spirits. Giving myself over to them in writing is a profoundest blessing.

Rituals, Yours—and Mine

I.

living by your words
as if i haven't enough of my own
ever
to make them stretch
that long distance
from home to here
from then to now

and all the new words
i've ever read learned
or shelved so neatly
can't explain myself to me
like yours always do

*past
memories*

sometimes that one gesture
of your chin and lips
my memory of
the sideways movement of your eyes
are the only words
from that language
i can manage
to put things in their place

II.

walked in on you today
closed the screened door quietly
so you wouldn't notice
just yet
stood watched you
mumbling shuffling about the kitchen
your long yellow-gray braid
hanging heavy down your back

Present

wanted to see you turn
just that way
hear that familiar exclamation
you snapping the dishtowel
landing it just short of me
shame on me for surprising you

you walk toward me laughing
don't change anything I chant silently
wiping your hands on your faded print apron
you lay them gently still damp cool
one on each side of my face
for that long long second

"When'd you come? Sit down, I'm making breakfast."
I watch the wrinkled loose flesh jiggle on your arms
as you reach to wind and pin your braid
hurry to find your teeth behind the water pail
pull up your peanut butter stockings
pull down your flowered housedress
and wet your fingers
to smooth the hair back behind your ears

III.

smoothing away time with the fluid line
of your memory
I am in place at your table
in the morning damp of your still dark kitchen
I wait for you to come
stepping through the curtained doorway
you enter intent on this day
restart the fire
fill, place the kettle
pull open the kitchen door

inviting daylight to come
welcoming it into your house—
bringing it into mine.

Margaret Behan

ARAPAHO ▮ CHEYENNE

Ha ba *in Arapaho means*
"Greetings, my friend."

"Red Spiderwoman" *is my Arapaho name that also translates into Cheyenne. My mother drew "Margaret Louise" out
of a hat of nurses' names and added my father's last name,
Behan.*

*Watonga, Oklahoma, was where I spent my childhood and
went on to Catholic and government boarding schools. I am
presently a creative-writing major at the Institute of American
Indian and Alaska Native Arts in Santa Fe, New Mexico.*

*My career has been making storyteller dolls out of the mi-
caceous clay. The dolls represent a figure telling a story or
legend to children. Originally, I started writing in order to
write stories for my storyteller dolls, but the writing has become
more than that for me.*

*I find time for my daughters, Olivia and Pam, my son,
Paul, as well as for my grandchildren, Elana and Justin.*

I presently reside in San Juan Pueblo, New Mexico.

Puberty

Magett was real curious if her and her older sister Umillnet were going to have babies.

Magett was a chubby jolly thirteen-year-old. Umillnet was a petite fifteen-year-old, a late bloomer. They lived three miles west of Watonga, Oklahoma.

On Magett's birthday, May 12, 1939, she wanted to know if her and her sister will have babies. She remembered that old lady Dog Woman was like a fortune teller, she knew the old lady lived in town, but didn't know exactly where.

In the evening while washing supper dishes Ma convinced Umillnet to look for Dog Woman after school.

Umillnet said, "I'm scared. I heard Dog Woman was like a witch."

Magett answered, "We will never know for sure, until we meet her, huh? Please, I want to know the unknown, can we please?"

Umillnet finally agreed by making her eyes big, and nodding her head yes.

Magett took it upon herself to tell her father they were going to be late from school that next day. He nodded his head yes and didn't question them. Magett anxiously went to bed. Umillnet did her usual thing. She read a few chapters of *Little Women* before going to sleep.

The next morning Magett jumped up out of bed and yelled with excitement and went over to Umillnet's corner of the room.

"Pevee woonott [good morning], Big Sister." Magett ran to the kitchen and began fixing breakfast oatmeal. Umillnet was slow, dragging her feet. They ate, and ran to the Whirlwind Country School. After school they got a ride to town with one of the teachers. They went to the section of town where the Cheyenne lived in *Red Spider Woman* a cluster of cabins. At the first cabin they came to they knocked on the door. Junior Starr answered and directed them to Dog Woman's cabin.

"I'm scared, let's go home please."

"No, we can't now, come on. You are such a scaredy-cat."

Magett knocked on the door; they could smell liver and onions cooking. Then there was a tall, slim, pretty old lady with her braids tied together in the back of her head, her glassy eyes piercing at them.

"We want to know if we are going to have babies."

Dog Woman laughed. She was so tickled she invited them in to eat. Cheyenne custom is when you go to a home to visit you sit down to eat. They did. There was no talk while they ate. They finished and the girls washed the dishes. Dog Woman instructed them: "Go and get me a set of Rocky Mountain oysters and come back and see me."

Magett looked disappointed: "Where are we going to get bull balls?"

"That is your problem, you get them if you want to know if you all are going to have babies."

Dog Woman pushed them out of her house, slamming the door. "Ha ha ha, bull balls! Bull balls!"

"Little Sister, now what?"

"Where are we going to get them?"

"This is crazy!"

"People are going to laugh at us when they hear this."

Magett was already thinking Uncle is the kind of guy that can do anything. So they walked toward home. Uncle's house was across from the school. Uncle and Esther had six kids all in steps. Umillnet could see what Magett was thinking.

"Uh-oh, this is embarrassing."

Magett had a determined look on her face. She knocked on the front door. Esther answered.

"Hi girls, come on in, supper is almost ready."

They went in and sat on the couch quietly.

"What do you girls want?"

Quickly Magett answered—"Nothing, we just came to visit."

Esther knew the girls didn't like her kids. She was curious why they were there. Magett got up and went into the kitchen to help Esther set the table.

"Where's Uncle?"

"Uncle and the boys went to get wood."

Just as she said that Uncle and the boys came storming in.

"We're hungry."

They washed their hands at the same time in the washbasin. They all sat down to eat hamburger patties, fried potatoes, and biscuits. Umillnet thought to herself, onions again, and the kids are getting on my nerves. She gave up the embarrassing idea and wanted to see how her little sister was going to handle it. Magett buttered up to Uncle.

"Magett, tell me what you want so I can rest."

"Uncle, let's go outside, this is private."

Umillnet held her breath, then heard Uncle crack up. He came in.

"Girls, better get home."

Umillnet ran out to where her sister was. They walked home quietly. As they were about to reach the front door Umillnet asked, "What did Uncle say?"

"He would keep an eye out for them. He wants the both of us to baby-sit his brats for a weekend so he and Esther can practice up on their stick game tricks.

Umillnet yelled, "Oh look what you've done—just forget it. It is stupid!"

They went into the house. Their father asked what all the loud noise was outside.

"We were just playing."

Their father said, "Supper is on the table."

At the same time they said, "I'm not hungry."

He asked, "Where did you eat?"

"Uncle's. We ate onions twice."

"Who cooked onions?"

"Esther."

"She must sure like onions."

"Shush! Umillnet."

They washed the dishes, cleaned up the kitchen, and went to

bed. Umillnet buried herself in her book to escape her little sister.

"Umillnet, wouldn't it be neat if I had a baby girl that looked like me?"

"Shut up! Enough! Enough, go to sleep."

Many weeks passed, school was out. All of a sudden Charles came running to the house. In between his huffing and puffing he was laughing.

"My daddy wants you girls."

"Hurry up."

Magett ran out of the house calling Umillnet, "Come on."

"No."

Uncle was butchering a bull a rancher had had an accident with. The rancher gave the bull to Uncle. Uncle handed a knife to Magett, saying, "Cut them off, don't just stand there."

Slowly she began to cut the hide that linked the patch. Charles handed her a piece of rag to put them in. "Come back and tell us. Remember our deal."

After all that wait now everything was happening. She had the jewels that are the key to her curiosity. She was in a daze, wondering what Old Lady Dog Woman was going to actually do with these things. She remembered to find Umillnet and go to Dog Woman's as quickly as she could. Finally they reached Dog Woman's house. Dog Woman already saw them; her curiosity had built too. As soon as they got there she commanded them to build a fire out by her woodpile. They hurried. When the fire was burning well she took the tied rag bundle, opened it, and cut apart the pair of balls, handing one to Umillnet and the other to Magett.

Dog Woman said, "At the same time both of you throw them into the fire and watch which one is yours, and tell me if it pops."

They watched very carefully. Magett's popped. She screamed happily jumping up and down, clapping her hands. Umillnet's did not pop.

"What happened?"

"Magett is the one that is going to have babies and Umillnet won't—but Magett's first baby she will give to you."

Nora Yazzie Hunter

NAVAJO

As a writer and poet, language is the voice of the land that is surrounded by the four sacred mountains of my Navajo people. That particular place of beginning, according to Navajo mythology, is that ...ch names, nurtures, and sustains me. It is the center of who I am: a place deep inside that reflects me as a human being.

I come from the Redhouse clan and am born for the Salt-water clan. My Navajo name, Nanezbah, means "returning from war." My identity through my clan connects me to earth, Redhouse, and to one of her primary elements, water from the ocean. Navajo history is one of suffering and survival; therefore, "returning from war" is my name, which serves as a shield that carries me through life, and it is a name that is inherited from my ancestors who have fought battles on my behalf and all future generations yet to be born, and who have left prayers and songs now in motion.

My poems are songs of celebration in honor of the gifts that come from the earth who heals, nurtures, and sustains. I honor her in this way for it is her voice that I hear when I begin an idea for a poem. Powerful influences of both my grandfather and my grandmother laid the basis of who I am as a poet and writer.

As a child, I was fortunate to have observed and participated in ceremonies performed by my grandfather, who was a sandpainter. The repetitive chants and words voiced in the songs and prayers were my first poetry.

My grandmother, who died at the age of 101, reminded me of earth's journey into old age, only to be reborn. She was a midwife and weaver. She helped bring new life into the world and the rugs she wove were old stories she told over and over, but were brand new each time she told them. She would wake up in the early hours of dawn and quietly perform the ancient task of gathering pollen to be used as a prayer offering.

My observations of these important acts were seeds my grandparents planted for my cultivation of creative imagination.

Old Great-Grandma

I drive a long stretch of dirt road
where you herded your sheep and goats on horseback
and remember the small oasis where lambs
were eaten by wet sand.
I stop my car to take a last look around and
remember the special place you reserved — place of prayer
to hide us from the Mormons and the rest of them.
The toys we made from rocks, sticks, and sand are still there,
seasoned in time, wind, and rain.
On this stretch of land that faces east I raced as Changing Woman.
You welcomed my return and molded me.
My young daughters will race, too, someday and know that your
essence underneath their feet will welcome them.
We return you to the earth as rain begins to sprinkle its blessings.

Janet Campbell Hale

COEUR D'ALENE

I am a Coeur d'Alene tribal member living for the first time as an adult on my ancestral land. My father was a full-blood Coeur d'Alene. I dropped out of law school because I realized I could not both practice law and do my serious work; I made a commitment to my work and that's where I've been ever since. I was first published at the age of twenty.

The Only Good Indian

It has always seemed to me that the heaviest penalty the servants of the Hudson's Bay Company were obliged to pay for the wealth and authority advancement gave them was the wives they were expected to marry and the progeny they should rear. What greater happiness to the father, what greater benefit to mankind than noble children. I never could understand how such men as John McLoughlin and James Douglas could endure the thought of having their name and honors descend to a degenerate posterity. Surely they were of sufficient intelligence to know that by giving their children Indian mothers, their own Scotch, Irish, or English blood would be greatly debased. . . . They were doing all concerned a great wrong. Perish all the Hudson's Bay Company thrice over, I would say, sooner than bring upon my offspring of such curse.

— H. H. BANCROFT,
The History of Oregon (1884)

One of my earliest memories is of being taken to Oregon City to visit McLoughlin House, which was Oregon's first museum.

Oregon City, just south of the metropolis of Portland, Oregon, came before Portland—Portland grew from it. My great-great-grandfather, Dr. John McLoughlin, founded Oregon City when he built his last house and his lumber mill there. Today Oregon City blends into Portland. McLoughlin Boulevard connects the two.

McLoughlin House is a magnificent two-story wood-frame house, a near-mansion. It looks as though it came from the East, as though it could have belonged to a New England sea captain. But it is a Northwest house and it belonged to the man who, as chief factor for the Hudson's Bay Company, founded Fort Vancouver (which is just north of what is today Portland, just across the Columbia River). Before Fort Vancouver there was nothing here. A valley. A river. Woods. Wilderness. The small city of Vancouver, Washington, grew from the fort.

"Don't touch," my mother warned me. "Don't touch a thing, you hear?" Not even the maroon-velvet-covered ropes that kept tourists from entering open bedrooms by restricting them to the narrow strip of red carpet that ran down the hallways and across the big rooms. "Look. Don't touch! Don't let go of my hand until we get out of here." Her tone told me she meant what she said.

The house contained a few things that had belonged to the McLoughlins: his writing table, a lacquered Chinese cabinet, a grand piano (for some reason our guide told us the piano had come via ship from Boston but didn't mention where the other things had come from), an Oriental rug, a beautiful long dining table with twelve chairs, each place set with the McLoughlins' elegant china and silver as if the family and their guests were about to sit down to dinner. All the rest of the furniture (like the high-canopied beds with the little stools people had to step onto to get into bed) hadn't belonged to the family, but were authentic period pieces. We were supposed to imagine that this was, more or less, the way the house had looked when the McLoughlins had lived in it, that this was the kind of furniture they would have chosen. My mother told me the people who had built this fine house for their later years and who lived in it for a long time and both died here were our relations. We were descendants. Of course, I didn't get it.

Did I understand that Gram, Mom's ma, was my grandmother? And that Gram's husband, who died before I was born, was my grandfather? Sure. Mom's dad, Sullivan, of whom Mom was so fond. My grandfather. Sure. I got that. I knew what grandparents were.

Well, these people, whose house this had been, were Gram Sullivan's grandparents. Gram's grandpa had been a very, very important man. Dr. John McLoughlin, who came from a place called Quebec, was chief factor for the Hudson's Bay Company a long time ago. This was sort of the same as being governor, my mother said. I didn't know what a governor was exactly. I was just a preschool child. So I didn't have an inkling what McLoughlin had been. Actually he had had more power, as chief factor, than any governor.

In those days the Northwest Territory stretched from California to Alaska. The Territory was held in joint occupancy by the United States and Great Britain. The Hudson's Bay Company was the quasi-government, and as chief factor, Dr. McLoughlin was its head. His word was law in the Northwest Territory. It was his domain. He was called King of the Columbia and Emperor of the Northwest (and posthumously, officially, the Father of Oregon). He became chief factor in 1821 and ruled for a twenty-one-year period that came to be known as "The Age of McLoughlin." That important man was my gram's grandpa, and his wife, Margaret (my mother's name too), was from a place called Ontario, and she was my gram's gram.

I held my mother's hand and looked up at their portraits, not understanding what these people were to me.

Dr. John McLoughlin (Mom and Gram insisted on the proper, Canadian, pronunciation: "McGLOCKlin," rather than the American "McLAWFlin") certainly looked formidable in his portrait, painted when he was in middle age. He was a powerfully built man (he stood six feet four inches tall—a giant of a man in his day— which was 1784–1854) with a stern countenance and dressed in a formal black suit. His hair, a long, wild white mane, flowed well past his shoulders. He was famous for his hair. I would learn much later that it was said to have turned white overnight when his canoe overturned on Lake Michigan during the Great Fur War, when he was in his twenties. The Indians of the Territory called him "The White-Headed Eagle."

Margaret McLoughlin is an old woman in her portrait, which is a photograph, not a painting. She is also wearing black. Mrs. McLoughlin is dressed like a white woman. *But she is not white. She is an Indian.*

She was a Chippewa, my mother told me. "Doctor McLoughlin was not ashamed of her," my mother said, as though it were mighty big of him not to have been.

Not ashamed of her? I studied her portrait. Solemn. Sad eyes. An Indian woman. What was there about her to be ashamed of? (My mother said things like that sometimes. I didn't like it.) I resented my great-great-grandfather then, the eminent Dr. John McLoughlin, disliked him even. How dare he have such a conde-scending attitude toward his own wife? I resented Dr. McLoughlin as if my mother's attitudes were his.

There is another memory that goes with the one of our visit to Oregon City.

"White people respect good Indians," my mother said rather casually as she sat darning socks and mending small tears in our clothes. I was about four at the time. I sat on the floor beside her chair, coloring in my (probably Carmen Miranda) coloring book. "Good Indians are clean and neat, hardworking and sober," she said. I wanted to get away from her. I hated it when she talked like that and I could not, even to myself, articulate my feelings because I was too young. I couldn't get away because it was raining. She wouldn't let me out. No escape. "White people look down on the other kind, the bad ones, the drunken, lazy louts." I stopped col-oring and went to a window and watched the rain pour. Mom's voice droned on.

She would often instruct me on being a good Indian, the kind white people approve of (and sometimes, when I was a little older, on being the kind of woman men respect). I would feel the resentment rise in my blood. Why should I care? Why don't they worry about being the sort of person I respect? Why should I have to be the one to live up to someone else's expectations? Anyway, trying to be a "good Indian" was a futile endeavor. Several years before Gram Sullivan was born, General Sheridan had made his famous remark regarding the only good Indian being a dead Indian. I didn't care to be a good Indian.

Gram Sullivan was born Angeline McLoughlin in Idaho or British Columbia in the Kootenay Valley near the international boundary in 1875. Her father (or her pa, as she called him) was the only surviving son of Dr. John and Margaret McLoughlin. David McLoughlin, Gram's pa, had gone to university and medical school in Paris, France (where his father's brother was then personal physician to the king of France). And of course his father was the wealthiest, most powerful man in the whole Northwest Territory. Yet, Gram's pa did what many half-breed Indian boys before him had done: he just saddled up his horse and rode away. He left the white world behind and wandered for a time before he came to the beautiful Kootenay Valley. He married a full-blooded Kootenay Indian woman named Annie Grizzly, who became Gram's ma.

Gram Sullivan was actually one-quarter white (that one-quarter coming from her paternal grandfather, Dr. McLoughlin), but Gram was a *dark* Indian woman, much darker than I. As dark as my other grandmother, who was a full-blood. She was part white, but she had the looks of a full-blood.

She was paralyzed on her left side and lost the power of speech when she suffered a stroke when I was about six. I have no memories of her before the stroke. To me she was always a mean-looking old woman sitting in a wheelchair, one arm in a sling. She couldn't speak, but she made ugly, scolding noises that sounded like swearing. She "swore" at everyone. She had a reputation for being mean. Before the stroke she was mean, and after, she was meaner still. She also had a reputation for not liking us, the children of my mother's second marriage. (She remained on friendly terms with my mother's ex-husband, who was white, and saw the children—a boy and a girl—from this marriage regularly.)

I do have one memory, not of her exactly but of a conversation, a short exchange between my mother and me before Gram's stroke:

We're at Gram's house in Spokane, in the bathroom. I'm crying because Mom's washing my face with cold water. "Why does Gram hate me?" I ask.

"She doesn't hate you. Don't think that. She hardly even knows you. She's just old and cranky. And . . . you remind her of someone else . . . someone she does hate." The words sink in, and I remember them always. *I remind her of someone she hates.* Who?

I thought my father must be the one I reminded Gram of, because she did hate him. That was no secret. My mother alone, of seven Sullivan children, married an Indian, went to live on a reservation, and had Indian kids. My mother's sisters all looked one hundred percent white, just like Mom. They were poor, uneducated, working class, yet made no effort to disguise the fact they looked down on us because we were Indian.

Clearly there was no love lost between my father and my mother's family. Surely he must be, I thought, the one I remind Gram of. People said I looked like him.

Though Dad never spoke a word against Gram or indicated in any way that he disliked her, he wasn't overly subtle when it came to what he thought of my mother's sisters: "So, you're going with your mamma to visit her sisters today? Good. I want you to do something, okay?" I nodded. Sure. Anything. "I want you to watch your aunts and listen to them. Observe them very carefully. You know why? Because the way those women are . . . that's just exactly the way women should not be." I could learn a lot from them, Dad said. Watch their every move. But don't let them catch me watching them. I took him seriously and I did as I was told. I furtively observed my aunts.

They were loud and aggressive and argumentative. My mother spoke softly (most of the time). They did not. They were rude and crude. They smoked and drank. They swore and said "shit" a lot. They made stupid, snide remarks about Indians, too, whenever they could. For instance, there was the time one of my aunts had seen a man looking into a neighbor's window. She went out in the dark night and fired her little handgun (which she kept for her "personal protection") into the sky and scared the Peeping Tom away. Though it was very dark, my aunt said she could tell the peeper was an Indian because he had an Indian shuffle. He fled into the night with an Indian shuffle, she said. Mom just ignored this reference, as she ignored all of their references and snide remarks. Then, most of the time, she fumed over them when we got home. She just laughed about the guy with the Indian shuffle, though, imagining him running and shuffling at the same time in a way that was so distinctive, her sister could tell, even in the dark, that he was an Indian.

So my aunts smoked, drank, swore, and were vulgar, not to mention racist. But they were kind to their mother. They took care of her for many, many years. They put up with her nagging (the noises she made to express her unhappiness) without complaint. Gram was known to knock her food away with her good arm, causing it to fly across the room. Once they brought her an alphabet, large plastic letters.

Since she didn't seem interested in writing when they brought her a pencil and paper, they thought maybe she would communicate with them by putting these plastic letters together to form words. They put the letters in front of her on a low table and explained to her what they had in mind. Gram got very, very angry and began yelling at them, making those awful noises of hers and then knocked the table over. She didn't want to form words, they thought. It was too tedious for her. (Much later, when I was grown, I remembered the incident and thought Gram had probably lost the ability to read or write, as stroke victims do. She probably couldn't form words with plastic letters any more than she could write with a pen. But that didn't occur to my aunts.) Gram was mean and cranky and hard to put up with. She had, in fact, always had a bad disposition. But they took care of her and were patient with her, too, and as kind as they could be.

They said she'd worked so hard when they were children. She had made so many sacrifices for them. "Now it's our turn," they'd say. "Now we must take care of her."

Their father, who had worked for Great Northern Railroad, had had some sort of work-related accident one winter day. He was pinned under something. It took a long time to free him. He'd been exposed to the cold for a long period of time. The result was frostbite. His toes had to be amputated, and he was out of commission for a long while.

That was long before President Roosevelt's New Deal. No workmen's compensation then. No state disability. No unemployment benefits. No Aid to Families with Dependent Children. Nothing. And six children to feed.

Gram Sullivan took in laundry (there were a lot of single men in railroad camps). Railroad men's clothes must have gotten very dirty. Of course she had no running water, no washing machine.

Gram worked hard as a laundress, harder than seemed humanly possible. Gathering laundry, chopping wood, building fires, hauling water, heating tubs of it and scrubbing, scrubbing the clothes on a washboard. Her hands got all raw. The skin on her knuckles cracked and bled. But she managed. Gram did it. She supported her family of eight for one whole winter and spring all on her own. "And now it's our turn," her daughters who weren't refined said when she got old, crippled, speechless, and crabby. And they did take care of Gram. They took good care of her.

Spokane, even today, is sort of a Wild West kind of town. Country-western music is, and has always been, very big in this region and lots of men wear cowboy boots and drive pickup trucks with gun racks. And it's conservative. Very conservative. It's surrounded by five Indian reservations (including my own, which is about sixty or seventy miles east of the city; the first Kootenay rez is about one hundred miles north). If you are an Indian in Spokane, you are always aware of it. There is not a great multitude of people from many diverse ethnic and racial backgrounds. (I don't recall ever seeing a black person in Spokane until I saw one walking down the street one day when I was thirty years old.) In Spokane no one ever mistakes me for Hispanic or Middle Eastern. No one there has ever asked me, as I've often been asked in New York and San Francisco, "What is your ethnic background?" They know what it is.

Even today, in Spokane, Indians pretty much keep to themselves and whites to themselves, though there are people on both sides striving for racial harmony. But there's a word that was used to describe an Indian, a "dirty," denigrating word, sort of like *nigger*. The word is *Siwash*. My parents first told me about that word and told me I should just ignore it if I heard it, that I should feel sorry for a person who would say it because such a person has a bad heart and is ignorant.

It was sort of like *squaw*, but worse. *Siwash*. It had the power to cut like a knife. "Dirty Siwash." The last time I heard it was on the street in Spokane when I was thirty-one. A group of young white men in cowboy boots who had obviously been drinking passed me. One of them turned his head and looked back but didn't slow his pace and muttered, "Siwash. Goddamned Siwash." I was startled. I'd even forgotten such a word existed. It still had the power, after all those years, to cut like a knife.

That was what my mother's first husband called her, she told me when I was older. Despite her beauty. Despite her white looks. Nobody could tell she wasn't white if they didn't know. Her husband knew. And he was one of those people my parents told me about. "Squaw," my mother's first husband would call her when he felt mean, which was a lot of the time. "Stupid Siwash squaw. That's all you are, you know. Just a Siwash squaw." The psychological wound she suffered when she left him for a full-blood must have been deep.

So Mom had had to suffer racial slurs, too, as I had when I was growing up. Probably not just at the hands of her first husband either. She and her white-looking sisters, after all, couldn't hide their mother very easily (nor, I think, did they wish to hide or deny her).

I didn't know Gram Sullivan before her hair turned white and don't remember her before she was an invalid and her daughters began to keep her hair cut short and neat and easy to care for. My mother and aunts said Gram's hair had been thick, blue-black, and smooth as satin. She often wore it, when she wasn't working (and it had to be pinned up), hanging loose. It fell nearly to her waist.

Gram Sullivan's hair was like black satin. The looks of a full-blood. But not the soul of one. Not like Poulee, my other grand-mother, who spoke not a word of English, never wore a pair of shoes in her life, and was nothing if not secure in her idea of herself, her acceptance of herself as an Indian woman. Not a Siwash. Not a squaw. An Indian woman.

My mother identified very strongly with her Irishness. Maybe because she looked Irish. Maybe because she was her Irish grand-parents' favorite person in all the world. Her happiest childhood memories were of staying with them on their farm. Mom knew all about County Clare, where they had come from, and she could speak with an Irish brogue just like theirs. She did speak with an Irish brogue, a little, every Saint Patrick's Day.

Mom enjoyed the social life of the railroad camps too. Feast days. Parties. Dances. Even a wake was a social event. Once, Mom won a local beauty contest. I don't know what the title was, but it was a little like homecoming queen in that the railroad men all voted for the girl they believed the fairest one of all. It was a highly coveted honor. Mom didn't expect to be chosen—partly because she didn't believe she was beautiful, ever, no matter what anyone said, and because she was years younger than the girls, of marriage-able age, who did expect to be chosen.

They were all gathered at this yearly event, a party and dance that children as well as adults attended. The time came to announce the homecoming queen (or whatever she was called). They called out the name: "Maggie Sullivan." That was Mom! The older girls, the girls who would be queen, were shocked. One of them wept.

But Maggie Sullivan was happy and she would never forget that time, not ever.

Gram Sullivan was the only non-white wife in that society. She didn't participate in any of it, Mom said. She had no friends. When her husband and children went to the wakes and parties and dances and feasts, Gram stayed home alone. She had things to do, she would say, you all go ahead and have a good time. Or she would have a headache. Or she would want to relax and enjoy a little peace and quiet. Mom said she thought Gram felt inferior because she wasn't Irish. I wonder if this was true. Did the woman who washed so much dirty Irish laundry that year her husband was disabled feel inferior because she wasn't Irish?

Gram loved her home in the Kootenay Valley and went back for visits. She didn't take her children with her, though, unless they were babies. Sometimes Gram's Kootenay relatives came to visit her. They could not (or would not) speak English. Gram and her relatives always conversed in Kootenay when they came to visit. She always dressed in white women's styles, but her relatives did not.

Mom remembered herself as a little girl hiding behind her mother's skirts and peeking at the Kootenay visitors. They wore moccasins and leggings and bright-colored clothing, and their hair (even the men's) was in long braids. They did not wear coats. They wrapped themselves in blankets (I imagine wool trade blankets from the Hudson's Bay Company) and wore exotic jewelry made of shells and animal's teeth and glass beads. Some of them wore earrings my mother especially admired that were large and made of some sort of shells. Mom coveted those earrings and imagined herself, when she was grown, wearing them. (Only Mom would be much too conservative to wear any sort of flashy jewelry, let alone Indian shell earrings.)

Mom was afraid of her mother's exotic relatives, but she was attracted to them, too, fascinated by them. She like the way they looked. She loved to listen to the smooth, flowing language she didn't understand. She knew Gram's Kootenay grandpa had been a chief, and she liked to imagine him and what he must have been like. For all her Irishness, I think Mom always felt a strong Indian undercurrent in herself.

My grandfather Sullivan was the youngest child of a large family. He was born in County Clare, Ireland, in about 1871. When he was just an infant his father slaughtered and butchered his own hog without paying the tax required by law. He was caught in the act by a British tax collector, who then tried to impose not only the tax but also a fine for attempting to evade the tax.

Times were bad in Ireland. The government did things to the Irish people—forbade them to speak Gaelic, collected all their potatoes and sold them back to them, imposed all sorts of taxes on them.

So the story goes, my grandfather's father was caught in the act. Still holding the knife he had used to butcher the hog, its blood still warm on the sharp steel blade, he killed the tax collector. He then went underground and, with the help of his friends in the resistance, got out of Ireland. His wife and children escaped by pretending to be the wife and children of his half-brother, whose name was not Sullivan. Friends and neighbors gave my mother's grandmother a gold broach the night before they left. It had a pair of manacled hands engraved on it symbolizing the oppression of the Irish people by the British government.

My grandfather must have been two or three when his mother snuck out of Ireland, snuck them all out, with the help of her brother-in-law. He and his family were part of those famous huddled masses yearning to breathe free. But he had no memory of the country he came from. (No feeling for it, either, as his parents had. No nostalgia. No desire to return to it.) He had no memory of the voyage, of arriving in America.

The Sullivans settled in New York City, which was not hospitable to Irish immigrants at the time. Employers advertised for help but noted NO IRISH NEED APPLY and some businesses put signs in their windows that said NO DOGS OR IRISH ALLOWED. My grandfather's parents never did like New York. Their older children soon reached adulthood and married and had children of their own. It looked like they would be stuck in that big, mean city for good.

Then, when the man who killed the British tax collector and his wife were past middle age, homesteading opened up in Idaho and Washington State. Good, rich farmland, free for the taking (which, of course, was available because the American government had taken it from the Indians of the West). Despite their age, and the fact that they had just one child at home (the almost-grown young man who would become my mother's father), the Sullivans went west and again had at long last a farm of their own! My mother never knew any of the cousins, aunts, or uncles Sullivan who remained in New York City.

My grandfather went to work for Great Northern when he grew up. Somewhere along the line, as he was laying tracks (no doubt in Kootenay country), he met an Indian girl named Angeline.

She must have seemed a strange Indian girl, not at all "shy" as Indian girls were always said to be. And she spoke English. Not just fluently but really well, like an educated person. And she could read and write too. A most unusual Indian maiden.

Angeline McLoughlin became Mrs. Sullivan and left the Kootenay Valley.

I was fourteen when Gram Sullivan died. She was eighty-five. I remembered that day at her house before she had her stroke when she made me cry and my mother told me I wasn't to think she hated me. "She's just old and cranky, that's all. And . . . you remind her of someone else . . . someone she does hate."

None of my sisters attended Gram's funeral, though most of her grandchildren and great-grandchildren did. We buried her in Spokane beside her husband. Then my parents and I went home to Wapato, and I didn't think of that crabby old woman for years and years.

Then suddenly, after a long time had passed, I began to think of her. I remembered her face and the photographs I'd seen of her when she was young and the stories my mother and aunts told about her. What had Gram really been like? Who, if anyone, had I reminded her of?

I read a book about Gram's tribe. The Kootenay was the only tribe in the region that had been matrilineal, the only one that had had women warriors.

I remembered a book my mother had owned, a biography of Gram's granddad, Dr. John McLoughlin, and his brother and sister, entitled *The McLoughlin Empire and Its Rulers*. It was a big, heavy, formidable-looking book. Royal-blue cloth with gold lettering. It looked important. It had been very important to Mom. To her it said she came from "a good family," whatever her (our) circumstances might be. From a good family . . . but down on her luck. She read it often, studied it. *Interpreted* her ancestors.

I was never interested in that book. I didn't like my mother's interpretations of the McLoughlin family. Their lives, I thought, had no relevance to my own. Who was Dr. John Mcloughlin, after all, but a big, rich white man who had exploited Indians in the old days? Father of Oregon. What did that mean? Helped settlers steal land. I wasn't impressed.

Of course I had to study Northwest history in school, and every Northwest-history textbook told about Dr. John McLoughlin. Once, just once, I raised my hand in class and told my teacher, "He was my great-great-grandfather." I must have been about eight years old at the time. My teacher didn't say a word, just stared at me, stared hard. Some of my classmates giggled. When I told my mother, she said I should never mention that I was related to Dr. McLoughlin. Nobody would believe me. I would be ridiculed. I never did mention it again. So why would I be interested in his life? Why would I want any part of him?

But now, years later, for some reason I *was* interested. Dr. John McLoughlin's life was relevant to Gram's life. And Gram's life, was, somehow, relevant to my own.

I got myself a copy of *The McLoughlin Empire and Its Rulers*. It was still a formidable-looking book. We were all there on a family chart: Gram's ma and pa and all Gram's children, including Mom (and even Dad's name was there, as Mom's husband), my sisters . . . and *me.*

In 1983 I applied for a sixty-day residency fellowship to go to the Center for the Study of the History of the American Indian at the Newberry Library in Chicago. I wanted to study the fur-trade era in North America, the white-Indian marriages of that time, and the mixed-blood people, who were (and are) a legacy of the fur trade.

I wanted to study the McLoughlin family, to study Old Fort Vancouver so long and so hard that Fort Vancouver in its heyday would take form in my imagination.

Fort Vancouver was many things, of course. Headquarters for the Hudson's Bay Company (that is, of the fur trade) in the Northwest Territory. It was a thriving cultural center, too, known as the Paris of the West. It was also a fully functioning military fort, not out of fear of the many Indian tribes that lived in the Territory, who were the business partners of the Hudson's Bay Company, but because American aggression was feared. Fort Langley, just south of what is today Vancouver, British Columbia (and a long way north of Vancouver, Washington), was the second fort McLoughlin built in the West, intended as a backup in case Americans attacked Fort Vancouver and put it out of commission.

The dispute over the boundary was a serious one. A war was nearly fought over it. Great Britain wanted the Columbia River to be the dividing line. This was why McLoughlin built Fort Vancouver on the north bank of the river. This was where Canada was to begin (where the state of Washington actually begins). Americans were not in agreement. In 1844 James Polk's campaign slogan was "54.40 or Fight," referring to where he wanted the border to be (that is, at the southern tip of Russian Alaska). Chief Factor McLoughlin built Fort Vancouver when Gram's pa was just a little boy. Her pa had grown up there. Before prep school in Montreal. Before university in Paris. Before he went native.

I wanted to imagine, if I could, Gram's early life before she left the People of the Valley and married Sullivan and became my mother's ma. What made her the way she was when I knew her? What had she been like before?

I was awarded the research fellowship and went to Chicago the summer of 1984.

Gram Sullivan's paternal grandfather, Chief Factor Dr. John McLoughlin, was born in 1784 in Rivière-du-Loup (River of the Wolf), Quebec. *His* grandfather, Captain Malcolm Fraser, came from Inverness, Scotland, to fight for the British on the Plains of Abraham. He was my first non-Indian ancestor in North America. Years later, now a colonel, Malcolm Fraser fought for George II against the Americans during the Revolutionary War. He defeated Montgomery (who was killed in battle) and the soon-to-be-infamous General Benedict Arnold at the Battle of Quebec on the last day of 1775. As a reward for saving Quebec—it had been a close battle, and Montreal had already fallen—His Majesty rewarded Colonel Fraser with the seigneury at Mount Murray, Quebec. But all of that is another story. His grandson joined the fur trade. He only meant to stay in the business for a brief while. But he met a woman named Margaret at his first post, a Chippewa Indian woman.

Margaret was no nubile Indian maiden. She was ten years his senior and the mother of four young children. She had been abandoned, as most Indian women involved in liaisons with white men of the fur trade eventually were, by her first white "husband."

Dr. John McLoughlin knew very well that he could not hope to return to Montreal and the genteel life he had imagined for ·himself with an Indian wife (not to mention four half-Indian stepchildren). John and Margaret married, and from then on his life was the fur trade. It had to be. Eventually he was appointed chief factor and went to the Northwest Territory, where he founded Fort Vancouver.

Gram's maternal grandfather was also born in the 1780s, but the exact date, the exact year, is unknown. (Like her other grandfather, he died before Gram was born.)

Gram's maternal grandfather was a Kootenay (which is an anglicized version of the tribe's name for itself: "Kul:nee," which means "People of the Valley"). He had been kidnapped, taken as spoils of war, by the Blood Indians, who were the bitter enemy of the Kootenay, when he was just a little boy. They kept him as their slave and were unimaginably cruel to him. His was a wretched existence growing up among the Bloods. At age fourteen he escaped and returned home to the People of the Valley.

Shortly thereafter a grizzly bear appeared to him in a vision and told him he was destined to become a great war chief and Grizzly himself, the fiercest, strongest, bravest one of all, would be his animal protector, would counsel him and ride into battle with him. That was how Gram's grandfather became Chief Grizzly—one fierce war chief—the most effective killer of Blood Indians that ever lived.

It appears as though Chief Grizzly converted to Catholicism in his later years. His children took Christian names. He did not. Maybe only his children and their mother converted and the English translation of his name, that is, of his animal protector, became their surname.

Annie Grizzly, Gram's ma, never learned English. Annie died when Gram was still a young girl, and Gram, the bossiest and eldest, took over the housekeeping and looked after the others. Her pa, who lived to be a very old man, never remarried.

Since they lived in a remote area where no school existed, I presume it was their pa (it had to be) who taught Gram and her sisters to speak English so well and to read and write.

When Gram's pa, David McLoughlin, left his wealthy, mixed-blood family and went native, there most certainly was a great deal of racial prejudice against Indians and those of mixed blood. There had always been, but it became more intense as the fur-trade era began to fade and the missionaries came, followed by floods of white settlers with their insatiable hunger for land.

I think David became disgusted with politics (he left Fort Vancouver shortly after his only brother was assassinated as part of a plot to oust his father from power). David had been, until then, a dutiful son . . . but he truly had no desire for power as his father had, no desire to head a dynasty. David preferred the wilderness and the native way of life. (I've read his letters. In one, to his best friend and cousin, David Michaud, with whom he'd studied in Paris, he wrote that the years in Europe seemed only a dream now that he was home on the frontier.)

"There's something wrong with every one of them," HBC governor Sir George Simpson said of mixed-bloods, he who had many Indian children by many different Indian women, most of whom he did not acknowledge and did nothing for. (Some of the Frasers had urged Dr. McLoughlin not to marry his Indian wife . . . and then not to educate his children: "A good education is wasted on a boy with Native blood.") David had grown up with anti-Indianism, though his father's wealth and authority and his own light skin had protected him to a degree. But he could hardly foresee the racism of the society that would replace the one he'd known, the society that would regard Indians as subhuman beings, as soulless savages to be done away with so that the West could be won.

He was just a half-breed who preferred the Indian way of life when he went to the wilderness and married a woman named Annie Grizzly and lived out his long life as an Indian. He could not imagine the sort of life the next generation of Indians, including his own children, would have.

When Gram was a year old, in 1876, General Custer led the 7th Cavalry to the Battle of Little Big Horn, which not one white man survived. Sitting Bull fled to Canada, where he was granted political asylum. Never were Indians more unpopular in the United States of America than in 1876 after Custer's Last Stand.

In 1879, when Gram was four years old, Carlisle Indian School, in Pennsylvania, opened its doors for the first time. Carlisle was the first government-run boarding school, the first attempt to assimilate Indians, en masse, into mainstream society.

They rounded up students-to-be, not extremely young children but older ones and adolescents, from reservations all over the United States and brought them by freight train to Pennsylvania. Many died of disease and homesickness. A few committed suicide rather than become "a white man's Indian."

Many people thought the best solution to what was commonly referred to as the Indian Problem (that is, what to do with the Indians who had survived the Indian wars, the ones living on reservations) was to kill them all off. To just exterminate them as though they were cockroaches.

The director of Carlisle, though, was humane and progressive. His motto was: "Kill the Indian and Save the Man." Get rid of everything Indian . . . his language and culture, his identity. Cut his long hair short. Make him wear white people's clothes. Then he would be all right.

Carlisle (whose most famous graduate was the great athlete Jim Thorpe) was considered a success. The government established more Indian schools, patterning them after Carlisle, in Oklahoma, Arizona, Nebraska, South Dakota, Utah, New Mexico, Kansas, California, and Oregon. It supported many other, church-operated residential schools. Whether run directly by the government or by a church through a government contract, all the Indian schools had the same goal: assimilation. The residential schools were notorious hellholes.

When men from the government came to Kootenay country, the Kootenay hid their children, but many were found and taken away. Gram and her sisters, though, were spared. There was no reason to haul them away to government school. They spoke English as well as, or better than, any white children around. And they could read and write like nobody's business. They were allowed to stay home.

When Gram was fifteen years old, in 1890, the slaughter at Wounded Knee occurred. Surely she was aware of it. It was big news. She read newspapers. She probably read anything she could get her hands on.

What did she think when she read about all those Indians in South Dakota who had been shot down like dogs because they, unarmed and all penned in, had been singing Indian songs, Ghost Dance songs, that made the white soldiers who guarded them nervous? (Did the newspapers of the day, I wonder, publish those photographs taken at Wounded Knee of the frozen corpses lying in the snow? Did the accounts in the papers tell how the soldiers took articles of clothing and even cut body parts from the corpses to take away as souvenirs of Wounded Knee? Did the newspapers print the photograph of the long trench the soldiers dug, of the Indian bodies all piled into it, the mass grave?)

What did Gram think about when she read, or heard, about the massacre at Wounded Knee and all the rest? When she read about the government's intentions to educate the Indian out of the Indian . . . when she read about her own people described as savages?

All the Indian nations were conquered now, restricted to reservations, forbidden to hunt buffalo, to practice their traditional religions. This was perhaps the darkest hour of the Indian people. The old way was gone, or at least deteriorating, breaking apart. The People of the Valley became poorer as time passed and their way of life, their traditional way, could not continue (not the way it had been in the days of Chief Grizzly).

Gram was aware of a world beyond the Kootenay Valley. I wonder if she ever daydreamed of the life her father had had before (which he would not discuss with his family) . . . did she daydream of seeing the places he'd seen: Paris, maybe . . . London? Did Gram ever wish she could go back to Oregon from whence her pa had come and reclaim something, at least, of what rightfully should have been hers? I have reason to think she did.

Chicago in the summer is hot, awfully hot for a person from the Northwest, and muggy. But not in the vaults of the Newberry Library, where precious old documents and books are kept. In there I had to wear a sweater to keep warm. My hands got cold.

The Oregon State Historical Society and the Oregon Pioneer Association invited Gram's pa to Portland in 1901 for "Pioneer Day," to be present at a ceremony honoring his father.

More than forty years had passed since David McLoughlin left white society. Much was made about how the old man wore Indian buckskins and didn't even own a suit of white man's clothes. George H. Himes, who held various offices in both the Historical Society and the Pioneer Association, wrote the old man a letter informing him that a suit and a pair of shoes had been purchased for him and would be sent along with a postal money order in the amount of $16 to pay for his train ticket and other expenses. Himes went on to say that he did not want David to feel that "This is a matter of charity," for poverty is no crime. "Whatever is done for you is done for the sake of honoring your father." Himes advised David to buy a round-trip ticket since he could "save a little" that way.

A Mr. Ryan wrote a letter to Mr. Himes telling him, "By request of friends of David McLoughlin I accompanied him to Spokane and took charge of the $16 you sent. Of this I expended from him the following sums:

"Round-trip fare from Spokane to Portland, $5.10 [he probably had to travel by horse from his home to Spokane, a distance of some 120 miles], and three meals, $1.05. TOTAL: $6.15.

"Bed at the Pacific Hotel, $.75;	$ .75
Shirt, $1.00; underclothes, $1.00	$ 2.00
Necktie, $.25; handkerchief, $.75	$ 1.00
Telegram, $.55	$ .55
Lunch to take on the train, $.50	$ .50
GRAND TOTAL	**$10.95**

"The balance of $5.05 I will give him with his ticket after I put him on the train to Portland. The old gentleman has lived in the woods so long that he is helpless as a child in a city."

Mr. Himes said about Gram's pa, "David McLoughlin was a

very well-educated man, but throwing himself away as he did, destroyed his future. In some respects the visit to Portland in June was not a kindly act. The motive was to, through him, pay tribute to his father. It was a revelation to David of his wasted life."

Reading that made me angry. I wished I'd been there. I would have told the old man not to go. Those people don't really wish to honor your father, I would have said to him. They don't have any understanding of who Dr. John McLoughlin was.

They believed David had "thrown himself away" because he'd chosen to live as an Indian. "Don't go, Great-grandpa," I would have said had I been there. "Don't do it. They're going to bring you all that way and dress you up in some stupid white man's suit and make a big deal out of the few cents they paid for it. Many years later a professor of Northwest history who is also a Historical Society member will write a book in which she interviews an old man who was a nine-year-old boy in 1901 and saw you at the Pioneer Day celebration and she will quote him as saying you were 'not well dressed at all' *in your cheap new white-man's suit* 'but rather unkempt and seedy-looking.' And they're all going to shake their heads over your life, which they will regard as wasted, and they'll pity you and write about how you married a *squaw* (as though this were evidence of a wasted life, an illustration of how low you had sunk)."

(They'll even tell *me*, when I visit the replica of Old Fort Vancouver in 1987, how Dr. John McLoughlin had had to marry a squaw because no white women were available on the frontier. A guide will tell me that, not realizing that Dr. John McLoughlin lived on the frontier partly because he had an Indian wife, not the other way around.) "Don't go," I would have said to Gram's pa if I could. "You were right to have left those people when you did. Don't go back. Not even for one day."

But I wasn't there, and he did go. Curator Himes and others wrote letters back and forth on the advisability of bringing a member of David's family to Portland to accompany him, since David was an old man and couldn't walk without the aid of a cane.

In the end they decided against it because, as they put it, no member of his family was "presentable" enough to come to the ceremony they were planning to honor David's father. *Presentable?* Who wasn't presentable? What were they talking about? Their clothing? Then it dawned on me: *presentable* was their euphemism for "white-looking." So. None of his family was light enough. David himself was rather light. His looks were acceptable to Oregon's Historical Society. But no member of his family was. Not Gram. They didn't want her there, nor any of her sisters. (They certainly wouldn't have wanted his mother there either, were she alive. She was too dark for them too.) Gram's pa, as old and feeble and forgetful as he was, made that long trip alone. And they believed they were honoring his father!

I also found, to my great surprise, an account by a woman who was a member of the Society concerning two young Indian women who had come to Portland a few years earlier: *They presented themselves as granddaughters of Dr. John McLoughlin and asked for assistance in seeking employment "and escape from their unenviable surroundings." They seemed to think they were deserving of some sort of special consideration because of who their grandfather had been. Because of their lack of education and unpresentable appearance they were not suited for any sort of employment save that of washerwomen. Unsuccessful in their efforts to find work, they left Portland and returned to their home.*

My gram! It had to be. Gram at the age of nineteen and one of her sisters! What a great distance they had traveled from their home on the Idaho-Canada border to Portland, Oregon. Did they ride their horses all that way or did they scrape up train fare? Gram and one of her sisters job hunting in 1895—as if they didn't realize they were Indian women and the limitations that imposed on them. I bet they were all dressed up, too, in job-hunting attire, in corsets and dresses with long skirts and bustles and high-buttoned shoes, trying their damnedest to look presentable.

They knew their grandfather had been named Father of Oregon

for all the help he'd given Oregon's pioneers. Lots of help—money and supplies. Once, several big canoes carrying one hundred settlers and their supplies overturned. Those people lost everything they had, and Dr. McLoughlin helped them.

Sometimes he even loaned pioneers livestock that belonged to the company, despite orders not to help. Settlement was not in the best interest of the fur trade. But he did help, because he was kind and because he knew that even if he and the company didn't offer any help at all . . . even if they let the settlers starve or freeze to death . . . that wouldn't stop the settlement of the West. Nothing would.

Gram and her sisters knew all about his acts of kindness and that he had helped the early pioneers, but I doubt that they knew that when Dr. McLoughlin died in 1854, there were many among Oregon's most prominent families who owed him money . . . a great deal of money! Eight pages of promissory notes written by people after whom streets were named in Portland. Eight pages of bad debts totaling $80,000. An immense amount of money in 1854.

And McLoughlin's magnificent house, which became Oregon's first museum (the one my mother took me to visit when I was a little girl), was confiscated by the state (along with most of his property) on the grounds that his land claims were made when the Territory was held in joint occupancy (as were everyone else's claims).

McLoughlin had been the representative of that hated British company. Hostilities were not forgotten once the border dispute was settled and Oregon was firmly American. But McLoughlin's many kindnesses and all the money he had loaned the good pioneers *were* forgotten.

The state allowed John and Margaret to live in their house (but not to bequeath it). When Margaret died in 1860, it became the property of the state of Oregon.

Many years later, when both Dr. and Mrs. McLoughlin were long dead, his many kindnesses were remembered at last (through racism lived on, and no bad debts were ever repaid). The beautiful house that had been confiscated by the state became a boarding-house for a while. Then it was a brothel. It was about to be de-molished when the Historical Society rescued it, salvaged it, turned it into Oregon's first museum. They named Dr. John McLoughlin the Father of Oregon and had a statue made of him and sent it to Washington, D.C.

But when two young women came along, two poor, shabby Indian women from somewhere up in Idaho along the Canadian border, looking for work, they were promptly dismissed. They seemed to think that they, as granddaughters of the Father of Oregon, deserved some sort of special consideration. Naive. So un-presentable they were unfit for any sort of employment . . . save that of washerwomen.

So young Angeline McLoughlin returned to the Kootenay Valley, where she did not, at least fully, belong either.

Did she ever hate her Indianness? At least sometimes? At least a little? She knew how unacceptable she was because of her looks (and maybe even an accent). I tried to recall a time—was there one?—when I hated my Indianness. Really hated it, not just been hurt by prejudice, but a time I really wished I were not, did not have to be, an Indian.

When I was six or seven years old, at Christ the King Elementary School in Omak, Washington, a little town adjacent to the Colville Reservation, I was the only Indian kid. Other Indian kids went to the public school, or to the Catholic mission boarding school. No play-ground equipment there. No swings or slides or teeter-totters. At recess the nuns organized the kids in hand-holding games like Red Rover and Drop the Handkerchief and London Bridge Is Falling Down. No-body would hold my hand. They refused to touch my brown Indian hands. Even when the nuns tried to make them.

I went home after school and filled a white enamel basin with water, then poured a cup of Purex bleach into it and soaked my hands. For a long time. As long as I could. My hateful brown hands. I hoped and prayed I could make them white. That I could make myself acceptable enough.

A year after Angeline's job-hunting expedition to Portland, she married a hard-drinking Irish railroad man from New York City (or County Clare, depending on how you looked at it) and had seven children with skin as presentable as snow. And every one of them married white, had white children. But then something went wrong.

One of Gram's presentable daughters, the girl who had once won an Irish beauty contest, left her white husband. She left her first miserable marriage for a dark man who spoke with an accent. A full-blood. A reservation Indian.

Years later there I was at my grandmother's house. I imagine I stood out among the little towheads who were my second cousins. (When we grew up I would hear my blond cousins tell people, "I'm part Indian," or "I have some Indian blood." Just a little Indian blood. A little is enough. Their great-great-grandmother was an Indian princess, you know.)

What did Gram think of, way back then, when she looked at me? At my Indian face, which was rather like her own? Did she remember the trip she and her sister made to Portland in 1895 "seeking employment" (as the Historical Society woman put it) and "*escape* from their unenviable surroundings," which they did not succeed in getting because they were too dark? Their Indian blood. Their Indian looks. No escape. Not then. Not yet. Who did I remind Gram of if not herself?

Jennifer Pierce Eyen

SHAWNEE

Writing for me is like child-birth—there's something deep inside me that must be born into the world. I believe that all art, all creative thought begins with Spirit and is interpreted through us into this place, this dream that we are sharing now. I give thanks every day that I am a writer. I can't imagine being anything else.

Wuski A-Baw-Tan (A New Dream)

A POEM DEDICATED TO OUR ELDER, HORSE MAN,
WHO PASSED OVER TO THE LAND OF THE
DEATH DREAM ONE STORMY NIGHT

Ningiwa eh gimewane chantoon
chena eh dasse gowa

Ningiwa papapanawe manese
pachan menquotwe

Ningiwa moqueghke
peshabon ni-pai-n' coi ono' ityi-yende
te eh Shawandasse h' tow-wa-ca'

Ilani ahuk getteminack negvech
Ilani ahuk naga ni-bog-we
Ilani gowa wapacoli gowa
Ilani ahuk naga aghqueloge,
Ilani ahuk di-ben-indis!

Ye ama pekon Ilani a-baw-tan wuski a-baw-tan!
Negvech, Ilani umbe to minikwewin alagwa!

A New Dream (Wuski A-Baw-Tan)

I have seen the rain speak
and the wind dance

I have seen the lightning knife
cut the sky

I have seen the hills
at the first light of day
whispering secrets
to the Southwind People's ear

I am happy now
I am no longer thirsty
I dance a warrior dance
I am not sick, I am free!

This night I dream a new dream!
Now, I come to drink the stars!

Paula Gunn Allen

L A G U N A ▮ S I O U X

I write for the same reason that
mountain climbers do what they do: because it's there. As a
younger woman I remember a few dreadful weeks when I wept
and raged because all I did was write when there were so many

ills to correct, so much to be done. Eventually, I came to un-
derstand that the pen is mightier than the lawbooks, and that
the image is where the action is begotten.

But I also understood that writing is indeed a sullen art,
as the poet claimed; my statement that accompanied some
exam for receiving my MFA I remember writing "writing re-
quires a number of small suicides—some of them fatal." I do
not write as therapy, as self-expression (whatever that means),
or as a way of being cool, acceptable, and part of the in-crowd
(whoever that might be). I write because I am aware that
whoever controls the image controls the population; that those
who define us determine not only our lives, but our concept of
our very selves, and that colonization begins and ends with the
definer, the contextualizer, and the propagandist.

Most of my work has been focused on getting other writers
into print, contextualizing their work so that it might become
comprehensible to an ignorant non-native world, and so that
native people, young ones, middle ones, and elder ones, could
find themselves in the pages of a book. More and more I am
pushing for native people to get heavily involved in media at
the popular level, on major networks, and especially in made-
for-television and made-for-theater films. We must get control
of those definitions, those contexts, and those images of our-
selves.

Going Home, December 1992

I left New Mexico, my home, almost twelve years ago. I was
depressed because the state had voted for Ronald Reagan. My
mother called me election night to crow: "We're so happy!" Her
voice betrayed a hint of gloat beneath its familiar warmth. At that
time, fury, or simmering rage at any rate, was how I moved from
one life stage to another, though it had been a capricious master.
It had motivated my writing, my curiosity, and my intellectual pur-
suits, and colored my career and my relationships, often disas-

trously, for a number of years. That year, just after Ronald Reagan's election, rage moved me to California. On that cold election night, I made my plans to escape the confinements of rage, disappointment, rejection, and fear. On Martin Luther King, Jr.'s birthday, I was headed west along the familiar highway to the Bay Area, a song by the Police ringing in my head: "So if you're dreaming about California. . . ."

A small trailer hitched behind my car held some household stuff, my typing table and chair, the three or four cartons of books that remained from thefts and giveaways, sales and trashing. With me in the car—named White Spirit by the dealer—rode my crystal ball, Mitse, my IBM electric typewriter, unnamed, my lover, M., and my precious backpack stuffed with poetry and fiction manuscripts, all named though unpublished. And thus, beneath a clear, cold January sky, emboldened by righteous rage and plentiful hope, I set out to seek the American grail in the promised Golden State.

Because my life had changed dramatically in the five years since I had last lived in the Bay Area, I wasn't certain what I'd find there, other than a familiar city where gays clustered, where voting Democrat was thought to be somewhat reactionary, where fringe politics and alternative spiritualities thrived. I believed I was heading to California where the Aquarian Conspiracy was alive and well. It was January 1981, and although I didn't know it, California was indeed a brand-new game.

Now it's December 1992. A little over a year ago we buried my mother. For the first time in years I returned to our homelands around Laguna. The day before her funeral, my children and I drove out to Laguna and Cubero, her first and longest homes and the place where I grew up. The land was the strongest link between us. We climbed the mesa behind my grandma's house in Cubero, a climb made difficult by someone's addition of a fence just where the sandstone rears up behind my grandmother's rock garden. We performed a small ceremony of remembrance for my mother, burning then burying the sage used the night before to soothe our grief. Nothing soothes it, really. The hard part is not being able to call her on the phone. In the time I've been gone, a score of family members and several friends have died, and I am not only sorrowing but old. Strange to be the old folks when you're not really out of childhood, however gray your hair under the wishful red dye.

I had not returned to Laguna or Cubero since my grandmother died seven years before. It was too painful to go where Grandma's chirpy voice no longer greets me with news of scattered family, where there is no cup of her strong black coffee, no Pepperidge Farm cookies stashed carefully against occasions, no little lunch. Too painful to go where there is no tiny grandma standing at the kitchen door, guiding me with her eyes and voice as I enter her rock garden, disappear behind the pussy willow bush she nurtured for thirty years, and climb toward the ancient sandstone cliffs that were so much my childhood home.

It was only when Mother died that I returned to Laguna, hoping to find her spirit on the mesas above her home, hoping to meet her on an odd volcanic rock we called "the Chair," spewn from an explosion thousands of years ago, landing miles away from the eruption. It was about the size of a Barcalounger, high backed with an inward curving seat. It stood sentinel near the highest point of the mesa, and I had spent hours there all through my growing up. I visited every time I went home. I went to the Chair on the mesa during marriages and love affairs, through breakups, pregnant, with children, alone. I took my best friend there. I took three husbands and two lovers.

So at Mother's death I returned, an aging and grieving woman. Mother wasn't there, only the wind, mysterious in its soughing; only faded memories, great, gaunt vistas, November light, and cold, cold wind. You can see the entire little village from the Chair; you can see eons of earth's life; you can see millennia of all that is past and returns no more. My mother climbed those mesas in her youth, like her daughter, like her daughter's daughter, like our sons. They were much different mesas then, overlooking a different world.

What I realized on that mesa on that bleak day before my mother's funeral was only that I had not known the woman at all—so private she was, so inward-bound. Who were you, I asked the wind?

The silence that holds it in the air was the answer I received: I am myself, and no other.

Mother used to tell me that I might have to go along with whatever was required. I might have to say a lot of things I didn't mean, didn't believe. But, she would say, touching her brow with an extended finger, they can't control what you think: that's for you alone. A few years ago we talked about that privacy. She repeated her lesson, adding: There's a line all the Indian people have that no one can cross. Behind that line I keep everything that is mine, that is me. I don't let anyone over that line. Maybe we're different that way, she said, pausing. Maybe that's what makes us what we are. It's not the same as "keeping secrets," no. It is simply recognizing that one's self is inviolate; the private soul is private, not public. It's neither commodity nor consumable. It is most like the center of silence that is the always flowing wellspring of life, like the spring that used to bubble up like a miracle just beyond the alfalfa field which was across the little arroyo from our old house in Cubero. The sweet, sweet spring where every day my mother went to draw water for her family's use.

Now, on this gloom-filled late December day nearly a year since Mother's death, and twelve years since I moved to California, I'm heading back down the highway, going home. My stuff has grown by leaps and bounds. Laden with possessions and bills, possessed of three grandchildren all lost to the red mists of their three separate mothers' rage, sans lover, sans mother, deserted by both rage and hope. I make my painful journey home, a wounded eagle returning to the ancient nest. Pursued by tornado warnings, brainfogged after a night of hurricane-like storms that beat around my daughter's Marin County home until dawn, I turn eastward on Highway 58 toward Bakersfield, toward home, toward Laguna and Cubero. I anticipate driving by the villages just after the new year begins. Speeding by them on I-40, I will remember scores of stories from my past life there, the people I knew, very old, lost, dead. I don't think I'll stop. I will speed around them, along the edges. The way of respect, the way of non-violation. My mother's and grandmother's way, the Laguna way. There is still a there, there, but not one I recall.

I left home premenopausal, debilitated from not-yet-diagnosed chronic fatigue immune deficiency syndrome; now postmenopausal, in better health after acupuncture, Chinese herbs, good chiropractic care, and a California-decreed upscale diet. Then, I was an angry daughter determined to flee the redneck politics of my home, my parents, and my bewildered childhood. I return a grieving daughter, a grieving granddaughter, a grieving grandmother, a single, aging woman whose own daughter rages somewhere in the California fantasy I'm leaving behind. My typewriter has transformed into a Powerbook, a portable printer, and a PC. My crystal ball is goddess-knows-where, replaced by eagle feathers, my great-grandmother's huge Acoma pot, and a beautiful basket that I think is Pima—or is it Apache?—also once hers. Broke again (or is it still?), I gotta sell them both, soon.

I will miss them, as I will miss the seductive heaps of fresh vegetables and fruit that grace California markets and street stands. I will miss the softly feminine California hills, the redwoods, the fog, the beneficent climate. I have lost much in these twelve years. The edge of the gathering storm I've so far outpaced is a fitting mentor for this newer, older phase. Mournful, sodden, the shaman sky mumbles companionably all around as I drive south then east: going always brings return.

On Christmas afternoon, just a few days before I left California, a package of photographs was delivered to me at my daughter's home. I reached for one stack eagerly because the photograph of a man holding a silver-tipped cane strongly reminded me of my uncle Ook, who died five or six years ago. Intrigued, I pulled it out of its covering and stared at it for a time, remembering Ook, smiling, torn. The last time I saw him was in a dream. He was happy enough, once again driving the old milk truck for Creamland Dairies as he had twenty or thirty years before. I guess he wanted me to know he was okay, or to see how I was doing. And I remembered him, a much younger man, dropping by to visit, tilting his chair at the oilcloth-covered table until my mother would say, "It's not a rocking chair! You're going to break it! You're going to fall!" And the time he did fall, *whump!* flat on his back. And the look on his face, the laughter. "Well, grace, did you enjoy your trip?" When he was ready to go on his way he'd amble toward the door, saying his customary "See you in the funny papers." I turned the photo over and saw it had been taken by a Laguna photographer, Lee Marmon, who is my cousin and Ook's, and who took the photos for my first wedding back in the 1950s. Of course the face looked familiar, though at the time I didn't recognize Walter Sarracino, past governor of Laguna Pueblo and also a relative, holding one of the governor's canes presented to the Pueblos by Abraham Lincoln.

I called my youngest son to look. Quietly we went through the stacks together, murmuring. Among hundreds of images were a precious few photos of home. They were, except for my children's presence, the best gift I received, even though I knew that most of the pictures, maybe all of them, had been taken years before and probably chronicled people dead, disappeared, or grown much older than their frozen images from another time. I realize as I drive beneath the lowering clouds that these wonderful photos, static and dead, preserve a subtle lie. Life in its unfolding does not stop, even though life and love both have their finite terms.

I am going home. I left in anger and return in grief. The road that unwinds before me cannot be the same one I took all those years ago. Even the mountains, soaring and serene, the great plains spreading below, the laddered mesas that climb the horizon to meet the rain-blest clouds will not be the ones I left behind. There is a new life brewing beneath the rain-bearing clouds, and I shall drive through the storm all the way to old heart's place, brand-new home.

Gloria Bird

SPOKANE

Rocking in the Pink Light

Because I came in during the late stage of my labor, I was given no dulling medication for pain—I had barely taken my place on the coldest of tables when the waters broke—and my son, newborn, opened his eyes blinking up at the nurses, at the light from the window, alert. His eyes are fiery black balls in which stars live and make him appear as holy as the ancient man who will later bless his new life. He moves then puckers his lips that are minute hearts of deep, deep red. I open my shirt, position his head to rest on the crook of my arm, the slight weight of his body supported by the remaining bulge of stomach which I am told will go down in a few days' time. My son shakes his head instinctively back and forth, back and forth. Between two fingers I position a nipple too big it seems for his mouth, which he finally grasps firmly into his open mouth. We stay like that, bundled together. I lean against the pillows and backrest of the bed for what seems like hours. Even after he is asleep I do not move him.

I want to embrace his magic, let it spin me motherly toward his small frame and galaxied face, his nose pressed to the fat of my left breast which I must hold so as not to smother him, but the ache spreads outward from my tender belly, the mother blood escaping from between my legs. I can feel the layer of dried sweat on my forehead and clinging to the loose strands of hair. I ease the backrest of the bed nearly flat, scoot down to sleep with my newborn son who breathes irregularly next to me, whose tiny heart I can feel through the layered swaddling fluttering the memory of distant dancing, muffled bells, shells, songs, and beating sticks wafting on winds to mark the periphery of celebration at home.

My son's shape is diamond; the skinflap covering his cranium rises and falls with his breath, his beating heart. The tip of the diamond reaches nearly to his forehead of thin fuzz backward to the spiral of long, straight black hair in which the unruly strand perches like a knowing flag marking a line of demarcation that predicts the sleeping infant's temperament and predilection; at its width, it is about an inch and a half. When later, at two months, the old lady we call Auntie Etty sees him for the first time she acknowledges our kinship by offering to hold him. She begins to unwrap the yellow blanket, removes his socks, lifts his nightgown. We are sitting in the P.H.S. Clinic waiting room. I dare not protest how the baby could catch a chill but watch her deft wrinkled hands silently as they move over his body: two long perfect feet (she appears to count toes), two hands as delicate as marble, the chiseled details of which outline the miniature moons of his nails (counts fingers), the sleek roundness of his head. There. She stops at the soft spot while he wiggles in her lap attempting to pull his limbs back in. She rings the ridge of skinflap with her fingertip. *Diamond,* she says, *what does it mean? I used to know but I have forgotten.* I can see in her eyes in their overt goodness that she knows but is weighing the consequences of her action, decides against putting the words where no words need be. I already know. She caresses the smooth of his stomach, pulls his gown down, hands him back in pieces: body, booties, blankets. He knows things already, which I don't say, but instead, *He makes no fuss, is a good baby,* to which she indulges me with a smile and nod and pats my hand.

I am dreaming of my son, resting in the warm spot away from the metal bars the nurse has pulled up so the baby will not roll off though my arm is draped over him while he sleeps, my body already keyed in to his imperceptible movements. We are caught together in the most basic of needs—his, simplified and crystalline, and mine, operating as refracted and reflected rays of light from moisture to create a rainbow opposite the sun. I sense that my will is no longer my own, the way it has been for eons for women who have birthed nations. I release my youth, my wandering eye, my solitude, the very corpuscles that seeped through my veins for this infant who is dependent on me, my body continuing to provide his nourishment the way it did while he still rocked inside of me, his added weight swelling my ankles as he grew seven, eight, then nine pounds and two ounces by the time he emerged. While still inside of me, stretching, he pounded against rib bone, the weight of his head pressed against my pelvis until I ached. My feet grew one size larger, and a filling from a calcium-depleted tooth fell.

We dream together: my lips move, my fingers curling around the curious sway of his backside particular to infants. *I am rocking in the pink light, swaying with sensations that tickle my underfoot, through the membrane I see my mother's face, her eyes large and round, a halo of light emanating from behind her form. She coos and ahs, removes the dampness from my bottom and I am dry, my belly full.* Someone is in the room.

I open my eyes. It is the baby's father, the one from whom I am estranged. He stands in the entrance of the room hat in hand. *Hi,* he says, *are you awake?* I tell him to come in, pulling the front of my robe to cover my exposed breast, the soft nipple slipping from the baby's mouth, the awkwardness acute in the cool air of the room in which we negotiate our new relationship to one another, sterile and unfamiliar. His face is as round as his son's, his eyes wide, too pretty for a man's I think, as brown as tree bark and well lit with intelligence. I can still feel his love for me, aching and hesitant. He smiles. I respond by motioning him to a chair next to the bed. *Want to hold him?* I ask, placing our son between us on the hospital bed where he can lift the baby without the intimacy of touching my body of which I am aware he is aware, the air of proximity thin as cotton this dance of separation remembers.

I can't believe you slept with him, my best friend said that next morning over coffee. Neither could I. We were too old for reckless pawing, the slobbering tongues, the ridge of his teeth as sharp as the razor edge of his need. Sometimes on the street he pulled me in, possessive in front of other men; he came to my work to talk domestics that built a wall around me so thick that "they" could see I was a monitored possession. Against my will, he would peck my cheek, ask *what time will you be home?* stressing that last word in a way that there could be no mistake about our living arrangements; then, when I did return, I was furious over his transparent behavior, his draping insecurities, his puppy-dog looks of repentance.

He sits between my newborn son and me beaming his fatherhood as if he were the one whose guts were split open, whose body had betrayed him in spasms of pain and humiliation in front of strangers who prodded at the tenderest of skin in private places, and whose center of being imploded in a single struggle to release the plug from which life was held precariously at both ends: the cord around his neck, the placenta refusing to dislodge. The baby's nose and throat were suctioned; I was scraped clean. His grin the final rope with which he draws me in, and he knows I hold no malice toward him; that although it is not love but care, duty-bound, I will never keep him from our son. And though I have put him out, I cannot shut him out completely. He will take the scraps; he would savor the remembered juices of my bones; and he will pretend that there is something *more* between us.

I watch as he strokes the shock of thick, black hair on the baby's head, and as the tiny fingers curl around his. He is pleased by the clarity of our son's distinctive coloring, the obvious similarity of the baby's features to his own, and in particular, as he removes the diaper to assure himself of our son's gender, a reality pinch that puffs up his manhood. When he says *my son*, I see my future waver like wet, heavy laundry hung in the wind. It is only a matter of time. The inarguable terms of parenthood lay stark black on white, as simple as the papers imprinted by our child's footprint above a golden seal, and in the too eager movements of his thick hands as he signs on the line marked FATHER with his full given name, claims responsibility for the hospital bill, and later signs the forms for my release and simultaneous bondage.

We are a family now, he says. Though my eyes say no, my

mouth remains closed, my head is nodding, yes. An awkward finality joins us together; at the center was our son who at this moment lay sleeping the sleep of infants who wake at three or four o'clock in the morning, whose cries wake the neighbors, and who suckle in those early hours desperately as if starving for touch, for comfort . . . who begin to put the pieces together at five years of age, suddenly cognizant of changes around them, who are jolted by the suspicion that something is missing, something amiss, whose eyes become distant and full of questioning how incomprehensible death touched down . . . and in the swirling black hole contained a creeping harboring of cancers, dark and mean . . . that one day will suck his father through to the other side . . . a son wanting to remember . . . but who?

Was I released then? and am I released now?

But in the room, the quietness evaporates as his scratching boots on slick linoleum suggest his hesitation. I look up. I cup my baby's head in the palm of my hand, the palm of my heart. I am still reveling at the body's fertility, the division of cells, and the truest mystery of procreation. I am kept awake by the sheer force of adrenaline though my body is fatigued, my face puffy with water weight and aged by incomprehensible pain.

He wants to come back. I watch him, handsome, clumsy, childlike in his inability to articulate his wants directly. Remembering how to read him, how he changes with the slightest scrap of hope, I say, *We'll see.* He takes my hand then, his sudden movement uncharacteristically determined, placing in it a stone, *For love,* he says: an electrifying crystal of the deepest amethyst, its sharp edges as jagged as the way my intuition has formed its defenses. He leaves before I am able to protest, before I am able to register what he has in fact resorted to in a last desperate attempt to change what is not within his power to change.

Once the father of my baby leaves, we return to our sleep. *I enter the pink light floating in liquid, call through the membrane that is as tight as a drum around. "Is this how you come, Love, transfixed from an outside source, a white witch's doing?" The question fills me with anxiety; I struggle to change the direction of the dream. I am following a purple string of light, one end attached to my son's navel, another to mine, and a third, trailing off to the horizon where the baby's father is sitting too close to a plum-colored bonfire. I can hear a soft chanting, move in closer to discern the words only to discover too late that as he makes a circling motion with his hands he is reeling us in, the baby and me.*

The room is dark when I awake. A telephone down the corridor rings. A cart rattles its metal clutter against the walls of braced nerve endings, stops at the door. A nurse enters flipping on the light switch. I close my eyes against the sudden glare. She checks the baby's bottom, disturbing him. She turns back my blankets and begins massaging the sore muscles of my midsection pressing down hard, rubbing. She moves my hand up, makes me continue rubbing, rubbing in a circular motion *so the uterus will contract*. I feel cramping. She hands me a green-and-white pill, *a stool softener*, a large white *painkiller* that sticks in my esophagus. She exits in a clatter of metal on metal. I am to be released in the morning.

I move the baby to the other side to feed him. He is sleepy and I have to push on his cheek to remind him to suckle, and the sensation of emptying relieves the pressure that has gathered there. As he becomes sated, the movement of his mouth slows to an on-and-off feeding. A clear liquid puddle forms at the edge of his mouth. I try to pull away; he won't let me, sucking faster in his sleep, already possessive, the bond of splitting cells that binds us all.

On the edge of sleep, I move my arm out to stretch touching the cold metal of the sidebar. The thud of the stone hitting the floor jars me awake. On the windowsill, wrapped in a shiny ribbon, is a potted plant of fat mauve-colored blossoms that stink like weeds. I slide from the bed to retrieve the crystal to plant it deep in the soil of the plant that will not come home with us when we leave. It glitters like a diamond in the moonlight but is as cold as city streets. I mean no harm, know I am not cruel enough to bear frail superstition like a fishhook. I make my way back to the bed feeling in the blankets for my son before climbing in to the still warm spot next to him. My last thoughts before I fall asleep jumble together: that our relationship is like a parabola, a conic section taken parallel to an element of the intersected cone; humans' feeble abilities would conceptualize a mathematical formula to express only a portion of the whole; yet, recognizing my basic mathematical illiteracy, that the formula has more to do with the theory of projectiles than imaging; still, all of history, both sides of our lineage, could make up the shape of the parabola that contains us in its cone like a cradle in which we are rocking toward that pink light, toward morning when I will name the baby Xavier.

Dian Million

TANANA ATHABASCAN

I am Tanana Athabascan and Nova Scotian. I was born in Alaska in 1950, and lived on the road with my family from Nenana to Anchorage, and all over the Kenai peninsula. I was removed from my home when I was twelve because we were having a particularly hard time.

I spent my young womanhood in foster homes, one in Washington, D.C., and in Hillcrest School for girls in Salem, Oregon. I started writing stories to remember my folks and what we were feeling.

I want to reflect on some of the confusion I experienced as a native woman looking for reasons in history and in human nature, for a myriad of experiences. I cared deeply about the forces that moved within, about the losses we endured and learned from. One was loss of children. Because I was first *concerned about how many native children were removed from Alaska in the 1950s I faced learning a whole history of the attempt to destroy our families.*

We must be very aware of the future that we portray in English. I think of English as a strange wing that sprouted, not grounded in the old thinking about the land, but one that we must learn to soar in.

The Housing Poem

Minnie had a house
which had trees in the yard
and lots of flowers

she especially liked the kitchen

because it had a large old cast iron stove
and that
the landlord said was the reason
the house was so cheap.

Pretty soon Minnie's brother Rupert came along
and his wife Onna
and they set up housekeeping in the living room
on the fold-out couch,
so the house warmed and rocked
and sang because Minnie and Rupert laughed a lot.

Pretty soon their mom Elsie came to live with them too
because she liked being with the laughing young people
and she knew how the stove worked the best.
Minnie gave up her bed and slept on a cot.

Well pretty soon
Dar and Shar their cousins came to town looking for work.
They were twins

the pride of Elsie's sister Jo
and boy could those girls sing. They pitched a tent under
the cedar patch in the yard
and could be heard singing around the house
mixtures of old Indian tunes and country western.

When it was winter
Elsie worried
about her mother Sarah
who was still living by herself in Moose Glen back home.
Elsie went in the car with Dar and Shar and Minnie and
Rupert and got her.
They all missed her anyway and her funny stories.
She didn't have any teeth
so she dipped all chewable items in grease
which is how they're tasty she said.
She sat in a chair in front of the stove usually
or would cook up a big pot of something for the others.

By and by Rupert and Onna had a baby who they named Lester,
or nicknamed Bumper, and they were glad that Elsie and Sarah
were there to help.

One night the landlord came by
to fix the leak in the bathroom pipe
and was surprised to find Minnie, Rupert and Onna, Sarah and
Elsie, Shar and Dar all singing around the drum next
to the big stove in the kitchen
and even a baby named Lester who smiled waving a big greasy
piece of dried fish.

He was disturbed
he went to court to evict them
he said the house was designed for single-family occupancy
which surprised the family
because that's what they thought they were.

II.

WITHIN THE ENEMY: CHALLENGE

Gail Tremblay

ONONDAGA ▮ MICMAC

When I think about the things
that shaped my work as a poet, I remember going to Catholic
school and being required to memorize poetry that had turn-
of-the-century rhymed and metered form. In third grade, I
memorized a poem called "October's Bright Blue Weather" by
Helen Hunt Jackson long before I knew she was a friend of
Emily Dickinson and wrote Century of Dishonor. Because I
was studying and reciting poetry, my grandfather dug out his
copy of Pauline Johnson's poems. He wanted me to know that
a Hau de no sau nee person was an important poet laureate,
and so I memorized a couple of her poems too. Because she
wrote in that same turn-of-the-century style as the poets I
studied at school, when I first began to write I also used rhyme
and meter. She gave me my first inkling that I could write
things about which I cared, things that were not acceptable to
the teachers at school.

It wasn't until I went to college that I really learned that
formal poetry was out of fashion with writers and poetry editors. I learned about free verse by reading Emily Dickinson,
Louise Bogan, Marianne Moore, Elizabeth Bishop, Theodore
Roethke, and Langston Hughes. But I have never lost my love
of rhythm and sound.

As a young woman learning to write in the early sixties
before there was much published by other native poets, I felt
lonely. I tried to give my teachers what they expected using as
models the poets they taught. But I was always looking for
American Indian poetry; I'd sit in the poetry section of the
library looking at titles hoping to find someone. The first contemporary poet I found was N. Scott Momaday, a slim volume

called Angle of Geese. *Just finding his book was very impor-*
tant for me. In the late sixties there were other books and
anthologies as well. It was then that I began to write some
poems based on personal experience and to write from my own
cultural perspective.

Indian Singing in 20th-Century America

We wake; we wake the day,
the light rising in us like sun—
our breath a prayer brushing
against the feathers in our hands.
We stumble out into streets;
patterns of wires invented by strangers
are strung between eye and sky,
and we dance in two worlds,
inevitable as seasons in one,
exotic curiosities in the other
which rushes headlong down highways,
watches us from car windows, explains
us to its children in words
that no one could ever make
sense of. The image obscures
the vision, and we wonder
whether anyone will ever hear
our own names for the things
we do. Light dances in the body,
surrounds all living things—
even the stones sing
although their songs are infinitely
slower than the ones we learn
from trees. No human voice lasts
long enough to make such music sound.
Earth breath eddies between factories
and office buildings, caresses the surface

of our skin; we go to jobs, the boss
always watching the clock to see
that we're on time. He tries to shut
out magic and hopes we'll make
mistakes or disappear. We work
fast and steady and remember
each breath alters the composition
of the air. Change moves relentless,
the pattern unfolding despite their planning—
we're always there—singing round dance
songs, remembering what supports
our life—impossible to ignore.

Carolyn Marie Dunn

MUSCOGEE ▪ SEMINOLE
CHEROKEE

"**M**argaret/Haskell Indian School" *came to me while doing research for a graduate class on Native American music taught by Charlotte Heth at UCLA. I was recording Muscogee Stomp Dance songs when I came across a recording of a Creek lullaby sung by a young girl named Margaret at Haskell around 1919. It struck me as odd that I, a young woman of Muscogee, Seminole, and Cherokee blood who grew up removed from my tribes and languages, should learn the words of a song from a record made by a little girl who was at boarding school as her language and culture were being forced from her. As I sat there listening, this poem came to be, and I believe it was from Margaret who* *wanted this story told. So, I can't take credit entirely for my poems and stories, as they are also the poems and stories of the spirits as well.*

My community is large and ever expanding. I have never known my tribal relations by sight; by phone and by name is all. But the relationships with them grow stronger every day. My immediate community in Arcata consists of an intertribal group of students, colleagues, and friends who are much more family now than anything else. I sing on two drums, the Humboldt State University Indian Student Drum, and the Mankiller Singers, an all-women drum group that serves as a great support for all of us women who sing around in the drum (we are known in circles as the Mankillers). We face all kinds of persecution here on the northern coast of California; my sister from Jemez was assaulted in front of her own home in a racially motivated attack just last month.

Language cannot describe the depth of feeling at this life, but I certainly try. It is my refuge, my release, my weapon, and my gift.

Margaret/Haskell Indian School

I am wandering.
It was a time long ago and we
well knew what was to come.
The tears fell like rain
from above the sky, red
red with blood and
we were remembering.

Sleep baby.
Sleep.

We were there,
not long ago.
We run and run,

we are not of this place
like shadows against the light
if we fall back enough away from the hard pressed eyes
of Pius X,
Saint Stephen and the Martyrs,
the lady Jeanne d'Arc
and John the Baptizer
their vacant gaze will not
fall on the
shadows
red with tears and
blood.

Mother had gone to find
turtle shells.

If I can remember
what it was like to
sing
to lift my voice and sing
of the songs
the songs of the trees
and life
and things I can remember
songs she taught me
maybe I could just see once
the blue sky and emerald
trees
just once.

She says she'll be back tomorrow.

We stand silent
against the cold pillar
the vacant eyes staring behind
into our backs

as if water
and bread
would make us clean
it is not those things but the
stars and
the sky
and the sun
and the trees
and the way I used to
lay on Grandmother's
soft breast and she would sing

sleep, sleep.

I stand apart.
We are the same, these shadows and I,
yet the differences pass
between us too far and
sometimes near
and if I sing,

bebi noja noja
noja

maybe I could go home

la ja hobo gan
ai yang gis

and lay my head
upon Grandmother's breast

ai yang gis
fak si nu

watching the stars
against the indigo trees

ta la da gis
naki do

nightchant fills my head
and I sleep

ai yang gis
bebe noja noja

with Grandmother with me
under tall trees and
bright stars

noya
noja.

Berenice Levchuk

NAVAHO

I am Kin yaa'áanii (Towering
House People) and born paternally for Tó dích'íi'nii (Bitter
Water People) of the Diné (Navaho). Although I now live in
Columbia, Maryland, with my family, I always come home to
the nurturing of the traditional hogan of my birth on the Diné
reservation. In my hogan, important kernels of my learning
came through chants, songs, stories, and my general presence
during what some now call the oral tradition. I am the first
member of my family to extend this tradition by putting my
thoughts in the form of written English prose and poetry. In

my own small way, I am attempting to convey an accurate representation of Diné thought to the reading public, especially to our native youth.

As a young girl, I began a lifelong effort to interpret between Navaho and English for parents, traders, teachers, missionaries, and others. I quickly learned that accurate translation is very important. Accuracy usually required not only a full explanation of the subject at hand, but also overcoming barriers to communication caused by inaccurate information and misinterpretations based on biased beliefs. Over the years, non-native so-called experts have been responsible for putting into print and sustaining far too much flawed writing and beliefs concerning native thought and symbolism. It is crucial that our native children and youth be given correct information about where they came from and who they are.

Leaving Home for Carlisle Indian School

The Navaho youth wears a cheap army-green suit, and the stiff shoes replace his comfortable moccasins. A wide-brimmed hat sits evenly on his freshly cut hair. He holds a red, print bandanna tied into a bundle. Perhaps some food and small personal items are in it. Devastation and despair show on the faces of his family. With departure imminent, the father, caringly holding his son's arm, urgently counsels him at the door. . . .

These Navaho images in E. A. Burbank's "Leaving Home for the Carlisle Indian School" were probably painted in the late 1800s. I imagine the drama of this scene to have been repeated countless times with countless tears shed across many thousands of miles.

The Indian Industrial Government Boarding School at Carlisle, Pennsylvania, received its first arrivals in 1879. Judging from old photographs, the youngest children were perhaps seven or eight years of age. Until it closed in 1918, about 5,000 Native American children and youth reportedly boarded at the school under the "Contract" system. Many would remain at the school into their early twenties. The school sent some teenagers and young adults on the "Outing" program to live with European-American families, called "patrons," to work on their farms and in their shops and to housekeep their homes.

When I first saw Burbank's painting in Hubbell's Trading Post in Ganado, Arizona, during the 1950s, I was unaware that other Native American children and youth had similarly left many different homelands far behind. They came from the western fringes of the Aleutian Islands, the interior of Alaska, the Southwest, the Southeast, the upper Midwest, and the upper Northeast. School records reveal many tribal origins: Apache, Cheyenne, Papago, Gros Ventre, Seneca, Laguna, Passamaquoddy, Winnebago, Chippewa, Nez Perce, Omaha, Chitimache, Clallam, Corelo, Cowlitz, Tsimpshean, Tlingit, Piegan, Cornplanter, Bannock, and many others. Filipino students from the state of Washington and students from Puerto Rico also attended the school.

This would have begun in the century preceding my own boarding-school experience. I remember all too often and all too well how devastated, frightened, broken-hearted, and lonely I felt when I arrived as a little girl in Ft. Defiance, Arizona. My schoolmates and I would board for nine months going to classes and working at the school. We spent only three short summer months at home with our families.

Now that I live within a day's drive I often visit what is now known as the Carlisle Barracks. During my first trip there, I expected to find little more than ramshackle buildings and neglected grounds. Instead, I was greeted by a sentry standing guard at the gate of a military facility.

"What is the purpose of your visit?"

"Why, to visit the old Indian school, of course." (I soon learned that many people have a variety of reasons for visiting Carlisle Barracks. It has existed since 1757, and is currently the home of the

U.S. Army War College and the U.S. Army Military History Institute. The Indian school was only a short phase of a long and varied history.)

"You will find the cemetery on the other side of the post behind the PX." (Cemetery? I hadn't asked about a cemetery.)

It was neat and well kept, with rowed uniform tombstones, about two hundred, in the typical veterans' cemetery style. But these were not the final resting places of the casualties of military campaigns. Rather, on these grounds, Mother Earth gives final comfort to her children, our ancestral children.

I was stunned and speechless upon seeing so many headstones. While most markers bore names, some were inscribed only with "Unknown." Tears soon blurred them from my vision. Perhaps I might know members of the descended families of some of these boys and girls, for example:

Lena Carr, Pueblo, June 11, 1887
Frank Cushing, Pueblo, July 22, 1881
George Ell, Piegan, April 7, 1891
Frederick Skahsojah, Apache, June 3, 1887
Thomas Suckly, Mandan, April 11, 1892
Percy White Bear, Cheyenne, July 22, 1899

As I walked softly among the graves of these sleeping children, thinking sacred thoughts, many questions flooded forth. Did they die of diseases such as tuberculosis, influenza, pneumonia, or measles? Or was it the cold dampness of the Pennsylvania winter, or overwork in the humid heat of summer?

I am reminded of a television documentary program about Asian immigrants. Some of these people went blind after coming to this country. No physical cause was detected. Culture shock, culture detachment, loss of support system, and homesickness were offered as possible explanations. Maybe the Carlisle students just died of homesickness.

The callousness and the arrogance of the U.S. government boarding-school system are legendary among my people. My grandfather is still passing stories down to me of his own boarding-school experience and his elders' experiences with boarding-school agents. "They would come through and steal the children, and take them off very roughly to boarding schools without regard for our feelings." This is a reasonably accurate literal translation of my grandfather's description as given in the Navaho language.

His elders told of children being kidnapped from their hogan or while they were out herding sheep. The elders also described how they themselves would be hidden by their parents among the family's belongings. Agents made no attempt to inform or explain to parents. Emotions ran so high that one Navaho father shot an agent for stealing his son.

Ironically, these were the same elders, as well as their children, who were expected to embrace and benefit from the education clause in the Treaty between the Navaho Tribe of Indians and the United States of America. Manuelito, an important and respected leader, and other Navaho headmen who signed the peace treaty had envisioned the importance of this treaty clause for the betterment of their people. But they undoubtedly never imagined the brutal enforcement measures that would be thrust upon them by the United States government. Such acts against children by men speaking of peace would have been unthinkable to the Navaho signatories.

The manner in which "the duty of the agent for said Indians to see that [their children are compelled to attend school] is strictly complied with" caused the people to feel that they were forced to sacrifice their children to the United States government. The people felt that the government not only wanted their land, they also now wanted their children. Tragically, these were the very people and their offspring who had been victimized by orders of General James H. Carleton's open war on Indians. They had also been paralyzed by "Kit" Carson's scorched-earth tactics. Carleton and Casson had murdered their relatives, burned and starved them out, rounded them up, and force-marched them on the Long Walk to imprisonment at Ft. Sumner from 1864 to 1868. Fear, distrust, resentment, and suspicion were justifiably present. Their thinking that

"Our children will probably never return to us from the foreign land, and we are helpless to resist" was indeed justifiable.

The same self-righteous, authoritarian attitudes that were imposed upon the people in Indian country persisted at Carlisle and other fledgling boarding schools. A plaque still seen among the buildings at Carlisle Barracks attests, "The way to civilize an Indian is to get him into civilization. The way to keep him civilized is to let him stay." The philosophy of Carlisle's founder and first superintendent, Lt. Richard Pratt, was to transform his charges into model civilized Indians through military-style disciplinary methods, regimentation, Christian indoctrination, and work at a trade. The Indian child must be separated from parents and homeland for prolonged periods of time, or these methods will not be effective, thought Pratt. He propagandized his ideas to Congress and the public here and abroad by displaying photographs of students posing "before" (long hair, beads, blankets) and "after" (short hair, school uniforms) their transformation.

My quest to find out about the children buried at Carlisle has taken me into Carlisle records housed in the United States National Archives in Washington, D.C. Although these records so far have yielded very little about the buried children, they do provide information about how the school carried out Superintendent Pratt's philosophy and policy.

"Ran 11/25/13" and "Trapped 12/30/13" proclaims the young man's official Carlisle school record, which also contains a copy of a memorandum authorizing an agent to apprehend and return the "deserter," who was twenty years old at the time, to the school.

One school agent's report stated, "C____ is happy in his home and is learning very rapidly. His deportment is good except that he calls to see a colored girl. He has been asked to not do this and if he continues to do it Mr. ____ will not employ him any longer." And later. "C____ seems discontent . . . on account of his wages . . . $8 per month is all he can earn at his present trade."

A school agent wrote the following in A____'s record in December 1911: "[A____] and Mr. ____ were plowing in a field . . . when I was there today. Each had a team and A____ was doing fairly good work. He does not seem to know English well and it is hard to make him understand. He goes ahead with chores about the barn without being told . . . I am favorably impressed with Mr. _____ and no doubt he affords a good home for the boy. *I have never been to the home*" (emphasis added).

L____ was sent home as an undesirable. The school wrote to her home agency's superintendent, stating that "no one was to blame but the girl herself" for becoming pregnant. The school also chastised the agency superintendent for sending an "undesirable" to Carlisle, as the school wanted "only students with desire and ambition." L____ became pregnant during her Outing in a Philadelphia suburb. Her patron wrote an indignant letter to the school denying that, contrary to rumor, his sixteen-year-old son had anything to do with it. After all, his son was of great character and was even a Boy Scout. Letters from L____'s patron and his wife portray attitudes that surely many more students than L____ had to cope with in silence, pain, and humiliation. They spoke of another "filthy" Indian student from Carlisle. They alleged that L____ had a "secret scheme," did not tell the truth, and received "suggestive correspondence" from a boy, the latter being learned by the wife going through L____'s personal belongings. The wife also expressed pride that they did not treat L____ like just a servant.

Although incomplete and probably selective in favor of the school's mission, Carlisle school records reveal some insight into the school's Outing program, Contract system, and student experiences. Outings were typically in Maryland, Pennsylvania, and New Jersey and lasted for varying periods of time—from a few weeks or months to over a year. Some Outings lasted as long as twenty-five months. The male students worked for their patrons, doing farming and blacksmithing in the countryside. Others did printing, clerking, and tailoring in towns or cities. The female students did laundering, cooking, sewing, and housecleaning in town and country alike. Those in the country were no doubt also expected to do other wife helper chores such as milking, gardening, and tending chickens.

When on campus at Carlisle, the students were trained in vocational skills, including a designated primary trade. The earliest students at the school were taught shoemaking and tinsmithing. In time, other trades were added, such as printing, carpentry, blacksmithing, harness-making, and tailoring for the boys; and cooking, laundering, and sewing for the girls. They received grades marked "excellent," "good," and "fair" for their trade skills and for something called "academic subjects."

Boys and girls were detailed to various vocational work and labor forces to construct some buildings at the school and to keep the school in operation. For example, the school gymnasium, still in use and now named for the famous Carlisle athlete Jim Thorpe, was constructed by Carlisle students in 1887. They also farmed, sewed, laundered, and otherwise worked at the school in order to be housed, taught, fed, and uniformed. Uniforms and regimentation pervaded school life.

Students came to Carlisle under "contract," which was essentially an agreement to stay at the school for a three- or five-year term without going home. Many students actually stayed longer, even as long as twelve years, at the insistence of the school. Parents pleaded through letters, often written for them, to have their daughter or son sent home.

Some students have become especially memorable to me, perhaps because theirs were among the first files I read. Among them was a ten-year-old girl from Chihuahua who worked as a laundress and housekeeper for various families until she left in her early twenties. I cried for her, remembering my own boarding-school work and chores. The socks to be darned and other clothing to be mended waited for me in the evening after I was released from my kitchen or dining room detail, year after year.

Day in and day out, from the first grade through the eighth grade, the other girls and I arose at 5 A.M. every morning to be on time for our 6 A.M. kitchen or dining room detail. We were dismissed from our detail at 8:15 A.M., just in time to clean up quickly, change clothes, and rush to class still smelly and sweaty from the kitchen. At noon, we hurried back to the dormitory to put on our work clothes before rushing to the kitchen or dining room in time to get things ready for lunch. Then we would clean up the facilities after lunch before running to the dormitory again to wash and change and scurry back to class, even more smelly and sweaty than before (only two showers per week were allowed). The supper rush began right after school, and lasted until everything was put away for the night. Our hands bled from lye soap—we washed dishes with powdered lye soap; we washed face and hands, showered, and shampooed with bar lye soap.

Furthermore, our unempathetic matron, the adult who was employed to be responsible for our well-being and for providing our nurturing, refused to give us any Vaseline for our chapped hands and faces. We children saw those large, institutional-sized jars of Vaseline that the matron stashed in her supply room. She stashed other things, such as new clothes our parents would buy for us, fresh fruit, and other food that our parents would send or bring from home. She took them for "safekeeping" until they rotted or became "lost" in her supply room. There was always some explanation why things from home were withheld "for our own good."

I suppose it was "for my own good" that the matron refused my request to go over to the hospital, only a block away, for medical attention when I got hit severely in the eye by a baseball. This caused excruciating eye and head pain accompanied by nausea. It lasted for days. I was not allowed to lie down inside and was chased out. I often wonder if the eye problem still afflicting me is related to this incident.

About a year later, the hospital provided eyeglasses for me, but the matron would never let me have them. I still wonder why she demanded $4 from a little child, knowing that I did not have the money to pay for something I now believe was provided free by the government hospital.

Sometimes unconscionable treatment progressed to cruelty. For example, upon someone's even minor infraction of a rule, we were all required to stand at attention for prolonged periods with arms fully extended toward the ceiling. No sooner than an arm wavered, then *wwwhhhaaappp* with the yardstick. Monitors tried to force one girl's deformed arm above her shoulder as she screamed in agony. As for me, I usually fainted and hit my head on the hard concrete, the same way as when they made us all line up outside in formation. I also wonder if my severe headaches that continue to this day are related to the many such falls I suffered.

Intimidation and fear were very much present in our daily lives. For instance, we would cower from the abusive disciplinary practices of some superiors, such as the one who yanked my cousin's ear hard enough to tear it. After a nine-year-old girl was raped in her dormitory bed during the night, we girls would be so scared that we would jump into each other's bed as soon as the lights went out. The sustained terror in our hearts further tested our endurance, as it was better to suffer with a full bladder and be safe than to walk through the dark, seemingly endless hallway to the bathroom. When we were older, we girls anguished each time we entered the classroom of a certain male teacher who stalked and molested girls.

Thus, I fully sense the inner turmoil that a Carlisle graduate must have felt as he wrote to the school eighteen years after leaving, trying to explain politely that the Carlisle plan was not very effective when it came to education. He arrived at Carlisle in 1896, as a boy of fourteen under a five-year contract. He spent eight years at the school and had six patrons. He wrote that he did not attain as good an education as he should have, because he had to work on the farm for so many years. His letter also disclosed that, while he was a student, he wanted to go back to school from his Outings, but the school wouldn't let him.

Appeals from ill and needful parents to have their children sent home to help them were denied. One child's record includes letters from the child's mother asking for the child to be sent home, because she was always getting sick at the school, while at home she had stayed healthy. Request denied. The school superintendent felt that the child should be broken with discipline to get over her "melancholia," and that the concerns of the mother only contributed to the child's problems.

I remember one boy who went home due to illness. Six weeks after arriving at Carlisle, he was hospitalized for hemorrhaging lungs with a diagnosis of pulmonary tuberculosis. After spending nearly two months in the school's hospital, he was determined to be strong enough to travel, so he was discharged due to "illness" to return to Wisconsin in January. This boy's home agency physician had signed a medical certificate of good health, which was required for admission, that his physical condition was suitable to attend the school. Perhaps this incident offers a clue to some of the children's deaths.

We must especially remember those who died at Carlisle and never returned home. Also, we must remember those who never came home because some misfortune had befallen them. I am very much touched by and proud of our persevering ancestors. Alone, they had to struggle to overcome great obstacles in their young lives. Their long journeys from home and living without the nurturing and support of immediate and extended families were traumatic and agonizing for them and their families.

Cruel and unconscionable policy and practices forever robbed the students of their natural childhood and youth. Their undeniable rights and needs as children and youth were stolen, taken away forever. They were also irreparably deprived and starved of their physical, emotional, and spiritual contact with their families and tribes during their childhood and youth.

There must be a healing of all generations of Native Americans who, as children and youth, have become stunted and crippled physically, emotionally, and spiritually by the boarding-school system. The boarding-school experience must be remembered and told in its true reality. Our blotting out of the painful memories of boarding-school days, recalling only the pleasant things and rationalizing that "maybe it was good for us Indians after all," only hinders the healing process. Those of us who have been scarred by the boarding-school system should unashamedly tell the whole story of this phase of our Native American holocaust.

The Navaho youth wears a cheap army-green suit, and the stiff shoes replace his comfortable moccasins. A wide-brimmed hat sits evenly on his freshly cut hair. He holds a red, print bandanna tied into a bundle. Perhaps some food and small personal items are in it. Devastation and despair show on the faces of his family. With departure imminent, the father, caringly holding his son's arm, urgently counsels him at the door. . . . My son, you are beginning on a new road; be careful, keep to the good path. If you remember the teachings the ts'aa holds, they will protect you and help you to endure.

Alice Lee

METIS ▪ PLAINS CREE

I am a Metis from Saskatchewan presently living in Calgary. My mother's tribe is Plains Cree. I am a poet.

Confession

self narrative poem

—insignificant / self-worth

Box like structure / —confessional booth

i remember
my first confession
i was five years old

Catholic residential school

there is a snake inside you
the priest said
i must get it out
so you will stop doing bad things

so detailed. Why?

—makes you uncomfortable

—Surfaces strongly the medical truths

i remember
his hands
under my skirt
inside my panties
looking for the snake

—what is the snake

the way he was touching me *[symbolic for what?]*
made me hurt inside
but i was too afraid *[repressed / unheard – minority colonized / nats living in fear / silence]*
to say anything

he said it was my turn
to look for his snake
he put my hand on him down there
i felt a hot hardness
i tried to pull my hand away *[trying to resist]*
but he held it tight *[held tight within the gov't system]*

i always sleep with the light on
the darkness makes me feel
a heat in my hand

Lois Red Elk

FORT PECK DAKOTA
TRIBE

I live under northern Montana skies (Fort Peck Reservation) and am owned by rolling plains. My ribs are tipi poles and my heart beats a badlands song. The year I was born a butterfly landed on my hand, wishing my blood to speak the language of our grandmother—Maka Unche. Being the firstborn I was taught to share and to take care of my siblings. I was given the name "She Rides a Roan Horse." The smoke of sweet grass and sage, sacred rocks, eagle plumes, loving grandmas, a kind father, and dreams are my early teachers. I'll never forget this child.

Then came a generation of white man's hell. I would have preferred a knife cutting out my heart than the denial of my right to learn my Dakota language by beating my parents; the foreign and racist years in public school; the years of sniveling, fearful-of-God Christians after my soul; and the assault on my female relatives by machoism and sexism till they became subservient, second-class housewives (Dakota women and men have always been equals). However, the crime against me didn't put me in prison forever. I claim this hell.

When I was twelve years old "the hell" turned me inward (to resist under my breath), then I wrote and rewrote my thoughts (poems) to resolve the pain of stuffing their prejudice against us. In high school I wrote notes to encourage my Indian friends—"Stay in school, keep your baby, don't take your life, you can quit drinking." I learned well.

My writing comes like movement of horse people in my blood. My grandmother's name is "Brings Her Sorrel Horse," and my father's Indian name is "Backtracks His Horses." I can always feel them approaching—the slow gait of repose; getting where they need to with clenched thighs; and with knowledge of their horses, they lean forward, watch flanks stretch, and can ride you into the ground.

For Thieves Only

Don't tell me
Your great-great-grandmother was an Indian Princess!

This Indian's cheekbones
Have been kicked by hate.
This hawk-shaped nose
Smelled her parents' fear.
This redskin's hands
Smothered a baby to protect a nation

I paid a price.
I know terror.
I took a life.

Don't tell me
Your great-great-grandmother was an Indian Princess!

This raven hair has been caked with blood,
And the color was never lost.
This heathen soul was nailed by a cross,
And the earth is still my relative.
This Indian heart was betrayed for 500 years,
And my people have continued.

I refuse dishonor,
I am tradition.
I have survived.

I am as keen as a diamondback,
Know the coming of thieves.
Meet me at my children's feet,
I'll show you what you never learned.

Velma Wallis

ATHABASCAN

I am one of a family of thirteen children, born in the rich fur-trapping country of Fort Yukon, Alaska, raised in my people's traditional Athabascan values. I *was thirteen when my father died, and dropped out of school to help my mother raise five younger siblings.*

Later, I passed my high school equivalency exam and moved by myself to a trapping cabin, a twelve-mile walk from the village, learning to live off the land as my Indian forebears had.

Two Old Women

The women were aware that, although they had been left behind to fend for themselves, the People had done them a good deed by leaving them with all their possessions. They suspected that the chief was responsible for this small kindness. Other less noble members of the band would have decided that the two women soon would die and would have pilfered everything except for the warm fur and skin clothing they wore. With these confusing thoughts lingering in their minds, the two frail women dozed.

The moonlight shone silently upon the frozen earth as life whispered throughout the land, broken now and then by a lone wolf's melancholy howl. The women's eyes twitched in tired, troubled dreams, and soft helpless moans escaped from their lips. Then a cry rang out somewhere in the night as the moon dipped low on the western horizon. Both women awoke at once, hoping that the awful screech was a part of her nightmare. Again the wail was heard. This time, the women recognized it as the sound of something in their snares. They were relieved. Fearing that other predators would beat them to their catch, the women hurriedly dressed and rushed to their snare sets. There they saw a small, trembling rabbit thay lay partially strangled as it eyed them warily. Without hesitation, Sa' went to the rabbit, put one hand around its neck, felt for the beating heart, and squeezed until the small struggling animal went limp. After Sa' reset the snare, they went back to the camp, each feeling a thread of new hope.

Morning came, but brought no light to this far northern land. Ch'idzigyaak awoke first. She slowly kindled the fire into a flame as she carefully added more wood. When the fire had died out during the cold night, frost from their warm breathing had accumulated on the walls of caribou skins.

Sighing in dull exasperation, Ch'idzigyaak went outside where the northern lights still danced above, and the stars winked in great numbers. Ch'idzigyaak stood for a moment staring up at these wonders. In all her years, the night sky never failed to fill her with awe.

Remembering her task, Ch'idzigyaak grabbed the upper rims of the caribou skins, laid them on the ground, and briskly brushed off the crystal frost. After putting the skins up again, she went back inside to build up the campfire. Soon moisture dripped from the skin wall, which quickly dried.

Ch'idzigyaak shuddered to think of the melting frost dripping on them in the cold weather. How had they managed before? Ah, yes! The younger ones were always there, piling wood on the fire, peering into the shelter to make sure that their elders' fire did not go out. What a pampered pair they had been! How would they survive now?

Ch'idzigyaak sighed deeply, trying not to dwell on those dark thoughts, and concentrated instead on tending the fire without waking her sleeping companion. The shelter warmed as the fire crackled, spitting tiny sparks from the dry wood. Slowly, Sa' awoke to this sound and lay on her back for a long time before becoming aware of her friend's movement. Turning her aching neck slowly she began to smile but stopped as she saw her friend's forlorn look. In a pained grimace Sa' propped herself up carefully on one elbow and tried to smile encouragingly as she said, "I thought yesterday had only been a dream when I awoke to your warm fire."

Ch'idzigyaak managed a slight smile at the obvious attempt to lift her spirits but continued to stare dully into the fire. "I sit and worry," she said after a long silence. "I fear what lies ahead. No! Don't say anything!" She held up her hands as her friend opened her mouth to speak.

"I know that you are sure of our survival. You are younger." She could not help but smile bitterly at her remark, for just yesterday they both had been judged too old to live with the young. "It has been a long time since I have been on my own. There has always been someone there to take care of me, and now . . ." She broke off with a hoarse whisper as tears fell, much to her shame.

Her friend let her cry. As the tears eased and the older woman wiped her dampened face, she laughed. "Forgive me, my friend. I am older than you. Yet I cry like a baby."

"We are like babies," Sa' responded. The older woman looked up in surprise at such an admission. "We are like helpless babies." A smile twitched her lips as her friend started to look slightly affronted by the remark, but before Ch'idzigyaak could take it the wrong way Sa' went on. "We have learned much during our long lives. Yet there we were in our old age, thinking that we had done our share in life. So we stopped, just like that. No more working like we used to, even though our bodies are still healthy enough to do a little more than we expect of ourselves."

Ch'idzigyaak sat listening, alert to her friend's sudden revelation as to why the younger ones thought it best to leave them behind. "Two old women. They complain, never satisfied. We talk of no food, and of how good it was in our days when it really was no better. We think that we are so old. Now, because we have spent so many years convincing the younger people that we are helpless, they believe that we are no longer of use to this world."

Seeing tears fill her friend's eyes at the finality of her words, Sa' continued in a voice heavy with feeling. "We are going to prove them wrong! The People. And death!" She shook her head, motioning into the air. "Yes, it awaits us, this death. Ready to grab us the moment we show our weak spots. I fear this kind of death more than any suffering you and I will go through. If we are going to die, let us die trying!"

Ch'idzigyaak stared for a long time at her friend and knew that what she said was true, that death surely would come if they did not try to survive. She was not convinced that the two of them were strong enough to make it through the harsh season, but the passion in her friend's voice made her feel a little better. So, instead of feeling sadness because there was nothing further they could say or do, she smiled. "I think we said this before and will probably say it many more times, but yes, let us die trying." And with a sense of strength filling her like she had not thought possible, Sa' returned the smile as she got up to prepare for the long day ahead of them.

Catron Grieves

CHEROKEE

I am of the Cherokee tribe in Oklahoma. I grew up near the Sugar Mountain dance grounds. This poem is for my community at Tailholt. I was sometimes raised by the traditional women when my mother was ill, as she often was. My father took me to Green Corn dances, and I learned to dance to tortoise shells laced to female legs and sacred chants. I grew up eating the things one gathers in the meadows, streams, and woods. We had animals and a garden. In my early years, my community had no electricity, no telephone, and two teachers for eight grades. I was a high school dropout. I went to Job Corps, and married young. A white man. It didn't work. I began college as an adult at night school, and now I am here, living with my daughter in Iowa City when I'm not at home around Tahlequah, Oklahoma.

Connuche

You asked me once for something really Native.
I said invite me to eat at your house.
"I don't cook very good," you said.
You implied that a recipe was required.

So this is connuche which is good in the fall
just after school starts.

Beat up hickory nuts very fine
until it can be mashed into balls.
Don't do that—just cover
with boiling water in a pan and stir
real good. Keep stirring and the shells
will separate from the goodies.
Strain this through a cloth
or find a sieve. Add mashed hominy
or if there's not much corn, a little cooked rice.
Heat this and serve it in a bowl,
like soup with a little salt.

But the best way to eat connuche
is with peaches and wild honey.

In a few weeks when the corn "Se lu"
is harvested
I will tell you about skinned corn,
you know hominy. And sa lo li,
squirrel, it makes pretty good dumplings.

Leslie Marmon Silko

LAGUNA

It begins with the land; think of
the land, the earth, as the center of a spider's web. Human
identity, imagination, and storytelling were inextricably linked

to the land, to Mother Earth, just as strands of the spider's web radiate from the center of the web.

From the spoken word, or storytelling, comes the written word as well as the visual image.

My earliest memories are of being outside, under the sky. I remember climbing the fence when I was three years old and heading for the plaza in the center of Laguna village because other children passing by told me there were ka'tsinas *there dancing with pieces of wood in their mouths. A neighbor, a woman, retrieved me before I ever saw the wood-swallowing* ka'tsinas, *but from an early age I knew I wanted to be outside: outside walls and fences. . . .*

The Pueblo people have always connected certain stories with certain locations; it is these places that give the narratives such resonance over the centuries. The Pueblo people and the land and the stories are inseparable.

[Excerpted from Yellow Woman and a Beauty of the Spirit: Essays on Native Life Today *(New York: Simon and Schuster, 1996).]*

Angelita La Escapia Explains Engels and Marx

Comrade Angelita stepped up to the microphone and announced she was not afraid to talk about anything the people wanted to know. She had no secrets and nothing to hide, so there was nothing to be nervous about; there was nothing they couldn't talk about. Was Comrade Angelita trying to get the villages to join up with the Cubans? How much were the Cubans paying her? Had they promised her Japanese motorcycles? What about chain saws? Wasn't communism godless? Then how could history, so alive with spirits, exist without gods? What about her and that white man, Bartolomeo? To questions about her private life Angelita was quick to snap back, "What about it?" with her jaw set so hard, the questioner was afraid to open his or her mouth again. Comrade Bartolomeo, she explained, was under arrest, about to be court-martialed for betraying the revolution with capital crimes against history.

"More about the traitor Bartolomeo afterwards, but first . . ." Angelita launched into a lecture.

"Questions have been asked about who this Marx is. Questions have been asked about the meaning of words like *communism* and and *history*. Today I am going to tell you what use this white man Marx is to us here in our mountain villages."

But right from the beginning, Angelita explained, she wanted no misunderstanding; nothing mattered but taking back tribal land. Angelita paused to sip orange soda and scanned the crowd for her "elder sisters." The "elder sisters" had complained that Angelita was hardly different from a missionary herself, always talking on and on about white man's political mumbo jumbo but never bothering to explain.

"Are we supposed to take what you say on faith?" the elder sisters had teased Angelita.

"Is this Marx another Jesus?" Jokes had circulated about Angelita's love affair—not with Bartolomeo or El Feo but with Marx, a billy-goat-bearded, old white man. The elder sisters laughed; here was the danger of staring at a photograph. A glint of the man's soul had been captured there, in the eyes of Marx's image on the page. The elder sisters said Angelita should have been more careful. Everyone had heard stories about victims bewitched by photographs of strangers long dead, long gone from the world except for a trace of the spirit's light that remained in the photograph.

It was time to clear the air, especially now that Bartolomeo was about to be court-martialed by the people. Angelita set down the empty soda bottle near her feet and pulled the microphone stand closer. She glanced at the elder sisters standing at the back of the crowd; they nodded at her, and Angelita took a deep breath and began:

"I know there is gossip, talking and speculation about me. I have nothing to say except every breath, my every heartbeat, is for the return of the land." The teenage troops yelled and whistled, girls and boys alike; the dogs barked and the crowd applauded.

If they could agree on nothing else, they could all agree the land was theirs. Tribal rivalries and even intervillage boundary disputes often focused on land lost to the European invaders. When they had taken back all the lands of the indigenous people of the Americas, there would be plenty of space, plenty of pasture and farmland and water for everyone who promised to respect all beings and do no harm. "We are the army to retake tribal land. Our army is only one of many all over the earth quietly preparing. The ancestors' spirits speak in dreams. We wait. We simply wait for the earth's natural forces already set loose, the exploding, fierce energy of all the dead slaves and dead ancestors haunting the Americas. We prepare, and we wait for the tidal wave of history to sweep us along. People have been asking questions about ideology. Are we *this* or are we *that*? Do we follow Marx? The answer is no! *No* white-man politics. *No* white-man Marx! No white-man religion, no nothing *until we retake this land!* We must protect Mother Earth from destruction." The teenage army cheered and even the older people had been clapping their hands.

"Now I want to tell you something about myself because so many rumors are circulating. Rumors about myself and Marxism. Rumors about myself and the ghost of Karl Marx!" There had been laughter and applause, but Angelita did not pause. "I will tell you what I know about Marx. His followers and all the rest I don't know about. This is personal, but people want to know what I think; they want to know if I'm Marxist." Angelita shook her head.

"Marxists don't want to give Indian land back. We say *to hell* with all Marxists who opposed the return of tribal land!" Market transactions had slowed as Angelita warmed up; and the people listened more attentively. Angelita could see El Feo and the others working their way through the crowd, recruiting volunteers to feed or hide their people's army regulars. "To hell with the Marxists! To hell with the capitalists! To hell with the white man! We want our mother land!"

Cursing the white man along with free soda pop put the people in a festive mood; they were accustomed to listening to village political discussions that continued for days on end. "Marxism is one thing! Marx *the man* is another," Angelita had said as she began her defense of Marx. So-called disciples of Marx had often disgraced his name, the way Jesus was disgraced by the crimes of his alleged "followers," the popes of the Catholic Church.

Angelita announced she would begin with her early years at the mission school on the coast where she had first heard the name. The old Castilian nuns at the mission school had called Marx the Devil. The nuns had trotted out the bogeyman Marx to scare the students if the older students refused after-school work assignments, free labor for the Catholic Church. Avowed enemy of the priests and nuns, of the Baptists and Latter-day Saints—enemy of all missionaries, this Marx *had to be* Angelita's ally! She had understood instinctively, the way she knew the old nuns had got the story of benevolent, gentle Quetzalcoatl all wrong too. The nuns had taught the children that the Morning Star, Quetzalcoatl, was really Lucifer, the Devil that God had thrown out of heaven. The nuns had terrified the children with the story of the snake in the Garden of Eden to end devotion to Quetzalcoatl.

Angelita paused to scan the crowd for reactions. Spies for the federal police or the army would use up the batteries of their little hidden voice recorders before she was finished. The people's army units could have vacated the village within a few minutes anyway. Screw the Christians! Screw the police and army! Angelita didn't care. They would not take her alive. Before she died, she must explain to the village people about Marx, who was unlike any white man since Jesus. For now—screw Cuban Marxists and their European totalitarianism!

Marx had been inspired by reading about certain Native American communal societies, though naturally as a European had misunderstood a great deal. Marx had learned about societies in which everyone ate or everyone starved together, and no one being stood above another—all stood side by side—rock, insect, human being, river, or flower. Each depended upon the other; the destruction of one harmed all others.

Marx understood what tribal people had always known: the maker of a thing pressed part of herself or himself into each object made. Some spark of life or energy went from the maker into even the most ordinary objects. Marx had understood the value of anything came from the hands of the maker. Marx of the Jews, tribal people of the desert, Marx the tribal man understood that nothing personal or individual mattered because no individual survived without others. Generation after generation, individuals were born, then after eighty years disappeared into dust, but in the stories, the people lived on in the imaginations and hearts of their descendants. Wherever their stories were told, the spirits of the ancestors were present and their power was alive.

Marx, tribal man and storyteller; Marx with his primitive devotion to the workers' stories. No wonder the Europeans hated him! Marx had gathered official government reports of the suffering of English factory workers the way a tribal shaman might have, feverishly working to bring together a powerful, even magical, assembly of stories. In the repetition of the workers' stories lay great power; workers must never forget the stories of other workers. The people did not struggle alone. Marx, more tribal Jew than European, instinctively knew the stories, or "history," accumulated momentum and power. No factory inspector's "official report" could whitewash the tears, blood, and sweat that glistened from the simple words of the narratives.

Marx had understood stories are alive with the energy words generate. Word by word, the stories of suffering, injury, and death had transformed the present moment, seizing listeners' or readers' imaginations so that for an instant, they were present and felt the suffering of sisters and brothers long past. The words of the stories filled rooms with an immense energy that aroused the living with fierce passion and determination for justice. Marx wrote about babies dosed with opium while mothers labored sixteen hours in silk factories; Marx wrote with the secret anguish of a father unable to provide enough food or medicine. When Marx wrote about the little children working under huge spinning machines that regularly mangled and killed them, Marx had already seen Death prowling outside his door, hungry for his own three children. In his feverish work with stories of shrunken, yellowed infants, and the mangled limbs of children, Marx had been working desperately to seize the story of each child-victim and to turn the story away from the brutal endings the coroners and factory inspectors used to write for the children of the poor. His own children were slowly dying from cold and lack of food and medicine; yet day after day, Marx had returned to official reports in the British Museum. Wage earning might have saved Marx's children, but tribal man and storyteller, Marx had sacrificed the lives of his own beloved children to gather the stories of all the children starved and mangled. He had sensed the great power these stories had—power to move millions of people. Poor Marx did not understand the power of the stories belonged to the spirits of the dead.

The crowd had listened patiently because there was plenty of orange soda, and because rumor had it that Cuban "advisors" such as Bartolomeo were soon to become part of history too. But certainly the most exciting topic for the people had been the handbills showing Menardo Flat-Nose Panson shot dead with his own pistol. People had questions about the handbills. What was the truth? The man shown lying on the handbills had been killed accidentally; Menardo had been shot at his own request. Angelita waved a stack of the handbills in front of her; she tore them to pieces dramatically and threw them high over her head like confetti. The handbills were the work of an enemy who had slandered the good name of all the tribal people in the mountains.

El Feo left the politics to Angelita, who got intoxicated on the subject of Marx even as she denied being a missionary for Marx. El Feo had confronted Angelita with his suspicions: somehow Angelita had been bewitched by the photographs and writings of Engels and Marx. El Feo had listened to Angelita go on and on about Marx and Engels. Angelita told El Feo about Engel's hearty sexual appetite.

They had already made love a number of times when El Feo had teased Angelita about her two other lovers, Engels and Marx. At first El Feo feared he had gone too far because Angelita's jaws had clenched and she had frowned. But El Feo had grinned and chuckled to keep the mood light, and Angelita had calmed down. She was no Marxist; she had her own ideas about political systems, and they had nothing to do with white men in Europe. But after Angelita had defended herself, she had showed El Feo photographs of Marx and Engels in books. She had remained quiet for a long time staring at the photographs. El Feo had settled back in the hammock to smoke a cigarette and watch the wild woman. Finally after a long time, Angelita had told El Feo the truth; the first time she had opened a volume of *Das Kapital*, she had been amazed at the blazing darkness of Marx's eyes. The photograph had been made when Marx was a young man. She confessed to El Feo she had never entirely believed what the old-time people said about photography until she had seen the photograph of Marx. A flicker of energy belonging to Marx and Marx alone still resided within the blazing eyes of the image; emanations of this energy had reached out to Angelita from the page. But it was only after she had heard his stories that she had fallen in love with Karl Marx. Both El Feo and Angelita had laughed and shaken their heads. Angelita warned El Feo never to repeat their conversation; enough rumors went through the villages about Angelita's lovers. They didn't need speculation about ghosts or spirits. They didn't need, and their army didn't need, ar   ors about sorcery. The village committees had to caution t people: generous financial aid would keep rolling in so long as all the "friends of the Indians" remained confident. Witchcraft rumors upset white people. That was a fact they had to live with.

Nora Marks Dauenhauer

TLINGIT

My early childhood was a traditional Tlingit way of life. We lived on a boat most of the year, except when we stopped in Hoonah where we lived in *my father's clan house and visited my uncle's clan house. When we stopped in Juneau we stayed at my grandfather's land at Marks Trail. Our home language was Tlingit, and only when we were in Juneau and had to make business deals did any of our family members speak in English. Our way of life included traditional Tlingit foods. Some were made at dry-fish camp, and others we gathered during their seasons. We lived on game meats most of the time. We bought only staple food from the stores in the towns where we stopped for fuel and to buy supplies and sell fish or furs. My family also maintained a traditional ceremonial life when it, as well as subsistence, was no longer the fashionable thing to do. On the other hand, my family was technologically innovative, with new kinds of tools and engines, fishing gear and freezers.*

I have tried to write from this sense of place and self. The body of my writing comes from living part of my life with elders who followed the traditional way. My writing is also greatly influenced by my research in Tlingit language and literature. I find great beauty in Tlingit language and literature. By writing, I feel that I'm passing on some of the intellectual and spiritual beauty of my family and people to my children and grandchildren, and to whoever else may read my books. One of my motives is to counter negative stereotypes and misinformation about my people. Another motive is to help others gain a better sense of self in confusing and adverse times.

How to Make Good Baked Salmon from the River

It's best made in dry-fish camp
on a beach by a fish stream
on sticks over an open fire,
or during fishing
or during cannery season.

In this case, we'll make it in the city,
baked in an electric oven on a black fry pan.

Ingredients

Bar-b-q sticks of alder wood.
In this case the oven will do.
Salmon: River salmon,
current supermarket cost
$4.99 a pound.
In this case, salmon poached from the river.
Seal oil or hooligan oil.
In this case, butter or Wesson oil,
if available.

Directions

To butcher, split head up the jaw. Cut through.
Remove gills. Split from throat down the belly.
But, but make sure you toss all to the seagulls
and the ravens, because they're your kin,
and make sure you speak to them
while you're feeding them.
Then split down along the backbone
and through the skin.
Enjoy how nice it looks when it's split.

Push stake through flesh and skin
like pushing a needle through cloth,
so that it hangs on stakes
while cooking over fire made from alder wood.

Then sit around and watch the slime on the salmon
begin to dry out. Notice how red the flesh is,
and how silvery the skin looks.
Watch and listen
how the grease crackles, and smell its delicious
aroma drifting around on a breeze.

Mash some fresh berries to go along for dessert.
Pour seal oil in with a little water. Set aside.

In this case, put the poached salmon in a fry pan.
Smell how good it smells while it's cooking,
because it's soooooooooooooo important.

Cut up an onion. Put in a small dish. Notice
how nice this smells, too,
and how good it will taste.
Cook a pot of rice to go along with salmon.
Find some soy sauce to put on rice,
or maybe borrow some.

In this case, think about how nice the berries
would have been after the salmon,
but open a can
of fruit cocktail instead.

Then go out by the cool stream
and get some skunk cabbage,
because it's biodegradable,
to serve the salmon from.
Before you take back the skunk cabbage,
you can make a cup out of one
to drink from the cool stream.

In this case, plastic forks,
paper plates and cups will do,
and drink cool water from the faucet.

To Serve
After smelling smoke and fish and watching
the cooking, smelling the skunk cabbage
and the berries mixed with seal oil,
when the salmon is done,
put salmon on stakes on the skunk cabbage
and pour some seal oil over it
and watch the oil run
into the nice cooked flaky flesh
which has now turned pink.

Shoo mosquitoes off the salmon,
and shoo the ravens away,
but don't insult them, because mosquitoes
are known to be the ashes of the cannibal giant,
and Raven is known to take off
with just about anything.

In this case, dish out on paper plates
from fry pan. Serve to all relatives and friends
you have invited to the bar-b-q
and those who love it.

And think how good it is
that we have good spirits
that still bring salmon and oil.

To Eat

Everyone knows that you can eat
just about every part of the salmon,
so I don't have to tell you
that you start from the head,
because it's everyone's favorite.
You take it apart,
bone by bone,
but be sure you don't miss
the eyes,
the cheeks,
the nose,
and the very best part—
the jawbone.

You start on the mandible
with a glottalized alveolar fricative action
as expressed in the Tlingit verb als'oos'.

Chew on the tasty, crispy skins
before you start on the bones.

Eiiiiiii!!!!!
How delicious.

Then you start on the body
by sucking on the fins
with the same action.
Include the crispy skins, and then
the meat with grease oozing all over it.

Have some cool water from the stream
with the salmon.

In this case,
water from the faucet will do.
Enjoy how the water tastes sweeter with salmon.

When done, toss the bones to the ravens
and seagulls, and mosquitoes,
but don't throw them in the salmon stream
because the salmon have spirits
and don't like to see the remains
of their kin thrown in by us
among them in the stream.

In this case, put bones in plastic bag
to put in Dumpster.

Now settle back to a storytelling session
while someone feeds the fire.

In this case,
small talk and jokes with friends will do
while you drink beer.
If you shouldn't drink beer,
tea or coffee will do nicely.

Gunalche'esh for coming to my bar-b-q.

Beatrice Medicine

LAKOTA

My writing and interest in cultural traditions stem from my Lakota parents—Martin Medicine and Anna Gabe Medicine. These interests began very early when I taught myself to read from the books in the house and the Sioux City Journal which we received in our home on Standing Rock Reservation in South Dakota. Perhaps it is significant that my father chose this particular daily—because of its title. Or perhaps it might have been that his Irish buddy from World War I days lived in Sioux City and came to visit us every summer. Whatever, my first "pretend" husband's name was chosen from that paper when I was about five years old. His name was Jack Bird and he was an African-American murderer. My mother was aghast!

Later, at about ten years of age, I read Anna Karenina. It was a summer-long endeavor. Then, in our public high school in Wakpala, the English teacher told us Lakota students to interview our parents and grandparents about our history, family stories, and place names on the reservation. All of us Lakota students became proficient writers.

I live in an old log cabin with no running water and only a wood stove. I love the plains, the buttes, and the creeks. Scaffold burials were placed on the buttes near my home. My ashes will be strewn on the butte where my band, the Sihasapa (Blackfeet band of the Lakota Nation), captured eagles.

Searching for the Bishop

The pope's visit to the Western Hemisphere brings back memories of the Catholic bishop's visit to my home community on Standing Rock Reservation in South Dakota. When we were "vanquished" or "conquered"—as it says in the history books—we Lakota people were corralled and placed on reservations. Our beautiful belief system—the Sun Dance—was prohibited. We were considered savages.

The Lakota Nation, called "Nadoweisiw-eg" by our traditional enemies, the Chippewa, was said to mean the "adders" or the "enemies" in their Algonquian language. This word was misinterpreted to "Sioux" by French immigrants. We called ourselves either Lakota, Dakota, or Nakota according to the Siouxan dialect which we spoke. We were a people—humans.

The people of Standing Rock are a reservation of mixed bands. Some of our leaders were Sitting Bull and Running Antelope of the Hunkpapa band; Sitting Crow of the Sihasapa (Blackfeet—another source of confusion) band; and various headmen from the Yanktonai and other bands. The headmen all attempted to maintain a sense of cultural cohesiveness and communication despite the push and pull of Christian missionaries and government agents, such as "Major" James McLaughlin. I often imagine the chiefs saying such things as this:

"Tahanshi! [Male cousin!] When you go to that meeting [church] and I go to this one, we'll find out what they are saying and wanting us to believe. We'll see if they worship the same Wakan Tanka." (*Wakan Tanka* translates from the Lakota language to mean "Great Holy" or "Great Spirit" or "God.")

The Lakota bands had been arbitrarily assigned to various Christian denominations—Catholic, Episcopal, Congregational. These different sects crosscut the indigenous tiospaye (extended families) on Standing Rock. We were to remain true to our assignments and not cross culture boundaries.

Because we were "worshipping" the one Christian God, it must have been incomprehensible for our great-grandfathers to believe that one god could be worshipped by so many different "meetings."

But nonetheless, no matter to what religious denomination, we tried to interact in rituals which approximated the aboriginal ones. Rites of passage such as birth, puberty, marriage, and death pulled us together as they still do. Our kinship ties, though anachronistic in some instances, bond us together in a Lakota identity.

But back to my search for the bishop. I remember that year. We were living in the Good Elk house. I was enrolled in the first kindergarten operated by the public school. It was the year that I made such a sacrifice to attend school, which I really enjoyed. But I made my demands. I insisted that my mother meet me at the gate every day when I returned home. On the days she didn't meet me, I did dire things: I pulled the tail off the paper cat I had colored black in school; I refused to go to the house when Uncle Sam Red Eagle came to get me. (I could do these things. I was the third child and birth-order names allowed such idiosyncratic behavior.)

I also remember that day as a bright, spring one. For the past few weeks, I had heard Aunt Susan, Aunt Hattie, Aunt Elizabeth, Aunt Rose, and all the rest of the Lakota women of the St. Mary's Society murmuring "Bishop he kte cha!—The bishop is coming!"

I honestly did not know what or whom the bishop was.

I knew that the parish priest was very much in evidence. He was non-threatening to our Lakota fathers. He and the women of the St. Mary's Society were busy planning a Lakota meal of dried venison, dried corn, wild turnips, and a fruit pudding made from wild chokecherries. Someone would bring fried bread.

Aunt Susan was organizing the choir. Hymns would be sung in Lakota. My older sister and female cousins were busy rehearsing.

So weeks of planning for the bishop's visit occurred. The day of the happening approached.

That bright, spring day I returned home and waited at the gate. My mother did not meet me, so I decided to go looking for the bishop. No one saw me leave because all the women were talking to the priest.

I went to the one-block main street of our prairie town. First, I looked into A. B. Johnson's Meat Market. Only a small group of my little old grandmothers were there buying meat for soup. Grandmothers Cross and Good Elk were there. Grandmother Walking Wind was leaving the store with a white package.

Then I went to the lone restaurant run by a German lady. It was empty. Hesitatingly, but bravely, I headed for the den of iniquity—the pool hall owned by the man married to the German cafe owner. He was a Bulgarian, with a strong accent and even stronger profanity. As my mother often said, "His every other word is 'damn!' " (We have no profanity in the Lakota language.) He greeted every man with a slap on the back and "Hau! [Lakota greeting to males] You old son-of-a-bitch!" or some other choice salutation. He was called "Crazy Jim" because of his accent and pungent phrases.

I thought, "If the bishop is a male, he's probably in there with the rest of the men—Lakota, Germans, Russians, or anyone else who happened to be in town."

Timidly, I peeked into the open door. I saw several younger Lakota men. One was my Uncle Sam Red Eagle playing pool with my other uncle, Sam Two Hearts. Good! They didn't see me.

I sneaked another look, as we say on Standing Rock. I saw a group of older men sitting at a round table—playing cards. I was in luck! I saw a white leather jacket like one my father owned. I felt somewhat braver. He was there.

I looked the third time. Crazy Jim saw me! He shouted, "What do you want, little girl?" I boldly stood in the open door. He asked, "What do you want?"

I said, "I came to see the bishop."

Everyone broke into guffaws and loud laughter. Some even gave the so-called Lakota war whoop!

I was ashamed. I wanted to be reassured. I ran to the white leather jacket and, pulling the sleeve, shouted, "Mother wants you to come home!"

Surprise! It was Ed Two Hearts—not my father! My father sat next to him wearing a red plaid shirt. Now everyone went into gales of laughter. Everyone, that is, except my mother's younger brother, Uncle Charlie. He had to uphold her honor.

I committed two errors in one day. The last one was even more disastrous than my search for the bishop. Ed Two Hearts was a cousin (Tahanshi—male cousin) to my father. This meant that he was in a joking relationship with my mother. The joking could assume sexual connotations.

Thus, to the assembled Lakota male minds, this attribution of fatherhood to him was even more amusing. Poor Mother!

My father came around the table and tousled my hair.

Uncle Sam Red Eagle said, "Give her a candy bar, Crazy Jim."

Crazy Jim let me select one. I chose a Denver Sandwich and walked home with my father, holding his hand.

Tiffany Midge

LAKOTA

I agree with a statement made by Judson Jerome, who said "Poetry should comfort the afflicted and afflict the comfortable." Much of my own work I'd like to believe falls into this category, by confronting painful issues facing native people of the past, the present, and the future. My writing attempts to challenge the romantic myths, satirize the stereotypes, illustrate profound gestures of love, and through humor and grace lend some insight into a magnificent, yet greatly misunderstood culture. Above all, my work reflects a personal journey—an autobiography of sorts. In a very true and literal sense, my writing became the center of my salvation.

I've found much peace through the creative process by risking to speak of the stories that strike hard into the locked internal landscapes—the scariest cupboards—of my being. Through releasing them, I've learned the true meaning of forgiveness.

Written in Blood

I surrender to *Roget's Pocket Thesaurus.*
I confess my crime of breaking into this container of words,
and slaughtering this poem with meta innuendo.

But I needed something. I wanted to gather the dust
of 84 warriors & 62 women & children. I robbed
from this vault of words, language of the enemy, in hopes

I could capture these people, allow their prayers to
reach Wovoka in the final hour before I end this poem.
I wanted to know that I'm not grieving merely from the guilt

of that European blood that separates me from two worlds.
I need to know that I can be allowed my grief.
Sadly I have failed. This 1961 Cardinal edition thesaurus

I depended upon has betrayed me. Betrayed my Indian kin.
With this language there are times I feel I'm betraying myself.
In my search for synonyms for *murder,* I find *Cain,*

assassin, barbarian, gunman, brute
hoodlum, killer, executioner, butcher
savage, Apache, redskin.

Yvonne Lamore-Choate

QUECHAN ▪ MOJAVE

I am an enrolled member of the Quechan tribe of California, but also claim Mojave and Maricopa as my lineage. I currently reside in the San Francisco Bay Area with my husband, Melvin (who is a Choctaw), and our sons, Lance and Chase.

I was encouraged to write my story by two very good friends who also happen to be teachers, Kathy Moran and Ramona Wilson. They wanted to share the story with Indian students in their class, most of whom had grown up in the city.

Like most of the Native Americans in the San Francisco Bay Area, I came here through the Bureau of Indian Affairs' relocation program in the 1970s. I am fortunate to live in an area where there is a large Native American community because I feel being able to keep in touch with my people helps me to survive this urban "madness."

Untitled

I was born in the Ft. Yuma Indian Reservation in 1945. My mother was Quechan and Mojave Indian, and my father was half Maricopa and the other half we didn't claim. I was always taught that to be Indian was something to be proud of, and I always felt it was a privilege to be Indian.

I guess you could say we were poor when I was growing up, but I didn't know it. We lived in a mud house and like most homes on the reservation at that time, it didn't have any running water or electricity. We got our water from a hand pump, and used kerosene lamps for light. We lived with my maternal grandmother a lot of the time because my father wasn't around much from the time I was born, until the age of seven.

My grandmother was my rock, the one stable person in my life I could depend on. She couldn't speak a word of English, but could understand it very well. I couldn't speak our language (Quechan), but understand it very well. She would speak to me in Quechan and I would answer her in English. I tried a few times speaking our language but was always afraid I'd say the wrong thing, so to this day I can only say a few phrases, but I can still understand all of it when someone speaks to me in our language.

My grandmother was a very tall woman, with long straight hair. She had tattoos running in horizontal lines from below her bottom lip to her chin, an adornment most women of our tribe wore at the time. I remember my mother had a very faint tattoo in the middle of her forehead.

More than anything, I liked staying with my grandmother because that's where all my cousins were. I was an only child, and didn't have any brothers or sisters to play with.

One of my favorite things to do during the summer at my grandmother's was to get up early in the morning to have her tortillas and scrambled eggs with potatoes and coffee. My mother said I was weaned on coffee and bean juice. After breakfast, my cousins and I would go swimming in the irrigation ditch, or if one of the grown-ups took us, we could go swimming at the canal, which was more fun because it was wider than the ditch and didn't have as many crayfish. It was fun when the grown-ups went swimming with us because they would make mud slides on the side of the bank, and we would slide down them and into the water. I guess you could say this was an early version of today's water slides.

I don't remember too much about the wintertime, only the summer, because that was the most fun. Sometimes in the summer I'd sit under the shade of a mesquite tree with my grandmother while she would dig for hours to find just the right-sized root to make a cradleboard. She would find a root about two inches in diameter, and maybe five feet long. She would soak the root for days, and when it was pliable enough, she would bend it into a hairpin shape and tie the ends together with wire. She'd hang the root in the tree until it was completely dried. I'm not sure how long this took; it seemed like weeks. At the same time as she was digging for this root, she would also get other little roots in order to form slats on the cradleboard. Once the cradleboard and the slats were dry, she would whittle holes on the inside of the dried root in order to put the slats in. When completed, it resembled a stepladder with a closing at the top.

She'd also braid the yarn ties that went around the baby in order to keep the baby tied to the cradleboard. If the baby was a boy, the color of yarn was black and white; if the baby was a girl, the color was red and white. I'm not sure what the significance of the colors were, but these colors were also used on someone when they died. If it was a man, they would put black marks on his face. If the person was a woman, they would put red marks on her face.

A shade was also made to go with the cradle; it was made out of the bark of the mesquite tree and woven. It was in the shape of an inner tube, and went around the cradle at the head.

The mesquite tree was used for many things. In the summer, around July, we used to pick the mesquite beans off the trees when they were ripe. They were yellow, and about the size of a green bean, and were sweet and juicy. When the mesquite beans dropped off the trees and dried, my grandmother would put them in a gunny sack. She would grind the dried beans to a fine powder, and mix the powder with water to make a sweet drink.

My grandmother also used the sap of the mesquite tree as a natural hair dye. She would take the parts of the bark where there was sap, and put that in a pail with some water. She'd leave it in the water for about two weeks. After two weeks it would be ready, and when she washed her hair, she used the sap water as a rinse. After using this rinse, her hair would be dark and shiny and healthy looking.

She sometimes used a charcoal-colored mud on her hair. She

said this was used for dandruff and she would have my cousin dive to the bottom of ditches or canals to gather this mud. She'd put the mud on her hair and work it in real good, shape it into a turban, and leave it to dry. She would leave the mud on until it was completely dry, usually about one full day, and then wash the mud out.

Because people on the reservation sometimes didn't have the transportation to get to town to shop, there was a white man who would come to the houses selling blankets. We called him the "Blanket Man." One day my mother put this mud mixture on my father's hair, and he looked so funny walking around with his head wrapped in mud and shaped into a turban. Well, the Blanket Man came to my grandmother's house and everyone ran into the house, leaving my father the only one to talk to the Blanket Man. He said he was so embarrassed because of the mud on his head!

My grandmother never wore shoes; shoes were only for special occasions. She always wore high-top black tennis shoes, and whenever we saw her with her shoes on we got all excited because it meant she was going to a funeral. This may sound gruesome, but the kids all looked forward to funerals because it was one of the few times all the kids on the reservation got together in one place, besides school, where we could all play and have fun.

I guess you could say funerals were a big social event for everyone. The deceased would be taken to the "cry house" or, as it was more commonly called, the "big house." It was called the big house because it was a large one-room building. If you broke it up into rooms, I guess it would average out to about four big bedrooms by today's standards. The floor was a dirt floor and had a lot of gravel. In one corner of the room was a wood-burning stove which was used during the winter. In the winter, my grandmother would take blankets for my cousin and me and we would sleep on the floor next to the stove to keep warm.

Next to the big house was a smaller building which was the kitchen. There was always something to eat in the kitchen: stew, beans, and tortillas. There was always a pot of coffee, whether it was winter or summer, and Kool Aid or iced tea for the kids.

There were chairs or benches set up for people to sit whenever they weren't dancing or whenever they weren't crying next to the body of the deceased. Whenever someone came into the big house from far away, the closest relatives would go with them up to the body and then they would all cry together. This was the proper way to mourn the dead. There was always someone there with the deceased—the body was never left alone. At intervals, there would be singing and dancing, or someone would get up to eulogize the deceased and they always spoke in the Quechan language.

On the morning of the fifth day, at about five in the morning, the women would put on dresses made of colorful ribbon over their clothes. They also wore large scarves sewn together and worn like a cape. The men wore colorful scarves around their necks like a tie.

Because in those days it wasn't required by law to use a casket, the body of the deceased was laid on a bed and covered with colorful scarves. When the time came to cremate the deceased, about six men would carry the bed slowly to the gravesite with the procession of singers, dancers, and mourners following behind.

The grave would be about six feet deep, mesquite poles were placed around the opening of the grave, and aeroweeds would be placed around and between the poles and, when completed, the structure looked like a fence. A black or red cloth would be placed around this fence, again the color of the cloth determined by whether the deceased was male or female. The mourners were given one last view of the deceased and then the deceased was lowered into the grave. When someone of our tribe dies, all new things are purchased for this person: clothes, blankets, suitcases, trunks, and anything the deceased might have enjoyed during his or her lifetime. By the time the blankets, clothes, and anything else that was purchased new were put in the grave, the mound was about five feet past the opening of the grave. The cloth around the fence would then be ignited, and everything would burn. At this point, the women would take off the Indian dresses and scarves, and place them on the fire. The men would do the same with the scarves around their necks. The singing and mourning would go on for about another hour, and the family would visit with friends and relatives who had traveled a long way for the funeral.

The fire would then be left to burn out, everything would fall into the grave, and eventually the body also was burned. There is someone who watches the fire, and when it eventually burned out, the grave is covered with dirt. Everyone is usually gone by this time. To me this is the loneliest sight—to see the fire burning and no one is around. It is believed that the spirit of the deceased sits in that gravesite for four days and four nights, and mourns for the ones left behind, and that on the morning of the fifth day, a relative that has gone before them will come to lead them to the other world.

Back in those days, when someone in the family died, everything was destroyed: homes, pictures of the deceased, anything the deceased had used would be burned, and the ashes buried. This is so the spirit of the deceased doesn't try to come after his or her possessions or back to a familiar place. For this same reason, we are not supposed to eat any grease or salt for four days after a funeral, and we must wash ourselves with cold water and smoke ourselves with the smoke from aeroweeds. The women also cut their hair as a sign of mourning.

I remember my grandmother was always moving from one site to another because we lost some real close relatives when I was young.

There was always something going on at my grandmother's; it seemed to be the gathering place for everyone—aunts, uncles, and cousins. One of my uncles used to read Archie comic books to me and my cousin, we would get a quilt and put it under the shade of a big tamarack tree, and he would be in the middle reading to us. What I liked was that he never read the book in English, he always read it in Quechan and the story seemed more exaggerated—by the time he was through with the book, we'd be in stitches! He used to say he was embarrassed to take me to town with him because I wasn't as dark and did not physically resemble any of his kids, and when I called him Daddy like my cousins did, people would look at him in a funny way like he had kidnapped me from somewhere.

At night we'd all sit outside because it was too hot to go in the house. My grandfather had all the kids go to the corral to gather dried horse manure to burn in order to make smoke to ward off the mosquitoes. While the grown-ups talked and smoked their cigarettes my cousins and I used to roll up newspapers or pages of the catalogues real thin, and try to smoke them like cigarettes. There was a bed outside the house and sometimes my grandmother let us sleep there. I remember one night while we were sleeping outside the neighbor's black horse got out of the corral, and when I opened my eyes there was this black horse staring at me. I flew into the house to sleep with my grandmother.

Once in a while my grandfather would let us go to town with him in the wagon, which was pulled by his two horses, Betsy and Nellie. This was a lot of fun because we got to go to the grocery store and have strawberry soda pop. Before he stopped off at the store, he made the rounds of all the alleys in town. He'd stop behind each store—J. C. Penny, the Emporium, Kress—because in those days if something was slightly damaged, it was thrown out. He would find a lot of nice things this way, sometimes even clothes. One time behind one store he found a porcelain bathtub and I remember he had the hardest time trying to get it in the wagon because it was so heavy. Well, he finally got it into the wagon and when we got home, he placed it under the hand pump, cleaned it out until it was sparkling clean, and pumped clean, cool water in it to water Betsy and Nellie. When he returned with Betsy and Nellie, there I was sitting in the water and it was all muddy and dirty! He just laughed and let me keep swimming in the tub.

My grandfather was a very gentle man, he never scolded or spanked us. He always wore this hat that resembled Smokey the Bear's hat, and wore Levi's and a blue workshirt with a black scarf tied around the neck. When he attended government boarding schools, he was given an English name, William Penn. One time when we were returning home from a trip to town, there were some tourists stopped on the side of the road trying to take a picture of us. My grandfather frowned on pictures and felt they had no right to take pictures of us. He stopped the horses, got down from the wagon, and told my cousin and me to sit still. He walked across the road and took the camera out of the man's hand and threw it to the ground; it broke into pieces. He never said a word, he just got back into the wagon and we rode off; the tourist just stood there waving and saying "Bye, bye."

Rita Joe

M I C M A C

I was born in Whycocomagh, Nova Scotia, in 1931 as a status Indian of the Micmac tribe because I was a foster child who had been shunted from home to home and from one reservation to another. I have a deep and abiding love for children. With eight of my own, I have nonetheless adopted two more and take care of two grand-children. I write always with children in mind. I write so that others may come to understand the right of my people to ed-ucation and dignity.

I have received the Order of Canada Medal from my coun-try, and an appointment to Privy Council by Queen Elizabeth. I am sixty-one years old with Parkinson's disease, but that doesn't stop me from creating. I am working to better the im-age of my people.

Expect Nothing Else from Me

Words no longer need
Clear meanings.
Hidden things proceed from a lost legacy.
No tale in words bares our desire, hunger,
The freedom we have known

A heritage of honor
Sustains our hopes.
Help me search the meaning
Written in my life,
Help me stand again
Tall and mighty.

Mi'kmaw I am;
Expect nothing else from me.

Mukk Skmatmu Piluey Koqoey Wja'tuin

Klusuaqann mu nuku' nuta'nukl
Tetpaqi-nsitasin.
Mimkwatasik koqoey wettaqane'wasik
        Lnueyey-iktuk ta'n keska'q
Mu a'tukwaqan eytnuk klusuwaqaney
        panaknutk pewatmikewey
Ta'n teli-kjijituekip seyeimik

Espe'k Lnu'qamiksuti,
Kelo'tmuinamitt ajipjitasuti.
Apoqonmui kwilm nsituowey
Ewikasik ntinink,
Apoqonmui kqama'lanej app;
Espipukua'lanej aqq mlkiknewa'lanej.

Mi'kmaw na ni'n;
Mukk skmatmu piluey koqoey wja'tuin.

Elizabeth Cook-Lynn

CROW CREEK SIOUX

I was born a Sioux (Dakota) Indian on One Crow Creek Sioux Reservation—in a public health hospital—in 1930. My journey (both literary and personal) has always, therefore, been a tribal one. Contemporary and historical struggles over land and tribal autonomy are my consummate commitment to the children and grandchildren of the tribal nations. And that, of course, includes my own.

I come from a family of Sioux politicians and native scholars. My grandfather, Joe Bowed Head Irving, and my father, Jerome, served on the Crow Creek Sioux Tribal Council for many years. My namesake grandmother, Eliza Renville Irving, was a bilingual writer for early Christian-oriented newspapers. And an elder grandfather was a native linguist instrumental in developing early Dakota-language dictionaries.

Aurelia

When the people of her Indian nation were first driven from their lands by the white farmers and politicians, they went to war. They fought terrible wars. Different from anything they had ever known. Wars that went on for decades. Wars that made them seem cruel and heartless and hate-filled and desperate, wars that took away their children and brought death to their communities in such numbers as they had never experienced before. They won more of these wars than they ever lost because their warriors were honorable men and their wives faithful, and, even after that, their singers composed victory songs with the central message *"Mitakuye ob wani ktelo! Epelo!!"*

Yet, in the end, the old people always told Aurelia they were to become just like the nations of the world before them, signing peace treaties with their aggressors that redefined them, drawing parameters to their homelands in different ways. They put down their weapons and relinquished their war ponies and set about making new lives in a reconstructed, yet familiar world.

Then, squatters came into their reserved lands. Gold seekers. German farmers, laborers, and Swedish ranchers. Norwegian, Dutch, English financiers. People from all over Europe and the new America who became labeled in history, pioneers: "those who venture into unknown or unclaimed territory to settle." "Trailblazers." But, they knew, the old people said. They knew that these lands were not "unknown," not "unclaimed." They knew, the old people said, that they were stealing from us.

Almost immediately, the Indians began telling stories amongst themselves of how the whites quarreled and fought over the land, women, gold, their pigs and oxen and cattle. Even the wild game that meandered into the settlements, surprised and unawares.

It was like watching great red ants, the old people said, scurrying back and forth, carrying objects twice their size, heads bent to the tedious tasks of their own making. Building. Building. And every now and then they fell upon one another, striking death to their own fellows, biting them until they were stilled. Remorselessly dragging the carcasses away into the mass of pebbles and stones. Then, oftentimes, in whatever ways suited them, they were striking out at Indians whom they began calling lazy and obstinate. This kind of thing went on for over two hundred years.

Even at the turn of the nineteenth century, when it was thought that Indians would soon disappear into the so-called "mainstream," the Indians wanted to rid themselves of these strange people, now called "wasichus," who had by then become their white overseers: the military first, then the missionaries, and finally the bureaucrats. How to do this became problematic.

Collectively, the tribes scared the wits out of the whites, whose only response was the knee-jerk one of calling out the soldiers. Individually, though, Indians didn't seem to the whites to be quite so threatening. Thus, federal policies intent upon further breaking up the Indian land estates were set in motion. And the rise of individual Indian leadership, oftentimes unconnected to the cultural ideologies and tiospayes of the past, began to occur.

Aurelia's maternal grandfather, Amos Chante Numpa Two Heart (he had an important name, one that was old and well known among the people), was quick to play the game. His father had gone to Carlisle, thus he too went off to boarding schools as a young man, though they were local, regional ones, where he was intent upon becoming literate and cunning and smart in the white man's ways.

Though he had probably never in his life read de Tocqueville, he had, years after Carlisle, the occasion, oddly enough, to read, quite by accident, through some of the papers of Lewis Meriam, the white scholar of American government who was laying the groundwork for what was to be called the "Indian Reorganization." Meriam was a scholar who brought to the attention of the public that Indians were, on the whole, making less than $100 per year, only 2 percent making $500. In other words, that the economic survival of the American Indian was at risk, something Indians had known ever since the peace treaties were signed. It was time, said those bureaucrats who read the report, to bring American Indian government out of "the blanket" and into the modern world of commerce and trade and economics.

Two Heart started reading these newly distributed reports at St. John's one spring day in 1932, while he was waiting for his daughter, Myrna, Aurelia's mother, to finish up her cleaning chores at the church. "Public health work and administration and relief work is inadequate," he read. "Living conditions are appalling."

Every week thereafter, he looked forward to the four-mile trip to St. John's where he sat in the priest's rooms, unbeknownst to and undiscovered by anyone, reading materials which were first acquired and, oftentimes, kept secret by the religious bureaucrats who had a hand in running the missions. He read just enough to know that the corruption and subsequent failure of governmental policy toward Indians was being discussed not just by Indians as he had presumed, but, astonishingly, by scholars and politicians everywhere.

Sometime later, when Aurelia was hardly out of her cradleboard, and when the U.S. Congress had set in motion the appropriate legislative apparatuses for individual Indian leadership to emerge, Two Heart filed his papers with the Bureau of Indian Affairs to run for "district" councilman. He won, of course, because he had many powerful relatives. But he had other attributes as well. He could, for example, speak excellent English and, fluently, all three dialects of the tribal language. He was, therefore, frequently asked to serve as translator in court cases involving his fellow tribesmen, and as consultant on other professional matters, thus gaining the well-deserved reputation as a man useful to the system of making Indian/white relations work.

But, most important of all, probably, he had the good luck to have married a woman with a great inheritance of "allotted" lands. Lands which he began selling off, piece by piece, to any white man who had the money, so that he could travel and purchase the things he needed to promote his own political career. He enjoyed being "classy." He wanted to be "somebody," never mind the irony of rising to a leadership position in the tribe with one hand, all the while diminishing its land base with the other. He became one of the first councilmen of his tribe under the Indian Reorganization Act, seen by some as the dubious distinction of being a collaborator, for others a position of great status and importance. He went to Washington, D.C., many times and, wearing an eagle-feather headdress which had once belonged to the revered Gray Plume, had his picture taken with dignitaries, presidents, state senators, and congressmen.

Two Heart carried on like this for twenty years, enjoying the fame. He continued to read everything he could get his hands on, and he developed into a great orator. Eventually, he went to Washington, D.C., and signed the documents for the flooding of the tribal lands for the hydropower development of the Missouri River. It was very nearly his last "official" act.

By this time he was an old man, and his heiress wife was landless, penniless, on the welfare rolls. She died in 1950, in her little one-room house down on Crow Creek, almost alone. At the last minute, Aurelia's grandfather rode into the yard on a bay stallion. He was just returning home from a local meeting of the tribes of the Agency, a meeting at which they discussed the great Corps of Engineers encampments above the river, the possibility of a $400 per capita payment to each and every tribal member. He went immediately to the bedside of his dying wife, just in time to witness her failed and agonized attempt to speak to him. But she passed into the next world mute, unexplained, unknown.

Even after that, he tried to discuss with others what her last words might have been. Many of her blood relatives who had watched him throughout the years neglect her and spend her inheritance wanted to respond to his inquiry truthfully, by saying, "She was probably trying to tell you to go to hell, Old Man." But, of course, in the interest of family harmony, they said nothing.

Aurelia's mother, Myrna, was one of several Two Heart daughters. Throughout her life, she had taken in, uncritically, the dealings of her father, and indeed held him in high regard. As a teenager, she had married a fellow tribesman, Albert Blue, but, if the truth were known, she always felt that she had married "beneath" her and, therefore, she treated her husband contemptuously. She bore several children and for most of her adult life worked as a cleaning woman for the church people, for the more prosperous whites in the area, for the people who ran the boarding schools. Myrna was an attractive woman whose flawless skin never seemed to age and whose black hair did not whiten as the years passed. She was a hard worker. She wore sensible, flat working shoes which she bought at J. C. Penny's and, always, winter and summer, a man's long-sleeved blue denim shirt.

Myrna Two Heart went through her life trying not to "be Indian," which meant, to her at least, that she refused to "talk Indian," didn't participate in tribal ceremonials, and ignored the tribal ways and her relatives as much as she could. She, like several of her brothers and sisters, eventually divorced. Then she married a white man, and never again spoke to the father of her children. Later on, Myrna divorced the white man and married another. She was caught up in the alcohol life of the cowboys, ranchers, and drifters who hung around Indian reservations.

Many generations of the Two Hearts and their relatives had lived on the place along Crow Creek, long before Aurelia's time. Through changing times that no one predicted. Through times of isolation and great oppression. When the tiny Aurelia was at last "given" by her neglectful mother to her father's people to be raised, in the mid-1930s, many of her mother's relatives wanted more than anything to leave the reservation, even if it was only to move to the tiny cow towns nearby which were filled with white people whose ancestors had grown to hate Indians. The Two Hearts wanted to live in those towns, to never come back to tribal lands. To become whites. Americans! To be the generation of Indians who would begin the new tradition of assimilation, seen, years later, as a desire rising out of ubiquitous oppression, continuing into the following decades, some say to this day.

When the unfortunate wife of Amos Two Heart died, back in the 1950s, the consequences of intervening decades could be clearly known and a new anxiety about the future, a new despair came upon the people.

Aurelia went dutifully to the old woman's funeral. Aurelia was, by that time, nearly a grown woman, a woman with a mind of her own, a woman who did not want to share her maternal grandmother's fate, or her mother's. She often fought against the slowly turning memories, vague and distasteful, when she could see herself as a youngster visiting her mother's people, hiding behind the bed in the back room as the drunken parties went on and on. Sometimes for days. Eventually, she would have to come out, hungry and thirsty, emerge from her hiding place, creep carefully around the kitchen table to avoid the rough, grasping hands of her mother's drinking companions. Though she had told her father's mother, Unci Mahpiya Blue, about these instances, her visits with her mother had continued, intermittently and fearfully, throughout her childhood, and she learned quickly to reject the legacy of the Two Hearts.

The funeral ceremony of the old mother was the final blow to Aurelia's sensibilities as a member of the family. The family of "new Indians" did not want to bury the old woman in the traditional ways, so they did not. For the four days that grandmother Two Heart was left at the funeral home in the nearby white man's town, unattended and bereft, her children and her husband's relatives, like thieving vultures, took over her house, eating and drinking as though in celebration of some joyful occasion, snooping through her boxes and trunks, and taking for themselves her fine, kept things. Arguing. Snatching from one another's grasp, greedily, the old woman's treasures which she had hoarded for her own "give away."

The "burial mass" was conducted at St. John's Catholic Church by the tall, smiling priest for whom Myrna had long served as housekeeper. Unnoticed, Aurelia stood beside Myrna and was thankful that the mother she hardly knew was sober on this solemn occasion. When Myrna, in a brief, sentimental gesture reached toward Aurelia to take her hand in her own, Aurelia turned away, unsmiling, grim-faced.

Later, the old woman's pine casket was lowered into a dark hole, prepared in the communal grounds which were filled with an entire century's human remains, her fellow countrymen, the relatives of her aloof and selfish husband, two tiny infants who had preceded her in death. Hidden living creatures such as the small animals and reptiles of the prairie lands, black tails, playful burrowing owls, prairie rattlers in the grass, red-tailed hawks in the sky, rarely showing themselves during these periodic disturbances, on that day kept surreptitious watch over the proceedings.

It was, as one might have expected, a gloomy and hasty affair.

Aurelia, who could not weep, looked up at the far hills. In the distance, the tall figure of a man, another secret participant, a pipe-keeper of the Santees whom Aurelia recognized as a knowledgeable relative of the deceased, uninvited by the family members and unseen by the others attending the Christian ritual, was standing on a small hill overlooking the gathering of burial participants. Aurelia squinted her eyes and clutched her handkerchief to her bosom, at once afraid, yet thrilled and thankful beyond words. The pipe-keeper seemed to be intently watching the comings and goings of the children and grandchildren. Alone, he seemed to wait until he saw the black-robed priest lead the small column of relatives to the graveside and make the sign of the cross.

Then he hunched down close to the ground, and he seemed to be thoughtfully and reverently fingering the pouch which hung from his neck. He opened a kerchief which he kept buttoned up inside his shirt, took out some sage, and began to roll the leaves into little balls. He cupped the sage in his wrinkled fingers and held it to his face to breathe in its sweetness and then, Aurelia saw, he began the prayer ritual.

Aurelia stared for several long moments. If she had been close by, she would have heard the holy man's sorrowful words: This was a good woman, I regret that she has not been cared for in the appropriate ways of our people. Look towards the West. I am standing there and looking towards you. (Wiohpeyata etun wan yo! Inawajin na ahitunwan nawajin yelo.)

Instinctively, Aurelia felt flashes of quick shame that she was present here at this obscene ritual, standing there amongst her mother's scandalous relatives, answering the smiling priest in thoughtless repetition: "Lord, hear our prayers. Lord, hear our prayers." She was confused. She was comforted by neither of the rituals, and, now upon the death of a fine old woman to whom she had never spoken more than a few words, she was even more certain that the discordant nature of her family history was a curse, an indelible, frightening impression in the movement of human life.

Helen Chalakee Burgess

MUSCOGEE

I am Muscogee (Creek), Katcv (panther) clan, and I belong to Tallahassee Ceremonial Grounds. Currently, I am residing in Norman, Oklahoma, where I am enrolled at the University of Oklahoma working on a master's-level secondary language arts teaching certification. I also studied journalism at Northeastern State University, Tahlequah, during the seventies and was employed as communication director for, first, the Cherokee Nation of Oklahoma where I was editor of the Cherokee Advocate and, later, for the Muscogee (Creek) Nation where I was editor of the Muscogee National News for ten years. I also served three years as deputy director of the Oklahoma Indian Affairs Commission before reentry into academics. Presently, I am working as an assistant to Professor Geary Hobson in the University of Oklahoma English Department.

I saw one of my roles as an Indian journalist as interpreting national Indian policy-making in ways that Creek people could relate to its consequences. I am thrilled now to be a part of a nationalistic effort of reinventing the enemy's language.

Rational

She don't look Indian all the time
      sometimes she does, sometime she don't
            . . . I overheard the old woman say

I knew her grandma at boarding school
      she was full-blood. Hokte has her eyes
      —her eyes know Indian ways, but
      she married a white man first
            . . . the two bandanna-wrapped heads
              years of practice, they were on cue

I remember her daddy used to carry
      ol' black bull snake in his pickup truck
      he would scare este hutke with it
            . . . more nods

I used to see her go to free will
      with her white grandma
      She didn't go to grave creek
      no more
            . . . no nods this time
              their black eyes met, realizing

nobody went to get her to take her
      there after her Indian
      grandma passed
            . . . again, twin nods

Chrystos

MENOMINEE

I began writing when I was
nine, as a way to keep myself company because at that time
there was only one other Indian family living near us and I
was not accepted at elementary school. I continued writing in
high school, when I was very enamored of the Beat poets,

whom I used to sneak in to see (pretending to be of age), and
also of existentialism. At that time I was writing for my own
survival and had no concept of publishing. During the time after
high school and for about ten years, I didn't write at all because
I was on the streets and in and out of nut houses. In about 1973
or 1974, I began keeping a journal again. I started writing poems
again, many of them reflective of the political work I had become
involved in. When I began this new phase, I was concerned with
making the real lives of First Nation people visible and address-
ing the political struggles we face. This continues to be the main
focus of my work. I have been most moved by my audiences, by
the love I have been shown, by the stories of personal survival
that so many women have shared with me, by all those who
have told me that my books have saved their lives—I can think
of no greater honor than to help others fight to survive, despite
all the forces arrayed against them.

The Old Indian Granny

FOR ANDY SMITH

begging silently with a paper cup under the viaduct
is there every Tuesday on my way to therapy
I give her a dollar
Today I almost gave her a twenty
because it's rainy gray cold
but I remembered my bills, late rent
& how much I owe my therapist
who is saving my life
Granny travels with me her sweet round brown face
appears in my dreams
I wonder if she drinks
to kill the pain of this graveyard they've made
this new world where her only place
is crouched on cement

as thousands hurry by turning away from her need
I used to drink too   use drugs   use women   use words
to chop out a place for myself   to tie off the ache
     You told me about all the Indian women you counsel
     who say they don't want to be Indian anymore
     because a white man or an Indian one raped them
     or killed their brother
     or somebody tried to run them over in the street
     or insulted them   or all of it
     our daily bread of hate
Sometimes I don't want to be an Indian either
but I've never said so out loud before
Since I'm so proud & political
I have to deny it now
Far more than being hungry
having no place to live or dance
no decent job   no home to offer a Granny
It's knowing with each invisible breath
that if you don't make something pretty
they can hang on their walls or wear around their necks
you might as well be dead

Linda Noel

CONCOW   MAIDU

I am Sierra soil and sunlight,
granite and snow, mountain and meadow, river ravine, acorn,
pine, cedar, and am constantly aware of the sharp edge of
coyote shadow. I am Concow Maidu.

I am from northern California. My people survived the California gold rush. That's why I write, to tell the stories that sometimes seem too painful, are too stark and sharp for most who are ignorant of truthful history. I have to tell it.

Understanding Each Other

"You're too wild,
woman."
"You don't drink
raw whiskey,
but when moon hangs
angled
you drink from
the tilted golden cup,
and
when salmon season
returns
you stand among
river willow shadow
humming,
all the time believing
fish understand
why you are there."

So he left me
to marry one
whose dreams
are laced in perfume
and dishwater suds.

Inés Hernández-Ávila

NEZ PERCE

PRESENTE

Soy Inés Tohmahtohlahkikt,
nacida en Galveston, Tejas,
el 28 de febrero de 1947.

Soy la hija de Rodolfo Hernandez,
obrero Mexicano-Tejano nacido en Eagle Pass,
*   Tejas,*
hijo de Sabas Hernandez y de Inés Torralba
*   Hernandez,*
los dos nacidos en el estado de Coahuila,
*   Mexico,*

Y de Janice Tzilimamuh Andrews Hernandez,
nacida en el noroeste, en Nespelem, Washington,
daughter of Thomas Ukshanat and Alice Tohmahwahli
*   Andrews,*
members of Hinmaton Yalatkit's (Chief Joseph's)
*   band*
of the Nimipu (Nez Perce people).

De buena suerte
que a mi papá le tocó un "leave" en Seattle
(él era Marine)
donde trabajaba mi mamá en el Boeing

Aircraft Factory
durante la segunda guerra mundial.
Si no, yo no existiera.

Soy madre de dos hijos,
Rodolfo Valentino Shimilpt y Tomás Carlos
    Kushtimni.

Y ahora,
a la edad de treintiseis años
I have found balance in my life
y entiendo que la vida se aprecia.
Si no, no es vida.

I have wandered on the sharp piedras
at the edge of desperation
often enough to know that I cannot
reject responsibility,
por más que quisiera.
To do so, for me,
would be to surrender my conciencia,
y entonces mi ser no fuera feliz.

Cada cabeza es un mundo
cada mundo tiene derecho de desarrollo
el mundo de mi propio corazón
está lleno de seres que saben respetar
que no presumen, ni desprecian, ni destruyen,
aunque vivimos en donde todo eso es natural.

I choose to walk barefoot on the piedras,
    adrede.
¿Y sí duele, pa qué nos hechamos mentiras?
But I am not alone.

Vamos abrazados
yo y mis compañeros y compañeras,
caminamos
juntos
cantando
y
SOMOS
un mundo claro corazón—
y
TODOS
barefoot.
De esto *se trata mi poesía.*

An Open Letter to Chicanas: On the Power and Politics of Origin

mothering text

Mis queridas hermanas: As many of you know, I am Nimipu (otherwise known by the French-imposed name Nez Perce), of Chief Joseph's band, on my mother's side. On my father's side I am Tejana/Mexicana—I was raised in a Chicano barrio in Galveston, Texas, but with my sometimes stubborn, always gentle, loving Indian mom always at my side. My dad, carpenter-fisherman-worker, with hands and mind of an artist, is Tejano/Mexicano, therefore mestizo, therefore at least part Indio—my mom, from the rez and the *montanas*, having come to the island to share her life with him. I am their daughter. Yet in the Indian/Chicano community I am often confronted with persons who tell me I must choose—Indians who complain about my Mexicanness, Chicanos who complain about my Indianness. Herein the politics of my own creativity and the politics within my creativity. My work, my word, is my response from being to and for myself first, and then to those persons who have faced the similar dilemma of wanting to understand the difference.

The weight of the role that has been imposed upon us as mestizas—that burden with its roots fundamentally interwoven with patriarchy and Catholicism (and the accompanying degrading dichotomy of the *mujer mala/mujer buena*)—we have already rejected. But what do we do with that outrage, that hatred, those intense resentments, and, finally, that fear that for so long was the main instrument used to keep us repressed and which dried up all the life energy of our beings—so that we would end up effectively spent and even turned inside out, with nothing inside to sustain us or nourish us?

About sixteen years ago, I was sitting in my home in Austin, Texas—my sons were asleep, and my lover, who knows where he was—and felt intensely depressed. I sat at my kitchen table, drank a whole bottle of wine alone, and smoked some weed (I gave up smoking marijuana about eleven years ago). Suddenly, I grabbed paper and pen and began to write: two poems came out that I believe are declarations of love and resistance for women. One is called "*Rezo*" ("Prayer" or "I Pray"). In this poem I called on the spirits of the female ancestors, and those feminine principles, to ask them to help us conquer our history and "put in order our House of Aztlan"—metaphorically, of course, I meant our Chicana/ Chicano community. The other poem was the following:

Cancion de Madre	Mother's Song
No llores, hija	Don't cry, my daughter
India de mi corazon	Little Indian girl-child of my heart
No llores	Don't cry
Ni pases esos corajes	Don't allow those rages to pass through you
Muy dentro de tu alma	So far into your soul
Hasta que te pierdes	That you lose yourself
te pierdes	you lose yourself
Y no te encuentras	and can't find yourself
Ten calma, mija	Be calm, my little daughter
Todo Pasa	Everything passes
Nacer	To be born
Renacer	To be reborn

Retenacer	To be reborn again
Es cosa natural	Is natural
Nadie tiene control	No one has control
Ni el Miedo mismo	*Not even Fear itself*
Echate a ese Miedo	Kick out that Fear
de tu vida	from your life
Y enfrentate con ti misma	And face your own self
O puedes o no?	Can you or can't you?
No llores, hija	Don't cry, my daughter
Todo pasa	Everything passes.

I didn't quite understand at the time, but I now know that the "*Cancion*" was the answer to the "*Rezo.*" I am the daughter in the song, and the mother is the most ancient mother of all—the original female energy, the female *principle*, in every sense of that word, call her by a name or many names—who in her consolation validates me, as an *India* and as a woman, and teaches me how to have courage, to be brave. But that mother is also me, mother to my self, as we all can be, and so I dedicate this song to all mestizas.

I feel that within each Chicana/Mexicana/mestiza there is that indigenous aspect that is connected with the collective consciousness of the red tradition of this continent—and that aspect reveals itself as a little Indian girl who for centuries has been abandoned, ignored, and unloved. We have wanted to erase her from our being—she doesn't know love, she doesn't know what it is to have confidence in herself or trust in others. In the most remote corner of our being—whether we are dark-, medium-, or light-skinned— she has hidden herself. She is cornered, repressed, and humiliated, encaged and without voice, without hope. She nourishes herself with the little vital energy that we cannot deny her—because she is a part of our being, our cultural essence. The spirits of her ancestors, her grandmas and grandpas—how they would like to free her, embrace her, and show her lovingly how to grow and become a complete woman, beautiful, powerful, and courageous. But they, too, have forgotten. It is very common to hear Chicanos say, "Well, yes, they say my grandmother was pure Indian, but no one knows what tribe." Of course, because that rarely is spoken of. Children are told not to behave like *indios*. When *raza* gets drunk and carries on, the next day the people often say, almost with a mixture of shame, laughter, and admiration, "The Indian in me came out." Out of where? Out of hiding? Out of the closet? Out on a prison furlough? Out of isolation?

Genocide is an instrument of imperialism, and both depend on cultural imperialism and the dialectic of terror to invade, violate, traumatize, exploit, and totally control human beings throughout the world. As long as the majority of mestizos/mestizas refuse to acknowledge the face and heart of the Indian man or woman inside themselves (again, *not to the exclusion* of the other aspects of their being and cultural heritage), they will not be able to realize themselves as complete human beings, in the sense of knowing their own origins, much less give true value to the indigenous peoples of the Americas or to the other autochthonous peoples of the world (and so, these people will continue to remain faceless masses, without individuality or personality)—a grave and sad situation for humanity, and for all so-called progressive movements today which mestizos/mestizas are involved in. Why and how so? Because I have noticed the overwhelming tendency on the part of many of my colleagues in academia, and in the community, some of whom are Marxist-oriented, for example, to reject and discount the indigenous perspective in their analysis of the issues that face us. Anything Indian is seen as unsophisticated and "primitive." Besides, they argue, race is not the primary issue, and furthermore, Indians are always talking about spirituality, respect for Mother Earth, and sovereignty. Why can't they (the Indians) just accept that their time is up, it's past, it's over and done with—it's history. Yes, I would say, it is history—repeating itself.

Eduardo Galeano writes in *Memory of Fire* that in 1563 an Araucano chieftain confronted the Spanish captain Bernal and demanded that the Spaniard's troops surrender to native forces. The Araucanian warriors had the upper hand, but the captain refused to surrender, even in the face of sure death. He tells the Indian chief that in the end they, the Spaniards, will win the war, for there will be "more and more of us." The chief asks, "How? With what women?" The captain says, "If there are no Spanish ones, we'll have yours . . . and we'll make children on them who'll be your masters!" And so, many times over, the scenario was and is played out between Indo and Español, whereby the energy was/is set in motion to sustain the hostility, the antagonism, the hatred today between Indio and mestizo. Perhaps surprisingly to mestizos, proud of their Spanish drops of blood, however few they are, Indios, "Skins," find it a cause for shame, for derision—"You don't talk about being Mexican." Why? Because your mother was raped and you were helpless to prevent the act—you are further evidence of it, constant presence. At another level, the Indio, the "Skin," often has the utmost scorn and contempt for mestizos who are running after the European-superiority lie. How dare they think they are better by aligning themselves with the rapist, the invader, the thief. The irony of our situation should not be missed. Many people would argue that the so-called Spanish (and Portuguese) "Conquest" was not as brutal in its decimation of indigenous peoples as were the genocidal policies in the North. I wonder. At least here in the North, Indians know they're Indians and they know what that means. In the mestizo community we have internalized the Western European, and now white American, oppressor's mentality that turns us against our very selves.

I have always been stubborn in my insistence (and I know I am not alone) that what is most precious about the Chicana/Chicano psyche is our originality. As orphans, because that has been our (mis)fortune (of course, for reasons expressly historic), we have had to dig out of our own insides what is ours—because there was no one who would accept us, much less teach us. Scorned by the Anglo-Saxon world, where we continue to drop out of schools in record numbers, and by much of the Mexican world, where frequently we are condemned for our *mocho-pochoness,* or assumed lack of sophistication, the Chicana and the Chicano have had to strengthen and develop ourselves in our own way—that is, we have had to recover and reevaluate what our culture is, not only through formal investigation and research, but also and in great part through our intuition and the dictates of our heart.

In the process of reintegration with our history as Mexicans, for example, we saw some interpretations that didn't seem right to us. One of the major cases is the history of Malintzin, who within the Mexicana/Chicana culture has come to signify more than her identity as an Aztec woman. Chicana writers and artists have confronted the pejorative manner in which the image and spirit of this symbolic mother of the first mestizo has been accused and punished over the centuries. Why does she even matter? Because first of all, Malintzin, or la Malinche, was named in the records of the so-called Conquest, and thus she acquired a face and place in history, and in the Mexican collective conscience, not only as mistress to Cortés and mother of his children, but also as the "tongue," the interpreter who traveled with the Spanish troops to secure the support of other native peoples; she is, from the men's historical perspective, the mother to be ashamed of, the arch-traitress, the Mexican Eve, the one who opened her legs and in giving herself over gave over the continent to foreign control.

For me, there is a relationship between la Malinche and marijuana in the Chicana/Chicano community. I've heard some of our *gente* argue that if you don't smoke *mota*, you're not Chicano/Chicana. I know it was said facetiously, but I have also heard Indians say the same thing about liquor. But liquor was introduced to the Indian community throughout the Americas to aid in their cultural devastation. In the case of Chicanos, however, there is another factor to be looked at: marijuana is an herb that has medicinal powers, but for the most part, it has been abused and exploited, and has worked against us as a people. I've noticed that the same Chicanos who make the arguments for *mota* often are not concerned with, and in fact dismiss, the efficacy of all other *hierbas* in terms of their healing properties. I know, also, that many males see *mota* as female. The herb and the woman, both abused, violated, and exploited by men for their femaleness, both considered "bad" by men, yet both sought after for that very "badness." In the circle of men, a woman can be accepted if she assumes her role in the "illicitness" of the setup.

One of the possible meanings of the *Malintzin* is derived from the root *malin-*, which is seen by some as associated with the Nahuatl word *malinalli*, or *hierba*. So Malintzin can be seen, in turn, as a human counterpart of the herb *malinalli* (in the Indian community she would also be called, as an herb, the little grandma, the little sister/older sister—she is a *relation*). The original meaning of the hieroglyph *malinalli* as defined by Mexican scholar Cesar Macazaga Ordono, in his study *Templo Mayor/Sagrario de la Vida: La religion agraria del Mexico Antiguo*, expressed the idea of life and death. From the skull is born the herb, year after year. Plants, flowers, life are reborn from the earth that has been fertilized by the bones of those buried there, and matter is renewed thanks to its own death. If we extend this understanding to Malintzin the person, we are given a nonjudgmental way in which to look at her life and her role in history, and we have one more piece of evidence to connect her to Mother Earth, and to that female principle that encompasses everything.

However, in typical male projection, and as if the men themselves had not mistook the Spaniards for gods, she is associated instead with the worst of all possible offenses—collaboration with the enemy. Mexicanos, especially the men, are outraged at their mother, their women, themselves. Why? Because they don't see their mother as a victim—they see her as a sell-out, one who gave herself—so they want to rid themselves of any trace of her, and the female aspect of themselves. They view Indios/"Skins" with the contempt they feel is befitting a supposedly weak and inferior race, just as they transfer their mistrust of Malintzin to mistrust for all women. Why? Because they have bought the father's story that is seeped in misogny and, having internalized the racism of Indian hating, they identify with him. When captain Bernal spoke his words to the Araucanian chief, he totally invalidated the power, consciousness, and presence of native women and what their response would be to this planned, forced utilization of their bodies as instruments to give birth to children who would turn on their own people and be programmed to devastate them.

For me, Malintzin is at the heart of the very issues that Chicanas are struggling with today—race, class, gender, sexuality, and voice. Because she is so well known, she is associated with all Indian women and with all of us as mestizas. She represents the indigenous feminine aspect of this continent—the continent itself as Mother Earth, which continues to be invaded, violated, exploited, tortured, and killed, just as indigenous peoples are throughout the Americas, in Guatemala, Bolivia, Peru, Brazil, Chile, wherever Indian people are. As an individual human being, Malintzin also had a major role in history at a monumental time, and so she must be looked at as an active woman, politically, sexually, culturally, a subject who made choices within the rigid framework in which she moved, just as today's Chicanas have done. It is not such a far cry to relate to this woman who has been condemned for her gender, her color, her politics, her sexuality, and for being brilliant and articulate. Let us not forget either that Malintzin was taken in slavery as a child; she is relative to that Indian girl child in all mestizas. To date she is not free, except in the dance community of the Aztec tradition.

Within the dance tradition of the Concheros of "la Gran Tenochtitlan," la Malinche is a path-opener, an *abrecaminos*, who cleanses and blesses the path with the smoke of the incense in her *sahumador* (a clay, chalice-like vessel that represents Mother Earth and which holds the embers that allow the incense to burn—the embers themselves representing the fire in the heart of the earth, and the life in woman's womb). The *sahumador* holds the sacred fire, which is said to protect the entire circle of each dance group. La Malinche is the front(line)—the vanguard, so to speak. Her is an arduous position, for on her depends the security of the path. That is, through the dance tradition (which has experienced syncretism) the positive image of la Malinche has survived. In this tradition I am a Malinche; I have been for eleven years. My role as a Malinche within a ceremonial context has helped me to understand how I am a Malinche in a social and intellectual context. We should consider the possibility that each Mexicana/Chicana could become a Malinche in the sense of being a path-opener, a guide, a voice, a warrior woman, willing to go to the front to combat the injustices that our people suffer. In this way our indigenous mother will be revindicated and we will be revindicated as well.

Who are the Malinches of today? As Tomas Borges of Nicaragua says of poets, "Anyone who loves their people with their whole heart and willingly commits to their defense and to the struggle for justice on their behalf." Rigoberta Menchu, the young Guatemalan Mayan leader, who learned the language of the oppressor, Spanish, and made it her own, just as she learned the Bible to use it as an organizing text and tool in her community. Elvia Alvarado, the Honduran *campesina/India* organizer, and Roberta Blackgoat, of the Diné Nation, resisting the relocation at Big Mountain—all of the women who have accepted their role as "tongues" and demanded that their voices be heard.

There are many Malinches—Sor Juana Ines de la Cruz; the Mexican feminists of the 1910 Revolution, such as Sara Estela Ramires, Juana Gutierrez Belen de Mendoza, Dolores Jimenez y Muro; Violeta Parra, the Chilena "mother of the New Song Movement"; the *boricua* sister Olga Talamanez and her other sisters who are now serving sentences in this society as political prisoners of the United States; Dolores Huerta, Raquel Orendain, Maria Salas, and all the other *campesina* women who have carried on the struggle for so many years, knowing only too well what it is like to be treated like Indians; all the women labor organizers who continue the tradition of leaders like Emma Tenayuca and Manuela Solis Sager; women such as Maria Jimenez and Isabel Garcia Gallegos, who steadfastly defend the rights of our relations "without papers," the undocumented workers; those workers themselves who brave the frontline of the U.S./Mexican border daily to exert their will to live and sustain their families; writers, poets, artists, like Angela de Hoyos, Gloria Anzaldua, Janis Palma, Joy Harjo, Jean LaMarr, Cherrie Moraga, Ana Castillo, Santa Barraza, and so many others, who dedicated themselves to cultivating their own originality so that their vision of us and of the world will be keen and just;

academicians who, in their investigations, find on behalf of our people, on behalf of our culture, on behalf of our women, but who are not afraid to call a lie for what it is and who speak out against learned patterns of abuse, violence, and victimization, whatever their source; and every single woman, Chicana/Mexicana/mestiza, who has refused unconditionally to accept any longer any form of oppression or violation of her self, whatever that source, and who has committed herself to a universal struggle for justice and dignity, as they say in the Indian community, for "all our relations."

To be revolutionary is to be original, to know where we came from, to validate what is ours and help it to flourish, the best of what is ours, of our beginnings, our principles, and to leave behind what no longer serves us. Not every Chicana/Mexicana was/is Aztec. We come from many tribes, many peoples. To begin to understand our origins in more than a superficial way is to begin to "find our way back home" to what is ours, as opposed to what has been imposed upon us. The day that each mestiza/mestizo truly searches for and finds her/his own roots, respectfully and humbly, and furthermore validates those peoples who still maintain their identity as original peoples of this continent of America, North, Central, and South—on that day we will be radical and much more capable of transforming our word, our universe, and our lives.

Lee Maracle

SALISH ▪ METIS

Born on the West Coast of British Columbia of Salish/Metis heritage, I am the mother of four and grandmother of two. Besides writing I make my living as *an empowerment and cultural reclamation counselor. I am a gifted orator and one of the most published native authors in Canada.*

Who's Political Here?

"Give me that, thanks," and I put the toilet paper back where it belongs, after catching it in midair before she managed to throw it into the toilet bowl.

"Excuse me." I grabbed the washrag and then both girls, removing them from the temptation of playing in the toilet by pushing them out of the bathroom, while my toothbrush vigorously scraped at my dentures. I strolled into the kitchen. My husband was standing there, looking kind of lost. He had that I'm-about-to-bawl-you-out look, so I started to ignore him before he even spoke.

"Do you think you could do laundry?" he said with the tone of voice that implies it has been at least a month since the last time I had done laundry and in between then and now I had been particularly unproductive. I put my teeth in, ran the water for coffee, and mumbled some sort of bored affirmation.

"Could you pass me that hat?" He doesn't. He says something about not having any underwear. I tell him that he certainly does have underwear, that it's in the laundry, and then I crawl over the table, grab the hat, and on jumping to the floor, snatch the matches from one girl's hand, then lean over to turn off the stove the other one has turned on. Thank Christ this kitchen is pathetically small. He leaves the room.

"Glgbltglgl-blk-th-blk," my youngest babbles, inflecting her nonsense in a way that suggests she knows what she is trying to say.

"Yeah, I know what you mean, I get that way sometimes too."

"Here, Mommy," the other little girl hands me her sister's shoes. She is three and really does know what's going on. We are all getting ready to go out. Mothers have an identifiably different sense of movement when they are getting ready to go out, and kids know it.

"Stiffen you leg, stiffen you leg . . . stiffen, that's it, after all. I stiffen my leg when I put on my shoes." I hold her on my lap and Tania tries to help.

She had reached the age of insistent and cheerful incompetence. I never discourage her assistance so everything we do takes twice the time.

"Who are you talking to?" He is back in the room.

"Columpa."

"She can't talk."

"You asked me who I was talking to, not who was talking to me. What are you going to do today?" I grab the stroller, a giant secondhand English pram that no longer has the bonnet or basket, just the frame and seat, and haul it over the porch to the sidewalk. He has to follow me to answer. I think this humbling exercise of following me around and answering my questions annoys him, but he thinks it too petty to mention. Further he is still a little pissed about the underwear shit—no pun intended. I come back in with him at my heels.

"I'm going to poster downtown." Terrific. He posters while I maneuver the logistics of shopping, nurturing, and fulfilling my laundress duties. I take the shopping cart and the two girls and go out again.

"Where are you going? To do the laundry?" If I had the emotional intensity I would either laugh or cuff him, because this last remark is so obviously a disguised accusation of my general recalcitrance, but I have lost the heart to do either.

"Sure."

"How come the cart is empty?"

"I haven't finished shopping" to him and "Take that out of your ear" to Columpa. "Only put your elbow in your ear": She tries, but fails, but keeps trying. At least her mind is off sticking the pencil in her ear and she doesn't cry when I put it in my purse.

"You said you were going to do laundry." He is whining now. There is nothing worse than hearing a grown man whine. Grown man. Since when have you known a man to really grow up, Lee. I agree that I am going to do the laundry, today, and put both girls in the stroller (back-to-back), and haul the shopping cart and kids down the lane. He is standing there on the porch looking dejected.

"Hey." I stop without turning around and try to bury the exasperation that wants expression. "You look like one of those sixteenth-century fishmongers, pushing her cart with grim determination." He finds this amusing. One, I don't look like a European anything, and two, the word is *fish-wif*. Fish-wif means fish-drudge and is the father of wife, but I don't say that. I roll the buggy and pull the cart. I couldn't laugh but I did manage to turn around and give him a condescending smile. He is not an idiot and resents my lack of appreciation for his joke. Another obstacle to hurdle.

"Bldthbldbld."

"Cambie wants a cookie," Tania tells me.

"Does she?" Beats me how Tania can understand her babble. Of course, figuring out that the kid wants a cookie can't be too difficult because even if it weren't true, it would at least shut her up and she'd forget what she really did want. Last but not least, Tania's desire for a cookie would be satisfied. I get the cookie, grumbling a whole bunch of stuff about how I never had them as a child, they probably aren't good for you, and so forth. They don't care much about all that.

En route to Safeway Columpa addresses every single citizen with a cute little "Hi," four or five times each. Every time she says it Tania insists I look at her and acknowledge her intellectual brilliance—until it about drives me to distraction.

"Hey."

"Sa-aay, Frankie. How are you?" When the only humans you have to talk to are under four and making demands or over thirty and barking out orders, and they all complain when they aren't fulfilled, you really appreciate some guy on the street saying "hey" to you, even if he is an obnoxious womanizer. He sidles over and asks what I am doing. I tell him I am on my way to Safeway to do a little shopping.

"Where are you going to put the groceries?"

"In the cart."

"How the hell are you going to wheel the cart and the kids home?" Men are not known for their resourcefulness. They are inhibited by their own self-consciousness. If it is going to look funny, they won't do it. I jump inside the cart's handle and hold the handle of the cart and stroller together, taking mincing little steps. Frankie laughs. I secretly curse him because my next-to-useless husband is downtown having fun postering while I have to shop and do the laundry and his jerky friend is laughing at me, but I don't let on I am mad.

He is looking at me now. I can hardly wait to turn forty. Then the men my age may be less obsessed with fucking. He offers help and I take it. I have to put up with gross physical nuances like having his arm accidentally brush my breasts, but I don't care. Under the coercive pressure of hauling fifty pounds of babies and another seventy-five of groceries a full five blocks, the stupid little rubs don't seem so bad. It's his great pretense at morality, his sneakiness, and his belief that I belong to my husband that really get to me. If I were to suggest we jump in bed, he would ask me about my husband; he does not think of him while he is brushing my tits, though. DING DONG.

I virtually run through the aisles, throwing things into the cart. The good-behavior mode of either of my children spans only forty-five minutes. I had wasted five precious minutes on the street talking to this fool and now they are getting restless. Screams, tears, and tantrums are next.

Frankie is wheeling the cart and I am at the buggy's helm. We are moving fast. The girls love it. Columpa suddenly drops off to sleep in the middle of an incoherent bunch of babble that has a complaining tone to it. She starts swaying back and forth. Tania tries to hold her up. She is just barely managing to keep her sister in the buggy. I can't help laughing.

"You look beautiful when you laugh." Too much. It is the sort of remark from a John Wayne movie—you know, he has just paddled some poor woman's backside, she's hollering falsely indignant, he says, "You know you're cute when you're mad," and then they roll around, passionately, in the hay. I wouldn't care one way or another about a tumble in the hay with this guy. Sex, love, and morals have never formed a triumvirate in my mind, and I'm still young enough to be gleeful over doing something I am not supposed to be doing. But the line was so bad. Still, I smile full in his face, encouraging him.

Tania is nodding out. At home, I put them both to bed, lock the door, and confront his amorousness. He doesn't resist. It's all so naughty and hence lovely.

"What about Tom?"

"Christ." I had forgotten that I knew he was going to say that. "How long has he been on your mind? When did you start thinking about him, when you were—"

He cuts me off. He just thought of it now.

"Well, in that case, we are all too late to do anything about it, so why don't we stop musing over hopeless things?"

The doorbell rings and I move to answer it. He grabs me and asks "what about him?" again. I wonder if some of the gray matter from his brain has sneaked out through his manhood. Jeezuss. The doorbell again. No time to convince this twit that people come in and out of my house all the time and it isn't anybody's business which of them I sleep with, most especially not Tom's. Frankie is not dealing with this at all well. He better not make some stupid suggestion about my leaving my husband or I will beat him to a pulp.

"Tom is in jail," and Don rolls in to take a seat.

"Great. You want dinner?"

Frankie comes downstairs and is calmly greeted by our mutual friend. Frankie's face is painted with thirty different shades of guilt. I try not to think about it. It didn't go by Don; the whole scene looks kind of funny.

"He is in jail," Don repeats himself with great patience, trying to articulate the significance of what he said.

"Yeah. I heard you. Do you want some dinner?" and I start banging the pots and pans. In 1974 I was still convinced that my whole reason for being was rooted in mothering my daughter, my husband, and *his* friends. Don expected me to get all excited. What was new? He probably got drunk and landed himself in the drunk tank again.

"For postering." Well. Pardon my heresy, but that was worth at least one belly laugh. He must be the only person in Vancouver to have been charged with postering.

"It is fifty dollars to bail him out."

"Fifty dollars. Well, I just happen to have it in my ass-hip pocket. When does he go to court?"

"Tomorrow."

"He can stay there until then."

Don looks at me, a little pained. I want to say, Look, a..hole, I do all the laundry, cook and clean after that man, type all his leaflets after midnight, and mother his two children so that he can risk postering downtown. Who is in prison here? *My* sentence is "until death do us part"; he's going to be there overnight. I don't say it; he wouldn't understand.

In the corner, Frankie has gone catatonic with guilt. Don turns down dinner—he is miffed about my not taking the "jail in the line of duty" seriously, as I ought. In some perverse fashion he thinks that turning down a dinner invite is going to offend me. This guy believes that I cook, clean, and mother because I really think it's the end-all and be-all in my life. He leaves mumbling.

"I don't know if this is right." Frankie is still bemoaning our tumble in the living room, rendered all the more disgusting for him by the knowledge that Tom was in jail while he had been helping himself to his lovely wife.

"Honey, if you are talking about morals, it was all wrong." I hear the girls scurrying around upstairs. Frankie keeps mumbling about Tom, how we shouldn't have "done it," etc., while I bang pots and pans. Boy, men are miserable. They do everything they can to get between your legs and then whine about it later. I could have hit him.

"Mahmm." My youngest is screaming and being hauled down the stairs by the oldest. She has hold of a toy that the other one is clinging to. Tania, in trying to get it away from her, is dragging the little one down the stairs. They are both crying, someone else is knocking at the door, so I put the toy on top of the fridge without bothering to tell them they can't have anything that they fight over, pick them up, coo a little, then answer the bloody door.

"C'mon in." A couple of Tom's friends come in and sit down. The conversation centers on his arrest. It's amusing. Arrested for postering. What next? I've heard that during the thirties they arrested people who made speeches without flying a Canadian flag, but this is forty years later. Maybe they'll start demanding that we get a permit to demonstrate.

"What do you say to the man? Uh, excuse me, sir, but, uh, can I have permission to demonstrate against you? I mean, it's like a kid asking his mom for permission to curse the jeezuss out of her." That remark brought laughter from me only. "Not funny?" I ask, serving coffee all around.

"Bad analogy," someone mumbles.

"Okay. . . . Don't put your fingers in the butter," and I move it out of the reach of my youngest girl. "Put the hat back on his head," to the older one. "Cream, sugar? . . . Practically speaking, fifty bucks is a bit of a wad. I don't have it."

They seemed to understand, though their faces look a little pinched. I resume cooking and someone suggests making a "run." I tell them that that is not a good plan. While Tom is home, I put up with that shit but I wasn't about to while he wasn't here. The room got a little stiff and quiet, the pair start to fidget, drink their coffee, mumble about things they have to do, then leave.

Frankie is upset. "Why'd you tell them that?"

"Because I don't want them partying in my house." I grab a diaper, change the baby, wash my hands, and tend dinner.

"Don't you think it was kind of rude?"

"Yeah, that's why I told them no."

"I didn't mean *them.*"

"I did. Pass the cloth next to your elbow." He does. He just can't leave it alone. Somehow, he has it in his head that Tom would have let these two buy beer, drink, and puke all over my house in full view of my toddlers, and while I agree he probably would have, he isn't here now and Frankie doesn't think it's okay for me to refuse them the dubious privilege of making fools of themselves in my house in Tom's absence.

"But . . . Tom . . ."

I remind him that he is not in a position to talk about what Tom allows or disallows as it was a definite given that Tom has never permitted his friends to help themselves to his wife. That hit home. He asks what we are going to do.

"We? I am cooking supper and you are sitting there waiting for it to be cooked, passing me this and that as I might require. Pass me the salt." He does. Cambie grabs it before I manage to intercept his bad pass. I have to lean into the pass and try to get it from her before she pours salt on the floor. I don't make it. It is in my hand upside down.

"These guys need a good licking."

"Yeah, I know, but they are all grown up so it is kind of hard to convince them to bend over."

"I mean your daughters." Now he has really gone and done it.

"Look, sweetheart, you are really pretty and your body worked the way it ought to, but father to my children you are not. Even if you were, I doubt very much that I would take your advice."

"Just look at them, they're wild." They are under the sofa playing in the box of shoes. The sofa is not really a sofa. It is two planks plunked atop four square bricks. They are too big to sit under it without raising the planks with their heads. It does look a little out of hand but they aren't hurting anyone so I don't bother telling them not to have fun. Toys they lack and if I don't let them play with whatever is at hand, I will have to run after them enforcing ridiculous prohibition laws with violence. I have neither the time nor the energy, much less the inclination.

"I never did want to be a cop, so I don't see why I ought to run around policing them." He doesn't get it. Supper is ready and I take them to the bathroom to wash up. The baby keeps trying to grab the soap, the elder is obsessed with rubbing her hands together to create bubbles and foam. I manage to rinse them off and herd them to the table.

"What about us?" Oh, good Christ, here it comes again. Tania says, "What does 'what about us' mean, Mommy?" . . . "Oh, never mind, he doesn't mean anything." . . . "Then why did he say it?" . . . "Well, what about us?" . . . "Pass the butter. Nothing." . . . "What do you mean, 'nothing'?" . . . "Yeah." . . . "Mommy, I don't want do peez." . . . "Eat them, they're good for you," and I plunk the food into the baby's mouth. "I really don't believe you, Frankie. I am married to your gawdamn friend for chrissakes." . . . "Gawdamn for chrissakes," Tania repeats the choicer words. "Well, why did you do it?" . . . "Look I did not do it by myself, number one, and number two, we both thought it was a good idea at the time." . . . "Don't put that in your hair." . . . "Pass me the rag, she put it in her hair."

"This is a gawdamn zoo."

"You better leave, Frankie." I don't need anyone calling my girls animals to their faces. I put some more food in the baby's mouth. Tania is studying her piece of meat. I tell her it's probably best to study the taste and never mind how it looks. The phone rings and I jump to answer it. The doorbell goes off and the baby stands up on wobbly legs and half crawls out of the high chair. I holler at Frankie to help her. The person at the other end of the line says "What?" Frankie is too late and I curse him. This really offends the other person. I have to hang up on her round about the time when she is asking me what is going on.

I figure it out while I am comforting my little girl. Frankie is all indignant that I used him. If I had been upset about him taking me for granted, everything would have been normal. I was supposed to be upset and shocked about what we did and he could not handle that I felt no remorse, no guilt, nor any sorrow. How can one man be so many different kinds of a fool? I never did learn to act ashamed so now he was going to make me pay by picking my life apart, including attacking my parenting skills and the conduct of my children. I wanted to tell Frankie that the lady on the phone was Tom's girlfriend . . . that he doesn't think I know about her . . . Tom thinks me a fool who believes the relationship is strictly political, but I can smell her all over him when he gets home after "serving the people" with her—whatever that means. I don't say anything because he would insist that that's different.

Frankie doesn't leave. The doorbell rings again and he goes to answer it. More of Tom's friends come in. They all discuss the "politics" of Tom's arrest.

"He was probably arrested because the subject matter of the poster was South Africa," someone says.

I resume doing dishes and mothering my daughters and only half-listen to the chatter. Some of it is pure theater. It seems absurd to me to attach a whole world analysis to a simple postering charge. It never occurs to anyone that maybe cops and businesspeople don't like their "property" smutted up with lefty posters. They act like it was part of a global capitalist conspiracy to arrest their leader, Tom. An attack on freedom of speech, at least.

"We don't have freedom of speech in this country," and I mumble out a little lesson in Canadian legalism. "Parliament is responsible to the crown, not the people; human rights, free speech, etc., are not part of our judiciary."

No one pays any attention. Patti has come over and joined the guys in the "rap." I can't figure out why she is so acceptable to them. When she talks they respond. I find her exaggerated, rhetorical claptrap annoying—they eat it up. I get the feeling from all of them that college kids puff up their minds in order to feel like they have some sort of meaning or universal order to their lives.

Patti has been having an affair with Tom. I don't mind that so much but I think it kind of cheeky of her to come by my house, expect me to wait on her hand and foot while she is helping herself to my husband, ostensibly behind my back. She is no ordinary woman. Most of the women who come to visit me, my friends, help with the dishes, the kids, stuff like that, while they're here. Not this one. She acts like me and the kids are dead except when she wants coffee. She has some sort of secret inside of her that inspires men to respect her brain and not intrude on her person by reducing her to a servant. I envy her position.

She holds her coffee cup up and says "thank you" to me. It's weird, but before I slept with Frankie I used to think of all this as normal. Now, I just look at her dumbly. Annoyed, she gets up and tries to pour herself a cup. The kids get in the way (perfect timing, girls), and she puts the cup down. She suggests making a "run." Again I say no and they all get this funny look on their faces like they're constipated. Patti asks why not.

"Because I said so." I go to the door and open it. The room empties of all the visitors except Frankie. He is not happy with the kind of person I'm becoming but he can't leave me alone. I go to put the girls to bed. Frankie sits downstairs in silence while I read them a story or two and make a couple up. At 9 P.M. I am lying on the sofa and Frankie mumbles that he doesn't understand me. I don't understand me either, I tell him. It seems kind of lame that I should think all of this adultery stuff a pile of cow dung, but it is what I think. I'm jealous of Patti, not sexually, but because my husband and his friends accord her her mind. I can't explain that to Frankie. I can't tell him that she has something that I obviously lack—something that tells all of the men around her that she is to be taken very seriously—and that I would like to have some of that. I sure as hell can't tell Frankie that he means nothing to me beyond that one sexual encounter which I don't care to repeat. What a mix-up. It's all too complicated and inexplicable for me.

"Go home, Frankie. Tom is in jail." I roll over and face the wall. Everything is fuzzy after that. Rolling, changing emotions float around inside me as I lie looking at the old hand-besmudged wall and wonder what is happening to me, why I don't care about Tom's incarceration the way the others do, don't feel its earth-shattering importance, and why all of a sudden I resent them not thinking I am clever. Somehow what I am feeling seems more important to me than Tom's incarceration, and I think they should see it that way too. The changing emotions roar around inside, taking up speed and intensity until fear starts to ride over it all like the surf in a stormy sea. Panic almost overtakes me when my old granny's face grins through the wall.

I had not seen or thought about her since the last tear I shed just after she died a dozen years ago in our backwoods bush home. I hang on to the picture of her face against the white wall I was still staring at. It calmed me some to see her. She was telling me that confusion is just like any storm—it rages, but at the end is the beautiful clear light of day. Stop it, and you lock your confusion up and stay that way. Let it roll, let it rage—and she fades.

I did. I had no idea that a storm of thoughts could be so exciting. Like a hurricane, crazy and destructive, some of it; sometimes like a flood and at other times a tornado, but always the thoughts and feelings were exhilarating. I don't remember much of what I thought about—not much of it settled down for me to hang on to, but the last thing I remember is seeing my girls and thinking, yes, they are wild. Wild, untamed, not conquerable, and I was going to go on making sure they stayed that way. A wicked little grin came over me while I was tossed about in the sea of my own storm, my wild little girls at my side and blessed sleep beckoning me home.

Gladys Cardiff

CHEROKEE

For me, the creative life is more a matter of finding what might be called a fitting and timely accord. The way something is expressed will have the stamp of someone's individual experience and personality, but I am uncomfortable when too much emphasis is put on the act of writing as creative in the sense of being highly individualistic, the *writer as autonomous and original inventor. I think of writing as both a creative and an ethical activity. Poetry is the expression of ideas, thoughts, and feelings brought out and into the larger world. Words are powerful. They have an effect—they can clarify or obscure, for instance, and quicken or blunt, heal or injure. This means gratefully and respectfully keeping in mind those who have preceded me, and who persevere today, and honoring that collective wisdom which continues to speak its values and shape community out of the mass.*

It has something to do with final words

a newspaper, glanced at by chance,
       the real event transcribed out of wreckage,

           21:24 *That keeps—that's come on.*
               What's happening? A light has come on.

It's 22:30. The pilots are puzzled. Wondering about that light.
      What's it say in the manual?
        This is what it says.
          (I don't get it.)

          ADDITIONAL SYSTEM FAILURE
          MAY CAUSE IN-FLIGHT DEPLOYMENT
          EXCEPT NORMAL REVERSAL OPERATION
          AFTER LANDING.

after landing
    24:11 OK
      24:36 OK
        Shall we ask the technical men?

25:26 Just, ah, just, its, its, its
      30:41 Jesus Christ (Sound of snap)
      (Sound of four caution tones) (Sound of siren) *Wait*
        a minute. Damn it.

The newspaper headline reads PILOT'S FINAL WORDS.
I'm sitting in a window seat in a cafe
In Seattle, where the plane was made,
and the co-pilot's mother lives.

Outside a cube of day school kids,
colorful as Iceland poppies,
are waiting to cross the street.
Their teachers have cautioned them
in red cord to keep them safe.

The site was difficult to find. Difficult to get to.

The red light has changed. The teachers bend down.
All hold hands, their teachers say.

Most of the bodies have been found, but not all
and many have been identified, but not all,
and the black box was recovered so we have
their words and a piece of paper with the word
FIRE scrawled on it. The write-up says the wreckage
is being carted off, bag by seat by panel, steel plates
from wings, shed roofs? a water trough for carabao, maybe.

The jungle canopy is already sliding over.
Shimmying vines, then, and wide spatulate leaves

spreading their folds. I think of how sea creatures
settle down over jagged edges, and of the laying on

of hands. I think of how I have to make a choice,
of how to put this down.

All things can be looted. Words are such slight threads.

and something always (something
not always love) grows up inside.
You can say too much, or too little.

or not say it well, or put it aside.

There are things so awful
and powerful, that you call them
by another name.

There are some things you know,
but do not say.

There are words so old
they must be honored when you come
to them, and only after
can they do their work.
Fire, circled, is like that.

Luci Beach

ATHABASCAN

I was born in Blanco, New Mexico, and lived near Chaco Canyon for the first five years of my life. Various parts of the Southwest were home until about eighteen years ago when I moved to Alaska. My father was Scottish and English. He was a teacher and loved hunting and fishing. He encouraged my understanding of tribal life-styles, especially of the Southwest and Oklahoma. My mother is Gwich'in, Athabascan, from Fort Yukon, Alaska. She was raised by my great-grandmother and is very well versed in oral history and tribal knowledge. I grew up identifying with being Indian. I attended Navajo Methodist Mission School in Farmington, New Mexico, for six years. I have always lived in or near tribal communities. It was not until my thirties that I realized that I was classified as a half-breed. I classify myself as Indian. The emerging native poets of the early seventies helped me to validate my feelings and helped me find my voice. I have witnessed many of the 'cides of tribal people: suicide, homicide, genocide. I am hopeful for tribal people, especially the warriors, healers, and amazingly creative survivors in a world that continually tries to eradicate us and our traditional way of life. This is especially important today as the politicians and oil money try to manipulate their way into the calving grounds of the Alaska National Wildlife Refuge. Since gold and oil, many can only perceive of raping our land and do not give it the love it deserves. The Gwich'in Nation in Alaska and Canada are facing their opponents head-on as tribes have since contact.

2 months rent due and 1 bag of rice

the kids and her
promise what they'll get each other
when they get money
bikes, trips to Hawaii-first class, a boat,
strawberries, a car, the moon and the stars

but when they sleep it's the rent
the rice and
that woman at AFDC
none of them wants to see

she tries to be thankful
but it returns
a sad song sung over and over and over

she feels old and tired
as one more grain of her being
slowly slips out

Winona LaDuke

CHIPPEWA

I am of Anishinabeg and Russian descent, of the Bear clan, of the Mississippi Band Anishinabeg, living and working on the White Earth Reservation on land recovery and environmental restoration.

I never had a sense that things were right in this society. As a person who was raised between two cultures—I'm half Indian and half non-Indian—I didn't feel comfortable with the way things were.

I guess what you do first is take it personally, and it's you who is the problem; I think that's the automatic reaction. Some people never get over that, I suppose. Then you try to figure out if there's something wrong with the bigger picture, which is what I came to from my perspective—that there's something wrong with the construct of society. So I decided to try to do some work on it.

Coming from where I came from, the government process of trying to deny native people our own identity is such a horrible process that it means most people are faced with a lot of extra problems. That process of trying to reclaim identity and rebuild community—because in reclaiming identity you also have to heal your community, where you're from—has really engaged me in the process of social activism.

Ogitchida Ikwewag: The Women's Warrior Society, Fall 1993

Maggie lit the cedar first in the small cast-iron pan. Two or three matches burned at once while the oil popped and cracked in the flat leaves. The flames jumped with each sound, and almost as quickly as they erupted, they died, leaving a glowing edge to match that of the glow; each time she stopped blowing, the smoke would billow from the cedar.

Carefully placing the small pan on the table's edge, she took off her glasses and leaned over the pan. She pulled the smoke over her head with each of her hands, and whispered to the cedar. She pulled the smoke over her body and began to turn around.

Elaine stood next to her and picked up the eagle feather with her right hand and the small pan with her left. She bathed the feather in smoke and used it to pull the smoke over Maggie as the older woman turned clockwise. "Megwetch," Maggie whispered as she finished. Maggie then helped Elaine pull the smoke around her.

Elaine returned to her seat in the northeast of the Circle as Maggie continued to smudge each woman in the Circle. When Maggie had cleansed all of the women, she sat down on the east of the Circle. Maggie began with prayers for the full moon. Then Maggie blessed the water and sipped from the bowl. Then she passed it on to her left, clockwise. Elaine, the last, completed her prayer and placed the water back in the middle of the Circle. As she finished, Maggie began a new set of prayers. As she prayed, the women listened intently, the rhythm of her voice occasionally punctuated with exclamations of agreement and support. Then the other women prayed.

The prayers were for children, family, health, clear thinking, and to be good people. The prayers had a cadence and a rhythm, which the exclamations only accentuated. Some prayers were filled with laments and crying, at which time the women on each side would often reach toward that woman and hold her hands while she prayed. Each of the women also prayed for herself, as this ceremony was also the time and place for even this type of prayer.

When they had all finished, Maggie led them outside to the fire. Again they each said special prayers and carefully placed their offerings on the fire. Complete, the women returned to the house and their places.

They were more lighthearted now, and Maggie began with the berries. Four bowls were placed in order and each woman ate from the bowls until they were gone. They shared the fullness of the harvest.

Then they began to share their concerns and ideas. This was the fall of 1993, the third season of the ceremony.

It was Danielle who brought the story forward at the Full Moon Ceremony in November. She started to talk about Frances Graves, the eleven-year-old daughter of one of the tribal councilmen.

"I watch that girl in school, and there is something going on at home. She cries most days, and is gone at least once a week," Danielle said. "The truth is, she's got bruises on her too, mostly on her wrists, that I can see. It looks like she trys to cover them up, but she is such a nervous girl that she ends up playing with her sleeves, or something, and then I see those bruises again.

"I found her in the bathroom crying more than a few times. She won't talk to me very much though." Danielle continued, "You all know that her mother is in Minneapolis, working, and she's got the job of taking care of those two young boys, and cooking for her dad. Everyone knows that her dad has a lot of power here on the reservation, but that's no reason to turn our heads. I think something is going on."

"I talked to her one day in my office," said Meredith, a guidance counselor at the school. "The girl told me that she respects her father a lot, and that he is a good man. I asked her if her dad treats her alright, and she just kind of looked down. 'It's hard for him,' the girl mumbled, 'with my ma gone, I sort of take care of all three of them.'

"I came right out and asked her then," Meredith said. "I said,

'Does your father touch you in private places?' That girl really looked bad then, but she said, 'No.' "

The truth was everyone knew that Fred Graves abused his daughter. It was an awful secret that women spoke of in hushed voices, and men pretended did not exist. Graves had been on the council for three terms now, and had a firmly entrenched power base. He controlled most of the jobs in his district, and people depended on those jobs for their families. Speaking out meant losing your job. Besides, most people figured, the girl seemed okay, and she wasn't the only one who had been through it. Most had survived, and some men actually felt that "the experience" was good; a rite of passage.

Danielle didn't think so, and neither did Meredith. The truth was that there had been a suicide a year before. A fourteen-year-old girl who had been abused by her uncle had blown off her head with a shotgun in a shack behind their house. There were a couple of other girls too, and one of them people already said that her grandfather and father were the same person.

The women all listened to the stories, and thought about their own lives and experiences. The truth was it did happen sometimes, but that didn't make it right. It was even worse if they let it continue.

The women watched as Fred Graves slowly pulled his car into the driveway at 115 Amik Street in the housing project. There were probably fifteen of the women, including Lucy St. Clair, Georgette Hand, Danielle Wabun, Maggie Jourdain, Meredith Dole, and Elaine, as well as three or four elders. Each woman listened to her own breathing as she sat. Elaine ran her hands over the smooth ricing sticks. In the fall, the sound of the sticks knocking against each other and the wild rice dropping into the canoe would make a soothing sound of harvest. This winter night, the sticks would make a different sound.

The girl sat frozen in the front seat of the new sedan. The burly man walked around the front of the car and opened the passenger door. "Get out and go inside," he said to the girl. Although her body was mature for an eleven-year-old, she was still a frightened girl. She slowly emerged and walked toward the house. She waited for the man outside the door, and he followed her in.

Lucy shifted her weight from one haunch to another as she braced herself against the cold. Tonight the moon was almost full, making it one of the coldest nights of the month. It was clear and she could see the northern lights dancing over the edge of the house. One light went on in the kitchen and another in the bedroom. Lucy tapped the ricing stick against the palm of her left hand, and waited.

Danielle saw the man retrieve two beers from his refrigerator, and pause to open one to take a long drink. He was facing the window, and Denise swore she could smell his alcohol and his smugness. He flicked off the light and went toward the living room. The television went on, and the man sat on the couch.

Maggie watched the girl in her room. The pink walls were covered with posters of Madonna and young men in bathing suits. A few old stuffed toys were packed against the window on a corner shelf for knickknacks. The girl had closed her door, and now sat fully clothed on the side of her bed. She carefully removed her shoes and walked to the window, scratching the winter frost to better look outside. Slowly she turned and walked back to turn off the light. She lay down, still fully clothed, and pulled her blankets around her.

It was twenty minutes later that the living room light went off, and the man walked away from the droning TV. As he opened the bedroom door, Lucy saw he was clothed only in his shorts.

Maggie made her way toward the bedroom window, and carefully placed the small stepladder near the window. She climbed and listened outside. She could hear the man swearing at the girl, and the girl crying as she tried to push him away. She waited about two minutes, and then motioned with her arm for the women to move forward.

Lucy had a key she had extracted as a favor from an old boyfriend at the Housing Maintenance office. She slowly slipped the key into the lock and turned the handle. Lucy and six other women quickly slipped inside so as not to let in the cold air, and moved toward the bedroom. Their steps were muffled by the late-evening cop show.

Lucy pushed open the door to the bedroom and looked at the man as he tried to force himself inside of the girl. His body was heavy against her as he held her arms down and had parted her legs. Her pants were on the floor, and his shorts were to his knees. As the door opened slightly, the girl looked toward Lucy and shame crossed her face. The man was too intent to notice until Lucy's stick was on his back.

"Get off her, you goddamn scumbag," Lucy said as she pushed the man. As he looked up, he gave a small cry, and the women surrounded the girl's bed. The man lifted himself up slightly and the girl broke free, running from the room. Maggie quickly grabbed her underpants and followed her into the bathroom.

As the man began to stand up, the ricing stick began to fall on his back, head, and butt. He managed a cry, and reached to pull his pants up. Before he could get very far, Danielle grabbed them with her ricing stick.

"Not so fast, you pissin' asshole," she said, and she yanked them off his legs. "Howah," she said, as she twirled them on her ricing stick, "Your ass stinks as much as your politics."

The man took ten or fifteen more hits before the women herded him toward the front door. Lucy turned on the porch light and as she did car lights went on to illuminate the block. "Get moving, you fuckin' jerk, you're a poor excuse for a man," Lucy screamed as she kicked him down his front stair. The man stumbled toward the snow, covering his head from the sporadic blows as the women herded him toward car lights, and the sound of horns.

As two women went ahead, and roused the residents of the project, more car lights went on, and soon people wrapped in blankets and coats were on their front porches. The man, naked from the waist down, was walked through the housing project by the women. As he passed, each family came out to look at their Tribal Council representative.

It was December of 1993. A small woman cried in her bathroom, and was comforted by an older friend. As Maggie helped the girl on with her clothes, she whispered, "Shhh, shhh, shhh, shhh, shhh, shhh," just as if she were calming a baby. "It's okay, my girl, it's not your fault. It's okay." Finally dressed, the girl sobbed again, and once more Maggie drew her close and hugged her.

It was December of 1993, and the Ogitchida Ikwewag had its first war party.

Wendy Rose

HOPI ▪ MIWOK

I am raising cactus and succulents, collecting dolls and figurines of female superheroes and villains, married twenty years to Arthur now, and have a cat named "Nudge" who just moved in one day.

The Endangered Roots of a Person

I remember lying awake
in a Phoenix motel. Like that
I remember coming apart accidentally
like an isolated hunk of campfire soot
cornered by time into a cave.
I live even now
in an archaeological way.

Becoming strong on this earth is a lesson
in not floating, in becoming less transparent,
in becoming an animal shape against the sky.

We were born
to lose our eyes in the Sun Dance
and send out lengths of fishline
for the clouds, reel them in
and smooth away all the droughts
of the world.

Sometimes Medicine People shake their heads
over you and it is this; to drop your bones
into the sand, to view yourself
bursting through the city
like a brown flash flood.
The healing of the roots
is that thunderhead-reeling;
they change and pale
but they are not in danger now.

That same morning
I went for coffee down the street
and held it, blowing dreams
through the steam, watching silver words
bead up on my skin. The Hand-trembler said
I belong here. I fit in this world
as the red porcelain mug
merges in the heat of my hand.

On some future dig
they'll find me like this
uncovered where I knelt
piecing together the flesh
that was scattered in the mesa wind
at my twisted-twin birth.

Jeane Jacobs

CHEROKEE ▪ CHOCTAW

I was born in northeastern Oklahoma in 1947 to parents of mixed blood: Irish, Cherokee, and Choctaw.

My earliest remembrance of telling stories was at the age of four. There were always lots of cats around and I carried them in a box or in the wheelbarrow. I told them stories about other animals and creatures from other worlds.

Not only did I like to tell stories, I loved hearing them. My favorite line to any older person was "Tell me about when you were a kid."

I would sit for hours next to my Aunt Delora on the porch swing and just listen. She told me stories about every member of our family. She started out naming the ancestors and where they came from and then she would remember some event in their lives. I soaked up every word.

Now I live in Los Angeles and those dusty afternoons on the porch seem so long ago and far away. But the stories live on in my soul. My characters come from that place in me that remembers my ancestors with great respect. My love for writing grows with my age and the need to put the words on paper increases.

One-Hundred-Dollar Boots

It was Friday night when the boys came home and told Gramma their dad was going to stay in town awhile. It was midsummer, I had just turned seventeen.

It wasn't the first time Uncle Franke stayed out late. Gramma said, "He's gotta whore around." So she left the kitchen light on, the bulb over the sink that made a yellow square shadow through the doorway across the linoleum in the dining room. The darkness that surrounded it stood like still water.

When Gramma got up to make coffee, no one had turned out the light. She figured Franke had stayed with one of his women friends and she didn't give it much more thought.

It must of been late afternoon when the phone rang and Sheriff Philpott asked to speak with "Tookah Daylight." I hollered out the screen door for Granpa to come to the phone. His forehead was wrinkled when he walked through the door; it was unusual for him to get a call.

"Yes, this is Tookah Daylight." Granpa plugged his open ear with the middle finger of the hand that had no thumb. "What's that about my boy, Franke?"

Gramma walked into the dining room drying her hands on the end of her apron.

"Okay, I guess you'll have to do that." Granpa's face lost all of its normal color and his eyes sunk full of water. He struggled with the phone receiver so that Gramma took it away from him and hung it up.

"What's the matter, Tookah?" Gramma asked in her normal soft voice. "What has happened to my boy?"

Granpa walked past all of us and went out on the porch. He sat in his three-legged chair and balanced himself against the wall. His face was as white as his hair, his bottom lip began to tremble.

"Old man, what has happened?" Gramma asked in a loud, angry tone. "Don't you get closed-mouthed with me. Where's Franke?"

"Don't know, woman." Granpa sounded like his throat was full of something bitter.

"Montee, you go around back and get the boys. I'll send them to town, they'll find out what's going on," Gramma demanded. She was different somehow, like she was scared of something, I hadn't seen her this way. Come to think of it Granpa had never acted like that either.

I started to jump off the porch when Granpa said, "No need, Nona. The sheriff is bringing Franke home."

"What? Is he alright? What then?" Gramma leaned in Granpa's face and when their eyes met she knew. She didn't say nothing else, just moved quietly into the kitchen and started pounding bread dough.

Haloka went in after her and sat at the table staring into her black coffee. The expression in her eyes was deep and distant. She didn't ask anybody any questions, she knew more about her grandson, Franke, than anyone. Uncle Franke was about five when Great-Grandfather Ocealah died and they found Franke roaming around in the woods calling out for the old man. He wouldn't sleep after that unless Haloka was near him.

There was an emptiness in my stomach, like a part of me was missing. I kept trying to shake it loose, expecting to see Uncle Franke's Chevy pickup speeding up the road with dust rolling behind it.

Granpa and I sat on the gray wood porch with silence heavy in the air between us, like fog on a dark day. I just sat there rolling cigarettes until I had a pile of twenty or so in the red Prince Albert can.

Then I noticed the dust on the road, Uncle Franke's pickup and right behind it was Sheriff Philpott in a patrol car with a red ball on top.

Granpa never moved, he didn't even look in the direction of the cars when they pulled in front of the house. Gramma and Haloka came out on the porch.

Sheriff Philpott, a short stocky red-faced man, pulled his ample body out of the official car and reached in to get a cowboy hat with its shiny star just above the brim. He walked a bow-legged stroll to the edge of the porch. "Mrs. Daylight," he nodded to Haloka. "Nona and Tookay. I hate to be the one to bring such bad news to you. I can assure you we will be investigating until we find out what exactly happened."

I looked up at Granpa, it was as if he hadn't heard a word the sheriff said. His eyes were glazed with wet shine. He leaned back against the wall with both arms hanging down to his sides.

Gramma was wringing her hands and twisting her apron tail. "What bad news you got to tell us, Buddy?" Gramma asked the sheriff. "Where's my boy, Franke?"

"Nona, me and you been friends a lot of years and God knows I loved your Franke. But, Nona, somebody up and shot him last night." He moved his fingers around the brim of the cowboy hat with one hand and pulled it in a circle with the other as he talked. His blue eyes clouded over with tears and a large lump came up on the center of his throat. "Believe me, Nona, I'm gonna find out who done this. Franke never done nothing to hurt nobody."

His words, "Somebody shot him," rang in my head over and over as I watched the skinny deputy help Sheriff Philpott carry Uncle Franke from the back of his pickup into the dining room. Somebody shot him. Why would anybody want to? Who would even be crazy enough to? Somebody shot him.

I managed somehow to drag my limp body into the dining room and just stood there watching. JoDee and Aunt Lela came through the back door with buckets of water. Haloka sat back staring into her coffee. Gramma began to cut Uncle Franke's jeans off of him. There was no expression on her face, just like she was making bread or digging potatoes, something she had to do.

JoDee cried a little but she heated water and soaked rags with lye soap. JoDee was baby sister to my mama and Uncle Franke. She was only a few years older than me and had been to college and now she was home for a while. She said she wasn't too impressed with the white man's world. In secret she told me about the white boy she fell in love with at school but his folks were real against him having anything to do with her because she was Indian. That only made JoDee hate white people more.

Uncle Franke's skin was gray and his stomach and chest were caked with brown-red sticky splotches. As I watched Aunt Lela scrub him down with the lye soap, the skin began to pull away from what looked like a hole just above his navel. She took her finger and stuffed something pink and lumpy inside the split. "Get me a big needle and some white thread, girl." She motioned to me.

I put my hand over my mouth and tore through the kitchen. I reached for Gramma's sewing box on the back porch and raced the entire thing into the dining room. JoDee managed to thread a large needle and handed it to Aunt Lela.

Aunt Lela's hands pushed and pulled at Uncle Franke's stomach with that needle until she had a jagged line of stitches. Then she leaned over him and chewed at the string.

The three women washed and dried Uncle Franke's heavy body. Gramma went into his bedroom and came back with his clean pressed jeans and white cowboy shirt, the one he wore when he sang at powwows.

They lifted and struggled with him until they finally had him dressed. That's when I noticed his hundred-dollar boots were missing. Aunt Lela covered him with a decorated red blanket. It hung across his waist and down over his feet so maybe we wouldn't notice his boots were gone.

I stared at him as JoDee combed his hair, tears rolling down her chin and onto his face. I thought he would laugh and push her away. But his mouth didn't show any hint of a smile. Where was my Uncle Franke's charming smile?

A severe pain came up in the middle of me. Uncle Franke was dead. At that moment I ran hard and fast out the back door, into the woods. My breathing turned to a low wailing noise that I had no control over. It just came out of me. This awful hollow sound.

I tripped on something and fell facedown in the red clay near the river. I dug my hands into the earth and let my body melt heavy in that spot with this horrible moan inside my stomach. "Uncle Franke dead. How could that be?"

I remembered the story of the old Choctaw Bone Pickers. How their fingernails grew so long they curled. It was their job to pull the rotten flesh away from the bones of the dead. Uncle Franke dead.

The soil seemed to cradle me as I cried. I felt like something sharp was cutting me from the inside out. I heard the sound of the hawk calling to me. I rolled over on my back and stared into the dim sunlight glistening through the trees. The brown spotted hawk swooped above me and back up again. Uncle Franke's voice said, "Only the rocks and mountains last forever."

I remember him saying that once after that tornado tore through our place and shattered his trailer into little shreds of splintered wood and metal. He just cleared away the debris and said he was thankful we were all okay.

I walked back toward the house as the sun was going down behind the trees. There were cars and pickups parked all around the yard. A roaring sound of many voices talking all at one time swallowed me up. JoDee walked off the back porch. "Come on Montee, we are having the wake tonight and you look a mess."

Before I could say anything she pulled me into the shed. "Here, wash yourself. I'll bring you some clean clothes." She slammed the gray wood door behind her.

I had never been to a wake. Uncle Franke told me once, "Them gawddamn Indians get so damn drunk, pass out all over the place. It takes them days to find out which one you suppose to bury."

The water in the washtub was warm and had tiny beads of soap floating around the metal edges. The sweet smell of JoDee's cologne lingered in the cloth.

I was washing my feet when JoDee came back with her straight black skirt and my blue ruffled blouse. She began brushing my tangled hair, pulling it back from my face. She braided one braid down the back, like hers. She helped me dress. When she finished with me she leaned in the mirror and spread the cherry pink lipstick over her lips.

When we walked through the back door, Aunt Lela and some tan wrinkled woman with no teeth were cooking in Gramma's kitchen. Aunt Lela's hair was twisted in a bun at her neck and she wore her Sunday dress. "You look real pretty, girls." She nodded when we passed by.

The smell of cornbread made my stomach churn and I took a deep breath when I stood in the dining room door facing Uncle Franke all stretched out on the table.

Gramma and Haloka sat beside each other in the front room near the window. Gramma's light blue shawl draped over her shoulders. Her graying hair pulled tightly and twisted in the back. Her soft skin seemed pale and her dark eyes were wet and red.

Haloka's gray eyes stared into space as she rocked slowly back and forth in her chair. Her snow-white hair in two braids over each shoulder. The deep creases of her tan skin set around her half-pouting lips. The purple shawl halfway wrapped over her arms and hanging across her lap.

I backed myself into the corner and slid down the wall, folding my legs under me on the cool linoleum. I stared at him, half expecting my stare to wake him up. I wanted my Uncle Franke to raise his head and smile at me. He just laid there, silent.

I watched and listened on into the night. Those damn Indians beat their drums, sang and cried until daybreak. They took turns walking past me, around the table, and back out the door, again.

It must've been around midnight when Jeffrey and Marcus circled the table. Marcus fell over his father's stiff body. He made deep, dark noises and I knew he felt that same emptiness inside of him that was in me. His shoulders shook and he wailed, "No, Dad. No, Dad, no." Jeffrey wrapped his long arms around his younger brother and lifted him up. Uncle Charlie stood behind the boys, staring at the red blanket. Then he guided them out onto the porch where they sat next to Granpa.

In the still darkness Armagettin made her way through the door. She lived just down the road from us, she said her grandmother was a slave but she appeared to have some white blood and Haloka teased her about being part Cherokee. Armagettin held Uncle Franke's hand and her body shook as tears streamed down her light yellow face. Her hair was long and waved down her back. She had always been a pretty woman and had trouble with men. She had a house full of children, there was some confusion as to who their fathers were. Gramma always said Armagettin had a kind heart, she just didn't know how to say no.

Gramma walked over to Armagettin and held her like she would one of her own children. She always believed that a couple of Armagettin's younger boys belonged to Uncle Franke because he would take money to her on payday and he worked on her house when she needed things done.

No one ever said anything about it or asked any questions. It was just accepted and that was that.

Haloka leaned over to Gramma and softly whispered, "Montee's dad is here." She glanced down at me then, the look in her eyes said, "It's okay."

I breathed an impatient breath and waited for the door to open. My father, Clayton Lonebear, spent most of his life drunk. He washed dishes at T. J.'s Steak House and drank. Uncle Franke told me it wasn't like that until my mama died. He said my dad was a good man and had been a hero in World War II. His marine buddies called him "the Kiowa Warrior." But I didn't really know much more than that.

I saw him once in a while but he never said two words, he just watched me, those black eyes seemed to stare right through me. Maybe I reminded him too much of Mama or maybe he just didn't know what to say.

Clayton Lonebear stumbled through the door, dressed in a birdbone breastplate and leather pants and moccasins. His face was painted black from his eyes down and red across his forehead. His long dark hair hung loose with an eagle feather tied on one side.

He strolled around the table with his eyes straight ahead. Then he stopped at Uncle Franke's face, he kissed him right on the mouth and then fell to his knees. He screamed from somewhere in the center of himself. The sound rang out like a lonely coyote. I felt the floor tremble under me.

He sat on his knees and cried, loud sobs until almost daylight and an older man came in to get him. I felt his sadness as the two of them struggled down the steps.

I drifted in and out of sleep most of the day, in the corner of the dining room. I couldn't seem to move, like I had something real heavy holding me in that spot. I kept dreaming about Uncle Franke's hundred-dollar boots. He had made some extra money a few months back and drove down to Dallas to pick up those boots, he had ordered them special. He was so proud when he came home. Gramma said he just wanted to impress the ladies when the powwow rolled around. We all knew she was right. Even Uncle Franke agreed.

It was dark outside and everyone had gone when I heard Granpa walk off the porch and take a piss. A few minutes later he slipped in the back door and into the bedroom. That was the first time since the phone call that he had moved from his chair. He hadn't even looked at Uncle Franke. It was as if, if he didn't see the body, Franke wouldn't really be dead. I understood that somehow. I wished I hadn't seen him that way.

The light was still on over the sink and that yellow shadow made its way across the floor when I heard someone shut a car door and walk up on the porch. The screen opened and a white hand sat the hundred-dollar boots on the floor.

My legs cramped as I tried to move quietly toward the door. I only caught the taillights as the car drove away. But there they were, those hundred-dollar boots with silver toe covers staring up at me. I lifted the red blanket and forced those boots onto Uncle Franke's cold feet.

That must've been the last tears I cried as I slid back down in the corner on that cool linoleum and watched and waited.

Marcie Rendon

ANISHNABE

My life is deeply moving—I live life intensely. Who inspired me? Jim Northrup (a writer), my mom, and all the native women who died without being heard.

You See This Body

you see this body
i mean
do you see this body

legs, are you a leg man?
let me tell you about these beautiful legs, leg man

they have walked and stood and squatted

walked across this nation on the Trail of Tears
stood firm at Wounded Knee
squatted to give birth to all humanity

oh yes, leg man, these sure are some beautiful legs

and you, hey you over there,
you like ass, you an ass man?

let me tell you about this ass
it's been kicked and shoved and beat
Nazi nuns, KKK, U.S. soldiers

feel it man, soft and round, good as new
some beautiful ass, huh?

you see this body
i mean
do you see this body?

hey man, you over there
see this smile and flashing eyes
sure can turn your head

hey man,
let me tell you 'bout this pretty smile
and flashing eyes

got me 'cross the Berlin Wall
free passage on a ship outta 'Nam
fed my kids quicker than the welfare line

amazing smile and flashing eyes
turned your head
just long enough

Anita Endrezze

YAQUI

I'm an artist as well as a writer/poet. When I paint I do it for myself primarily, while when I write it's for others. I don't write for an audience, however, but I do have the idea that others will read what I've written. When I paint I'm often dissatisfied with the end results. I don't think I have a true vision for art; that is, I'm not able to create something entirely new. I love colors and shapes and I try for that in my writing with the images I create. When I write I feel a deep satisfaction upon completion. And I know when something is finished. I think what I do in writing is original. I'm a very visual person and I delight in my senses. Art and writing are deep parts of myself.

I'm inspired by many writers, but especially by women

The Constellation of Angels

Above the city, the constellation of angels glows. In the tidal waters, mud-red fish race against the infiltration of air. In the tribal dreams thick with broad leaves and clans of red fish and moons, the perceptive ones sigh. Those who have lost their tribes, their dreams, world over, feel their eyes sealed with concrete and wake aching to see the world.

Wake aching like an orchid burned black from the cold, its Kirlian aura unfurling vermillion into the teethy shadows. If an orchid ached, what of the human soul?

From the temple of the dream-walkers, I emerge, standing with one cloudy hand on the dark red maples, breathing the lunar downpour of air.

It is the temple of the reedy rivers, its doors made of shifting sand and yellow canaries. There are many doors; I am one of them. My eyes can be as glittery as dragonfly wings. I emerge and see the young woman who lives in the dark cracks of the city. Her lips are swollen; there is a black bubble of skin, the blood inside welling up and thickening. Her stomach is rounded with a new human hungry for wholeness. She is remembering that her man hit her. She saw the bottle in one of his fists, and from the other, stars. He gave her stars with his fists. His long warrior's face was oily. She said she was sorry. She is a bearer of souls and fleshes out their bones with tiny veins and nerves that flinch at the sound of her heartbeat. She apologizes for his anger at life.

Mary is my Other: my special human. The top of her head feels like sunshine. I divide myself into grasses swaying in the wind. In the time before, I walked with the wind, which came from the lack of hooks and seams, from animals huddling over the unearthed, I came from a certain blindness, the great eye. I came to watch over the humans, with their thick thighs and golden arms. Or their skin dark as grapes, and those with skin the color of almonds. Whenever I leave them and reenter the temple, into the nets of turquoise butterflies, I am astonished at my lightness.

Mary lives in a cold house. It has three rooms, but she lives in one, the kitchen. There she washes her underwear and hangs them over the backs of the two chairs to dry. She has a table. Around it she has piled newspapers and in the middle is a space where she places her older baby so it can be safe. Her man has big heavy boots that do not always care about what they step on. When he wears them, the house shakes. She's a good mother. She take care of him, too. She washes his clothes. She feeds him. And when he is not drunk, she understands the logic of shadows and becomes one.

She's a chameleon; she wears her self-effacing camouflage the way a rose wears its thorns.

When he hit her, he was thinking of another woman. He hadn't been home all night: he'd been with this other woman and seeing Mary made him feel guilty. He hit her and when she fell down, he understood her better. Her legs turned sideways to protect her stomach and he forgave her for being. Although for a second, his foot ached to kick her. But she had said she was sorry and he knew she wouldn't give him any trouble. The other woman had big brown nipples and small eyes that seemed to be the same color as gin. He had, for a moment, felt as if he were being skinned alive, but then she moved her hips and closed her eyes and she was very different from Mary, whose belly was baglike. The other woman had pretty hair but he couldn't remember her name. He might see her again on the streets or, most likely, he wouldn't. He remembered the green army jacket she wore, with nothing underneath it so that her breasts hung free, ready for grabbing. He had seen her a few times before that, smoking outside the cafe, but she had always ignored him. Then, last night, she had been too drunk to remember she'd rather be alone than with him. Sometimes he got lucky that way with women.

He talks to himself a lot. His mantra is "fuck." Sometimes he barks the word: fkkk! Other times, it stretches out so long he can't remember the beginning of the word: fuuuuuuuu. . . . It's his favorite response to daylight, a broken shoelace, the car that almost hit him, his last smoke. It's as if he never got past his second of conception: fuck! He's not my responsibility but often I put my hand on his head. His thoughts are like an onion made of ash: no center. Diffused in a scornful breath. But my touch calms him. He remembers that his great-grandparents were healers. He remembers that his ancestors coaxed corn from the desert. He remembers what he could've been. I see his soul: it has a rind on it, thick and knotted.

Mary, on the other hand, sings her thoughts. Yesterday she said to herself, "My friends are all gone. One who told stories we all loved to hear . . . and the other who lived in a house on the hill. Even I am gone from the still stones and the woods. I should only love a tree, with its owl eyes, its blue feathers, its crow's voice. A tree is better at forgetting than I am. It has centuries of blue to reach out to, while I am only lessened through the loss of friends who say their roots are elsewhere. Who says that trees lost by having only wooden hearts?"

And who is to say that Mary is lessened by needing that man, the father of her children? Human love and need confuse me. Sometimes good comes out of bad. I watch the young men on West Second Avenue, shifting their weight from one foot to the other, smoking and spitting, waiting for the next needle. In their chests, something rattles. Something is broken. It is Life. And then, the young women, with their thin bodies, their deep bodies, their eyes stubborn and wasting. They need some man to talk to. Are they lonely or do they just need money?

Sometimes there is nothing but badness substituting for Nothing. Mary is not like that. She doesn't drink. She doesn't smoke. She doesn't use drugs. But she does need him. That's her emptiness.

In the temple, which is the other frame of my existence, music has eyelids and breasts are made of sunlight. There are roosters with feathers like red poppies, stonefulls of water, and salt candles that smell like the warrior sea. What is real is variety and we experience water breathing and sometimes a single stem of beautiful darkness.

I understand the way Mary thinks. But unlike myself, she is not what she thinks. Often she is a contradiction. It is not the difference between intellect and feeling, or even between the body and the soul. There is a vast difference between the Mary of the trees with the wooden hearts and the Mary of apologies.

In the temple, we dance further than trees can see, singing into oldness the white stars and the delicate blue veins of babies.

Mary walks to the store. She tucks her baby in the nest of her arms, so that it is resting on the baby unborn. She makes a list in her head. Soap. Milk. Bread. Peace and quiet. She can smile at that.

The baby has a tooth that shines when the sun strikes it. She squirms in Mary's arms. Mary has only gone a little way so she turns around and goes back home.

He's sitting at the table, staring at his hands. "Hi, babe," he says to Mary. "Forget your money?"

Mary shakes her head. "Here," says Mary, handing him the baby. "I'll be back in a few minutes. I have to get our dinner."

"Can't you take her?" he asks. His head hurts and his ears feel like there's a big tree growing in each of them, the roots digging into his brain.

"She's too restless and I have to carry the bags back. You can come with us or you can just let her crawl around."

"Shit."

Mary's not sure if that means yes or no. She can see he's in pain and balances carefully between the pain that will explode into anger or the pain that will wear him down to agreement. She wheedles him. "You don't have to do anything, just see that she doesn't hurt herself."

He grimaces. "I feel like shit."

Mary places the baby down by his feet. She watches him for a few minutes, massaging the lower part of her back. Then she leaves.

When she reaches the store, she only buys as much as she can carry. At the checkstand, the clerk talks to her. "You know your husband, he can't come in here anymore. The boss told me to tell you that. Your husband disturbs the other customers. Please tell him not to come here anymore."

The clerk speaks very slowly as if Mary is from another country. Mary keeps her head down with embarrassment and nods. She picks up her two bags of groceries and goes outside.

Then another dream-walker comes to me, looking like a woman made out of marine lilies. She is the spirit-helper of the baby in Mary. Lilies looks at me with her green eyes. "This baby be like the paper shadow of birds, be like a hand without bones. This baby be sick and no dancing will give it wings or earthly firmness. What we have are eyes that are sticks and a heart that is a butterfly in a cage."

We speak a little longer. We are saddened. I knew something was wrong, could feel the baby crying out for wholeness. Lilies touches my shoulders and steps back through the door. It was good of her to tell me.

Mary stops with a startled look on her face. The bags fall from her hands. There is a terrible pain encircling her. She kneels on the sidewalk, her face white . . . chalky white   like the inner sky of an egg   like a fluted white shell   O, White Shell clan woman!   the woman with the black hair carried the jar on her head   she has a face like a baby with such big eyes and round cheeks she places one foot slowly in front of her   it looks like the flipper of a seal

she stumbles
and when the jar falls, it breaks
                    and her soul falls out
shimmering   shimmering   and half-liquid but without the glow
of a star and the woman's baby face is broken
                    into tiny mirrors of eyes
and the hair coils into rivers of red-black waters

here the hands wave their gelatinous fingers
here the ears are closed and flat as a rock
here the mouth is sealed shut and shaped like a horse's hoof
here the tongue is an empty funnel
little baby-woman: her soul has burned a spirit hole
into the temple of the sky

a constellation of angels with the lidless eyes of adders
welcomes her, saying:
    here is the altar of innocent eyes
    here is the refuge from a gather who has a bottle for a god
    here is the starry mother who is strong enough
to keep you whole
    here is your brightness and a crown of candles . . .

On the sidewalk, the blood flowed and Mary lost her second little heart. She lay dully, hearing voices around her, the pain racking and cramping. There was nothing I could do but to press my spiritual hand over her own wildly beating heart and breathe the peace of doves over her head. It is an ancient symbol but useful. It is hard to lose a baby within, unformed, deformed, unseen, but known to every cell in a woman's body. Mary was only feeling the physical pain now; later, I knew, she'd feel her own heart breaking at the loss.

I heard the ambulance coming. There were people huddled around her and a woman cradled her head.

The grocery clerk crossed her arms. "Don't they know they shouldn't drink when they're pregnant?"

A man shook his head. "Looks like she was all beat up."

"She gonna lose that baby," said another woman in a trembling voice. "All that blood. Someone do something! Where's the goddamn ambulance?"

The siren was getting louder. Mary felt like she was floating. She could see ashen-faced spirits reaching out their transparent hands, their black palms pulling out the dead fetus and unraveling the cord of life. The baby floated up and looked down at her mother.

I took the child's feathery hand and we walked toward the temple, the Flower World. With each step, our eyes grew brighter and on our left, jade deer with rattles around their hooves nodded at us, dancing, shaking their antlers. From the antlers, clouds of shells and colored birds scattered. On our right, two water drums shook the earth and flowers changed into butterflies. From behind us, the waves of flowers unfolding from the sea. From in front of us, holy trees set forth blossoms of wind and brown-skinned spirits danced in welcome.

The child shook free from my hand and joined the dancers. Her little body was patterned in flowers.

In the other world, her mother was carried into the ambulance. There was the smell of asphalt, the bitter odor of medicines, and the sweet smell of blood flowering between her thighs.

III.

TRANSFORMATION:

VOICES OF THE INVISIBLE

Wendy Rose

HOPI ▮ MIWOK

The Poet Haunted

Ghosts are attacking me, crowding up from
my childhood like coyotes or priests
rosaries rattling between claws and teeth.
I want my infancy back, another chance
for things to be different, for the ghosts
to return gravebound in the summer.
In these yellow dunes stretching
like buttes through galaxies of
remembered pain
are golden ages given
to the drunk and crazy
but never to the haunted or
the remembering.

Ghosts these fathers
Ghosts these children
Ghosts these clans
Ghosts these pictures
Ghosts these afternoons
Ghosts these pills
Ghosts these kittens
Ghosts these hospitals
Ghosts these fires
Ghosts these bullets
Ghosts these horses
        Captured bits of thunder
        pushing in from the Pacific
Ghost winds, sliding
        the warmth of myself through it all

like a red unicorn weeping, fooled again
by an ancient virgin;
Ghosts of myself fooled
Ghosts these virgins
Ghosts these brothers
Ghosts these mountains
Ghosts these buffalo
Ghosts these lovers
Ghosts these stars
Understand now
how ghosts are made
Ghosts these thirty years;
I sleep, they
stride by
Ghosts these walkers
I am left
to bandage the marks
from their incessant
mouths
Ghosts among ghosts
Ghosts left alive
Ghosts these mirrors
Ghosts of myself

Debra Calling Thunder

ARAPAHO

I am an Arapaho, a woman of
the Blue Sky People, a nation from long ago. And we love
words because words are life, binding all things sacred—the
heavens and earth and generations.

Words sing in our blood. They are the prayers and entreat-ies that ascend to the Creator Above, the songs our grand-mothers and grandfathers cried from the edge of genocide, the circle of dreams that whisper of eternity.

Words are the breath of time, and we love words because we love life and because words are in us.

May our words and the words of all grieving nations be strong.

Voices of the Invisible

There are voices behind the wall—our voices, disembodied, spoken as if by beings unseen.

From the silence arise words conjured from invisible mouths, and laughter without smiles, and songs without celebration, and wailing without tears.

The air is crowded with words—wondrous and beautiful words that rise invisible and unheard and then are swallowed by time. The air is crowded with words—words that bind us to eternity, that carry the stories and dreams that are the gifts from generations past, the songs of victory and mourning that compel us to seek tomorrow.

We are the invisible ones, the People of the Sky, the people of dreams whose voices cannot be bound by pain. We are the people of prayers, who stand small before the Creator, who entreat him, so that the strand of time that holds us to eternity might not be cut and our words slip into silence.

I give this song to Our People, to all the generations, and empty my soul before them.

Words are gifts, our grandparents say, and they give us many words so we will remain a nation, a circle of people.

My grandmother, Cleone Thunder, is nearly ninety now, an age she says is not so old. Days disappear, falling furiously into time, but love remains, and words and songs and stories.

She tells us the stories of our beginning when the Creator above rejoiced and we and many others came to exist, and the circle of our lodges grew large. Only a short time ago, she says, Our People roamed the earth following the great buffalo herds that stormed across the plains, the expanse of time and dreams.

The buffalo sang to us, and their song was their life. The buffalo sang to us so that we would grow strong. And the Old People would gather together many words to make prayers to the Creator. They would gather words as they walked a sacred path across the earth, leaving nothing behind but prayers and offerings.

Now the buffalo days are gone and we are here, living on a reservation in houses, no longer in a circle of tipis, but still as a tribe. Many of us have fallen into material poverty, but we are rich in relatives and songs and beauty.

The transmission of these words is how we keep alive what is left of the oral traditions, the gift of the Old People who loved us from long ago even though we did not yet exist. The words of long ago have bound us together, those of us who are like a victory song, like an eagle feather, like the thunder when it laughs.

When my grandmother was young, she lived in the old way—in a tipi near the Wind River—with her great-grandmother, Hoh-dah-wan, who gathered wood although she was old.

Hoh-dah-wan lived during a time when the people wandered the earth, starving because the buffalo were nearly gone. She gave my grandmother the stories of the Sand Creek Massacre, when the U.S. Cavalry in 1864 attacked a Cheyenne and Arapaho camp under an American flag and a white flag of truce.

On that November morning in what is now Colorado, our traditional homeland, Hoh-dah-wan saw old people, women, and children being hunted down by soldiers. She saw rape and mutilation of women, whom Our People considered sacred. There were soldiers cutting open the bellies of pregnant women and fashioning toys from the breasts and female organs of dead women. There were orders given to the soldiers to seek out and kill the young girls because "they breed like lice."

She saw the people fleeing in the snow, running to the riverbanks, hoping the earth would shelter them from the nightmare.

After it was done, the soldiers looted the camp, stealing sacred objects and human bodies which they beheaded—including those of my grandmother's two uncles—as the spoils of their "victory." The elders say the loss of sacred objects continues to hurt the tribe.

The U.S. Army used the human remains for medical research. It later gave some of the remains to the Smithsonian Institution in Washington, D.C.—our country's national museum—for display as curios.

In October 1992, a Smithsonian anthropologist came to talk to the spiritual elders of our tribe about the repatriation of Arapaho human remains, and funerary and sacred objects. My grandmother and I were there.

The Smithsonian had made the return of the massacre victims' remains a priority, he told us that day, nearly 128 years after the massacre. He said that the government began taking the remains of tribal people to continue medical studies begun on the bodies of Civil War soldiers.

No, my grandmother told him, it was because white people considered us savage and uncivilized. But they were wrong.

My grandmother is among the first Arapahos to know only the confines of a reservation and who did not learn the sacred ways of the women's Quill Society.

Her mother, Grass Woman, the daughter of Black Coal and the granddaughter of Hoh-dah-wan, was one of the last of the seven medicine women who carried the Quill Society's medicine bundles. Until her time, the women had passed on knowledge of the society to successive generations.

The seven medicine women supervised the making of quill ornaments used to decorate tipis, moccasins, buffalo robes, and cradles with designs representing prayers for health and long life. The women made gifts of the quillwork so that blessings would follow the people as they traveled the four hills of life.

The ceremonies of the society have disappeared with other aspects of Arapaho life, and our grandparents say they long for the old ways. There is a loneliness for Arapaho words, they say—the quiet, flowing words of the storytellers that spilled into the thin, winter light and into the hearts of the people, the words that bound generations and were stronger than death.

In 1878, the Northern Band of Our People settled on a reservation in Wyoming that they share with an enemy tribe, the Shoshone. The federal government set about turning them into farmers and Christians by allotting families land and outlawing the tribe's ceremonies. Smallpox threatened the tribe, which numbered only several hundred.

Black Coal, one of our last traditional chiefs, gave part of his land allotment to the Catholic Church for a school. That way, he said, the children would no longer be sent to faraway boarding schools, exiled from the words of Our People.

His son, Sumner Black Coal, had been one of the first Arapahos to be taken to boarding school, where Indian children were punished for speaking their tribal languages. The sons of the Arapaho chiefs and subchiefs were taken so the people would no longer fight and the future leaders would not learn Our People's ways.

After the school at St. Stephen's Mission was built, the elders, the chiefs, and the warriors would go into the classrooms and tell the children to get a white man's education. The buffalo days were gone, they told them, and you are the ones who will make a new life for the people.

In 1958, the federal government and the state of Wyoming put a radioactive waste dump near the school. It wasn't cleaned up until thirty years later.

The children were not sacred to them.

In 1890, Smithsonian ethnologist James Mooney described Our People as "devotees and prophets, continuously seeing signs and wonders."

The government had sent him to study our tribe, because it expected us to become extinct and our words fall into silence. It was during this time that many of the sacred societies, including the Quill Society, began to die out, and soon their ceremonies slipped away and their prayers were heard no more upon the earth. It was also during this time that Our People began to follow the way of the Ghost Dance, crying out to the Creator and bewailing the loss of the buffalo and a way of life.

Have pity on us Father, they prayed. Have pity on us for we have nothing left.

We buried my cousin last month. He was seventeen.

Before we buried him, the priest said words, incantations. He told us that all of us were all to blame because we failed to speak, we failed to listen. He said that we loved alcohol too much and our young ones too little.

His words cut into the silence and into our hearts.

Then we heard the songs given to us by the Old People, the healing words that arose above the circle of the drum. They sang to us so that we would be strong and the people endure. We have done it many times before—given our young ones back to the earth, who catches our tears, and to the Creator above.

We have done it many times before, we the Sky People who are tied together by time and blood, who have shared laughter and tears, life and death.

In July 1992, my family visited the Plains Indian Museum in Cody, Wyoming, where traditional cradleboards were on display, including an Arapaho cradleboard made around 1890 from sack cloth and dyed porcupine quills.

A little girl asked her mother what the quill ornaments were.

Toys, her mother said.

She did not know they were the captive prayers the grandmothers had prepared for the young ones.

She did not know that like the sacred prayers of the grandmothers and the songs of the buffalo, too many of our children have fallen silent.

Debra Haaland Toya

L A G U N A ▮ J E M E Z

The memories I have of my youth, and those of my grandparents, are, essentially, my writing. I think often about the times I visited my grandparents in Winslow and in Mesita. Hours seemed like days while waiting for my grandpa to return with deer. He never left the deer alone until after their spirits were sent away. I would find him sleeping in the garage with them next morning. I recall dancers and the sound of my grandpa's voice next to a hollow drumbeat. Climbing the red mesa about Mesita and taking baths in a galvanized tub after six of my cousins are also important to me.

I include myself in the memories my grandmother has of watching dancers in a house below the village, when she was seven. She never knew the dancers were coming, only that her mother cooked an unusual amount of food and they walked to that house after dark. They sat on the floor until dawn and watched—it was then that the dancers returned from whence they came.

Winslow, Arizona, is my birthplace because my grandma and grandpa Toya lived there, and my father was in Okinawa at the time. He went away as often as the U.S. Marine Corps would have him go.

I recently traveled to my ancestral lands in Norway, and I now include myself in the memories attached to my relations there.

It is only through combating the disease of alcoholism that

I have found the words to express my meaning of life. With my memories and experiences, I wish to benefit my Indian community, as well as those who listen. The honesty with which I need to write I find in children—I look to them to remember and to learn.

Hunter's Dance in Early Fall

Ga-wash-truht in Mesita, in early fall
in late night.
Unending silence
but for the hooting and hollering.
Their Kachina sounds
from the west side of the village.
I lie awake in the back of my uncle's Chevy pickup
counting a trillion stars
in and around obsidian sky.
Respect of the sacred prevents me from looking with my eyes.
I begin to hear them
when they climb the hill
next to the burial grounds.
From ancient history,
sounds so familiar to the soul of the village,
the natural want for dogs to bark is silenced.
I hear jingle of bells
deer hoof fragments knocking vacant turtle shells
green gourd rattles, and the Hunters' calls.
120 moccasins padding a path
through the center, past the Kiva and Sacred Heart Mission
to the old plaza, under the old, old cottonwood
its crooked arms entangling the moon and star light.
They dance there.

A white canvas sheet, rolled up
with cedar and prayers for the drum
the *os-stchoots*—

beat by *Naw-ish*.
Deep, flat, pulse
with the dancers' right feet.
They sing the language
Kat'sina understand.
This first dance for *stra-nis-gee-ya-she*; the Great Spirit;
God
They leave for the kiva.
My pores, like a sponge, soak in
free-roaming blessings
brought by these messengers of God.
Hundreds of years of prayers and worship fill my body
like the sound of the distant train filling the air
at this moment.
I sleep under the scintillating sky
awaiting the eastern light and my dance.

Arlene Fire

DAKOTA

I like to put down on paper my
own personal feelings, like if I feel lonely today, I will write.
Instead of getting on the phone and calling up someone, pouring out my feelings to someone who probably couldn't care less,
I write. Writing is a way to release personal feelings of loneliness, personal feelings which help me to remember my childhood and the happy times, many many happy times.

I always liked to go to school, I always wanted to see the
pictures in the books, the big tall buildings called skyscrapers.

What is a sky scraper? Who could be big enough to scrape the sky? Of course these were all coming out of the mind of a very young child just learning to read. And the airplanes, just what was it that kept them up there in the sky?

Then one year, 1983, I realized the necessity to have a degree, and eventually a good-paying job doing work I earnestly enjoyed. I went back to South Dakota to go to college even though I've been out of school since I was nineteen years old. I went to Sinte Gleska College (Spotted Tail College). My first semester as a freshman was totally disastrous. I passed only one class, Freshman English II with a B. That night after I had my scores on my semester tests and I showed my grades to my auntie, Hazel Schweigman, I felt so helpless, so stupid, so dumb. But a few days later, I made up my mind to go back to school, try again, and take the classes over again. The next semester, I did just that. This time I passed. Eventually, I made the dean's list.

I also taught two of the Native American classes. This coming summer, I will go back to Pine Ridge and finish my ninth year of Sun Dancing.

Hard-To-Kill-Woman

In 1986, I did my "hanblechia." I prepared myself for two full years to do this "hanblechia" and I looked for the right medicine man to put me up. I was ready now and the only person that was left was Titus, who is my relative. I told him I wanted to "hanblechia" and I gave him an old pipe, filled my old pipe and gave it to him and smoked it. I told him I was waiting for him 'cause I knew no one else could put me up. He said, "I was waiting for you to come to me and I'm glad because we're related. It's good." He put me up there for my "hanblechia" with two other women.

One of these men that was always chasing me, he told me, "You shouldn't go up." 'Cause he went up and something happened. He must not have been ready, because the spirits took him and they drug him down that hill he was on, and they just rolled him. There was cactus on him, cuts on him, and he was just wandering around. They went to pick him up and he was just wandering around the hill in a daze. He wasn't even himself. It took him a while to come back to his own sanity, so he was trying to tell me not to do it. When I was up there all that night and that day, he was down there in that camp, 'cause he was going to see how I was, how I made it. I did, I made it.

I did everything the way this medicine man, Titus, told me to do, to prepare. I had to have a dress to wear that I made specifically for that, that I never wore before, that no one wears. You make your own dress for that "hanblechia." I had to have a star quilt, I had to have a pipe that's never been used before, I had to have a feather and an abalone shell tied together, also never used before. I had to have a knife, never used, never touched, I had to have a bow, this "wasnabi," which is dried weeds and cherries, all these dried things, a brand-new pail and dipper, and I had to have all my tobacco ties, my flags, my felt with one large tobacco tie. That feather that I tied onto the abalone shell, instead of tying it in front of me like most people do, tying it to a stick in the ground in the west, Titus tied it on my head when we came out of the sweat. I'm sure there was a meaning for that, but he never did tell me what those meanings were.

Before we went into the sweat that night, before they put us up, we picked seven rocks, just seven good-sized rocks. You line them up in a row, all those seven rocks, they just belong to you. You pick seven people to stand behind each one of those rocks and look and tell you what they see and tell the medicine man what they see, and everyone else is listening.

I had my seven friends there and they picked up seven rocks and they each looked at the rock and they each saw something different, and each thing that they saw related to something in my mind that happened to me. My closest friend saw this brown-colored horse rearing up and that was my Indian name, Brown-Colored Horse Woman. The last man that looked at the rock, he saw a badger. That related to Titus, because one of his spirits was a badger spirit, so it all fit into place. There were four men that the other people saw, and it all fit together. This older lady, an elderly lady, she's the only one that was old, she saw two big hills. No one was standing out there, nothing, just two big hills. To me that meant that I should Vision Quest twice, but it turned out this hill that I was on was a big hill, and behind it there was an even larger big hill, right across the creek. All of it fit together.

You go up on the top of the hill and you stand up there and you stay all night and all day with your pipe. You don't sleep, you don't eat, you don't drink, you don't smoke cigarettes, you don't do anything. You just stand out there and you pray with your pipe. You pray for your meaning in life, that if there's a meaning in life for you, then show it to me, and if it takes longer than one Vision Quest, then tell me that too. That's what you pray for. I prayed for my education, I prayed for my writing, I prayed for good health for myself and my family, for my relatives, and for the people that were sick. I just prayed for everything good to happen to the Indian people everywhere, 'cause we were all having such a hard time.

Those prayers take a long time because before I pray one of those prayers, I pray to the west, the Grandfathers. To me, the Grandfathers in the west are the Grandfathers that came first. They're like the rock: the rock that came first went and sat in the west and he was black and there was nothing before anything else, so it was black. In the process of the creation, it somehow turned red, and then that was to the north. So I prayed to the north, to the old Grandfathers after the first Grandfather, and I prayed and asked him to help me because they're wise, they're old people. The next prayer that I prayed was to the east, to the sun, because the sun gives life. It gives everything to earth that helps the earth survive. Then to the south I pray to the spirit world, because that's the white and the white represents the spirit world. Then I pray to Grandfather, which is in the universe, everything. Then I pray to Grandmother Earth, which is the earth we live on today and everything comes from there. Everything together I pray for, like the Grandfather that's black, the one that's red, the one that's yellow, the one that's white, the one that's blue, and finally the Mother

Earth, and she's green. Then there's the four races, there's the animals, the birds, and then there's the water, the air, and it takes time. These things are sacred. You don't just pray just because they're there. You pray for the use that you can get from the plants, the medicine, the healing in the plants that you get, and the survival from the food, the water, and the unity that we can have as Indian people by respecting all of these things: the ceremonies, the sweat lodges, the Vision Quests, the Sun Dances, and through the other ceremonies that Indian people perform.

It took a long time, and it seemed like it was going to be dawn, because I could hear different kinds of birds that were starting to make noises. I heard someone walking toward me from the north, because I sat facing west with my pipe, and I froze because I could hear this person walking, I heard steps in the grass. I didn't want to look but yet something wanted me to look, so I turned and I looked toward the right and I could see my aunt, the one that had just passed away. She was standing there and she looked so nice, she wasn't sick anymore, she looked healthy. She asked me in Indian, "Arlene, what are you doing here?" I looked at her consciously and I said, "Auntie, remember what we talked about?" She said, "Oh, yeah." I said, "That's why I'm sitting here like this." She said, "Oh, okay." She just agreed with me. Then, just like that, she went away. When she was there, it was like daylight, everything was bright. Then the dark came back again.

I sat there and I thought about that for a while. I remembered that before he put us up, Titus said, "One of you girls is going to see my grandmother. She's going to come and talk to one of you." I expected one of us to, but I didn't know it was going to be me. I was thankful, so I prayed that she came to me and talked to me. I prayed for her spirit wherever she was going right then because it takes a year for the spirit to go back where it comes from. I prayed that her journey would be a safe journey, that she wouldn't have a hard time getting back to where she was going.

I didn't pray for a while again after that, I just rested awhile. Then I heard someone else walking behind me, coming from the east, and it just put chills up my back, 'cause I could hear this rubbing together, something dry rubbing together. It was scary, to me that was really scary because I couldn't identify the sound and I couldn't imagine what it could possibly be. It came closer, the footsteps grew slow and heavy, and they came closer and closer. They stood right behind me and I was just petrified. I mean, I didn't know what to think. I could smell this real old, old leather, like musty leather. I thought someone was just playing a trick on me, because sometimes the spirits will do that. They think they'll scare you, they'll do things like that to you. I turned around to my right and I looked to see, but it was still dark, and there was this real old man. He was old and his hair was long and gray. When I turned to look, he was standing looking at me, bending over. He had an old cane in his right hand. I turned away from him, 'cause he scared me, 'cause his hair was long, hanging down, but he didn't look ugly, he was just a really old, old man. I thought, maybe it's just my imagination, 'cause I'd never seen nothing like that, but I could smell the leather, it was so strong. Pretty soon, real slow, he said to me, "Who are you? Why are you sitting here like this?" I didn't answer him. He asked me again. I didn't know what to do, I didn't know who he was, and I didn't want to answer. What if he was just a spirit—you know, one of those "Iktomi" spirits that'll fool you? I thought, if I answer him, then he'll take me, something will happen to me, he'll take me, I may never come back. So I didn't answer him. He said, "Well, sit there then," and he didn't say anything mean or ugly, he just said in Indian, "Just sit there." I could hear him walk on over the hill and that's a steep hill, and I could hear him walking up that hill just as easy as you please, and I could hear his cane, every once in a while it hit a rock or he'd push it down in the dirt. He went into the water, 'cause there was a creek right there, and he just disappeared.

By that time it was getting to be morning, it was getting to be daylight, and I thought I heard some voices. I looked up, I looked around, but I didn't hear anything. All of a sudden, I heard this song. These people were singing this song, and I never heard this song before. It was an Indian song, but it wasn't a Sun Dance song, it wasn't a ceremony song, it was an Indian song I never heard before. That was up the creek a ways and there was a house there. I thought, well, maybe that's a peyote song because I never heard one of those before and maybe those people up there were having a peyote ceremony. That's what I thought, and I listened, but it got louder and louder, like it was coming closer and closer. It lasted for a while, maybe half an hour. By that time it was getting light, so I thought to myself, if it really gets light, I can see who these people are that are coming closer and that are singing. I waited and I watched, but it got more daylight and more daylight and they stopped singing and nobody came over the hill. So I thought, well, maybe they went back to that house over there, maybe they just did something this way and then went back up north to that house. I waited and it got really light and I waited to see the cars, 'cause it was daylight and you could see the house and there was only one car there and no movement. There were no people there. I could never figure that out, why did strange music come, why did I hear that? It was really different. You could tell it was a ceremonial song and it just continued and continued, but I could never understand what it meant. That was the third thing that happened.

After it got to be daylight, it was getting toward early morning, and you could see everything, it was just nice and bright. There was a big pine tree in front of me, facing the west. I was looking at the pine tree and I was still praying for the things that I saw and the things that I heard, and I was thankful that I made it through this night. I had till the evening to go, so I needed strength because it was gonna be hot that day, it was July. I just prayed and all of a sudden, out of nowhere, a huge eagle came from the west and circled four times. Each time he circled he came closer and closer to me. I was thankful to see this big eagle. He came really close to the tree and just like that he became tiny, like the size of a butterfly, and he just vanished. He just vanished. The butterfly was just this small eagle then. I thought that was amazing and I was glad, I was thankful, and that was four things and the circle was complete.

I'm deathly afraid of coyotes, and all the evening before we were put up, you could hear the coyotes. One of the elderly women said to me, "Oh, they're hungry." They were just teasing us, those elderly people. "When you girls sit up there, they're gonna come up and sniff you and see if you have anything to eat." We had bowls, I had a bowl of dried cherries and dried meat and dried fat, and you mix it all together and you put it there and you offer that to the spirits. The coyotes could have that if they wanted, but that's part of the ceremony. You need to put that out there. We heard these coyotes before anything ever happened, but when I was up there, I didn't hear one. I never saw one that night, not during the day either, but during the afternoon, after the sun started passing toward the west, I heard a whole bunch of coyotes way to the south. One of the girls said they were chasing cattle that were back there close to where she was. She said all night they were close to her and they were howling, and she was just over on the next hill past the ravine. She could see them and hear them, but I couldn't hear them, and I was so thankful for that—I probably would have got up and ran. The spirits test you. That was one thing that I was thankful for—that they didn't test me with that coyote. One thing my grandmother used to say when I was a child was, "If you're not good, them coyotes are gonna come and get you." All night long you could hear them outside.

That day it was so hot. There were clouds so that it seemed like it shaded just where I sat. I got sunburned, but I didn't feel the heat. The wind was so nice, it was just so breezy. During that afternoon, Titus and this other girl came up and they gave me some medicine, and he said the spirits asked him to bring that up to me. I wasn't having a hard time. I wasn't thirsty, I wasn't sleepy, I wasn't tired, and I wasn't hot either. I didn't need the sage to put in my mouth, and he gave me something else to put in my mouth if my mouth got too dry, but that never happened. But he said, "Take this medicine." I had to face the north and he put it into my mouth, and it was bitter and nasty-tasting. He said, "You're going to throw up, but you have to do that. Whatever it is that's in you, it has to come out. Don't throw up where you're sitting, bend over in the corner, throw up right there." I thought, I won't throw up, I'll be all right. Not too long after he left, my stomach really felt funny. I was praying to the spirits to help me. Pretty soon I felt that I couldn't hold it in anymore, so I still held my pipe and I put the blanket down and I leaned over the tobacco ties, and everything just came out. After it came out, I felt like I was not alive. I felt like I was light, like there was nothing heavy in me. Even after we got back down to the sweat and went through the sweat and were going to eat, I still felt light, and I didn't have any pain. I never asked, "Why did they tell you to do that?" I never questioned Titus, I just believed that it was something that was to be done.

There isn't that much difference for a woman and a man in the Vision Quest. It comes to you, like something kept telling me, there's things that I have to do, there's things that should be done, and why are you waiting, what are you waiting for? These come to you like in dreams, like I'll just be sitting there and no one's around and someone'll call me, and I'll look. I'll look in that direction just as plain as day, and there's no one. A lot of different things, a lot of little things add up. Someone'd call me and I'd get up and I'd say, "What?" They'd say, "Remember you had something to do? Did you forget?" They'd always talk to me in Indian, never talk to me in English. I wouldn't understand it at first so I'd pray about it in Indian, get tobacco out and make tobacco ties and ask for an answer, ask them to show me what it is I should do. They'd show me little pictures, like a filmstrip, right in front of my eyes, just one right after the other, and I could see myself doing different things, and the Vision Quest was one of them. I said, I can't believe this, this is too hard for me, but they would wake me up at night, and I would see these little pictures go by. So I stopped being afraid and I said, "Okay, I'll do it, 'cause that's what's important and I need to do that and it's going to help someone, plus I'm going to be helped. It's gonna be hard and I don't even know how to do some of those things, but I'll do it."

Roberta Hill

O N E I D A

I write for myself to discover what the energies beyond my mundane life, my daily consciousness, have to share. I want to be alive to the moment, smack up in my face and on as many levels as I can tune into. I write for the people I've met in this world, for all the people I love—husband, children, lovers, relatives, and those who have passed on. I respond to the fires and rainstorms other writers have led me to feel and remember. I write to encourage feeling for the awesome beauty and deep mystery of life on earth. We have the responsibility to ensure life continues in a good way.

To Rose

My sister, between us lie
fifteen rivers and a race track
and the weather here is snow and more
the same. Just when we thought
spring came, the rain grew fat
and fell twinkling on the muddy fields.

You always wanted to bear
the biggest burdens and took them
in your easy stride as you laughed
and cried against their weight.

Now your heart and body must meander
in another mode, so you can live,
my dear one. Toss your list
in a river and head east
for a while. Yes,
we've been dispossessed, but our dreams
keep strong our effort
to resist oppression.

Because you have the same spirit
as summer flowers, the land here
won't wake without you, Rose.
The sumac remains sullen
and his velvet buds can't break.
New songs can't struggle
against this constant snow.
Come home to the lakes
that love you. Flashing
waves will make you raise
your arms and shout with joy.
Come to ridges and fields
for the time
it takes to heal your heart.

Salli M. K. Benedict

AKWESASNE MOHAWK

My Mohawk name is Kawen-
notakie. It means "She carries a good word, or brings a good
word." My folks used to joke and say it meant "She walks as

she talks—in short, walkie-talkie." They named me well . . .
I talked and walked pretty early, and since the time that I
could talk . . . I was a storyteller.

Elders told me stories, and I would repeat them carefully
to others with my own animation and color. I'm sure that it
amused them, to watch me repeat their words. I didn't know
what shy was then. That's where they got to see their words
and wisdom transmitted to a successive generation. For me, it
was fun to tell traditional stories to others. I got lots of atten-
tion and praise and I felt like a wise old five-year-old who
knew everything in the whole world . . . Yep! . . . had the
whole world figured out by the ripe old age of five.

In my life, I have seen the importance of the transmission
of culture from one generation to another. I'm part of the
generation that got to see the Mohawk language just about
disappear. I had the language till about the time I started
school. For me the language is still in the pictures of a five-
year-old. When I hear the Mohawk language, I don't translate
the words, I interpret the images. For me the language is im-
agery and color. It is poetry in its most natural state. I would
say it's pretty much cheating to translate Mohawk words or
ideas into English . . . Because presto! . . . It's poetry. It's much
prettier than English. English seems to have lost its roots, and
people have to work at it more, to get up images and the color
and the beauty.

The Serpent Story

Many many years ago, when there was still much magic in the
world . . . and the waters of many rivers were crystal clear . . .

There lived a lady water serpent . . .

To the Mohawk people she was known as an "Oniarekowa." They
named her Tsiakotsiakwin. Few had ever seen the water serpent,
but those who had talked about her great beauty.

She was a very beautiful creature and she possessed many magical powers. She used her power to make the underwater world beautiful, and to make the underwater people and its creatures happy.

Even though the water serpent had many underwater friends to keep her company, she was very lonely.

She was the only water serpent in the whole world and longed to have a friend of her own kind.

One day two Mohawk men who lived near the river got into their boat. They were Teharasakwa and Skaroniati.

It was a beautiful day, and the sun's reflection sparkled on the water.

They caught many fish by the end of the day. Teharasakwa loved and respected the water and its beings. He always gave thanks to the Creator for the fish he caught.

He pulled out his pipe and his sacred tobacco to smoke and to give thanks.

Then the calm motion of the water made him daydream. He thought about what it would be like if he had been made a water serpent by the Creator. And he thought about what it would be like to live underwater with the underwater beings in their beautiful world.

Just as he was about to put his pipe away, it flew out of his hands and into the water.

The water was very clear, so when he looked down he could see his pipe sitting on a log. He thought that he could reach it. So he bent down over the side of his boat to pick it up.

It was so much deeper than he thought. As he stretched to reach for it, he felt his body being pulled into the water.

Down he went into the underwater world. It was beautiful! He looked around for his pipe and saw that it was being held by the beautiful water serpent.

He thought that she was a beautiful creature, but he could see the great loneliness in her eyes.

He wondered how she was able to stay underwater for such a long time. The lady water serpent knew what he was thinking. She told him to breathe underwater. He was overcome with her charm and beauty and the world around him.

She told him that she had heard his daydream and decided to give him the chance to see what it was like. She then asked him to stay with her in her world. He had fallen in love with the water world, its beings, and the lady water serpent. But he could not decide to leave his old world and friends.

With every change of decision in this magic world, his body changed. He changed from man to water serpent, and then from serpent to man, as he tried to make up his mind.

Finally, he told her that he should go back to the surface to live because his friend was probably very worried about him.

So he changed back into a man and swam to the top.

He was almost to the boat where his friend waited when he thought again how nice it would be to live in this enchanted world with the lovely water serpent.

With the thought, his body changed into a water serpent as it had before.

He dismissed the thought from his mind and continued to the top. He did not know that his body did not have time to change back to normal. He broke the surface of the water and called out his friend's name: "Skaroniati," he said.

Skaroniati turned to the sound of Teharasakwa's voice but he stared into the eyes of a male water serpent.

Teharasakwa looked at the fear in his friend's face and then looked at himself. He did not belong in his old world with his new body.

He said to his friend, "I am Teharasakwa . . . your friend. Let no one use my name. It is no longer the name of a man. It is now the name of a water serpent.

"I am returning to live in a new and wonderful world. I will be happy there."

So Teharasakwa returned to join the lady water serpent, to live there the rest of his life.

Luci Tapahonso

NAVAJO

I was born in Shiprock, New Mexico, where I lived until my early twenties. I grew up in a large, extended household in which Navajo was the primary language. Though I am now in a predominantly English-

functioning environment, I consider Navajo language to be the undercurrent, the matrix through which everything in my life filters through. It is the language that soothes, comforts, and it cradles the extremes of expression—sheer happiness and unbearable grief. Yet English is the language we must use to function in American society. Writing is, at times, an exhilarating challenge because I must, as near as possible, find the English version of what are essentially Navajo concepts or expressions. It is the beauty of the Navajo language—the sounds, the pauses, the rhythm of songs, prayers, conversation, and oratory—that infuses every aspect of my daily life, and provides sustenance away from the Navajo community. Writing is a way of sharing the memories and voices of family and relatives, and a way of survival. It is, at once, selfish, and it is also a celebration of and a sharing with others the nurturing sense of equanimity that the traditional Navajo lifestyle is rooted in.

As an English professor, my community is made up of students, colleagues, and the city of Lawrence, Kansas; my community is also that of my mother's and father's relatives, my siblings' children, my own children and their children, and that of the Navajo people, and the history and beliefs we represent.

What Danger We Court

Sister, sister,
what danger we court   .
without even knowing it.
It's as simple as meeting a handsome man
for lunch at midnight.

Last Friday night
at the only stop sign for miles around,
your pickup was hit from behind.
That noise of shattering glass behind your head,

whirl of lights and metal as two cars hit your pickup—
the silent frenzy by tons of metal spinning you
echoes the desert left voiceless.

Sister, sister,
what promises there must be for you
when you walk the edges of cliffs—
sheer drops like 400 feet—
vacuums of nothing we know here.
You turn and step out of the crushed car dazed
and walk to help small crying children from another car
and you come home, sister,
                    your breath intact,
                    heart pounding
                    and the night is still the same.

Your children cry and cry to see you
walking and speaking gently,
                    your voice gathers them in.

                    What danger we court.

It is the thin border of a miracle, sister, that you live,
The desert surrounding your house is a witness
to the danger we court and

                    sister, we have so much faith.

Marla Big Boy

OGLALA LAKOTA · CHEYENNE

I was born on the Pine Ridge Reservation in South Dakota. My mother is a Blackhorse. My grandmother is from the Conroy family. My great-grandmother, a Conroy, descends from Crazy Horse. My father is a Big Boy from Kyle, South Dakota. The Big Boys are the green-eyed full-bloods. My Aunt Louise said the light eyes come from a red-haired Frenchman five generations ago who married a full-blood, whose children then married full-bloods.

I am an Indian woman with two children. I write to tell stories for my children. My children are the continuation of my family. My poetry is inspired in part by my family because it helps me explain who I am and where I've come from.

I write to release emotions in a safe place. To heal myself by seizing ideas and turning them into events that develop into what I want. Writing is therapeutic to me.

There is an Oglala saying that the family is as strong as its women. I want my writing to capture the strength, the love, and the tenacity of women.

"I Will Bring You Twin Grays" is about two fictional persons, Delia and her sister. They portray the Lakota women I've heard in oral stories my grandfather told me about women who lived a long, long time ago. Delia and her sister live in pre-contact time. "Pre-contact" refers to the time before the invasion of the white people. Intertribal war was common and taking women prisoners showed the captor's courage. Sometimes the captured women integrated into the family and *sometimes they escaped and went home. These women were strong then and we are strong now.*

I Will Bring You Twin Grays

When the Osages captured you at the stream
I cried
You were snatched by a raiding party of no-good Osages
Delia, my sister
At morning I prayed for you
to have a warm fire and plenty to eat
An orange sunrise recaptured the stars like
I'm going to recapture you, my sister
        The spirits will protect you in Osage country

Gramma and I sang a traveling song for you
Father prepared the pipe
        I will bring you Twin Grays

            Mom said an Osage will slit a Sioux throat just
            to show they are better than us

Grampa named you after his mother
He said you have her laughing eyes
Her soothing voice
        Gentle singing brings tears to his tired eyes

Whirlwind Chaser came back and brought the news
You were given to a man who needed a wife
Skilled and industrious
Be a smart wife and bead him a leather belt
Show him you are a loyal captive
When trading season comes he'll want you there
So he can get a new blanket

I will finish quilling a dress to match your starry eyes
To trade for Twin Grays as fast as lightning
Horses that really go
Then I'll come to bring you home
My sister

Luci Tapahonso

NAVAJO

All the Colors of Sunset

Even after all this time, when I look back at all that happened, I don't know if I would do anything differently. That summer morning seemed like any other. The sun came up over the mountain around seven or so, and when I went to throw the coffee grounds out, I put the pouch of corn pollen in my apron pocket so that I could pray before I came inside.

During the summers, we sleep most nights in the *chaha'oh*, the shadehouse, unless it rains. I remembered early that morning I had heard loud voices yelling and they seemed to come from the north. Whoever it was quieted quickly, and I fell asleep. Right outside the *chaha'oh*, I knew the dogs were alert—their ears erect and eyes glistening. Out here near Rockpoint, where we live, it's so quiet and isolated that we can hear things from a far distance. It's mostly desert and the huge rocks nearby, *tsé ahił ah neeé*, whale rock and the other rocks, seem to bounce noises into the valley. People live far apart and there are no streetlights nearby. The nights are quiet, except for animal and bird noises, and the sky is always so black. In the Navajo way, they say the night sky is made of black jet, and that the folding darkness comes from the north. Sometimes in the evenings, I think of this when the sun is setting, and all the bright colors fall somewhere into the west. Then I let the beauty of the sunset go, and my sadness along with it.

That morning I fixed a second pot of coffee, and peeled potatoes to fry. Just as I finished slicing the potatoes, I thought I heard my grandbaby cry. I went out and looked out toward my daughter's home. She lives across the arroyo a little over a mile away. I shaded my eyes and squinted—the sun was in her direction. Finally, I went inside and finished fixing breakfast. We were going to go into Chinle that afternoon, so I didn't go over to their house.

Later that morning, I was polishing some pieces of jewelry when I heard my daughter crying outside. My heart quickened. I rushed to the door and she practically fell inside the house. She was carrying the baby in her cradleboard and could hardly talk—she was sobbing and screaming so. I grabbed the baby, knowing she was hurt. When I looked at my granddaughter, I knew the terrible thing that had happened. Her little face was so pale and wet from crying. I could not think or speak—somehow I found my way to the south wall of the hooghan and sat down, still holding my sweet baby. My first and only grandchild was gone.

I held her close and nuzzled her soft neck. I sang over and over the little songs that I always sang to her. I unwrapped her and touched slowly, slowly every part of her little smooth body. I wanted to remember every sweet detail and said aloud each name like I had always done, "*Díí nijáád wolyé, sho'wéé.*" This is called your leg, my baby. I asked her, "*Nits'iiyah sha'?*" and nuzzled the back of her neck like before. "*Jo ka i.*" This time she did not giggle and laugh. I held her and rocked, and sang, and talked to her.

The pollen pouch was still in my pocket, and I put a bit into her mouth as I would have done when her first tooth came in. I put a pinch of pollen on her head as I would have done when she first left for kindergarten. I put a pinch of pollen in her little hands as I would have done when she was given her first lamb, as I would have done when she was given her own colt. This way she would have been gentle and firm with her pets. I brushed her with an eagle feather as I would have done when she graduated from junior high. All this and so much more that could have been swept over me as I sat there leaning over my little grandbaby.

She was almost five months old, and had just started to recognize me. She cried for me to hold her and I tried to keep her with me as much as I could. Sometimes I took her for long walks and showed her everything, and told her little stories about the birds and animals we saw. She would fall asleep on our way home, and still I hummed and sang softly. I couldn't stop singing. For some reason, when she was born, I was given so much time for her. I guess that's how it is with grandparents. I wasn't ever too busy to care for her. When my daughter took her home, my house seemed so empty and quiet.

They said that I kept the baby for four hours that morning. My daughter left and then returned with her husband. They were afraid to bother me in my grief. I don't remember much of it. I didn't know how I acted, or maybe that was the least of what I was conscious of. My daughter said later that I didn't say one word to her. I don't remember.

Finally, I got up and gave the baby to them so they could go to the hospital at Chinle. I followed in my own truck, and there the doctor confirmed her death, and we began talking about what we had to do next. Word spread quickly. When I went to buy some food at Basha's, several people comforted me and helped me with the shopping. My sisters and two aunts were at my home when I returned. They had straightened up the house, and were cooking already. Some of my daughters-in-law were cooking and getting things ready in the *chaha'oh* outside. By that evening, the house and the *chaha'oh* were filled with people—our own relatives, clan relatives, friends from school, church, and the baby's father's kin. People came and held me, comforting me and murmuring their sympathies. They cried with me, and brought me plates of food. I felt like I was in a daze—I hardly spoke. I tried to help cook and serve, but was gently guided back to the armchair that had somehow become "my chair" since that morning.

There were meetings each day, and various people stood up to counsel and advise everyone who was there, including my daughter and her husband. When everything was done, and we had washed our faces and started over again, I couldn't seem to focus on things. Before all this happened, I was very busy each day—cooking, sewing, taking out the horses sometimes, feeding the animals, and often just visiting with people. One of my children or my sisters always came by and we would talk and laugh while I continued my tasks. Last winter was a good year for piñons so I was still cleaning and roasting the many flour sackfuls we had picked. At Many Farms junction, some people from Shiprock had a truckload of the sweetest corn I had ever tasted, so I bought plenty and planned to make *ntsidigodí* and other kinds of cornbread. We would have these tasty delicacies to eat in the winter. We liked to remember summer by the food we had stored and preserved.

When we were little, my mother taught all of us girls to weave, but I hadn't touched a loom in years. When I became a grandmother, I began to think of teaching some of the old things to my baby. Maybe it was my age, but I remembered a lot of the things we were told. Maybe it was that I was alone more than I had ever been—my children were grown. My husband passed on five years ago, and since I was by myself and I had enough on which to live, I stopped working at a paying job.

After all this happened, I resumed my usual tasks and tried to stay busy so that my grandbaby's death wouldn't overwhelm me. I didn't cry or grieve out loud because they say that one can call the dead back by doing that. Yet so much had changed, and it was as if I was far away from everything. Some days I fixed a lunch and took the sheep out for the day and returned as the sun was going down. And when I came back inside, I realized that I hadn't spoken to the animals all day. It seemed strange, and yet I just didn't feel like talking. The dogs would follow me around, wanting attention —for me to throw a stick for them, or talk to them—then after a while they would just lie down and watch me. Once I cleaned and roasted a pan of piñons perfectly without thinking about it. It's a wonder that I didn't burn myself. A few weeks later, we had to brand some colts, and give the horses shots, so everyone got together and we spent the day at the corral in the dust and heat. Usually it was a happy and noisy time, but that day was quieter than usual. At least we had taken care of everything.

Sometimes I dreamt of my grandbaby, and it was as if nothing had happened. In my dreams, I carried her around, singing and talking to her. She smiled and giggled at me. When I awoke, it was as if she had been lying beside me, kicking and reaching around. A small space beside me would be warm, and her scent faint. These dreams seemed so real. I looked forward to sleeping because maybe in sleeping I might see her. On the days following such a dream, I would replay it over and over in my mind, still smiling and humming to her the next morning. By afternoon, the activity and noise had usually worn the dream off.

I heard after the funeral that people were whispering and asking questions about what had happened. It didn't bother me. Nothing anyone said or did would bring my sweet baby back—that was clear. I never asked my daughter how it happened. After the baby's death, she and her husband became very quiet and they were together so much, they seemed like shadows of each other. Her husband worked at different jobs, and she just went with him and waited in the pickup until he was through. He worked with horses, helped build hooghans, corrals, and other construction work. When she came over and spent the afternoon with me, we hardly talked. We both knew we were more comfortable that way. As usual, she hugged me each time before she left. I knew she was in great pain.

Once, when I was at Basha's shopping for groceries, a woman I didn't know said to me, "You have a pretty grandbaby." I smiled and didn't reply. I noticed that she didn't say "*yée*" at the end of "*nitsóíh*" which would have meant "the grandbaby who is no longer alive." That happened at other places, and I didn't respond, except to smile. I thought it was good that people remembered her.

About four months after her death, we were eating at my house when my sisters gathered around me and told me they were very worried about me. They thought I was still too grief-stricken over the baby, and that it was not healthy. "You have to go on," they said, "let her go." They said they wanted the "old me" back, so I agreed to go for help.

We went to a medicine woman near Ganado, and she asked me if I could see the baby sometimes. No, I said, except in dreams.

"Has anyone said they've seen her?" she asked. I said that I didn't think so. Then she said, "Right now, I see the baby beside you." I was so startled that I began looking around for her.

"The baby hasn't left," she said, "she wants to stay with you." I couldn't see my grandbaby. Then I realized that other people could see what the medicine woman had just seen. No wonder, I thought, that sometimes when I woke, I could feel her warm body beside me. She said the baby was wrapped in white.

She couldn't help me herself, but she told me to see another medicine person near Lukaichakai. She said that the ceremony I needed was very old and that she didn't know it herself. The man she recommended was elderly and very knowledgeable and so it was likely that he would know the ceremony, or would at least know of someone who did.

Early in the morning, we went to his house west of Many Farms—word had already been sent that we were coming. The ceremony lasted for four days and three nights, and parts of songs and prayers had such ancient sacred words I wasn't sure if I understood them. When the old man prayed and sang, sometimes tears streamed down my face as I repeated everything after him— word for word, line for line, late into the night—and we would begin again at daybreak the next morning. I was exhausted and so relieved. I finally realized what my grief had done. I could finally let my grandbaby go.

We were lucky that we had found this old man because the ceremony had not been done in almost eighty years. He had seen it as a little boy and had memorized all the parts of it—the songs, the advice, the prayers, and the literal letting go of the dead spirit. Over time, it has become a rare ceremony, because what I had done in holding and keeping the baby for those hours was not in keeping with the Navajo way. I understood that doing so had upset the balance of life and death. When we left, we were all crying. I thanked the old man for his memory, his life, and his ability to help us when no one else could. I understand now that all of life has ceremonies connected with it, and for us, without our memory, our old people, and our children, we would be like lost people in this world we live in, as well as in the other worlds in which our loved ones are waiting.

A. A. Hedge Coke

CHEROKEE ▮ HURON

I am a mixed Canadian: Native Huron and Tsalagi (North Carolina), French Canadian and Portuguese. I grew up mostly in North Carolina but also in Canada during the summers. We stayed with various relatives in other areas as well and I spent a great deal of time in South Dakota.

I have gone from working in the fields of tobacco in North Carolina and sweet potatoes to working for an international Indian organization based in Los Angeles. I have had a very varied life. Two things which affected me a lot are my father's belief in traditional values and my mother's insanity. I still deal with this in my work as it is still a big part of my life.

I always wrote. As soon as I could write words, I used them in different ways to describe my feelings, observances, and experiences. I often felt like a witness as a child and wrote volumes which I never showed to anyone hoping that someone would find them when I died. I believed I would die very young given the circumstances of my youth and my extreme close calls *with death. These included reactions to local anesthetics and antibiotics, attempts made on my life by people very close to me, and severe automobile wrecks. I lived in battering situations as a child and as an adult. I am lucky to be alive now.*

A lot of my work also deals with abuse and its effects on the psyche. We have to stop this current before it floods our very existence. I believe in change. Some we experience through no fault of our own and others we create as a means of correction. The latter part of change is often a direct result of the former.

The Change

Thirteen years ago,   before bulk barns and
fifth-gear diesel tractors,
we rode royal blue tractors with
tool boxes big enough   to hold a six-pack on ice
In the one-hundred-fifteen-degree   summer
heat   with air   so thick with moisture
you drink as you breathe.
Before the year dusters sprayed
malathion over our clustered bodies,   perspiring
while we primed bottom lugs,
those ground-level leaves of tobacco,
and it clung to us with black tar so sticky we rolled
eight-inch balls off our arms at night and
Cloroxed our clothes for hours and hours.
Before we were poisoned   and
the hospital thought we had been burned in fires,
at least to the third degree,
when the raw, oozing hives that
covered ninety-eight percent of our bodies
from the sprays ordered by the F.D.A.
and spread by   land owners,
before anyone had seen

automated machines that top and prime.
While we topped the lavender
blooms of many tiny flowers
gathered into one,   gorgeous.
By grasping hold below the petals
with our bare, calloused hands
and twisting downward, quick, hard,
only one time,   snapped it off.
Before edgers and herbicides took
what *they* call weeds,
when we walked for days
through thirty acres and
chopped them out with hoes.
Hoes, made long before   from wood and steel
and sometimes (even longer ago)
from wood and deer scapula.
Before the bulk primers came
and we primed all the leaves by hand,
stooped over at the waist for the
lower ones   and through the season
gradually   rising higher   until   we stood
and worked simultaneously,
carrying up to fifty pounds of fresh
leaves under each arm and sewing it onto
sticks four feet long on a looper   under the
shade of a tin-roofed barn,   made of shingle,
and poking it up through the rafters inside
to be caught by a hanger   who
poked it up higher in the rafters   to another
who held a higher position
and   so   they filled the barn.
And the leaves hung down
like butterfly wings,   though
sometimes the color of
luna moths,   or Carolina parakeets,   when just
an hour ago   they had been

laid upon   the old wooden
cart trailers pulled behind
the orange Allis-Chalmer tractor
with huge, round fenders and only
a screwdriver and salt in the toolbox,
picked by primers so hot
we would race through the rows
to reach the twenty-five-gallon
jugs of water placed throughout
the field to encourage and in attempt to
satisfy our insatiable thirsts
from drinking air which poured
through our pores without breaking
through to our need   for more
water   in the sun.
Sun we imagined to disappear
yet respected   for growing all things on earth
when quenched with rains called forth
by our song and drumming.
Leaves, which, weeks later, would be
taken down and the strings pulled
like string on top of a large dog food bag
and sheeted up into burlap sheets
that bundled over a hundred pounds
when we smashed down with our feet,
but gently smashing,
then thrown up high to
a catcher on a big clapboard trailer
pulled behind two-ton trucks and
taken to market in Fuquay-Varina
and sold to William Morris and
Winston-Salem   for around   a buck a pound.
Leaves cured to a bright leaf,
a golden yellow with the strongest
aroma of tobacco barn curing
and hand-grown quality

before the encroachment of
big business in the Reagan era
and the slow murder of method
from a hundred years before.
When the loons cried out in
laughter by the springs and
the bass popped the surface on
the pond, early on, next to
the fields,   before that time
when it was unfashionable to
transplant each individual baby plant,
the infant tobacco we nurtured, to
transplant those seedlings to each hill
in the field,   the space for that particular plant
and we watched   as   they would grow.
Before all of this new age, new way,
I was a sharecropper in Willow Springs, North Carolina
as were you   and we   were proud to be Tsa la gi
wishing for winter   so we could make camp
at Qualla Boundary   and Oconaluftee
would be free of tourists and filled with snow
and those of us who held out forever
and had no C.I.B.s would be home again
with our people,   while the B.I.A. forgot to watch.
When we still remembered that before   even the Europeans,
working now shoulder to shoulder with descendants
of their slaves they brought from Africa
when they sold our ancestors   as slaves   in the Middle East.
Then the tobacco was sacred to all of us   and we
prayed whenever we smoked   and
did not smoke for pleasure   and
I   was   content and free.
Then they came and changed things
and you left me for a fancy white girl
and I waited on the land
until you brought her back

in that brand-new white Trans Am,
purchased from our crop,   you gave her
and left her waiting in a motel,
the nearest one was forty miles away,
but   near enough   for you
and   for her   and I knew though
I never spoke a word to you
about it, I knew and I kept it to
myself to this day   and time   and
I never let on
until I left   on our anniversary.
I drove the pickup
down the dirt path   by the empty fields
and rented a shack for eighty dollars
the one with cardboard windows
and a gillespi house floor design,
with torn and faded floral paper on walls
and linoleum so thin   over rotted board
that the floor gave if you weighed over
a hundred pounds,   I did not.
With no running water of any kind,   or bathroom.
The one at hilltop,   where I could
see out across all the fields
and hunt for meat when I wanted
and find peace.   I hear you remarried
and went into automated farming
and kept up   with America.
I watched all of you   from the hill
and I waited for the lavender blooms
to return   and when it was spring
even the blooms   had turned white.
I rolled up my bedroll,   remembering before
when the fields were like waves on a green ocean,
and turned away,   away from the change
and corruption of big business on small farms
of traditional agricultural people,   and sharecroppers.

Away,   so that I could always   hold this concise image
of before   that   time   and it
floods my memory.

Linda Hogan

CHICKASAW

For me, the act of writing comes
out of my deepest wanting of justice and survival. I began
writing with a sense of urgency about stories that were begging
to be told. I wanted to speak the value of human beings, and
the absolute significance of all the rest of living nature, to show
others that everything is alive and worthy of care. As a Chick-
asaw, I feel committed to the telling of Indian story, culling
the lies out of history to find what is beneath them, and then
speaking those found truths. I consider this writing the work
of the heart and I am still hopeful enough to think the world
might be changed by the words and the telling.

Skin

The men wore human skins
but removed them at night
and fell to the bottom of darkness
like crows without wings.

War was the perfect disguise.
Their mothers would not have known them,
and the swarming flies could not find them.

When they met a spirit in the forest
it thought they were bags of misfortune
and walked away
without taking their lives.

In this way,
they tricked the deer.
It had wandered into the forest at night,
thinking antlers of trees
were other deer.

If I told you the deer was a hide of light
you wouldn't believe it, or that it was a hunting song
that walked out of a diviner's bag
sewn from human skin.
It knew it could pass
through the bodies of men and could return.
It knew the arrow belonged to the bow,
and that men only think they are following
the deaths of animals
or other men
when they are walking into the fire.

That's why fire is restless
and smoke has become
the escaped wings of crows,
why war is only another skin,
and hunting,
and why men are just the pulled-back curve of the bow.

Dana Naone Hall

NATIVE HAWAIIAN

"Looking for Signs" has to do with an old coastal road in the Makena area of Maui. This road helped to focus Native Hawaiian concerns about what is essential in maintaining Hawaiian culture.

Four hundred years ago, the ruler of the Island of Hawai'i, 'Umi-a-Liloa, advised the Maui chief Kiha-a-Pi'ilani to undertake a project that would benefit the people. Kiha-a-Pi'ilani's response was to build a road that circled the Island of Maui.

It gives me deep and abiding pleasure to write the words "four hundred years ago" in order to relate a story from the long tradition of our people; and it gives me a deep and abiding sense of belonging to this place when I walk or drive on the sections of Alaloa, attributed to Kiha-a-Pi'ilani, that still exist today. I think of those whose names are no longer known to us, who shaped and fixed in place on steep slopes the ancient road, and who walked before me on the sandy dunes carrying nets and gourds full of water.

We are continually imagining the past, what it was like for our ancestors fifty years, ninety years, more than a thousand years ago. Sometimes the past is made visible as in the presence of the old road, and our use of the road is a way of preserving a link to an older part of ourselves and keeping open a way of being in the future.

Looking for Signs

Aunty Alice said it first
there had been ho'ailona
ever since we took up
trying to keep the old road
from being closed in Makena
on the island where Maui
caught the sun in his rope.
The foreign owners of a half-built
hotel don't want their guests
to taste the dust
of our ancestors in the road.
They want them to step
from the bright green clash
of hotel grass to sandy beach
and the moon shining on a rocky coast.
The last hukilau in that place was ten years ago,
but people still remember
the taste of the fish and the limu
that they gathered on the shore.
When tutu gets sick
the only thing that brings her back
is the taste of the ocean
in soup made from the small
black eyes of the pipipi.
In her dreams opihi
are growing fat on the rocks.
She is old and small now
in her bed above the blue ocean
wrapped in the veil of her dream
like the uhu asleep
after a day of grinding coral into sand.
It was at this house one Sunday
that relatives who stayed home from church
saw a cloud of dragonflies appear

over the ocean and fly through the windows.
Higher up the mountain someone else
dreamed of seeing Pele's canoe
on the water the red sail of Honua'ula
coming toward land.
One weekend the family slept
at another beach along the old road—
the old road that is the old trail.
Uncle Charley took us all to the heiau
mauka of the beach.
From the beginning he has said
the road will not be closed.
When we came back,
Ed, one of the boys from Hana,
was standing in the shallow water
sending the sound of the conch shell
and the winding breath of the nose flute
across the channel to Kaho'olawe
through the ear of Molokini.
Later, we listened
to Uncle Harry joke with the kupuna.
Tutu was there and she stayed
all night sleeping in the sand
with the 'aumakua all around.
The mo'o clucked in the kiawe,
while pueo flew through the dark
cutting across the path
of the falling stars,
and mano ate all the fish but one
in the net that Leslie laid.
As for us,
what is our connection to Makena?
You pointed out that we live on
one of three great rifts out of which
lava poured in ages past
to form the mysterious beauty of Haleakala.

Two gaps press in on the rim of the mountain
like a pitcher with two spouts.
Ko'olau separates us from Hana
and Kaupo divides Hana and Makena,
but there is no gap between us
and Makena lying at the bottom of the youngest rift, where the
sweet potato vines covered the ground.
This morning, coming back along the coast
on our side of the island
where the road bends at Ho'okipa,
I saw a cloud shaped like a pyramid
and a car driving out of the sun.

Mary Brave Bird

LAKOTA

In 1973, inside Wounded Knee, during the siege, volunteers set up a clinic. Mostly this was the work of our women. There were frequent firefights and as a result we had a number of people with gunshot wounds. I remember a sign tacked to the wall of our homemade "hospital": Bleeding Always Stops If You Press Down. *This was meant literally, but for me it was symbolic—in my mind Indian women are always pressing down hard to stop the bleeding of their hearts. It is not easy to be a native woman. I am proud of Indian women, proud of their courage in adversity, for holding the tribes together. After five hundred years of being held in subjection, we are finally standing up on our hind legs. Together with my sisters from many tribes, I am a birth-giver,*

*a rebirth-giver, fighting to ensure a life for unborn generations.
I am a Sioux woman!*

We AIM Not to Please

They call us the New Indians.
Hell, we are the Old Indians,
the landlords of this continent,
coming to collect the rent.

— DENNIS BANKS

The American Indian Movement hit our reservation like a tornado, like a new wind blowing out of nowhere, a drumbeat from far off getting louder and louder. It was almost like the Ghost Dance fever that had hit the tribes in 1890, old Uncle Dick Fool Bull said, spreading like a prairie fire. It was like the old Ghost Dance song Uncle Dick was humming:

> Maka sitomniya teca ukiye
> Oyate ukiye, oyate ukiye . . .
> A new world is coming,
> A nation is coming,
> The eagle brought the message.

I could feel this new thing, almost hear it, smell it, touch it. Meeting up with AIM for the first time loosened a sort of earthquake inside me. Old Black Elk in recounting his life often used the expression "As I look down from the high hill of my great old age . . ." Well, as I am looking from the hill of my old age—I am thirty-seven now but feel as if I have lived for a long time—I can see things in perspective, not subjectively, no, but in perspective. Old Black Elk had a good way of saying it. You really look back upon ten years gone past as from a hill—you have a sort of bird's-eye view. I recognize now that movements get used up and the leaders get burned out quickly. Some of our men and women got themselves killed and thereby avoided reaching the dangerous age of thirty and becoming "elder statesmen." Some leaders turned into college professors, founded alternative schools, or even took jobs as tribal officials. A few live on in the past, refusing to recognize that the dreams of the past must give way to the dreams of the future. I, that wild, rebellious teenager of some years ago, am nursing a baby, changing diapers, and making breakfast for my somewhat extended family. And yet it was great while it lasted and I still feel that old excitement merely talking about it. Some people loved AIM, some hated it, but nobody ignored it.

I loved it. My first encounter with AIM was at a powwow held in 1971 at Crow Dog's place after the Sun Dance. Pointing at Leonard Crow Dog, I asked a young woman, "Who is that man?"

"That's Crow Dog," she said. I was looking at his long shining braids. Wearing one's hair long at that time was still something of a novelty on the rez. I asked, "Is that his real hair?"

"Yes, that's his real hair."

I noticed that almost all of the young men wore their hair long, some with eagle feathers tied to it. They all had on ribbon shirts. They had a new look about them, not that hangdog reservation look I was used to. They moved in a different way, too, confident and swaggering, the girls as well as the boys. Belonging to many tribes, they had come in a dilapidated truck covered with slogans and paintings. They had traveled to the Sun Dance all the way from California, where they had taken part in the occupation of Alcatraz Island.

One man, a Chippewa, stood up and made a speech. I had never heard anybody talk like that. He spoke about genocide and sovereignty, about tribal leaders selling out and kissing ass—white man's ass. He talked about giving up the necktie for the choker, the briefcase for the bedroll, the missionary's church for the sacred pipe. He talked about not celebrating Thanksgiving, because that would be celebrating one's own destruction. He said that white people, after stealing our land and massacring us for three hundred years, could not come to us now saying, "Celebrate Thanksgiving with us, drop in for a slice of turkey." He had himself wrapped up in an upside-down American flag, telling us that every star in this flag represented a state stolen from Indians.

Then Leonard Crow Dog spoke, saying that we had talked to the white man for generations with our lips, but that he had no ears to hear, no eyes to see, no heart to feel. Crow Dog said that now we must speak with our bodies and that he was not afraid to die for his people. It was a very emotional speech. Some people wept. An old man turned to me and said, "These are the words I always wanted to speak, but had kept shut up within me."

I asked one of the young men, "What kind of Indians are you?" "We are AIM," he told me, "American Indian Movement. We're going to change things."

AIM was born in 1968. Its fathers were mostly men doing time in Minnesota prisons, Ojibways. It got its start in the slums of St. Paul taking care of Indian ghetto problems. It was an Indian woman who gave it its name. She told me, "At first we called ourselves 'Concerned Indian Americans' until someone discovered that the initials spelled CIA. That didn't sound so good. Then I spoke up: 'You guys all aim to do this, or you aim to do that. Why don't you call yourselves AIM, American Indian Movement?' And that was that."

In the beginning AIM was mainly confined to St. Paul and Minneapolis. The early AIM people were mostly ghetto Indians, often from tribes which had lost much of their language, traditions, and ceremonies. It was when they came to us on the Sioux reservations that they began to learn about the old ways. We had to learn from them, too. We Sioux lived very isolated behind what some people call the "Buckskin Curtain." AIM opened a window for us through which the wind of the 1960s and early '70s could blow, and it was no gentle breeze but a hurricane that whirled us around. It was after the traditional reservation Indians and the ghetto kids had gotten together that AIM became a force nationwide. It was flint striking flint, lighting a spark which grew into a flame at which we could warm ourselves after a long, long winter.

After I joined AIM I stopped drinking. Others put away their roach clips and airplane glue bottles. There were a lot of things wrong with AIM. We did not see these things, or did not want to see them. At the time these things were unimportant. What was important was getting it on. We kids became AIM's spearheads and the Sioux set the style. The feathers stuck in the hatband, the bone chokers, the medicine pouches worn on our breasts, the Levi's jackets on which we embroidered our battle honors—Alcatraz, Trail of Broken Treaties, Wounded Knee. Some dudes wore a third, extra-thin braid as a scalp lock. We made up our own songs—forty-niners, honoring songs, songs for a warrior behind bars in the slammer. The AIM song was made up by a fourteen-year-old Sioux boy. The Ojibways say it was made up by one of their own kids, but we know better.

We all had a good mouth, were good speakers and wrote a lot of poetry, though we were all dropouts who could not spell. We took some of our rhetoric from the blacks, who had stated their movements before we did. Like them we were minorities, poor and discriminated against, but there were differences. I think it significant that in many Indian languages a black is called a "black white man." The blacks want what the whites have, which is understandable. They want *in*. We Indians want *out*! That is the main difference.

At first we hated all whites because we knew only one kind—the John Wayne kind. It took time before we met whites to whom we could relate and whose friendships we could accept. One of our young men met a pretty girl. She said she was Indian and looked it. She told him, "Sleep with me." In bed, in the middle of the night, he somehow found out that she was Puerto Rican. He got so mad that she was not a real skin that he beat up on her. He wanted to have to do only with Indian girls and felt tricked. He had run away from a real bad foster home, seeking refuge among his own kind. Later he felt ashamed for what he had done and apologized. Eventually we were joined by a number of Chicano brothers and sisters and learned to love and respect them, but it took time. We lived in a strange, narrow world of our own, suspicious of all outsiders. Later, we found ourselves making speeches on campuses, in churches, and on street corners talking to prominent supporters such as Marlon Brando, Dick Gregory, Rip Torn,

Jane Fonda, and Angela Davis. It was a long, drawn-out process of learning and experiencing, this widening of our horizons.

We formed relationships among ourselves and with outsiders. We had girls who would go to bed with any warrior who had done something brave. Other girls loved one boy only. Usually a boy would say to a girl, "Be my old lady," and she might answer, "Ohan, you are my old man." They would go find a medicine man to feather and cedar them, to smoke the pipe with them, to put a red blanket around their shoulders. That made them man and wife Indian style. Then they slept under the same blanket. The white law did not recognize such a marriage, but we would respect it. It might last only a few days. Either of them could have a run-in with the law and wind up in jail or be blown away by the goons. We did not exactly lead stable lives, but some of these marriages lasted for years. Short or long, it was good while it lasted. The girl had somebody to protect and take care of her; the boy had a wincincala to cook his beans or sew him a ribbon shirt. They inspired each other to the point where they would put their bodies on the line together. It gave them something precious to remember all their lives. One seventeen-year-old boy had a twenty-two-year-old girl-friend. He called her "Grandma." He had a T-shirt made for her with the word GRANDMA on it, and one for himself with the legend I LOVE GRANDMA. He was heartbroken when she left him for an "older man." Some of the AIM leaders attracted quite a number of "wives." We called them "wives of the month."

I got into one of these marriages myself. It lasted just long enough for me to get pregnant. Birth control went against our beliefs. We felt that there were not enough Indians left to suit us. The more future warriors we brought into the world, the better. My older sister Barbara got pregnant too. She went to the BIA hospital where the doctors told her she needed a cesarean. When she came to, the doctors informed her that they had taken her womb out. In their opinion, at that time, there were already too many little red bastards for the taxpayers to take care of. No use to mollycoddle those happy-go-lucky, irresponsible, oversexed AIM women. Barb's child lived for two hours. With better care, it might have made it. For a number of years BIA doctors performed thousands of forced sterilizations on Indian and Chicano women without their knowledge or consent. For this reason I was happy at the thought of having a baby, not only for myself but for Barbara, too. I was determined not to have my child in a white hospital.

In the meantime I had nine months to move around, still going from confrontation to confrontation. Wherever anthros were digging up human remains from Indian sites, we were there threatening to dig up white graves to display white men's skulls and bones in glass cases. Wherever there was an Indian political trial, we showed up before the courthouse with our drums. Wherever we saw a bar with a sign NO INDIANS ALLOWED, we sensitized the owners, sometimes quite forcefully. Somehow we always found old jalopies to travel in, painted all over with Red Power slogans, and always found native people to take us in, treating us to meat soup, fry bread, and thick, black coffee. We existed entirely without money, yet we ate, traveled, and usually found a roof over our heads.

Something strange happened then. The traditional old, full-blood medicine men joined in with us kids. Not the middle-aged adults. They were of a lost generation which had given up all hope, necktie-wearers waiting for the Great White Father to do for them. It was the real old folks who had spirit and wisdom to give us. The grandfathers and grandmothers who still remembered a time when Indians were Indians, whose own grandparents or even parents had fought Custer gun in hand, people who for us were living links with a great past. They had a lot of strength and power, enough to give some of it to us. They still knew all the old legends and the right way to put on a ritual, and we were eager to learn from them. Soon they had us young girls making flesh offerings or piercing our wrists at the Sun Dance, while young warriors again put the skewers through their breast and found out the hard way where they came from. Even those who had grown up in cities, who had never been on a horse or heard an owl hoot, were suddenly getting it together. I am not bragging, but I am proud that we Lakotas started this. The old grandmothers especially made a deep impression upon me. Women like Lizzy Fast Horse, a great-grandmother, who scrambled up all the way to the top of Mount Rushmore, standing right on the top of those gigantic bald pates, reclaiming the Black Hills for their rightful owners. Lizzy who was dragged down the mountain by the troopers, handcuffed to her nine-year-old great-granddaughter until their wrists were cut, their blood falling in drops on the snow. It is really true, the old Cheyenne saying: "A nation is not dead until the hearts of its women are on the ground." Well, the hearts of our old full-blood women were not on the ground. They were way up high and they could still encourage us with their trilling, spine-tingling braveheart cry which always made the hairs on my back stand up and my flesh break out in goose pimples whenever I heard it, no matter how often.

We did freak out the honkies. We were feared throughout the Dakotas. I could never figure out why this should have been so. We were always the victims. We never maimed or killed. It was we who died and got crippled. Aside from ripping off a few trading posts, we were not really bad. We were loud-mouthed, made a lot of noise, and got on some people's nerves. We made Mr. White Man realize that there were other Indians besides the poor human wrecks who posed for him for a quarter—but that should not have made them kill us or hide from us under their beds. "The AIMs is coming, the AIMs is coming" was the cry that went up whenever a couple of fourteen-year-old skins in Uncle Joe hats showed up. The ranchers and the police spread the most fantastic rumors about us. The media said that we were about to stage bank robberies, storm prisons, set fire to the state capitol, blow up Mount Rushmore, and assassinate the governor. The least we were accused of was that we were planning to paint the noses of the giant Mount Rushmore heads red. Worst of all we were scaring the tourists away. The concessionaires at Rushmore and in all the Black Hills tourist traps were losing money. It was only right to kill us for that.

I think it was their bad conscience which made the local whites hate us so much. Bill Kunstler, the movement lawyer who defended us in a number of trials, once said: "You hate those most whom you have injured most." The whites near the reservations were all living on land stolen from us—stolen not in the distant past, but by their fathers and grandfathers. They all made their living in some way by exploiting us, by using Indians as cheap labor, by running their cattle on reservation land for a mere pittance in lease money, by using us as colorful props to attract the eastern tourists. They could only relate to the stereotyped song-and-dance Indian, locking their doors and cowering behind their curtains whenever we came to town, crying: "The AIMs is coming, get the police." Always a day or two after we made our appearances all the gun shops in the place were sold out. White folks took to toting guns again. They carried revolvers wherever they went, slept with loaded .38s under their pillow, drove around with big-powered rifles in racks behind the seats of their pickups. It was rumored that the then-governor of South Dakota, who once vowed to put every AIM member behind bars or six feet underground, had imported a special, quick-firing, newly invented type of machine gun from West Germany and installed it in the dome of the state capitol, where he spent hours training the gun on Indians who happened to walk by, zeroing in, moving the gun silently back and forth, back and forth. It may be only a story, but knowing the man, I am prepared to believe it. I did not mind their being afraid of us. It was better than being given a quarter and asked to pose smilingly for their cameras.

We were not angels. Some things were done by AIM, or rather by people who called themselves AIM, that I am not proud of. But AIM gave us a lift badly needed at the time. It defined our goals and expressed our innermost yearnings. It set a style for Indians to imitate. Even those Native Americans who maintained that they wanted to have nothing to do with AIM, that it ran counter to their tribal ways of life, began to dress and talk in the AIM manner. I have had some conflicts with the American Indian Movement at some time or another. I don't know whether it will live or die. Some people say that a movement dies the moment it becomes acceptable. In this case there should be some life left in its body, at least in the Dakotas. But whatever happens, one can't take away from AIM that it fulfilled its function and did what had to be done at a time which was decisive in the development of Indian America.

The Sun Dance at Rosebud in the late summer of 1972 will forever remain in my memory. Many of the AIM leaders came to Crow Dog's place to dance, to make flesh offerings, to endure the self-torture of this, our most sacred rite, gazing at the sun, blowing on their eagle-bone whistles, praying with the pipe. It was like a rebirth, like some of the prophecies of the Ghost Dancers coming true. The strange thing was seeing men undergoing the ordeal of the Sun Dance who came from tribes which had never practiced this ritual. I felt it was their way of saying, "I am an Indian again."

The Sun Dance was also an occasion for getting to know each other, for a lot of serious talk. I was happy watching the women taking a big part in these discussions. One of the AIM men laughingly said, "For years we couldn't get the women to speak up, and now we can't get them to shut up." I just listened. I was still too shy and too young to do anything else but stay in the background.

The people were tensed up. Everything was in ferment. The mood was bitter. News reached us after the Sun Dance that Richard Oaks, from the Mohawk tribe, a much loved and respected leader at Alcatraz, had been murdered by a white man. Not long before that a Sioux, Raymond Yellow Thunder, a humble, hardworking man, had been stripped naked and forced at gunpoint to dance in an American Legion hall in Gordon, Nebraska. Later he was beaten to death—just for the fun of it. Before that a millionaire rancher had shot and killed an unarmed Indian from Pine Ridge, Norman Little Brave, and gone unpunished. Norman had been a soberminded churchgoer, but that had not saved him. It was open season on Indians again and the people were saying, "Enough of this shit!" It was out of these feelings of anger, hope, and despair that the "Trail of Broken Treaties" was born.

I am still proud that it was born at Rosebud, among my people. That is probably bad. The feeling of pride in one's particular tribe is standing in the way of Indian unity. Still it is there and it is not all bad. The man who first thought of having caravans of Indians converging upon Washington from all directions was Bob Burnette. He had been tribal chairman at Rosebud and he was not an AIM member. Other Indian leaders of this caravan, such as Hank Adams, Reuben Snake, and Sid Mills—Sid and Hank from the Northwest, where they had been fighting for native fishing rights—were not AIM. Neither were the Six Nation people from upstate New York or the representatives of some southwestern tribes, but though they had not started it, it was the AIM leaders who dominated this march in the end.

The Trail of Broken Treaties was the greatest action taken by the Indians since the Battle of Little Big Horn. As Eddie Benton, the Ojibway medicine man, told us: "There is a prophecy in our tribe's religion that one day we would all stand together. All tribes would hook arms in brotherhood and unite. I am elated because I lived to see this happen. Brothers and sisters from all over this continent united in a single cause. That is the greatest significance to Indian people . . . not what happened or what may yet happen as a result of our actions."

Each caravan was led by a spiritual leader or medicine man with his sacred pipe. The Oklahoma caravan followed the Cherokees' "Trail of Tears," retracing the steps of dying Indians driven from their homes by President Andrew Jackson. Our caravan started from Wounded Knee. This had a special symbolic meaning for us Sioux, making us feel as if the ghosts of all the women and children murdered there by the 7th Cavalry were rising out of their mass grave to go with us.

I traveled among friends from Rosebud and Pine Ridge. My brother and my sister Barbara were among this group. I did not know what to expect. A huge protest march like this was new to me. When we arrived in Washington we got lost. We had been promised food and accommodations, but due to government pressure many church groups which had offered to put us up and feed us got scared and backed off. It was almost dawn and still we were stumbling around looking for a place to bed down. I could hardly keep my eyes open. One thing we did accomplish: in the predawn light we drove around the White house, honking our horns and beating our drums to let President Nixon know that we had arrived.

We were finally given a place to sleep in an old, dilapidated, and abandoned church. I had just crawled into my bedroll when I saw what I thought to be a fair-sized cat walking over it. I put my glasses on and discovered that it was a big rat, the biggest and ugliest I had ever seen. The church was in an uproar. Women screamed. Mine was not the only rat in the place, as it turned out. An old lady who had hitchhiked two thousand miles from Cheyenne River to get to Washington complained that the toilets were broken. It was the first week of November and there was no heat. An elderly Canadian Indian dragged himself around on crutches. His legs were crippled and he could find no soft place to rest. A young girl shouted that there were not only rats but also millions of cockroaches. A young Ojibway man said that he had not left the slums of St. Paul for this kind of facility. I told him that I had expected nothing else. Did he think Nixon would put him up at the Holiday Inn with wall-to-wall carpeting and color TV? Everywhere groups were standing huddled together in their blankets. People were saying, "They promised us decent housing. Look how they're treating us. We ain't gonna stand for this."

Somebody suggested, "Let's all go to the BIA." It seemed the natural thing to do, to go to the Bureau of Indian Affairs building on Constitution Avenue. They would have to put us up. It was "our" building after all. Besides, that was what we had come for, to complain about the treatment the bureau was dishing out to us. Everybody suddenly seemed to be possessed by the urge to hurry to the BIA. Next thing I knew we were in it. We spilled into the building like a great avalanche. Some people put up a tipi on the front lawn. Security guards were appointed. They put on red armbands or fastened rainbow-colored bits of cloth to their ribbon shirts or denim jackets. They watched the doors. Tribal groups took over this or that room, the Iroquois on one floor, the Sioux on another. The Oklahoma Indians, the Northwest Coast people, all made themselves a place to stay. Children were playing while old ladies got comfortable on couches in the foyer. A drum was roaring. I could smell kinnikinnick—Indian tobacco. Someone put up a sign over the front gate reading INDIAN COUNTRY. The building finally belonged to us and we lost no time turning it into a tribal village.

My little group settled down in one room on the second floor. It was nice—thick carpets, subdued light, soft couches, and easy chairs. The bureaucrats sure knew how to live. They had marble stairs, wrought-iron banisters, fine statues and paintings depicting the Noble Savage, valuable artifacts. I heard someone speaking Sioux. I opened a door and there was Leonard Crow Dog talking to some young men, telling them why they were here, explaining what it all meant. Somebody motioned to me: "Quiet! Crow Dog is talking!" Young as I was, Crow Dog seemed an old man to me, old with responsibilities, but he was only thirty-two then. It did not occur to me that one day I would bear his children.

The takeover of the BIA building had not been planned. We honestly thought that arrangements for our stay had been made. When the promises turned out to be the same old buffalo shit, as one of the leaders put it, we simply occupied the BIA. It was a typical spontaneous Indian happening. Nobody had ordered us to do it. We were not very amenable to orders anyhow. It's not our style. The various tribal groups caucused in their rooms, deciding what proposals to make. From time to time everybody would go down into the great hall and thrash out the proposals. The assembly hall had a stage, many chairs, and loudspeakers. Always discussions opened with one of the medicine men performing a ceremony. I think it was a black civil rights organization which brought in the first truckload of food. Later various church groups and other sympathizers donated food and money. The building had a kitchen and cafeteria and we quickly organized cooking, dishwashing, and garbage details. Some women were appointed to watch the children, old people were cared for, and a medical team was set up. Contrary to what some white people believe, Indians are very good at improving this sort of self-government with no one in particular telling them what to do. They don't wait to be told. I guess there were altogether six hundred to eight hundred people crammed into the building, but it did not feel crowded.

The original caravan leaders had planned a peaceful and dignified protest. There had even been talk of singing and dancing for the senators and inviting the lawmakers to an Indian fry bread and corn soup feast. It might have worked out that way if someone had been willing to listen to us. But the word had been passed to ignore us. The people who mattered, from the president on down, would not talk to us. We were not wanted. It was said that we were hoodlums who did not speak for the Indian people. The half-blood tribal chairmen with their salaries and expense accounts condemned us almost to a man. Nixon sent some no-account underling to tell us that he had done more for the American Indian than any predecessor and that he saw no reason for our coming to Washington, that he had more important things to do than to talk with us— presumably surreptitiously taping his visitors and planning Watergate. We wondered what all these good things were that he had done for us.

We had planned to have Crow Dog conduct a ceremony at the grave of Ira Hayes, the Pima Indian who had won the Congressional Medal of Honor at Iwo Jima, and who had died drunk and forgotten in a ditch. The army, which was in charge of Arlington Cemetery, forbade this ceremony "because it would be political, not religious." Slowly, our mood changed. There was less talk of dancing and singing for the senators and more talk about getting it on. Dennis Banks said that AIM was against violence, but that it might take another Watts to bring home to the reporters that the media were ignoring us: "What do we have to do to get some attention? Scalp somebody?" It was on this occasion that I learned that as long as we "behaved nicely" nobody gave a damn about us, but as soon as we became rowdy we got all the support and media coverage we could wish for.

We obliged them. We pushed the police and guards out of the building. Some did not wait to be pushed but jumped out the ground-floor windows like so many frogs. We had formulated twenty Indian demands. These were all rejected by a few bureaucrats sent to negotiate with us. The most we got out of these talks was one white official holding up an Indian baby for a snapshot, saying, "Isn't she sweet?" We had not come for baby-kissing or for kissing ass. The moderate leaders lost credibility. It was not their fault. Soon we listened to other voices as the occupation turned into a siege. I heard somebody yelling, "The pigs are here." I could see from the window that it was true. The whole building was surrounded by helmeted police armed with all kinds of guns. A fight broke out between the police and our security. Some of our young men got hit over the head with police clubs and we saw the blood streaming down their faces. There was a rumor, which turned out to be true, that we had received an ultimatum: "Clear out— or else!"

I felt the tension rise within the building, felt it rising within me, an ant heap somebody was plunging a stick into, stirring it up. I heard a woman screaming, "They are coming, they are going to kill us all!" Men started shouting, "Women and children upstairs! Get upstairs!" But I went downstairs. I saw the riot squad outside. They had just beaten up two Indians and were hauling them off to jail. We barricaded all doors and the lowest windows with document boxes, Xerox machines, tables, file cabinets, anything we could lay our hands on. Some brothers piled up heavy typewriters on windowsills to hurl down on the police in case they tried to storm the building. Young men were singing and yelling, "It's a good day to die!" We started making weapons for ourselves. Two or three guys discovered some archery sets and were ready to defend themselves with bows and arrows. Others were swinging golf clubs, getting the feel of them. Still others were tying pen knives to fishing rods. A letter opener taped to a table leg became a tomahawk. Floyd Young Horse, a Sioux from Cherry Creek, was the first to put war paint on his face in the ancient manner. Soon a lot of young men did the same. Many wrapped themselves in upside-down American flags—like the Ghost Dancers of old.

I took apart a pair of scissors and taped one half to a broken-off chair leg and went outside to join the security. My brother was one of the guards. He saw me and laughed. He had been four years in the marines and taught me to take apart, clean, and fire a .38. Seeing me with my measly weapon broke him up. "What are you going to do with that thing?" "Get them in the balls before they can hit me!"

At last the police were withdrawn and we were told that they had given us another twenty-four hours to evacuate the building. This was not the end of the confrontation. From then on, every morning we were given a court order to get out by 6 P.M. Came six o'clock and we would be standing there ready to join battle. I think many brothers and sisters were prepared to die right on the steps of the BIA building. When one of the AIM leaders was asked by a reporter whether the Indians were not afraid that their women and children could get hurt, he said, "Our women and children have taken this risk for four hundred years and accept it," and we all shouted "Right on!" I don't think I slept more than five or six hours during the whole week I was inside the BIA.

Every morning and evening was crisis time. In between, the negotiations went on. Groups of supporters arrived, good people as well as weirdos. The Indian commissioner, Lewis Bruce, stayed one night in the building to show his sympathy. So did LaDonna Harris, a Comanche and a senator's wife. One guy who called himself Wavy Gravy, who came from a place in California called the Hog Farm and who wore a single enormous earring, arrived in a psychedelically decorated bus and set up a loudspeaker system for us. At the same time the police cut all our telephone wires except the one connecting us with the Department of the Interior. A certain Reverend McIntire came with a bunch of followers waving signs and singing Christian hymns. He was known to us as a racist and Vietnam War hawk. Why he wanted to support us was a big mystery. Cameramen and reporters swarmed through the building; tourists took snapshots of our guards. It was as if all these white people around the BIA were hoping for some sort of Buffalo Bill Wild West show.

For me the high point came not with our men arming themselves, but with Martha Grass, a simple middle-aged Cherokee woman from Oklahoma, standing up to Interior Secretary Morton and giving him a piece of her mind, speaking from the heart, speaking for all of us. She talked about everyday things, women's things, children's problems, getting down to the nitty-gritty. She shook her fists in Morton's face, saying, "Enough of your bullshit!" It was good to see an Indian mother stand up to one of Washington's highest officials. "This is our building!" she told him. Then she gave him the finger.

In the end a compromise was reached. The government said they could not go on negotiating during election week, but they would appoint two high administration officials to seriously consider our twenty demands. Our expenses to get home would be paid. Nobody would be prosecuted. Of course, our twenty points were never gone into afterward. From the practical point of view, nothing had been achieved. As usual we had bickered among ourselves. But morally it had been a great victory. We had faced white America collectively, not as individual tribes. We had stood up to the government and gone through our baptism of fire. We had not run. As Russell Means put it, it had been "a helluva smoke signal!"

Beth Brant

MOHAWK

I began writing at the age of forty. A Bald Eagle brought me the gift. In these fourteen years of writing I have tried to convey and speak the truth about my people. When Eagle came to me, He did so when I was ready to accept the challenge and responsibility that such a gift brings. It has not been easy, but writing is like life—you either do it fully, with compassion and strength, or you cheat yourself and others of that joy. I have been moved by many things— a Blue Heron taking flight, Salmon leaping and fighting their *way to re-create, my grandsons asking me "why," a native woman telling me her story of survival, an Elder touching my hand and telling me I am doing a good job, corn pushing through the soil, being held by my life-partner, Denise, giving birth to my daughters, beginning a story, reading another native's words. I want to bring lasting beauty to this world we inhabit. I want to justify my father's pride in me. I want to tell that I don't write as an "individual," but as a member of many communities—Indian, working class, gay and lesbian, feminist, recovering, human, mammal, living entity among other living entities. I write for my People and because of my People.*

Stillborn Night

Wind.
Outside my suite, wind screams.
There is no rain, unless my tears can be called so.
I have heard over the wires, the phone held weakly—
My fourth grandson is dead.
Unable to make the journey of birth, he has become a
spirit.
I am unable to be with my daughter, my son-in-law, my
grandson that
lives.

The wind. The wind has cut power lines, has uprooted trees,
has
canceled flights.
But the ringing of the telephone remains
constant.
Through the wires, I hold my family. Voice becomes the
means to
love and comfort.
My daughter cries—"Mama, why did he have to die?"

Tim cries—"Mom, I'm scared."
And I think about the careless words that are said by people when
a baby has not completed the passage to this world.
"You'll have another one, you're young and healthy." "It's better
this way."
I can only say—"I love you." "I know you're scared." "I'll be home as soon as I can." "I don't know why he died." "I will miss
him too."

But I did know that he would die. All these months—I knew
—and I curse this knowing and want to scream like the wind outside my
suite.
My immediate thoughts are for my daughter—how to ease her pain,
wanting to take that pain and absorb it for her, my lovely daughter.
This is what a mother wants to do.
The grandmother wants the impossible.
To hold a baby in her arms. To rock him. To sing to him.
To imagine the first time he looks at me in recognition and smiles at
his grandma.
I bought no baby clothes, no rattles, none of the little things
that signal the celebration of a new being. I assembled no medicine
bag for him, no filling the pouch with gifts to keep him strong and
balanced in his journey of life.
I told myself I was being careful. This had been a difficult and
dangerous pregnancy. I was being careful, I told myself. I

did not want to presume the outcome.

But when I wandered through stores, I would go to the
baby clothes
and hold them in my hands, fingering colors. I picked up
rattles
and shook them, then laid them down. I looked at tiny
shirts and
diapers, smelled baby powders. I wanted to wonder if this
baby
would have thick, fine black hair like his brother, Benjamin.
I
wanted to wonder what the mixture of Tyendinaga and
Kanawake would
produce this time. He was to be named Brant Montour,
family names of
the grandmothers of this child.

I bought no baby clothes. I kept this secret of knowing
from everyone, even the woman who shares my bed and
my life.

I went with my daughter to doctors' offices. Went with her
to have tests. She talked of looking forward to being home
again, not having to go to work, looking forward to the
night feedings, the smell of baby's head, Benjamin's
reactions to having a baby brother, the solidifying of a
marriage that has been at risk for years. I listened.

This past year my thoughts have only been of Benjamin—
his terrible anger and confusion of his daddy leaving him,
his four-year-old fears of abandonment. Even while my
daughter needed so much from me during this time—love,
support, money, time—my thoughts have been of
Benjamin. He would come to see me, but would not spend
a night or weekends, fearing his mother would not be
there when he went home. If his daddy left him, why not
his mama?

When does this dysfunction end?

Upon hearing my daughter was pregnant, I cried. She was

trying to "save" a marriage that, by all accounts, was dead. The wind. I stand next to the window listening to the moans of air.

I call the hospital again. This time my daughter tells me that Benjamin is there. They have told him. He comes on the line.

"Grandma, Brant Montour died."

I'm so sad. I say, "Are you sad?"

"No," he says, that little-boy voice so sweet and pure. "He's with Great-Grandpa. He flew right here to be with him. He's an Indian angel too."

Despite my sorrow, I laugh. "Is that so?"

"Yeah, Grandma, so you don't need to be sad. Great-Grandpa is changing Brant Montour's diaper right now."

I can hear my daughter and son-in-law laughing in the background. Jill comes on the line. "Of course I didn't tell him that. He has it all figured out himself."

I stand once again next to the window. I think of my dad changing the diaper and I smile. He was so sick and weak before he died. But perhaps Benjamin sees a great-granddad who is strong again, who laughs at children's antics, who gives big hugs. This is how I imagine the Spirit World. A place of my relatives, joking, walking, eating, strong.

The wind has begun a new sound. A steady keening.

I turn on the radio. There are reports of accidents, of trees breaking and flying onto homes, of people afraid of the natural. There are no reports that an Indian baby ended his struggle to live inside his mother. There are no reports of strong and loving sisters who are taking care of their own. There are no reports of a lonely grandma, who knew this moment would come, but waited in silence.

There is a final call.

"Mama, I'm holding him in my arms now. He looks just like Benjamin. He has black hair. He's so sweet. His right arm isn't developed. And his left arm is twisted. The doctors

think his lungs and heart just didn't grow the way they were supposed to. He's so tiny," and her voice breaks.
My heart turns over. I want to sob, but more than that, I want to give my daughter what she needs. My desire to caress my daughter's hair, stroke her back, croon to her. Old images scatter across my memory. Giving birth to her, hearing the words "another girl," rocking her as she sucked her bottle, her frightened face as her father and I began our daily ritual of violent acts and words, her joyous face when she gave birth to Benjamin.
I croon, I murmur, I pretend I am strong. My voice takes on the rhythm of the wind outside the window.
And I am stunned by the knowledge that my daughter is facing this pain head-on. She is not taking shortcuts through grief. She is holding her dead child in her arms and she is grown up. Why does this surprise me? This courageous woman is my daughter. How could I not have seen it before? What does it take for a mother to see this?
Tim's voice comes on the line. He tells me about the night, about the stillborn night. My anger at him dissolved weeks ago, as I know what it takes to grow up in native homes. I also have remembered what is required to grow up in native homes. Gentleness, patience, love, acceptance.
Tim and Jill have given each other these very gifts that have been difficult to give. This long night, they have given these. I talk with him for a while, then return to my daughter. She retells the stillbirth, gathering details around her like folds of material. She is to retell this story for months after. Each telling confirms the reality that she carried a baby inside her. That Brant Montour was a life.
It is four in the morning. The wind has calmed to a song-like murmur.
I stand next to the window again. Sometime during this night, the spirit of Brant Montour passed over my head, passed over the lands of Tyendinaga and Kanawake, passed over into the world of his ancestors.

I look out the window onto the grounds of the campus. What people walked here? What spirits still swirl underneath the carefully clipped grass? I open the window and lean out to inhale the air, made fresh by the wind. My tears dry instantly on my face. I whisper his name into the cold air. I am comforted by the saying of his name out loud.

In one year I have lost two of my family. My father—role model, hard worker, reader of books, listener to beautiful music, loving parent, arrogant Mohawk, humble Mohawk, handsome man, learned man, loving man. Brant Montour— only a blurred vision of the baby, the boy, the man he would have been. The songs I would have taught him, the games I would have played with him. Just a blurred vision, and one I knew would not come to be. Still, I loved him.

In the plane, on the way home. There is no wind this morning. The sky is very blue and clear.

I mentally gather the things to bury with him. A medicine bag for another kind of journey. He will need a small toy to play with, a carved Turtle from his clan, a carved Bear from his father's, sweetgrass, tobacco, a stone from the earth, a bird's feather, a shell, an arrowroot biscuit. I assemble these gifts in my mind.

My arms ache. I will never hold him. My eyes are full of salt water. I will never see him.

My grandson.

Chrystos

MENOMINEE

As I Leave You

doors of dead roses close   stargazing lilies   a garden we grew
Tree you gave me in celebration of our union droops
     white blossoms
as I go down stairs I've swept
Spring opens this same season we first kissed when I dreaming
believed we rode the same pony
I dress in blue   least favorite color   to remember
     how cold I am
wearing your old coat inside
I cut my fingers call it accident
Gray walls of loss push me to earth
I stare out over water I almost gave up for love of you
A torn spiderweb is silver lace delight wet with tears
I can't see anything tomorrow stretches a hard barren line
Still reeling your last betrayal dances on the grave of our bed
cries *Pity me*   throws rocks comets pain in your eyes
say you didn't mean this
or rather you expected I would endure it
as I have before
I don't have the time
Briars are opening in the fields
There will be wild roses blooming while I sit here
without the home we built
My hands on a cold chisel learned to repair foundation cracks
I didn't see this one coming never thought you'd cut

me this way as you've held me drying my tears
    over this same story
with different women
A crow comes for me this evening to take me
    where your telephone pleas
begging forgiveness cannot ring
Here is your treason my darling
in our small fragile country
clasp her close
for I am gone in silence
will not return

Emma LaRocque

PLAINS CREE ▪ METIS

Like most children in North America, I grew up with comic books and movies, which is to say, I grew up with the glorified white man locked in moral combat against the much dehumanized "Indian." School only reinforced the images projected by popular culture. Columbus and, later, the cowboys were not only innocent victims of the irrational violence of bloodthirsty savages, but always the winners.

Perhaps more than anything else, this gross misrepresentation and brutal objectification of aboriginal peoples in mainstream culture made me a writer and a scholar. While the portrayals puzzled and shamed me, I knew we were not savages. This "knowing" drove me to question and to search. Then years later when I uncovered the self-serving white supremacist myths behind the images, I had to expose the lies. Such hate literature had to be exposed to the light of justice. And always, I wanted to express the consummate humanity of my nokom, *my* ama, *my* bapa, *my brothers and sister.*

I write also because I love words. I don't just write for political or "personal healing" reasons, I write for the love of writing. I see writing as a personal challenge for creativity, imagination, and skill. I come from a long female line of great storytellers. I try to do in English what my nokum *and* ama *did in Cree.*

Ultimately, writing is a process of confronting what is human in oneself as well as in others. Good, honest writing makes us tell the truth about the oppressor and the oppressed in us all. This is also why we must write about "all our relations." This will be my next level of writing.

Tides, Towns, and Trains heritage pride

I was born in the morning in the dawn of 1949 in a one-room, kerosene-lit log cabin, into a small family in the small Metis community of Big Bay, Alberta, near the town of Lac La Biche. I was born into a world of people whose roots of pride, independence, industriousness, and skills go back to the Red River Metis, back to the Cree. I was born into a world of magic, where seeing and hearing ghosts was a routine occurrence, where the angry Pehehsoo (thunderbird) could be appeased by a four-directional pipe chant, where the spirits danced in the sky on clear nights, and where tents shook for people to heal. When my mother brought home from town a comic book of Henry Wadsworth Longfellow's *Hiawatha*, which I later learned was a "classic," I could identify with its world. The magic and natural world of *Hiawatha* were my world too!

Yet I was not born into a garden of Hiawathian paradise. Our own humanness and the effects of European colonization were very much with us. Even as we lived off the land, we also lived off the railroad, and by fighting forest fires and picking rocks and sugar beets in the "deep south" of Alberta. Even as we ate moose, trout, and berries, we also ate canned Spork, sardines, and white sugar. Even as my grandmother's lover shook tents in the ancient ceremony of the Cree, we were kissing the Stations of the Cross in the annual pilgrimages of the Roman Catholic Church. And even as my mother chased away Pehehsoo, soon after I entered school I was lecturing her about the physics of thunder and lightning. And even as my father spoke of smelling the swooping night-spirit dancers, I lectured him about the gaseous flickers of aurora borealis. Even as we chanted to drums, jigged to fiddles, and laughed, we were also crying, hurting, and burying grandparents, aunts, uncles, brothers, and sisters who were felled by tuberculosis and other diseases. And even as we generously shared foods and other kindnesses with each other, there were those amongst us whom we feared. And there were those from town whom we feared. Violence stalked among us.

I was born into a complex community that was open to natural change but that simultaneously experienced forced change. Change was not and is not new to Indian and Metis culture. The issue is to differentiate between change that is imposed and change that comes from free choice. And change that is forced is oppression. Oppression over time, such as that of the colonizing of native peoples in Canada, has had various and varying effects on different generations. I believe changes came slower for my parents than for me, but my parents experienced changes that were more directly forced upon them by Canadian society, especially in regard to their children and schooling. It may be harder to unravel the effects of changes that were at once forced and at once sought after. Schooling was forced on me too, yet I actually fought my parents in order to go to school. At the time, I did not know that school was an institution of colonization invading and disturbing the way of life of my family, my community, my ancestors. Nor could I have anticipated the school's denigration of native peoples, which was to affect my self-image profoundly. And what could I make of the violence by white and native alike in the playground as well as in the classroom?

Even though I soon hated school, I idealized learning, and unknown to me I internalized much of what Metis author Howard Adams calls the "white ideal." Early in my childhood I quite consciously rejected the roles expected of me by my family and community, namely, to attend to household chores and eventually to become someone's wife. So I kept on going to school. I kept on going. And I kept on going.

My going to school presented numerous complications for my family. Living off the land was a family affair. Parents and children were engaged in the various activities associated with trapping, hunting, working on the railroad, fire fighting, gardening, processing food and animal hides, sewing clothing, making tools, cooking, healing, fishing, berry picking, creating and re-creating, the sum of which formed a well-integrated, functioning culture. Our culture cut across all seasons and some geography. However, in the early 1950s, forced schooling and governmental confiscation of Metis trap lines in the northeastern area intercepted the seasons, geography, and rhythm of our culture and, hence, our family life. My parents had to juggle between a land-based lifestyle, which was available to us only at Chard (a little whistle-stop on the Northern Alberta Railroad [NAR]), and a lifestyle that could accommodate school, which was available only in the Lac La Biche area. The distance between Chard and Lac La Biche was only 100 miles numerically speaking, but it seemed much greater, because we were crossing more than the muskeg. But we managed. My mother stayed at our home near town so we children could go to school, and my father shared a trap line with my favorite uncle and worked seasonally for the NAR at Chard. My father came home regularly every two to six weeks, and we joined him in Chard whenever school was out.

Chard was our haven. At Chard we had our second cabin (the first one being at Big Bay) just a few yards from the railroad. On the rail line between Lac La Biche and Fort McMurray there were Metis hamlets about every 20 to 25 miles. Metis men worked as section hands for the NAR and the women worked tirelessly at home. I have many fond memories of our numerous family trips on the train, going back and forth between town and Chard. I learned to play poker from the best on those train trips!

Just prior to my reaching grade seven, we learned about a dormitory that was opening at Anzac, between Chard and Fort McMurray, for Metis children whose parents lived along the NAR line. We would board at the dorm and go to a public school nearby. To get to Anzac, we would board the train, stay for two weeks, and then come home for a weekend. I had no idea what this place would be like; I only knew I had to get away from the town school. And just as I had demanded to go to school in the first place, I pushed my parents to let us go to Anzac Dorm. Even now it hurts me to think of the loneliness, the powerlessness, and the emptiness my parents must have felt, watching us moving away from them.

At the tender age of thirteen, I boarded the old NAR train on my way to Anzac. For more than a decade I was to board that train over and over again on my way somewhere in pursuit of "higher" education. For more than a decade I was to visit my parents only for short periods whenever economically possible, and then to take that train again away from them. It was never without enormous heartache. I still remember standing at the back of the coach waving goodbye to my mother as she stood on the tracks waving back. I would watch her until the steel ribbons blurred together by the distance and by my tears. I knew she was crying too. And I remember the joy of arriving. The train could not go fast enough (and it could not—it barely mustered 20 miles per hour). Finally, we would creak and rumble into Chard. My parents would be standing by their cabin, waiting, hoping. When they could determine it was really me coming toward them, my mother would break into a little jog, hesitating, then running to greet me. And she always had such delicious food ready for me. All too soon there would be the devastating pain of leaving them again. I remember it all, still, as if it were yesterday.

Each time I took that train away from them I was not only leaving a family and a place I loved so much, I was leaving a culture, a familiar way of life, for a world that was, initially, foreign, frightening, and, at times, excruciatingly lonely. With each train ride the distance between my two worlds grew, not only in miles but in ways that no words in English could ever adequately describe. What kind of a society forces families into such heartbreaking, no-win situations?

I was born into a wave that has haunted my heart and influenced my research and understanding of the human being as the oppressed and as the oppressor. The late 1940s to the 1960s was the tidal wave of the town—in which, like headlights of a car in the night coming closer and closer, the town loomed larger and larger. It was not just one town; it could be any town, anywhere in Canada. Town consisted of "white" people who spoke English with various accents: French, Anglo-Saxon, Ukrainian, Syrian, Chinese. To us, they were all white and they owned and ran everything. Restaurants. Stores. Offices. Schools. Churches. Hospitals. Rooming houses. Barrooms. Jails. And even the very corners of the streets we walked on. In Cree, we called them *ooh-gu-mow-wuk* (the governing ones).

Going to town was a major event, for in the 1950s we went only occasionally. For me, it was almost always a very unpleasant experience. *Ooh-gu-mow-wuk* stared and glared at us. Sometimes they called us names, like "squaws" and "bucks." Sometimes they yelled at us, "Go back home, dirty Indians." And sometimes, my parents stayed to visit with their friends and relatives on the streets, in secret wine circles, or in barrooms because they had no access to the recreational and tourist facilities in town. We, the children, waited in movie houses, looked at comic books in cafes, or, if late into the night, waited vigilantly in hotel lobbies. Sometimes fights in barrooms spilled onto the street—then, to be sure, there were the police. In the 1950s, there were few fights for there was little excessive drinking—but there would still be the police. Many times I saw police roughing up and/or picking up native people, among them my uncles, my aunties, and even my mother. Years later I was to learn, with horror, that there were times when the police picked up defenseless women just to assault them!

If we did not go to town, the town came to us; with the town came the priests. Wherever the Metis went, the priests went. They carried their portable god and confessionals. Priests functioned as catechism enforcers, baptizers, and buriers of the dead. I do not have any happy memories of priests. I remember them as austere-looking, authoritarian men with big dark beards who dressed in black. They taught an extremely simplistic version of heaven and purgatory, as if they were afraid we would fathom the contradictions of theology. They would pop in unexpectedly once or twice a year demanding confession, while my mother scurried to feed them. I especially remember one priest who, holding hands with my fifteen-year-old cousin, led her into the woods. I asked my mother why he carried such a big flashlight in the front of his pants! In retrospect, I wonder why no one stopped that priest.

Town brought disease. Throughout the first half of this century, thousands of native people were felled by tuberculosis. My community did not escape. People with advanced TB were shipped off to Edmonton, and often their bodies were shipped back. We had no money. We spoke no English. Edmonton may as well have been Russia, it was that inaccessible to us. Even the town hospital was inaccessible. It was only in the late 1950s that municipal health workers discovered our hamlet (which is only six miles from town) and started to immunize children against TB and polio. By the time I was ten years old, I had lost more relatives and neighbors than an average white person will ever lose in a lifetime. What emotional and ideological havoc all these deaths must have wreaked on us. What questions and doubts the medicine people must have had about their knowledge and their Cree and Christian gods. We, the survivors, walk in grief for much of our lives. There are ever-new diseases that stalk our communities.

Then there were the storekeepers in town, and town storekeepers in each hamlet. Storekeepers probably had the greatest power of any whites who had a connection with us. They acted as post office workers, bankers, translators, and managers of our family allowance, old-age pension, and paychecks. In the 1950s and much of the 1960s, there was no social assistance, but the storekeepers acted in the manner of welfare agents. They kept the accounts, doling out credits against debits. They determined the price of goods, furs, and berries. They watched us like hawks when we shopped in their aisles.

In this era, native people, including my parents, never fought back. They tolerated the stares, the dehumanization, the violence, the price-fixing. One time, I challenged the books of an old-timer, a storekeeper who was always very friendly, accepting of, and dependent on his native customers. He was buying blueberries from us and his arithmetic did not match mine. I exposed the discrepancy and made him pay us the correct amount, but my parents were mortified—not at him, but at me! *"Keyam, keyam,"* they ordered me. *Keyam* means, among other things, let it be—don't rock the boat. Don't question. Don't challenge.

My parents were reflecting centuries of colonial conditioning: fear and obey *ooh-gu-mow-wuk*. The flip side of this can be found in missionary and fur-trade journals in which colonizing Europeans assumed governing positions and considered any native expression of independence or resistance as "haughty," "impetuous," or "arrogant."

Quite early in childhood, I became aware of the serious gaps between the world I was born into and the world of the town with which we had to deal.

From grade one onward my student life has been filled with discomfort, loneliness, and anger. Before I understood racism intellectually, I experienced shame and alienation from teachers and textbooks that portrayed Indians as backward savages. And of course, the cowboys-and-Indians movies and the attitudes in town did not help. Yet I knew that there was absolutely no connection between such biased portrayals and the consummate humanity of my parents, brothers and sister, my *nokom* (grandmother), my aunts and uncles. But what does a child do when she knows from a place that had not yet been "documented"?

As a child, I never spoke up in classrooms or in playgrounds. As an adolescent, I felt shame and confusion. But in my late teens, I began to speak out. I began to talk back to teachers, missionaries, farmers, bus drivers, train conductors, cab drivers. To those whites I considered friends, I made special attempts to explain. Years later I came to understand that, like many native individuals before me, I had been forced into the position of being an apologist for "my people."

At the age of nineteen, I started what has become my career: the university. In several classes, but mostly from reading on my own, I learned about colonization, racism, slavery, and poverty. I read Harold Cardinal's *The Unjust Society*, and could identify with nearly every page. Finally a native person had articulated what I had been experiencing! I came to understand that our economic poverty and marginalization, our landlessness and our fragmentation, and all the hostility and stereotyping around us were neither accidental nor isolated, nor were they due to some "cultural difference" or innate deficiency in us. Racism and injustice, deeply entrenched in all major institutions, tore our communities apart and broke people down. This oppression was rooted in a racial, religious, and patriarchal ideology that claimed that whites were civilized and their manifest destiny was to enslave blacks and overtake Indians, both of whom were considered savage. In Canada, racism was and is the foundation and the justification for colonization.

For years I, like my parents before me, had been conditioned to fear and obey *ooh-gu-mow-wuk* and to *keyam*. All our lives, priests preached the acceptance of one's "station" in life; evangelicals preached personal sin as the cause of all grief. My parents explained disease and misfortune as a manifestation of "bad medicine." Life was a matter of fate and personal stupidity. In addition to all this, I was indoctrinated in grades seven to nine by well-meaning Mennonites at Anzac Dorm; I was taught to adopt the beatitudinal posture of meekness and of forgiveness and prayer for those who would devastate us. At the Prairie Bible Institute in southern Alberta (where I took grades ten to twelve), I was brainwashed never to question, never to challenge. There, medieval rules were equated with godliness. And on our town streets, Pentecostals yelled: "Prayer moves mountains" and "Take it all to Jesus."

I was born into a whirlpool of *keyams* and karmas. But I was born asking. I was born, as poet Joy Harjo writes, "with eyes that can never close." Even when blindness struck me in my early teens, I saw—at home and in town—what no one wanted to see. As a child, in the safety of my own home, I asked and challenged incessantly. In elementary school, terrified of my peers and teachers, I was cowed into deadening silence. As a vulnerable teenager, desperately in need of a framework to live by, I clung to religions that had simplistic "answers" to life.

Discovering earth-shaking concepts usually changes a person. Moving away from the concept of the "personal" to the "sociological" was, for me, a revolution. Learning that poverty and other problems in my community were due to some traceable oppressive processes was for me liberation from shame and confusion. I became politicized. What was more, I was politicizing on at least two fronts: as a native and as a woman. The early stages of decolonization entail much anger. I was as angry about the subjugation of female persons in my hamlet, and in my town, and in churches, as I was about the oppression of native people. I was shedding innocence and layers of myths, leaving patriarchal and paternalistic "friends." I was taking on new theories, pushing past boundaries. I soon found myself confronting people who made sexist or racist remarks. I lectured to my family and relatives, on the one hand about racism in town, and on the other about sexism and the sexual offenders in our communities. I was explaining these issues to whoever would listen, and, incidentally, even educating professors along the way.

Clearly embarrassed, my family tolerated me. My other relatives avoided me. My real friends said little. The "ordinary Canadian" whites reacted with disbelief, defensiveness, and shock. I had become the Uncomfortable Mirror. What no one understood was that I was in a revolution of many layers and there is little that is comfortable or "quiet" in such a revolution. I also soon discovered that there is nothing easy about trying to educate either the oppressed or the oppressor. Nor is there anything particularly angelic about either group. Both are afraid of self-inspection and change. The familiar is safer than the unknown.

There was nothing simple or static about the world my parents or I grew up in. Later as I pursued higher education I was confronted with many contradictions, ironies, and resistance. What does a native woman scholar do when she has had to "master" the very authors and materials that have always left her with the knowledge that they "see" but do not see? Today as a historian I document what I have always known.

Sometimes my feelings of being flung across the ages are highlighted in the most memorable of ways. In the summer of 1977, my mother and niece came from Alberta to visit me. In so many ways, it was a very important visit. It was the first time Mom, a woman who had traveled centuries in her lifetime, had had the opportunity to travel miles from her home, the first time to come to my world. Unknown to us, it was the last time she would travel in full health; in but a few years she would embark on that journey of no return.

Among many good memories I have of this visit, one incident stands out. We visited the Manitoba Museum of "Man" and Nature, where there was a display of a northern native campsite and its attendant cultural tools. In an instant, Mom recognized everything, and her whole person beamed. With great animation, she began to identify each tool and to explain its usage. She described, for example, how specific moose bones had to be shaped and honed with precision so that moose hides could be scraped without damage. She went on at great length in Cree to detail the technologies of her world. My niece and I stared at her in wonder and in pride. At times white audiences formed around us. I found myself interpreting to them parts of my mother's impressive lecture.

Besides the fact that we rediscovered my mother as the great orator, educator, and walking encyclopedia of culture that she was, the significance of this episode is how poignantly it illustrates the gaps in experience and knowledge between academic perception and native reality. What academics and other members of white society have filed away as "artifact" or "historic," my mother (and all our family members, for that matter) knew and used in everyday life. My mother, who did not ever have the opportunity to read English, experienced the museum display as an affirmation of her living culture. She would have been astonished and amused had she been able to read the descriptions, which dated the materials as prehistoric.

I was not amused. I have walked, feeling cold and lonely, in Canada's archives, libraries, cathedrals, martyr's shrines, museums, and forts that venerate priests and settlers at the awful expense of Indian and Metis peoples. I have cringed each time I came upon a historic site, a tourist shop, or Parks Canada's pale plaques. I have noted that at every important juncture and place in my life or in my family's life, our culture and perceptions have been either chronologically misplaced, fragmented, belittled, infantilized, denied, or disagreed with by the vast majority of non-native Canadians representing all walks of life.

Only recently have I begun to discuss violence, especially sexual violence, in my classes and in my public presentations. I have been stunned at the speed with which I have been labeled, lied about, and psychologized. But again, I can no longer be silent. I come from a long line of silenced women who have been victimized, as if war had been declared on their persons. My *nokom*, my mother, my aunties, and my sisters of many colors across this land have been victims of violence. All kinds of violence. Perpetrated by all kinds of boys (yes, boys) and men. From grandfathers, stepfathers, fathers, brothers, cousins, sons and nephews, and strangers. From peddlers to priests and police. From poor men on Main Street to rich men in business suits. There is also violence by and between women that must be addressed.

But where is the outrage? Who grieved and raged for that fostered fourteen-year-old Indian teenager who was raped seventeen times at Lac Brochet, her place of origin? I was rendered speechless when a prominent woman in government sat in my living room during elections and actually tried to justify the actions of those rapists.

I have seen enough. I have heard enough. I have read enough about the human condition (including some very naive and irresponsibly liberal criminology studies by white, middle-class men who clearly know not what they write). I know enough not to entertain naive or bleeding-heart notions about the nature of man, whether he is the oppressor or the oppressed: at the bottom is the woman or the girl.

Recently I was invited to address a federal Human Rights Commission "hearing" on the place of minority women in society. I raised the issue of violence and suggested that the commission work toward persuading the United Nations to list rape as a crime against humanity. A number of commissioners were clearly uncomfortable. After all, had they not asked me to speak (softly, apparently) on racism and "cultural differences"? Were they surprised to hear that violence/oppression of women is not a "cultural difference" but a universal human illness? And why is it that a problem global in scope continues to be called "deviant" by so many sociologists?

Later it came to my attention that at a dinner hosted by the Human Rights Commission, one of the commissioners labeled me "radical." For two decades now I have been chasing down and debunking stereotypes. I have learned that for every image I "de-feathered," another one popped up. Once I was "disadvantaged"; now I dare to be a "radical." Should not a human rights officer know all the ingenious ways whites psychologize natives, and men censure women? This is the nature and function of stereotypes: as long as a power struggle exists between peoples or between the sexes there will be new convenient stereotypes for those in power.

Stereotyping, labeling, blaming, denying, censuring, or psychologizing are all patterned responses in a colonial or patriarchal society. Just as native people are the Uncomfortable Mirrors for white Canadians, conscious women are the thorns in the flesh in a sexist society. And just as very few people want to see the underbelly of Canada, fewer still care to look into the caves of men.

It has not been easy to be framed an Uncomfortable Mirror. It is not easy to hear about "the Indian problem" everywhere one goes, or to see stereotypes almost everywhere one looks. It tests my patience to be baited, excessively challenged, or branded. I have had to live with the echoes of my own words, even the echoes of my research and analyses, because no one could receive them. This disheartening and lonely place is exacerbated by the fact that there are not many native writers or scholars with whom to share.

Educating for change is exciting but exacting. While preservers of tradition and the status quo can assume authority simply from their positions, seekers of change must always "prove themselves." And resistance can wear out a person. My bones know the places where my soul has been scorched.

So sometimes, just sometimes, I do wish I could stay with the fence-sitting side of Canada. I wish I could teach only statistics so that my students would stay sleepy, or simply tell jokes so that my audiences would keep on laughing. Sometimes I wish I could "tone down" the fire in my voice that aggravates those who want to hear a demure Indian princess. Could I write poetry without politics? And why do I not dress more traditionally? At times, I wish I could "live and let live," tolerate the moral majority, accept everybody, and, as some have chided, "understand that we mean well, we are all human, be accepting, be bigger than us." I wish I could be happy just being nice, being with my nice friends talking about nice things, going to board meetings and church or believing in karma. If only I did not expect so much from others, or from myself. I wish I could believe in feasibility studies, inquiries, conference resolutions, and royal assents. Maybe I could be a yuppie, or even an "ordinary" Canadian. I know my bones would like this very much. I wish I could dance for Wisakehcha with my eyes closed. I wish I could say *keyam*.

But I was born asking, and with eyes that can never close. The real wishing I do entails the transformation of people and of society. But how shall we transform the oppressed and the oppressor? And upon whose shoulders, whose consciousness does the task of transformation fall? I cannot trust ideological formulas. And I cannot be satisfied with conformity. I have known the shadows. I have heard the voices crying in the night. I have seen the sleeping. I know

> the sorrow of the poor
> the sorrow of woman
> the sorrow of native
> the sorrow of the earth
> the world that is with me
> in me
> of me.

I have been flung across the ages—and I have been the one to take the train, to ride the tides, to learn English, to cross the chasms. But who will know my world, my mother, my Cree?

Susan Power

Y A N K T O N N A I   S I O U X

I *am a Yanktonnai Sioux, originally from Chicago, although many of my relatives live on the Standing Rock Sioux Reservation, which straddles both North and South Dakota. I've written poetry since I was about five years old, and I think it's the cathartic writing process that has kept me sane. In my poetry I could sort through the conflicting values and belief systems I was taught by being raised with one foot in the Indian world and the other in mainstream society. My writing always reflected my experience, which frequently rendered it controversial in the classroom. Many of my teachers regarded my poems and essays as rebellious. I didn't*

feel rebellious. I felt honest. When I was eleven I wrote a play
titled "Funeral of a Beloved Wino," which was my recounting
of a funeral I'd attended in the uptown area of Chicago for
Big Tom, an intelligent but haunted Winnebago friend who
drank himself to death. My English teacher worried about me,
told my mother that I should try to be more like my classmates.

As the only Indian in every school I attended through
twelfth grade, I knew I was different. But I didn't see it as a
liability. I thought of it as an advantage. I felt I had a secret,
another world I could retreat to when the dominant culture,
for all its material success and political power, felt empty and
meaningless. In the Indian world there were living stories:
ghosts, mischievous spirits, bad medicine and good medicine,
people with real problems, problems of survival. The Indian
world always seemed immediate and startlingly real, a place
where things happened. In the other world of the preparatory
school I attended, experience felt abstract, refracted through the
distancing process of intellectual analysis.

Beaded Soles

I am beading moccasins for my husband, Marshall Azure. I am
beading the soles so he can walk clear up to the sky. There was a
fuss about letting me have a needle. They take it away at night so
I can't use it as a weapon.

The Chicago Indian Center took up a collection for me to get
whatever I needed, and I asked for cut beads, sinew, and buckskin,
so I could make a pair of death moccasins for Marshall to wear
into the next world.

They're taking his body home to Fort Yates, North Dakota, on
the Standing Rock Sioux Reservation. I won't be able to attend the
services. It's just as well though, because I know Father Zimmer's
Sermon for a Dead Indian by heart. Anybody who grew up on the
reservation can recite it backwards in their sleep. He likes to call
heaven "the Happy Hunting Ground," but it is an Anglo heaven

Father Zimmer describes. The streets are paved with gold I think would burn my feet, and the gates are of mother-of-pearl I know would blind my eyes. He makes heaven sound like a great bureaucracy; the most sophisticated filing system in the world where all your sins and virtues are entered like tax statements to the IRS.

Father's eyes change from blue to gray when he talks about heaven. His sharp overbite slices the words as they leave his mouth. He doesn't realize that Herod Small War will negate him. Herod will talk over the body of Marshall Azure in Dakota (Sioux), and Father Zimmer will nod as though he understands. Herod will explain to Marshall that Indian heaven is democratic, it is home, it is the place where we shall all meet again to join in the Great Powwow which goes on well into the night. In Indian heaven the Dakota people wear moccasins with beaded soles and dance on air. Herod will tell Marshall to look for us later on, to meet us on the road when it is our turn to make the journey.

Even I will make it to Indian heaven, where I will dance all night with my husband, Marshall Azure, carrying our son Jasper in my arms.

On the reservation memory is a sap that runs thick and deep in the blood. Ancient jealousies, enmities, and alliances are preserved until they become traditional. In my family memory was a soldier's navy blue tunic, stiffened on the left side with a spatter of sacred brown blood. As a little girl memory lured me into my parents' bedroom closet where the tunic was kept on a hanger, covered by a flour sack.

My fingers unpinned the bottom of the flour sack to stroke the coarse material. It bristled under my fingers. I bit the tip of my tongue and slowed my breath. When I refolded the hem of the flour sack and repinned the garment, I wanted to leave memory behind me in my parents' bedroom closet, but memory pinned my shadow to the ground. Some days I imagined I could feel God's thumb pressing on the crown of my head.

The soldier's tunic belonged to my great-grandfather, Lieutenant Henry Bullhead, an Indian policeman sent to arrest Sitting Bull.

Lt. Bullhead was shot in the side by Catch-the-Bear—one of Sitting Bull's followers—and the lieutenant shot Sitting Bull as he fell. It was said that Henry Bullhead's wound wasn't serious, that he would have lived if Sitting Bull hadn't fallen across him. The holy man's blood was enough to kill his enemy. Henry Bullhead's blood washed away as Sitting Bull's blood drenched the policeman's jacket, poisoning the lieutenant's wound.

As it turned out, Lt. Bullhead got off easy. He died and his body was brought back to his family. They buried him dressed in a fresh uniform, his hands folded across his chest like a white man.

Henry Bullhead left his sin behind him, scraped from his soul the way caked dirt had been knocked off his boots. The sin was left to his children.

My great-grandfather's sin against our own tribe came down through the generations like it was packaged in our genes. When a Bullhead made a misstep in life people would say, "What can you expect from a Bullhead?" Our word was doubted and we were considered unlucky. This last was true.

My father owned a horse we called *Ista Sa*, Red Eyes, for the angry glowing eyes in his black face. No one could safely approach him except my father, yet every morning the horse's mane and tail were plaited in tight knots which my father spent a half-hour untangling. It was said that mischievous *heyoka* spirits the size of small children played tricks on the dangerous horse to tease my father.

My mother never had success with her canning. No matter how careful she was the chokeberry jelly would ferment and the tomatoes would spoil until the mason jars exploded.

Our cabin burned to the ground in 1939 when I was nine years old, and the next year my father was killed by a bolt of lightning. He had just been paid for helping a white rancher break in a herd of wild ponies. He was found by the side of the road leading to the reservation, five silver dollars in each hand. My mother tried to give me one of the silver dollars so I could have something of my father's, but I wouldn't touch it. I imagined the scorched silver was evil.

My mother had always been generous but after my father's death she gave away anything she considered frivolous rather then absolutely necessary. People trained themselves not to compliment her clothes, house, or vegetable garden because whatever they admired she would present them. I had been in Father Zimmer's catechism class long enough to believe she was doing penance.

"*Ina* [Mother], are we repenting?" I finally asked her. Our small house was nearly empty. My mother was busy altering a dress for the wife of Mr. Mitchell, the reservation agent. We didn't own a sewing machine but her stitches were neatly uniform. She looked up from a flounced skirt.

"I don't understand," she said impatiently. She needed to finish the dress, which was to be worn that evening.

"Giving everything away. The blankets even."

"You're Dakota," she scolded. "I thought I raised you to be generous."

"But almost everyone else has more than us now."

"Greedy. Do we have to be like everyone else?" She was dismissing me. "Do you think we're like everyone else?"

No, I had never thought that. But perhaps we could have been. I never forgave my mother for marrying the grandson of Henry Bullhead. She could have chosen wisely. She'd had her choice of any Sioux, Cheyenne, or Assiniboine. My mother was a Sioux-and-French beauty, one of three Arshambault sisters who specialized in collecting hearts. And here she had chosen my father, taken his name, helped him create a child in his own image. She hadn't refused him the way I'd refused the silver dollar, not wanting what my father had to give me.

My father was a tall, quiet man with a tremendously thick mustache. I believed the heavy mustache was what kept him silent, making it too difficult for him to lift his upper lip. I was an awkward version of my father, stretched to his height—nearly six feet tall—as a grown woman. People said I was like him, they called me handsome, but I felt too strong to be attractive. My hands and feet were too broad, my hair too thick. I could chop wood like a man and carry three times the load of kindling my mother carried.

People expected me to be an old maid. I had two strikes against me: my size, and the fact that I was a Bullhead.

My mother tried to reassure me. "Remember the Dakota War Women," she said. She reminded me about the Sioux women who chose to join their husbands in battle. "Your grandma killed this many of the enemy," my mother would say, holding up both hands to spread ten fingers. "She was one of the best fighters and everyone wanted her for a wife. The best thing is to fight side by side."

I almost smiled. I couldn't imagine my mother riding into the dirt and blood, her face painted black like a Sioux warrior. The *Songs of Insult* flung at the enemy would never sound mocking on her sweet tongue.

"Dakota men will respect you. They will value your strength," she promised.

Maybe Dakota men had seen too many movies in Bismark. Movies where Jean Harlow pouted, Greta Garbo was silent, Merle Oberon fainted, and Claudette Colbert's eyes widened in innocent confusion. Either that, or the long shadow of memory stretched across my face like a veil so I was hidden from consideration.

I was twenty years old before Marshall Azure came looking for me. He showed up on washing day when my sleeves were rolled up and my arms looked like they extended forever. He came right up to me in back of our house, hands on his hips. When he looked me in the face our eyes were level.

"You remember me?" he asked, trying to puff himself taller. I nodded, feeling ready to crack down the middle with a smile.

"You're a Bullhead," he teased.

"You're a fathead." Words we had spoken before, in the school-yard of Saint Joseph's Catholic Indian School in Bismark. The school had anticipated a showdown between us, the two tallest Dakotas in the third grade. Minnie, a Gros Ventre girl with a rapid tongue, spread the news when the time came. She must have seen it in our eyes.

We circled one another slowly, carefully balanced, working our toes into the ground like digging springs. The first move wouldn't happen until we'd offered the words. We stood toe-to-toe, square-matched in height and frame like a reflection.

"You're a Bullhead," Marshall said, tapping me on the chest with a forefinger.

"You're a fathead," I spat, toeing the dust so it kicked across his shins. We rolled on the ground, becoming dark earth. The struggle was even and lasted until Sisters Michael and Fatima pulled us apart. Blood was in Marshall's mouth, smearing his teeth. I felt a knot rising on my forehead. We smiled at one another, sudden allies.

For the rest of our school days we were conspirators. We whispered Sioux together in the halls and play yard, defiant of rules prohibiting it. We talked about the Sun Dance and Herod Small War, a powerful *Yuwipi* man. We wrote perfect essays the nuns tacked on the wall, and secret essays we passed back and forth through a great underground system of resistance. Essays on what it was to be Indian, what it was to refuse to forget.

Now Marshall stood before me, a grown man. He was still restless in his own body, squirming a little in the sun. He had the pigeon toes of a traditional dancer, and a straight Sioux nose so old-fashioned it was almost arrogant. His top lip lifted in a permanent sneer, reminding me of Kicking Bear, one of Sitting Bull's contemporaries. His skin was so even in its warm color I imagined old women had gone over it with their flat thumbs, smoothing and blending.

"I'm back," Marshall said. I wanted to run my own thumb across the plane of his forehead.

"Took you long enough," I answered. I put my arms around him in welcome.

Marshall and I went down to Mobridge, South Dakota, to get married. We went to Happy Sam's place, about twenty miles out of town. Happy Sam was a white justice of the peace who specialized in Indian weddings. At powwows he handed out brochures which were so attractive most people on the reservation had one tacked up on their cabin wall.

The cover pictured a handsome Sioux couple wrapped together

in a star quilt. Their heads were bowed, the target of a pointing finger reaching down from a pulpit in the upper-left-hand corner. Beneath the couple was printed:

HAS THE CHURCH RENOUNCED YOU?
DOES THE CHURCH STAND IN THE WAY OF YOUR ETERNAL BLISS?

The following pages described how Happy Sam could make dreams come true. He married all comers—No Questions Asked.

We left the reservation and the state of North Dakota to get married because Marshall came from an important Sioux family.

"Your blood is from the Black Hills," his mother liked to say, exaggerating its purity. His family didn't want him linking his name to mine, marrying into the long shadows. But Marshall had a mind of his own.

Happy Sam was plucking a wild turkey when we pulled up. He was pasted with blood and feathers. He dropped his work and ran up to our car before we ever made a move to get out.

"You're sure you're going through with it?" he asked, wiping his hands on the seat of his overalls. "*And* you got the money?" Happy Sam hadn't smiled yet the way he did on the last page of the brochure. Marshall nodded. Happy Sam smiled. "I'll go wash up then," he said.

I watched him walk back toward his clean-painted two-story house. It was a soft blue that melted into the sky. I watched him climb the steps to his porch and open the front door. Just inside I could see a narrow hallway, the floor covered with an Oriental carpet runner. Happy Sam walked right across that runner in his blood-and feathered clothes. I'd heard that he had Oriental rugs throughout his house in rich colors like wine red and royal blue. He had real Chantilly lace curtains at every window and tatted doilies on each piece of furniture.

Happy Sam's two sons appeared from somewhere behind the house. One carried an accordion and the other a fragile guitar that looked very old. They could have been twins, both about fifteen years old, all corners in their clothes, standing on long, skinny feet.

Their hair was the color of a match flame, silver-white at the roots burning to yellow at the tips. They leaned against the house and stared at us. The accordion made me remember that back in the thirties Happy Sam had toured throughout the Dakotas with Lawrence Welk's band. He must have passed the music on to his sons.

When Happy Sam returned he was dressed in a worn black suit which had a plum purple shine in the sun. He wore black-and-red striped moccasins on his feet, and a warbonnet on his head with feathers trailing all the way down his back to brush against the ground.

He motioned for us to stand beside him in front of the house. I realized then that we would be married outside, like every other Indian couple he led to eternal bliss. I had heard that when it rained or snowed he would move as far as the porch, but that an Indian had never set foot on his Oriental rugs or sat on a piece of his doily-covered furniture. Somehow I had imagined that Marshall and I would be exceptions. We were dressed so carefully and standing so straight. We had combed our hair again before leaving the car.

Marshall seemed unhappy about something. He was cracking the knuckles of his thumbs over and over, their pop like the snapping of wishbones. He waved his hand at Happy Sam's warbonnet.

"You don't have to wear that," he said.

"You pay the full price, you get the full treatment," Happy Sam told him, fingering the folded bills already tucked in his breast pocket.

"Where'd you get that anyway?" Marshall asked him.

"Satisfied customers," Happy Sam answered. "Satisfied customers. But you don't have to worry," he told Marshall. He opened a ragged pamphlet. "I have respect." He snapped his fingers at his sons who launched into a bouncy song, something like a polka.

I wanted to remember the words Marshall and I gave one another, the promises we spoke into the wind standing on a South Dakota plain. But I don't remember the vows. I don't even remember saying my name, Maxine Bullhead.

Instead I see the limp turkey resting on a bench, its broken neck dangling over the side, beak dipped toward the ground. I see Happy Sam's sons in the background, their instruments slack in their hands, mouths open and eyes crawling over the grass. I see Happy Sam sweating in his suit, wetting the feathers of the warbonnet which framed his face. And I remember feeling the sudden weight of sin—tired, well-handled sin passed from hand to hand —slam against my heart.

"You're married," Happy Sam told us as I struggled to catch my breath.

"It's over," he said when I didn't move. Happy Sam pulled off the warbonnet and wiped his dripping forehead on the arm of his suit jacket. He slung the warbonnet over his shoulder and walked his boys into the house.

Marshall took my hands and squeezed them too hard. "Let's get out of here," he whispered. And we did.

It was five years later that Herod Small War caught me after church. "You visit the doctor," he counseled, smiling around his teeth.

I tried not to hope too hard. I tried not to let my dreams run loose. But it turned out Herod was right; Marshall and I were finally going to have a child. Between us we knew he would be a boy named Jasper. We knew what he would look like. In bed together at night we drew pictures in the air. Jasper would be a singer, his voice would cry and sing, bringing back the old days. Jasper would be eloquent like the ancestors, we would close our eyes to hear him speak. Jasper would expand our married circle, increasing the love between us. Jasper would forever seal the busy mouths of rumor-weavers who strung their looms each morning with deft tongues, claiming our childlessness was proof of what marrying a Bullhead would do.

Marshall worked hard at whatever jobs he could get. He helped local farmers with harvesting and rode with ranchers to tend cattle. He threshed, branded, and butchered. He dreamed as hard as I did.

On my last visit to the Indian Health Clinic before the delivery, the doctor called the two of us into his office. He was a new doctor from somewhere in the east where people spoke too quickly. His glasses kept slipping down his nose. He looked frightened. The three of us sat in silence for long moments. Marshall shifted. We were both too large for the small, hard chairs.

Suddenly the doctor was telling us, "The baby is already dead. It happens sometimes. We can't find a heartbeat."

I wanted to offer my own. *Give Jasper mine*, I thought. *Give him something of mine to warm his blood.* The doctor's voice was pitched too high, on the verge of hysteria. I wondered why this doctor was so upset for us.

Marshall had risen. He was arguing with the doctor. I wanted to rise too, but Jasper weighted me down like an anchor. Marshall told the doctor his science wasn't the last word, it was only good up to a point. Marshall looked stronger than I'd ever seen him. He looked like he could hammer the doctor into the ground with just a few more sentences.

That's why he's upset, I realized. *He's afraid of us.* Who knew what a wild Indian would do to a white doctor from the East? Too much John Wayne. Too many Hollywood hatchets dripping stage blood. I calmly watched the doctor in his terror, purposely concentrating on him to keep my mind from slipping off sideways, running out of the clinic, and scrabbling on all fours to the top of Angry Butte where its last trace of understanding would explode into slivers of howling sound.

The baby was due that week so the doctor told me he wouldn't induce labor for two days. It was still possible for me to deliver naturally and avoid an operation. Marshall was convinced there was hope. He worked harder than ever.

When I was alone I kept my eyes busy, off the rounded hill of my stomach rising like a burial mound. I had my mother make special moccasins for Jasper, just in case. But I wouldn't allow them in the house. The ancestors might become anxious to fit them on his feet.

Marshall took me to the Indian Health Hospital when I went into labor. The pain made me happy. The pain stretched a smile across my face. Marshall shivered in the car. His hands drifted over the steering wheel, locking and unlocking. Slim twists of praying tobacco were spread on the dashboard, their spicy smell sweetening the air. Marshall was watching the straight, empty road.

"Don't give up," he told me. They could have been my son's words.

"No," I told my husband, "we won't." Pain was my son's voice. He was trying to be heard. I listened and listened. My body strained to hear until the whole world became the angry voice of pain and the scent of tobacco.

When we arrived at the hospital Marshall stayed with me until I was taken away to a yellow room.

"He's run off," I heard one of the nurses tell the doctor. She smiled at me and her features pinched together. "We'll get this over with as soon as possible," she said.

No. Don't give up. Voices were filling my head. My brain was swollen and tight with voices until I felt them exploding from my body: rushing from my ears, singing from my mouth, falling from my eyes, rising from my pores.

"Poor soul," the nurse was whispering, "he's probably off getting drunk." She placed her hands on my knees and I felt voices stab her flesh and soar to the ceiling.

"I see it time and again," the doctor said. He didn't touch me. He was looking at his clean white hands as the voices slipped inside his jacket to lick his skin.

"It was a mistake to repeal," the nurse said. I knew what she meant. The Indian Liquor Law prohibiting Indians from buying liquor, which had been repealed only two years earlier. She was flushed and smug. She didn't notice that the voices had tipped her cap and were chewing on the nipples of her breasts.

"You're almost there," the doctor told me. "It'll be over soon."

No. Don't give up. The voices punctured his eyes.

Eventually the pain became quiet. The voices died. They scattered like petals, and the doctor and nurse crushed them underfoot. My son, Jasper, was silent in the nurse's arms.

"I want him," I told her. She shook her head, no, and moved toward the door.

I sat up and touched my feet to the cold floor. "You bring him to me right now," I told her, starting to rise.

"You'd better let her," the doctor said as he left the room.

I held my son Jasper in my arms. His body was light as a rag doll's, but his head was heavy. His thoughts must have petrified, layer upon layer. He was beautiful like my mother. His lashes were very long, brushing down the rim of his cheeks. His body was perfect. It was hard to believe anything was wrong.

"*Abu*," I whispered. "Sleep. *Abu*." In the few minutes the nurse left me I let go of Jasper's spirit. I put my lips to the unfused well of his soft spot, whispering "*abu*," until it became a mother's song, and rocked him away.

When he returned later that same day, Marshall's hair was wet, making it spike and separate like quills on a porcupine. His face was dirty, oiled with dust, sweat, and tears. He took my face in his hands. They smelled of tobacco and were hot, as if he had just snatched them from a fire. When my tears hit his hands I expected a spitting hiss.

"It didn't work," he whispered, looking not at me but at a corner of the room where two yellow walls met in a gray shadow. "We prayed. We called on everyone we could remember, and see what happened." He was talking to himself, I thought. "See what happened," he insisted.

Marshall had driven to Herod Small War's place to pray for Jasper. Their voices had joined me from across thirty miles and held me up when I brought death into the world. The ancestors they called on for help were sleeping. The ancestors were peeking at us from behind their hands but wouldn't look, and wouldn't answer.

"It's because I'm a Bullhead," I told my husband, and I moved my eyes to the same spot in the corner of the room he had watched so carefully. I thought the gray shadow moved. I thought it quivered before settling back against the yellow walls.

I had felt empty after the delivery, light and hollow, ready to float up to the ceiling except for my heavy tears. But now I felt the familiar weight of old sin. Marshall had brought it back. He had seen its shadow in the corner. Its poison was released through my body, filling up the emptiness from my toes to the cracked-bone splinters of my mind.

"I'm a Bullhead," I repeated, and Marshall nodded. He took back his hands and stuck them in his pockets. His skin had cooled and dried, and my tears had ended. The only trace of them was a fine salt dust on my face and his fingers.

Two months after Jasper was buried brochures arrived from the Bureau of Indian Affairs. They were neatly folded, printed on slick white paper proclaiming: CHICAGO—THE CITY BEAUTIFUL!

The photographs caught my eye. They pictured elegant homes with broad staircases, grand pianos in apartments, flowers on every table; sailboats drifted on Lake Michigan, skirting the skyline; well-dressed Chicagoans smiled a welcome. I collected brochures from neighbors who were settled. I like to stand them in a semicircle on the kitchen table so that when I rested my chin on its surface the brochures rose above my head like the city itself. I surrounded myself with Chicago's promises.

"I want to go to Chicago," I told Marshall one morning. He was eating oatmeal at the kitchen table, his bowl thrust into the center of my paper city. Marshall pushed the bowl away from him, nearly destroying the delicate lake shore I'd created.

"So, you've got Relocation fever." It wasn't a question. He had seen the paper city rise.

"I want to get out of here," I nearly cried. Marshall's silence reminded me of my father's. I wanted to fill it up with all my reasons, but I didn't, because the truest reason of all was too large for my mouth. I couldn't tell Marshall that I believed Chicago would wash me in a clean light. Chicago would never know I was a Bullhead. The ancestors and *heyoka* spirits with their long memories would never see me in Chicago. I would walk barefoot on Oak Street Beach as Maxine Azure and the sun would be so bright on my head I wouldn't have a shadow to fall forward or behind.

"Don't you know it's just another one of their tricks?" Marshall scolded me. He took down the brochures, placing them in a neat pile. His hands played with the corners. "They figure if they move us out into the cities they'll get the last bit of land."

I believed him, but I didn't care. If the government was putting one over on me, I was putting one over on higher powers. I was young enough to turn into Maxine Azure and have children we would raise in the city.

Marshall started to reach for me; his right hand moved to cover my own. But instead it jerked back to the brochures, tapping their edges on the table to even them up. His incomplete gesture made me cold the way I'd been cold every night since Jasper was buried. Marshall and I no longer fit together at night like a married puzzle but kept to our own side, chilled separately by the moon. Sometimes his hand reached out to rub my back, but the hand was always cold and stiff.

Marshall was watching me. He'd never stared at me like that before because we were raised to understand it was rude. I could tell he pitied me. His eyes were sad and careful.

"Whatever you want to do, Maxine, that's what we'll do." I knew he would take me to Chicago because he felt sorry for me, something I would have hated a few months earlier. But now I just wanted to get away. I imagined in Chicago I would become the real Maxine, and my husband's pity would be transformed into wild admiration.

So we moved. Our house was government property to be turned over to another Sioux family, and our relatives took the furniture. Sitting Bull had been reburied in Mobridge, South Dakota, by white businessmen hoping to attract tourist dollars, but I went to his old grave anyway to walk the sacred ground. I visited Jasper before we left, smothering him with sage and wildflowers. "You'll always be my first child," I explained to him.

When Marshall and I drove away from Fort Yates, North Dakota, I felt the road was lined with eyes. It wasn't until we'd left the reservation and hit the highway that we drove unseen. I wondered if that was what I had wanted all my life; to be invisible so that the sin lodged inside me would wink out, drained of all its terrible power.

In Chicago Marshall and I pretended things were different. We went to the Field Museum and Marshall Field's Department Store. We stood beside the stone Water Tower. We had conversations about city life; the noise and traffic, all the different tribes we met at the Chicago Indian Center. We pretended to be angry at the BIA for fooling us, sending us pictures of the North Shore where the wealthy lived when we were caught in slum areas, chased from room to room by tenant cockroaches.

Mostly we worked hard. There was a lot of competition for jobs. I finally landed a waitressing job at an all-night cafe under the elevated train. All week I worked the late shift, coming home after midnight. Sometimes strange men walked closely behind me, so I took to strapping a thin knife to my forearm, just inside my sleeve. Marshall got home even later. He was the night watchman for the Indian Center. I liked having a key to the Center, pretending the building was mine to be divided into large apartments for all the Indian people living in Chicago. Before I found my own job I would bring Marshall a late supper, and we'd sit for hours listening to the radio. Once I started work I missed the chance for us to be together because we slept most of the day, and when we weren't sleeping the bright light made us shy, highlighting the fact that very little had actually changed.

Marshall's increasing silence was too much like my father's. It had a power I couldn't ignore. It could fill the room, doubling on itself, leaping from floor to wall to ceiling like a runaway flame, or it could drain the room like a sump pump sucking at the bottom of my shoes.

I became homesick and wrote more often to my mother. One evening on my way to work I stopped by the post office just before closing to pick up a package. My mother had sent us *wasna*—a Sioux delicacy. She had packed the small round balls consisting of ground chokecherries and cornmeal in wax paper inside a coffee can. On impulse I decided to call in sick to work, and share the *wasna* with my husband.

I enjoyed the cold walk back to the Indian Center. I had never seen so many trees together as in the city, and I liked to walk on the bright leaves collecting on the ground.

I unlocked the heavy front door of the Indian Center, shutting it behind me with my hip and shoulder. The coffee can was cold from the walk and my cheeks were numb. I had no idea where Marshall would be; the building covered half a city block and was five stories high. I started down in the basement, slowly making my way to the fifth floor. Of course he was in the last place I looked, the chapel on the top floor. An Indian minister held services there every Sunday which I liked to attend because his sermons were always on the edge of losing control. I imagined it had something to do with the setting; blood-red velvet drapes dropped from ceiling to floor, covering the four walls. The air was thick and oppressive. I had the feeling I was inside a human heart.

This time when I entered the chapel I noticed a drape had fallen from the wall. I heard voices. I don't remember walking toward the voices but I must have, because suddenly my feet trampled red velvet. Somehow the coffee can had fallen and its plastic lid popped off. Precious *wasna* rolled across the carpet. I found my husband wrapped in red velvet like a king, another woman curled to him.

Marshall jumped away from her when he saw me. He wasn't careful and his movements exposed her body. Her face made no impression, it was very white and the features seemed smudged. Her black hair was thin and stringy. But her body offended me. Stretch marks on her breasts and belly marked her fertile; she had children. Her nipples were the pressed shape of a nursing mother; they had lived.

Marshall stood before me in his shorts. I realized I was still his height.

"What're you doing here?" he asked me. He looked desperate. He couldn't look me in the eye so he discovered the *wasna*. "Wasna . . . ," he whispered stupidly.

I had choices then. I felt one in each hand. It was the sin that decided me, my great-grandfather's original sin swelling to fill me, pushing my organs aside, displacing my heart. I became the sin that was inside me from the time of my birth, and wrestled my husband to the ground.

I pinned his legs between my own and he twisted, slippery with sweat. The chapel was silent but for our breath like two snakes spitting fear. Our hands were clasped, finally warm again as they had been when we made Jasper. We wrenched arms, rolling over and over the *wasna* until it crumbled, dusting our bodies. I pushed Marshall's face into the red velvet, my knee on his neck, but he reared and threw me off. Now he was on top, his body crushing me. For a confused moment I wondered if we would make love.

The sin saved me. It was speaking aloud, its voice echoing in the chapel.

The blade. The blade.

Marshall was sitting on my ribcage and my arms were raised above my head. *He has no respect. He thinks you killed Jasper.*

The sin spoke Sioux now. *The blade.*

Marshall had relaxed for a moment. We were both tired but I was fueled by sin. In that instant I reached inside my sleeve and pulled out the knife, slim and light as a razor. I stabbed Marshall in the heart. It was a completed act.

I held Marshall in my arms as he died, and our last words were all in Sioux so the shaking white woman wouldn't understand.

"I'm sorry," he told me, his pierced breath breaking the words apart. "We should never have left."

I shook my head. It wasn't Chicago or Relocation. But I could only whisper, "I love you," and cover his body with my own to keep him warm.

When the police came I said goodbye to my husband, and I could walk in a straight line. I knew who I was. I knew as I sat in the squad car watching the dark streets of Chicago. I was Maxine Bullhead.

I am beading moccasins for my husband, Marshall Azure. I am beading the soles so I will see his flashing footprints in the sky.

Marshall is teaching Jasper to dance the old way. I can see them moving together when I close my eyes. Lt. Bullhead is dancing with an eagle-feather fan. His body shakes with joy when he bends at the waist. Sitting Bull is singing the song. His voice is high. He is smiling because they are all together.

I cry over my beadwork and prick my fingers. It is hard for me to sit up straight on the edge of my cot because sins weigh me down, heavy as cannonballs welded to my shoulders.

Sins are at the center of my headache, slicing my thoughts into wedges. The sins are a pounding fluid, ripping through my arteries with a hot fire like gunshot in the bloodstream.

Beth Cuthand

CREE

Born in northern Saskatche-wan, I am a poet, educator, and activist of the Little Pine Cree, Scots, Irish, and Blackfoot Nations. My short stories and poems have appeared in aboriginal and feminist journals and magazines.

I am the mother of two grown sons, and I teach at En'owkin International School of Writing in Penticton, British Columbia. I live in a log house overlooking Lake Okanagan with my two cats, a dog, and an intriguing cast of housemates.

Dancing with Rex

There's lightning in the sky
horses prancing in the wind
light and dark
playing tag around the big top.

There's dust devils flinging sand
on clouds traveling in groups
and Indians at a powwow
promenading around the big top.

Aunty with her handbag crosses
her hands demurely over her ample lap.
She sits tut-tutting at all the
young clouds looking to score.

Me and Rex are brushing the dust
off our boots. His canine teeth
glint in the light of lightning
and his heart beats audibly in time to the drums.

A nice sedate owl dance is starting,
under the big top.
Hey Rex, says I, shall we dance?

Well now girl, says he, can you keep up with me?

Hey Rex, says I, if I step on your feet
or grin too wide, it's just me
having a good time. Don't sweat the small stuff.

Rex laughs a big laugh, so big
you can count his teeth.
Hey girl, that's all I want to know.

So we dance and Aunty watches us closely.

She doesn't like Rex
says he acts too smart,
shows off and never takes things seriously.

We dance in time
ta-dum
ta-dum
ger-thunk
(that's Rex stepping on my feet)

Hey don't sweat the small stuff.

Rex laughs so long and loud
that the old ladies shake their heads
and even the young men
    laugh nervously.

nila northsun

SHOSHONE ▮ CHIPPEWA

*writing helps keep my sanity. es-
pecially when i'm involved in relationships which is all the
time and when i'm not it's cause for even more writing. most
of life is tragically comic so i guess i try to point that out with
irony in my work.*

    *a turning point in my life that involved the act of writing
was when i got this word processor. before i kept a spiral note-*

book under my bed and wrote at bedtime and usually got too
sleepy to put very much down, or if i had alcohol in me i
couldn't read my own writing. but now i take time to sit in
the evening at the word processor which i gifted myself with
last christmas, and can turn out three or four pages in an hour.

i don't really know who my "community" is. for the most
part i find it hard to believe somebody would read poetry. i
become amazed when somebody writes or tells me my poetry
really meant something to them, like they weren't alone.

99 things to do before you die

cosmo mag came out with a list
of 99 things to do before you die
    i had done 47 of them
or at least my version of them
like make love on the forest floor
spend a day in bed reading a good book
sleep under the stars
learn not to say yes when you mean no
but the other things
were things only rich people could do
and we certainly know
you don't have to be rich before you die
things like
dive off a yacht in the aegean
buy a round-the-world air ticket
go to monaco for the grand prix
go to rio during carnival
sure would love to but
no maza-ska
money honey
so what's a poor indian to do?
come up with a list that's more
culturally relevant

so my list includes
go 49ing at crow fair
learn of 20 ways to prepare
    commodity canned pork
or fall in love with a white person
fall in love with an indian
eat ta-nee-ga with a sioux
learn to make good fry bread
be an extra in an indian movie
learn to speak your language
give your gramma a rose and a bundle
    of sweet grass
watch a miwok deer dance
attend a hopi kachina dance
owl dance with a yakama
curl up in bed with a good indian novel
better yet
curl up in bed with a good indian novelist
ride bareback and leap over a small creek
make love in a tipi
count coup on an enemy
bathe not swim in a lake or river
wash your hair too and don't forget your pits
stop drinking alcohol
tell skinwalker stories by a campfire
almost die then appreciate your life
help somebody who has it worse than you
donate canned goods to a local food bank
sponsor a child for christmas
bet on a stick game
participate in a protest
learn a song to sing in a sweat
recycle
grow a garden
say something nice everyday to
    your mate

say something nice everyday to
    your children
chop wood for your grandpa
so there
a more attainable list
at this rate
i'm ready to die anytime
not much left undone
though cosmo's
have an affair in paris while
discoing in red leather and sipping champagne
could find a place on my list.

Wilma Mankiller

CHEROKEE

I am a Cherokee mother and grandmother. My husband Charlie Soap and I live in rural Adair County, Oklahoma, on land allotted to my grandfather at the turn of the century when the United States tried to destroy the Cherokee Nation in part by taking land we had held in common, dividing it up, and allotting it to individuals. Since the occupation of Alcatraz Island in 1969 I have been involved in Indian rights issues. I was elected first female deputy chief of the Cherokee Nation in 1983, elected first female chief in 1987, and reelected again in 1991. So much of what I have chosen for my life's work requires almost constant interaction with other people. Writing allows me to spend time in solitude telling stories about people who have taught me *how to live. I also sometimes write simply to name things that I feel but cannot articulate verbally and I write to give others a little glimpse into the complex world of contemporary Cherokee people.*

Keeping Pace with the Rest of the World

This cold gray day seemed right for what Pearl had to do. It was a simple thing really, taking her Grandma Ahniwake to the Indian Hospital—except that Ahniwake, at sixty-eight, had never been to an American doctor. She had always gone to traditional Cherokee doctors.

Ahniwake was ready when Pearl arrived. "Do you need help with anything?" Pearl asked quietly.

"If you can find my cane, I'll be ready to go. My legs are very swollen today and my left leg hurts when I walk." She did not tell Pearl that she discovered her toes were purple when she woke up that morning.

As they walked to the car Ahniwake remarked, "You know, it's been almost a year since I've been doctored. Not since Charlie Christie passed on. It will be good to feel well again." Pearl knew how long it had been. She had taken Ahniwake to other Cherokee doctors, and they had even gone to the Creeks and the Euchi but no one knew the medicine to help her. "Grandma, remember last summer when we went to see that Creek medicine man and we had to wait all night for him to finish his clan ceremony before he could talk to us?"

"Yes. And when he told us that the Creeks had also lost the secret of the blood medicine, he seemed as sad as we were." Ahniwake looked out the window at the stark beauty of early winter and said, "He was sad, Pearl. Very sad."

Pearl drove on and Ahniwake continued speaking. "When Charlie Christie passed on, we lost many of our medicine secrets. Charlie once told me that many young people came to him and told him they were interested in learning about medicine but that he couldn't teach them because they weren't willing to accept the pure lifestyle of a Cherokee doctor. For some healing ceremonies, the songs will not allow themselves to be sung by anyone except the purest of spirits."

Although she had heard the answer many times, Pearl asked her grandmother. "Is everything Charlie knew lost?"

Ahniwake was quick to say, "No. The way it was told to me, as long as Cherokee people continue to honor our ancestors and our creator through good living and our ceremonies, the roots, herbs, and medicine songs will be available to us. When it is right, these things will be shown to our people again. They are never really lost, as long as we are not lost. I wish Charlie had passed on the medicine to help me, but when it is right his knowledge will be shown to our people again."

Again they rode in silence, each lost in her own thoughts. After a while, Ahniwake laughed and said, "I hope Maude and Thelma don't find out I've gone to the clinic. Lots of times we've talked about the way things have changed—about how our people don't plant big gardens anymore, put up food for the winter, raise chickens, hunt squirrel, rabbit, and deer, or go to Cherokee doctors. I told them I would *never* go to a modern doctor, an American doctor who did not know how to heal an illness, only to cut it out." She continued fretfully, "I wish I didn't have to go. I feel almost ashamed."

The Indian Hospital was just as Ahniwake had heard it to be. The hallway and waiting room were full of people. They reminded Ahniwake of cattle waiting to be herded through a gate. When she and Pearl were seated, Ahniwake commented, "Most of these people don't much look like Indian people."

After hours of waiting, a nurse finally took Ahniwake and Pearl into a small white room. A young man entered the room, introduced himself, and began to ask questions. Pearl let him know that Ahniwake did not speak English well, and Dr. Brown began to talk to Pearl as he examined Ahniwake.

Ahniwake thought he looked like a young schoolboy—except for his eyes. He examined her with cold gadgets that matched his cold eyes, occasionally asking questions which Pearl translated. Ahniwake noticed that he made hurried notes in his folder and she commented to Pearl, "He must have a poor memory."

After fifteen minutes Dr. Brown said, "She appears to have severe diabetes, but we can't tell for sure without further tests. She also has high blood pressure and there's some indication of heart problems. We need to keep her in the hospital for some more tests. It shouldn't take more than a day or so." The doctor had already begun reading his next patient's chart when Pearl began to translate all he'd said for Ahniwake. He stopped reading to look up when Ahniwake blurted out, "No!" and started out of the room.

Pearl grabbed Ahniwake's hand and pleaded, "Grandma, it's serious. After these tests, a medicine will probably be prescribed to help with your legs. What else can we do? We've already tried to find a healer among our own. Where else can we go?" Though Ahniwake was wary of the young doctor she finally agreed to stay. "I've gone this far," she sighed. "I'll see this through to the end."

While Pearl finished filling out papers, Ahniwake was taken by wheelchair to a room more spacious than the examining room but it too was colorless and cold. Pearl waited until the nurse helped Ahniwake settle into bed before asking her what she needed from home. As Pearl was leaving, Ahniwake called out, "And don't forget to bring my hairbrush." She liked to brush her thin waist-length hair and rebraid it every night.

With Pearl gone, Ahniwake suddenly felt exhausted. She lay back on the smooth, soft pillow and fell asleep. She almost immediately slipped into a dream of her youth. She was dancing alongside her husband-to-be, Levi Buckskin, at a summer ceremonial dance. Everyone was laughing and happy. Levi and the other men sang ancient Cherokee songs while Pearl and the other women kept the rhythm with the sound of turtle shakers strapped to their lower legs. They all circled the fire, circled each other, circled the four directions of the world.

Suddenly, Ahniwake felt one of her turtle shakers slipping so she stepped out of the line of dancers and leaned down to tighten the straps. While she was stooped down, she felt chilled, the night seemed darker, and she was instinctively afraid to look up. When she finally forced herself to look up, all the other dancers had gone, the fire had died, and the only person she saw in the moonlight was a young blond man wearing a white jacket. He moved toward her and she somehow knew she had to dance with him so she managed to shakily stand up and wait for him to join her. She linked her left arm through his right arm and they began to dance. But instead of the familiar Cherokee songs she had heard earlier, he sang a fast, loud cowboy song while twirling her around so rapidly she tripped and fell to the ground. She was out of breath, there were sharp pains in the left side of her chest, she could not get on her feet again. He jerked her up, laughing in a way that frightened her even more and told her that she had to keep pace with the rest of the world.

She was still twirling around in this terrible dance with the strange blond man when Pearl shook her awake. It took her a moment to shake off the dream. It left her drained and frightened. At home she never had bad dreams—her house was well protected against such things. Though Pearl stayed to talk until Ahniwake felt sleepy again, Ahniwake did not tell her of the dream. When she fell asleep again, she slept dreamlessly through the rest of the night.

The next afternoon, the doctor came in to talk to Ahniwake. He talked very slowly, and she understood part of what he said. ". . . remove part of your foot . . . possible loss of your left leg." Ahniwake merely stared at him till he finally left the room. He returned shortly with a woman who spoke to her in Cherokee. Ahniwake did not respond. She was looking out the hospital window at the parking lot. Pearl had just parked the car and was getting out. As Pearl walked toward the hospital, Ahniwake thought how like a very young girl she looked, tall and slim with long, straight black hair.

Ahniwake sat up and waited for Pearl while the translator explained that the doctor had to remove part of her left foot to save her left leg and ultimately her life. When Pearl entered the room and saw the three of them and noticed the look on Ahniwake's face, she asked, "What's wrong here?"

After the doctor explained, Pearl turned to Ahniwake and was not surprised when she merely said, "Take me home." She knew Ahniwake would never consent to surgery, Pearl sat on the edge of the bed and dutifully repeated all that the doctor had said about her worsening leg. Ahniwake was adamant. "Pearl, I have asked you to take me home." Pearl knew it was pointless to continue pleading with her so she helped Ahniwake get dressed and collect her things; together they left the Indian Hospital.

Though she felt no better now than when she had left home the day before, Ahniwake told Pearl, "I am so happy to be home. I don't care if I can't walk again without a cane, I never want to go to that hospital again. I don't know why I agreed to go. That place may be okay for white people but it's not for Cherokees! What kind of medicine would require removal of parts of the body to heal an illness?"

While Pearl made a pot of strong coffee, Ahniwake continued, "I've heard of other people with blood problems like mine who were treated at the Indian Hospital. First they had their toes removed, then their foot, then their leg, and later they died anyway." More to herself than to Pearl, Ahniwake added, "He did not know my clan, my family, my history. How could he possibly know how to heal me?"

There was one Seminole doctor Pearl had heard people talk about. It was said that he could heal almost any illness. She decided that she would try to get some sleep and then take a day or so off from work to go to Seminole and search for him.

The next morning, after checking to be sure Ahniwake had everything she needed, Pearl went to find the Seminole doctor. After many wrong turns and telephone calls to Seminole friends, she finally found Billy Joe Harjo's house. He seemed to be expecting her. After she explained Ahniwake's symptoms in detail, Billy Joe said, "I have doctored some people with your grandmother's illness. Many of our people suffer from blood problems, but most get insulin from the Indian Hospital so the need for my medicine is not great, but I do have some."

Pearl was very excited. "When can you see her? Should we bring her up here or can you go to her house?" she asked. Billy Joe said he thought it would be better to go to Ahniwake's home.

Noting her relief and exhaustion, Billy Joe invited Pearl to spend the night. He told her to rest and that he would gather the medicine in the morning and travel to Ahniwake's house in the evening. Pearl slept well, woke up early the next morning, and began the long drive home. She stopped at her house, picked up a change of clothing, and finally arrived at Ahniwake's house in the late afternoon.

When she entered the small, warm house she received no answer. She went to the bedroom and found Ahniwake sleeping soundly. Pearl called her name repeatedly, and finally began to shake her. When Ahniwake didn't regain consciousness she decided to get help. With mounting panic she went down the road and got one of her cousins to help put Ahniwake in the car. Not knowing what else to do she took her to the Indian Hospital. Only after she got there and the interns and nurses began immediately to attach wires and cords to Ahniwake's body did Pearl allow herself to wonder if she had done the right thing. Her grandmother had told her she never wanted to come back to this hospital. "Maybe I should have tried driving back to Seminole," she thought. "But then I might have missed Billy Joe on the road," she realized. She consoled herself that she had done the only thing she could have under the circumstances.

One of the interns called the doctor who told Pearl that her grandmother was in a diabetic coma and would not regain consciousness until the insulin took effect. He advised Pearl to go home and come back in the morning. They planned to keep Ahniwake in the intensive care area and Pearl would not be allowed to stay in the room. Pearl looked at Ahniwake, thinking that she looked beautiful and untainted even with all the wires attached to her. Pearl hated to leave her in this unfamiliar place. She went into the waiting room for a couple of hours and then, finally, after another peek at Ahniwake, went on home.

Hours later, Ahniwake began trying to get through the veil of drugs and illness to figure out where she was and what was happening. She felt strange, as if she was in a space between something incredibly beautiful and the present world. She knew she was on the edge of the most significant feeling a human could experience, more powerful than childbirth, or the love of young Levi, or the feeling after a cleansing ceremony. Yet she lingered there on the edge and did not go over quite yet.

Ahniwake broke through to see a fire in the center of a white room. After she was able to focus her eyes, she realized it was not a fire but a bright light. She was in that hospital again! There were tubes in her hands, on her chest. She tried to call out but there was even a tube in her throat. She managed to turn her head slightly toward the sound of voices. She could see two men in white talking by the swinging doors. One started walking toward her. To her absolute horror it was the same man who had appeared in her dream. The doctor walked behind him and said, "It won't do much good to try to talk to her even if she's conscious. She doesn't speak English." The young bad-dream doctor replied, "She should have kept pace with the rest of the world," and laughed the same frightening way he had in her dream. As he got closer to her bed, she felt a sharp pain in her chest and as the bad-dream doctor reached toward her she tried to move away and could not. He leaned down, linked arms with her, and began to sing the loud cowboy song he had sung in her dream. She gave in and they began to dance that same fast, whirling dance until she again stumbled and fell. But this time she fell much further. She floated into the soft arms of her Mother Earth and lay nestled there near the fire—waiting for the Creator, waiting for her life to be complete.

Pearl was up early the next morning. She wanted to get some of Ahniwake's things before going to the hospital. She also needed to find out what had happened to the Seminole doctor. She telephoned Billy Harjo's and found out that he had gone to Ahniwake's house while they were at the hospital and finding no one there had returned home. She wanted to take care of all her other errands too so she and Ahniwake would be free just to talk when she arrived at the hospital. She knew her grandmother would be mad because she'd taken her back to the hospital but they would talk about it.

Pearl was sure she could convince Ahniwake that she'd done the only thing she could. They had always enjoyed each other's company. They would talk for hours, more like girlfriends or sisters than grandmother and granddaughter. Because of Ahniwake, Pearl had learned the Cherokee language and knew many of the ancient tribal stories.

The past few days had been so extraordinary that when Pearl got to Ahniwake's she paused for a moment to absorb the familiarity of the house. She had always liked this house. Levi had built it when he and Ahniwake were very young. It was lighted by coal oil, heated by wood, and Ahniwake still drew her water from a well out back. Pearl's own father had been raised in the wood-frame house and Pearl herself had spent many years there. It was warm with memories and if a house could be friendly, then Ahniwake's house was definitely so.

Pearl got to the hospital in the late morning. When she stopped at the nurse's station to ask for the room number of Ahniwake Buckskin, the nurse said, "You need to talk to the doctor."

Pearl felt a surge of fear. Questions went rapidly through her mind. What was wrong? Was Ahniwake still in a coma? Was she still in the emergency room? What was it? The nurse asked her to sit down but Pearl leaned against the nurse's station and watched the hallway until she saw the doctor. As he came toward her she knew that he had no good news for her. Before he could say anything, Pearl surprised herself by yelling, "What have you done to Grandma? I want to see her now. Where is she?" Pearl knew she was shouting to keep the doctor from talking and to keep herself from thinking.

The doctor put his hands on her shoulders and said, "Pearl, Ahniwake died of a heart attack last night. I can't explain it. We decided to perform an emergency amputation of her left foot. It's really a relatively minor surgical procedure. She was in the recovery room. I was there with her. I thought I saw her move her head slightly so I went over to examine her. She suddenly looked terribly frightened, as if I were some sort of monster. She had a massive heart attack. There was nothing we could do."

Pearl shook his hands off her shoulders, slapped him as hard as she could, and left the hospital.

Pearl went to her uncle's house and asked him to go to the hospital to get Ahniwake and let the rest of her relatives know of Ahniwake's death. Pearl then went to Ahniwake's house to wait for the others to arrive for the wake. She built a fire in the old wood stove and sat and watched the flames. She knew she should put on coffee and stew or beans for the many relatives who would come to see Ahniwake one last time but she did not move from her place in front of the fire.

It was now almost dark and the house was lighted only by the fire. She suddenly felt warm, as she had often felt when she and Ahniwake were together and her eyes were drawn to a certain spot in the fire. She leaned forward and looked more closely. There, in the back of the flames, she saw Ahniwake with old man Charlie Christie on one side and Levi Buckskin on the other. Ahniwake looked very happy but Pearl began to weep. They could not speak to each other across the worlds that separated them but Pearl knew the message Ahniwake was sending. Once again she heard Ahniwake saying, "As long as the Cherokee people honor our ancestors and our Creator, the roots, herbs, and medicine songs will be available to us. These things will be shown to our people again. They are never really lost as long as we are not lost."

There in the warmth of these words, Pearl knew what it was she had to do. She vowed to do all in her power to restore and revitalize the traditional Cherokee way of life as a tribute to Ahniwake and to the lives of other Cherokees who are yet unborn.

Louise Bernice Halfe

CREE

Many, many events have moved me in life. Meeting my mate. I'm still awed by the celebration of our twenty-two years together. Each birth of my two children, their tiny fingers, breast-feeding, and watching them grow taller than I. The loss of an infant, the heart-wrenching struggle of battling with emotions I thought must be wrong. The loss of my brother and of my grandfolks. Obtaining a degree in my late thirties. Putting on weight, taking it off. I don't find it easy to answer the question that has moved me most deeply in life. How do you measure a cup of air? Each journey, each process moves. Sometimes beyond our comprehension. Life-Death-Life—that is what moves us so profoundly.

Pāhkahkos

Flying skeleton
I used to wonder where
You kept yourself.
I'd hear you rattle about
Scraping your bones.

I opened a door
You grinned at me through a
Hollow mouth
Pierced my heart with your
Socket eyes.

Lifted your bony hands
To greet me . . . and I
With a soundless shriek
Ran.

Upon my back you jumped
Clinging to my neck you hugged
My mound of flesh.

For a thousand years you were
A companion who would not leave
Bones heavy.

You knocked your skeleton
Skull upon my head
And I felt your leaden feet.
I dragged and dragged until

I could not carry
your burden more
I pried you loose
Bone after bone.

We stood face to face
Pāhkahkos, your skeleton frame
All exposed
And I, lighter than I could stand

I fed you the drink of healing tears
And you ran your skeleton fingers
Down your face and onto mine.

I gave you a prayer cloth
And weaved a blanket of forgiveness
And you covered us both, skeleton and flesh

I gave you the smoke of truth
And you lit your Pipe to life
and lifted it to your ghostly mouth,
and to mine.

My Pāhkahkos companion,
My dancing skeleton
My dancing friend

We carry our bundles
Side by side
Hands held.

Odilia Galván Rodríguez

LIPAN APACHE

I am a descendant of tribal people who moved across this country as a way of life. After several generations, what had once been a way of life became a very different existence and survival was based on the availability of farm work. When my father, a Korean War veteran, returned home from the war he had visions of a better life for his children. Instead of having us follow the crops from Texas to Illinois like the rest of our family, he chose to work as a laborer in the Chicago steel mills. The reality was that our family experienced much of the same economic hardships and this, coupled with the terrible isolation of urban nuclear family life, made it impossible for my parents to stay together. I experienced firsthand what alcohol can do to our people, how *families and lives are torn apart by this drug. I began writing at age fifteen. The immense turmoil of my family's life and the world around me offered no solace. Writing became my escape, my survival.*

I was a teenager during the late sixties and early seventies and was aware of the great changes the country was experiencing because of national opposition to the Vietnam War and the freedom and power struggles of people of color. As a result of my early involvement in political struggles, I have been a community and labor organizer, have served on countless boards and commissions, and have even taken to the streets. Most of my activist work now is related to my writing.

I write about the world that I see and would like to change. I dream the world for generations to come and write. I write about what makes me angry, joyful, and what I love most in the world. I listen to my voices: the grandmothers and grandfathers who see what's going on, what we are doing or not doing to the earth and ourselves. My writing calls them from the other side.

Last Rites

FOR SEAN

I stop the clocks in the house   cover mirrors with sorry purple cloth / eating hard boiled I sit on furniture bare of its cushions telling the four corners of your life on earth / what do I know of your living?   you were always home for me / to listen   to argue me to stay in this town I'd say doesn't fit you   can't take it back you'd say / I would always laugh knowing it meant you really just wanted me to stay. /

your body should have been washed in the finest herbs and flowers   then wrapped in soft cloth / instead they slit you open like a fish   inspected you like so many sides of beef left you ripe / bleeding the blood where they would find the drugs they say took you into the next world / you should

have been body-painted blue have been given a special tattoo so your ancestors would recognize you / those hunters
and gatherers you were so proud of would call you back
let you inside the special red door /

fashioning you a new age tombstone   your new car and
the fence in front of it / I put up a bouquet of freesias
calla lilies and birds of paradise / your pictures hanging from
colored ribbons flutter free on the chain link / soon other
friends' gifts appear   candles   crystal bowls full of water
and chocolate / no gravesite more befitting   the parking
lot of the City where your spirit still saturates /

in three short days my offerings like your body become
ashes swimming in a black night / while our drums beat
you a warrior's farewell   sage wafting our prayers up to
the turquoise sky / your last wish of me is granted   I am
here planted   not remembering where or why I was going
away

Louise Erdrich

TURTLE MOUNTAIN CHIPPEWA

Y ou can be married to the most
wonderful man on earth. You're still a woman. You can be
married to the Blessed Virgin. You can be married to the pope.
You can be ass-deep in money, charged with success like a
brand-new car battery. You can have fifteen-minute labors and
perfect breasts and you're still a woman. Can't get around it

TRANSFORMATION ▮ 411

> *. . . I am not a scientist, not a naturalist, not a chef, not an expert, not the best or worst mother, but a writer only, a woman constantly surprised.*

The World's Greatest Fishermen

1

The morning before Easter Sunday, June Kashpaw was walking down the clogged main street of oil boomtown Williston, North Dakota, killing time before the noon bus arrived that would take her home. She was a long-legged Chippewa woman, aged hard in every way except how she moved. Probably it was the way she moved, easy as a young girl on slim hard legs, that caught the eye of the man who rapped at her from inside the window of the Rigger Bar. He looked familiar, like a lot of people looked familiar to her. She had seen so many come and go. He hooked his arm, inviting her to enter, and she did so without hesitation, thinking only that she might tip down one or two with him and then get her bags to meet the bus. She wanted, at least, to see if she actually knew him. Even through the watery glass she could see that he wasn't all that old and that his chest was thickly padded in dark red nylon and expensive down.

There were cartons of colored eggs on the bar, each glowing like a jewel in its wad of cellophane. He was peeling one, sky blue as a robin's, palming it while he thumbed the peel aside, when she walked through the door. Although the day was overcast, the snow itself reflected such light that she was momentarily blinded. It was like going underwater. What she walked toward more than anything else was that blue egg in the white hand, a beacon in the murky air.

He ordered a beer for her, a Blue Ribbon, saying she deserved a prize for being the best thing he'd seen for days. He peeled an egg for her, a pink one, saying it matched her turtleneck. She told him it was no turtleneck. You called these things shells. He said he would peel that for her, too, if she wanted, then he grinned at the bartender and handed her the naked egg.

June's hand was colder from the outdoors than the egg, and so she had to let it sit in her fingers for a minute before it stopped feeling rubbery warm. Eating it, she found out how hungry she was. The last of the money that the man before this one had given her was spent for the ticket. She didn't know exactly when she'd eaten last. This man seemed impressed, when her egg was finished, and peeled her another one just like it. She ate the egg. Then another egg. The bartender looked at her. She shrugged and tapped out a long menthol cigarette from a white plastic case inscribed with her initials in golden letters. She took a breath of smoke then leaned toward her companion through the broken shells.

"What's happening?" she said. "Where's the party?"

Her hair was rolled carefully, sprayed for the bus trip, and her eyes were deeply watchful in their sea-blue flumes of shadow. She was deciding.

"I don't got much time until my bus . . . ," she said.

"Forget the bus!" He stood up and grabbed her arm. "We're gonna party. Hear? Who's stopping us? We're having a good time!"

She couldn't help notice, when he paid up, that he had a good-sized wad of money in a red rubber band like the kind that holds bananas together in the supermarket. That roll helped. But what was more important, she had a feeling. The eggs were lucky. And he had a good-natured slowness about him that seemed different. He could be different, she thought. The bus ticket would stay good, maybe forever. They weren't expecting her up home on the reservation. She didn't even have a man there, except the one she'd divorced. Gordie. If she got desperate he would still send her money. So she went on to the next bar with this man in the dark red vest. They drove down the street in his Silverado pickup. He was a mud engineer. Andy. She didn't tell him she'd known many mud engineers before or about that one she'd heard was killed by a pressurized hose. The hose had shot up into his stomach from underground.

The thought of that death, although she'd only been half acquainted with the man, always put a panicky, dry lump in her throat. It was the hose, she thought, snaking up suddenly from its unseen nest, the idea of that hose striking like a live thing, that was fearful. With one blast it had taken out his insides. And that too made her throat ache, although she'd heard of worse things. It was that moment, that one moment, of realizing you were totally empty. He must have felt that. Sometimes, alone in her room in the dark, she thought she knew what it might be like.

Later on, the noise falling around them at a crowded bar, she closed her eyes for a moment against the smoke and saw that hose pop suddenly through black earth with its killing breath.

"Ahhhhh," she said, surprised, almost in pain, "you got to be."

"I got to be what, honeysuckle?" He tightened his arm around her slim shoulders. They were sitting in a booth with a few others, drinking Angel Wings. Her mouth, the lipstick darkly blurred now, tipped unevenly toward his.

"You got to be different," she breathed.

It was later still that she felt so fragile. Walking toward the Ladies' she was afraid to bump against anything because her skin felt hard and brittle, and she knew it was possible, in this condition, to fall apart at the slightest touch. She locked herself in the bathroom stall and remembered his hand, thumbing back the transparent skin and crackling blue peel. Her clothing itched. The pink shell was sweaty and hitched up too far under her arms but she couldn't take off her jacket, the white vinyl her son King had given her, because the pink top was ripped across the stomach. But as she sat there, something happened. All of a sudden she seemed to drift out of her clothes and skin with no help from anyone. Sitting, she leaned down and rested her forehead on the top of the metal toilet-roll dispenser. She felt that underneath it all her body was pure and naked—only the skins were stiff and old. Even if he was no different, she would get through this again.

Her purse dropped out of her hand, spilling. She sat up straight. The doorknob rolled out of her open purse and beneath the stall.

She had to take that doorknob with her every time she left her room. There was no other way of locking the battered door. Now she picked up the knob and held it by the metal shank. The round grip was porcelain, smooth and white. Hard as stone. She put it in the deep pocket of her jacket and, holding it, walked back to the booth through the gathering crowd. Her room was locked. And she was ready for him now.

It was a relief when they finally stopped, far out of town on a county road. Even in the dark, when he turned his headlights off, the snow reflected enough light to see by. She let him wrestle with her clothing, but he worked so clumsily that she had to help him along. She rolled her top up carefully, still hiding the rip, and arched her back to let him undo her slacks. They were made of a stretch fabric that crackled with electricity and shed blue sparks when he pushed them down around her ankles. He knocked his hand against the heater's controls. She felt it open at her shoulder like a pair of jaws, blasting heat, and had the momentary and vo-luptuous sensation that she was lying stretched out before a great wide mouth. The breath swept across her throat, tightening her nipples. Then his vest plunged down against her, so slick and plush that it was like being rubbed by an enormous tongue. She couldn't get a handhold anywhere. And she felt herself slipping along the smooth plastic seat, slipping away, until she wedged the crown of her head against the driver's door.

"Oh God," he was moaning. "Oh God, Mary. Oh God, it's good."

He wasn't doing anything, just moving his hips on top of her, and at last his head fell heavily.

"Say there," she said, shaking him. "Andy?" She shook him harder. He didn't move or miss a beat in his deep breathing. She knew there wasn't any rousing him now, so she lay still, under the weight of him. She stayed quiet until she felt herself getting frail again. Her skin felt smooth and strange. And then she knew that if she lay there any longer she would crack wide open, not in one place but in many pieces that he would crush by moving in his sleep. She thought to pull herself back together. So she hooked an arm over her head and brought her elbow down slowly on the handle, releasing it. The door suddenly sprang wide.

June had wedged herself so tight against the door that when she sprang the latch she fell out. Into the cold. It was a shock like being born. But somehow she landed with her pants halfway up, as though she'd hoisted them in midair, and then she quickly did her bra, pulled her shell down, and reached back into the truck. Without groping she found her jacket and purse. By now it was unclear whether she was more drunk or more sober than she'd ever been in her life. She left the door open. The heater, set to an automatic temperature, yawned hoarsely behind her, and she heard it, or thought she did, for about a half mile down the road. Then she heard nothing but her own boots crunching ice. The snow was bright, giving back starlight. She concentrated on her feet, on steering them strictly down the packed wheel ruts.

She had walked far enough to see the dull orange glow, the canopy of low, lit clouds over Williston, when she decided to walk home instead of going back there. The wind was mild and wet. A Chinook wind, she told herself. She made a right turn off the road, walked up a drift frozen over a snow fence, and began to pick her way through the swirls of dead grass and icy crust of open ranchland. Her boots were thin. So she stepped on dry ground where she could and avoided the slush and rotten, gray banks. It was exactly as if she were walking back from a fiddle dance or a friend's house to Uncle Eli's warm, man-smelling kitchen. She crossed the wide fields swinging her purse, stepping carefully to keep her feet dry.

Even when it started to snow she did not lose her sense of direction. Her feet grew numb, but she did not worry about the distance. The heavy winds couldn't blow her off course. She continued. Even when her heart clenched and her skin turned crackling cold it didn't matter, because the pure and naked part of her went on.

The snow fell deeper that Easter than it had in forty years, but June walked over it like water and came home.

2
Albertine Johnson

After that false spring, when the storm blew in covering the state, all the snow melted off and it was summer. It was almost hot by the week after Easter, when I found out, in Mama's letter, that June was gone—not only dead but suddenly buried, vanished off the land like that sudden snow.

Far from home, living in a white woman's basement, that letter made me feel buried, too. I opened the envelope and read the words. I was sitting at my linoleum table with my textbook spread out to the section on "Patient Abuse." There were two ways you could think of that title. One was obvious to a nursing student, and the other was obvious to a Kashpaw. Between my mother and myself the abuse was slow and tedious, requiring long periods of dormancy, living in the blood like hepatitis. When it broke out it was almost a relief.

"We knew you probably couldn't get away from your studies for the funeral," said the letter, "so we never bothered to call and disturb you."

She always used the royal *we*, to multiply the censure of what she said by invisible others.

I put down the letter and just stared, the way you do when you are hit by a bad thing you can do nothing about. At first it made me so angry that Mama hadn't called me for the funeral that I couldn't even feel the proper way for Aunt June. Then after a while I saw where I was staring—through the window at the level of the earth—and I thought of her.

I thought of June sitting tense in Grandma's kitchen, flicking an ash, jiggling a foot back and forth in a pointed shoe. Or smartly cracking her purse to buy each of us children a dairy cone. I thought of her brushing my hair past my waist, when it was that long, and saying that I had princess hair. Princess hair! I wore it unbraided after she said that, until it tangled so badly that Mama cut precious inches off.

June was raised by Great-Uncle Eli, the old bachelor in the

family. He'd taken her in when Grandma's sister died and June's no-good Morrissey father ran off to high-time it in the Cities. After she had grown up and looked around for a while, June decided on my uncle, Gordie Kashpaw, and married him even though they had to run away to do it. They were cousins, but almost like brother and sister. Grandma wouldn't let them in the house for a year, she was so angry. As it turned out, it was an off-and-on marriage anyway. Being so much alike they both liked to have their fun. Then, too, June had no patience with children. She wasn't much as a mother; everyone in the family said so, even Eli who was crazy about his little girl.

Whatever she lacked as a mother, June was a good aunt to have—the kind that spoiled you. She always kept an extra stick of Doublemint in her coat pocket. Her neck smelled fresh and sweet. She talked to me the way she talked to grown-up people and never told me to play outside when I wanted to sit at the edge of a conversation. She had been pretty. "Miss Indian America," Grandpa called her. She had stayed pretty even when things got so bad with Gordie that she ran off alone, "like a no-good Morrissey," people said, leaving her son King. She always planned that she would make it somewhere else first, then send for the boy. But everything she tried fell through.

When she was studying to be a beautician, I remember, word came that she had purposely burned an unruly customer's hair stiff green with chemicals. Other secretaries did not like her. She reported drunk for work in dimestores and swaggered out of restaurants where she'd waitressed a week, at the first wisecrack. Sometimes she came back to Gordie and they made the marriage work for a while longer. Then she would leave again. As time went by she broke, little by little, into someone whose shoulders sagged when she thought no one was looking, a woman with long ragged nails and hair always growing from its beauty-parlor cut. Her clothes were full of safety pins and hidden tears. I thought now that her one last try had been Williston, a town full of rich, single cowboy-rigger oil trash.

One type I know is boom trash, the ones that bat around the

state in big pickups that are loaded with options. I know, because I worked with them, that to these types an Indian woman's nothing but an easy night. I saw it laid out clear, as I sat there at my table, how down to the limit that kind of life would have gotten June. But what did I know, in fact, about the thing that happened?

I saw her laughing, so sharp and determined, her purse clutched tight at the bar, her perfect legs crossed.

"Probably drank too much," Mama wrote. She naturally hadn't thought well of June. "Probably wandered off too intoxicated to realize about the storm."

But June grew up on the plains. Even drunk she'd have known a storm was coming. She'd have known by the heaviness in the air, the smell in the clouds. She'd have gotten that animal sinking in her bones.

I sat there at my table, thinking about June. From time to time, overhead, I heard my landlady's vacuum cleaner. Through my window there wasn't much to see—dirt and dead snow and wheels rolling by in the street. It was warm but the grass was brown, except in lush patches over the underground steam pipes on the campus. I did something that day. I put on my coat and went walking down the street until I came to a big stretch of university lawn that was crossed by a steam-pipe line of grass—so bright your eyes ached —and even some dandelions. I walked out there and lay down on that patch of grass, above the ground, and I thought of Aunt June until I felt the right way for her.

I was so mad at my mother, Zelda, that I didn't write or call for almost two months. She should have gone up the nun's hill to the convent, like she wanted, instead of having me. But she had married Swede Johnson from off-reservation, and I'd arrived premature. He'd had the grace, at least, to go AWOL from army boot camp and never let his face be seen again. All I knew of him was pictures, blond, bleak, and doomed to wander, perhaps as much by Mama's rage at her downfall as by the uniform. I'd been the one who'd really blocked my mother's plans for being pure. I'd forced her to work for money, keeping books, instead of pursuing tasks that would bring divine glory on her head. I'd caused her to live in a trailer near Grandma so that there would be someone to care for me. Later on, I'd provided her with years of grinding grief. I had gone through a long phase of wickedness and run away. Yet now that I was on the straight and narrow, things were even worse between us.

After two months were gone and my classes were done, and although I still had not forgiven my mother, I decided to go home. I wasn't crazy about the thought of seeing her, but our relationship was like a file we sharpened on, and necessary in that way. So I threw a few books and some clothes in the backseat of my Mustang. It was the first car I'd ever owned, a dull black hard-driven car with rusted wheel wells, a stick shift, and a windshield wiper only on the passenger side.

All along the highway that early summer the land was beautiful. The sky stretched bare. Tattered silver windbreaks bounded flat, plowed fields that the government had paid to lie fallow. Everything else was dull tan—the dry ditches, the dying crops, the buildings of farms and towns. Rain would come just in time that year. Driving north, I could see the earth lifting. The wind was hot and smelled of tar and the moving dust.

At the end of the big farms and the blowing fields was the reservation. I always knew it was coming a long way off. Even in the distance you sense hills from their opposites—pits, dried sloughs, ditches of cattails, potholes. And then the water. There would be water in the hills when there wasn't any on the plains, because the hollows saved it, collected runoff from the low slopes, and the dense trees held it, too. I thought of water in the roots of trees, brown and bark smelling, cold.

The highway narrowed off and tangled, then turned to gravel with ruts, holes, and blue alfalfa bunching in the ditches. Small hills reared up. Dogs leaped from nowhere and ran themselves out fiercely. The dust hung thick.

My mother lives just on the very edge of the reservation with her new husband, Bjornson, who owns a solid wheat farm. She's lived there about a year. I grew up with her in an aqua-and-silver trailer, set next to the old house on the land my great-grandparents were allotted when the government decided to turn Indians into farmers.

The policy of allotment was a joke. As I was driving toward the land, looking around, I saw as usual how much of the reservation was sold to whites and lost forever. Just three miles, and I was driving down the rutted dirt road, home.

The main house, where all of my aunts and uncles grew up, is one big square room with a cooking shack tacked onto it. The house is a light peeling lavender now, the color of a pale petunia, but it was never painted while I lived there. My mother had it painted for Grandma as an anniversary present last year. Soon after the paint job the two old ones moved into town where things were livelier and they didn't have to drive so far to church. Luckily, as it happened, the color suited my Aunt Aurelia, because she moved into the house and has taken care of it since.

Driving up to the house I saw that her brown car and my mother's creamy yellow one were parked in the yard. I got out. They were indoors, baking. I heard their voices from the steps and smelled the rich and browning piecrusts. But when I walked into the dim, warm kitchen they hardly acknowledged me, they were so involved in their talk.

"She sure *was* good-looking," Aurelia argued, hands buried in a dishpan of potato salad.

"Some people use spoons to mix." My mother held out a heavy tin one from the drawer and screwed her lips up like a coin purse to kiss me. She lit her eyes and widened them. "I was only saying she had seen a few hard times, and there was bruises. . . ."

"Wasn't either. You never saw her." Aurelia was plump, a "looker." She waved my mother's spoon off with a caked hand. "In fact, did anybody see her? Nobody saw her. Nobody knows for sure what happened, so who's to squawk about bruises and so on . . . nobody saw her."

"Well I heard," said Mama, "I heard she was with a man and he dumped her off."

I sat down, dipped a slice of apple in the bowl of sugar-cinnamon topping, and ate it. They were talking about June.

"Heard nothing," Aurelia snapped. "Don't trust nothing you don't see with your own eyes. June was all packed up and ready to come home. They found her bags when they busted in her room. She walked out there because"—Aurelia foundered, then her voice strengthened—"what did she have to come home to after all? Nothing!"

"Nothing?" said Mama piercingly. "Nothing to come home to?" She gave me a short glance full of meaning. I had, after all, come home, even if husbandless, childless, driving a fall-apart car. I looked away from her. She puffed her cheeks out in concentration, patting and crimping the edges of the pies. They were beautiful pies—rhubarb, wild Juneberry, apple, and gooseberry, all fruits preserved by Grandma Kashpaw or my mother or Aurelia.

"I suppose you washed your hands before you put them in that salad," she said to Aurelia.

Aurelia squeezed her face into crescents of patient exasperation. "Now Zelda," she said, "your girl's going to think you still treat me like your baby sister."

"Well you are aren't you? Can't change that."

"I'm back," I said.

They looked at me as if I had, at that very moment, walked in the door.

"Albertine's home," observed Aurelia. "My hands are full or I'd hug you."

"Here," said Mama, setting down a jar of pickles near me. "Aren't you dressed nice. Did you get your top in Fargo? Was the drive good?"

I said yes.

"Dice these pickles up." She handed me a bowl and knife.

"June went after Gordie like he didn't have no choice," my mother decided now. "She could at least have kept him happy once she got him in her clutch! It's just clear how Gordie loved her, only now he takes it out in liquor. He's always over at Eli's house trying to get Eli to join him for a toot. You know, after the way June treated him, I don't know why Gordie didn't just let her go to ruin."

"Well, she couldn't get much more ruined than dead," Aurelia said.

The odd thing about the two—Mama with her flat blue-black ponytail and rough gray face, Aurelia with her careful permanent, high rounded cheeks, tight jeans, and frilled rodeo shirt—was the differenter they acted the more alike they showed themselves. They clung to their rock-bottom opinions. They were so strong in their beliefs that there came a time when it hardly mattered what exactly those beliefs were; they all fused into a single stubbornness.

Mama gave up discussing June after Aurelia's observation and began on me.

"Have you met any marriageable boys in Fargo yet?" Her flat gray thumbs pursued each other around and around in circles, leaving perfect squeezed scallops. By marriageable I knew she meant Catholic. I shook my head no.

"At this rate I'll be too old and stiff to take care of my own grandchildren," Mama said. Then she smiled and shrugged her shoulders lightly. "My girl's choosy like me," she said. "Can't be too choosy."

Aurelia snorted, but contained her remark, which probably would have referred to Mama's first husband.

"Albertine's got time," Aurelia answered for me. "What's her rush? Believe me"—she addressed me now with mock serious vigor—"marriage is not the answer to it all. I tried it enough myself."

"I'm not interested anyway," I let them know. "I've got other things to do."

"Oh my," said Mama, "are you going to be a career girl?"

She froze with her hands in the air, seemingly paralyzed by the idea.

"*You* were a career girl," I accused her. I handed her the pickles, all diced into little cubes. Mama had kept books for the priests and nuns up at Sacred Heart since I could remember. She ignored me, however, and began to poke wheels of fork marks in the tops of the pies. Aurelia mixed. I watched my mother's hands precisely stabbing. After a while we heard the car from the main road as it slowed for the turn. It would be June's son, King, his wife, Lynette, and King Junior. They drove up to the front steps in their brand-new sportscar. King Junior was bundled in the front seat and both Grandma and Grandpa Kashpaw were stuffed, incredibly, into the tiny backseat.

"There's that white girl." Mama peeked out the window.

"Oh, for gosh sakes." Aurelia gave her heady snort again, and this time did not hold her tongue. "What about your Swedish boy?"

"Learnt my lesson." Mama wiped firmly around the edges of Aurelia's dishpan. "Never marry a Swedish is my rule."

Grandma Kashpaw's rolled-down nylons and brown support shoes appeared first, then her head in its iron-gray pageboy. Last of all the entire rest of her squeezed through the door, swathed in acres of tiny black-sprigged flowers. When I was very young, she always seemed the same size to me as the rock cairns commemorating Indian defeats around here. But every time I saw her now I realized that she wasn't so large, it was just that her figure was weathered and massive as a statue roughed out in rock. She never changed much, at least not so much as Grandpa. Since I'd left home, gone to school, he'd turned into an old man. Age had come upon him suddenly, like a storm in fall, shaking yellow leaves down overnight, and now his winter, deep and quiet, was on him. As Grandma shook out her dress and pulled bundles through the back window, Grandpa sat quietly in the car. He hadn't noticed that it had stopped. "Why don't you tell him it stopped," Grandma called to Lynette.

Lynette was changing King Junior's diaper in the front seat. She generally used paper diapers with stick-'em tabs at her home in the Cities, but since she'd been here my mother had shamed her into using washable cloth diapers and sharp pins. The baby wiggled and fought her hands.

"You hear?" King, already out of the car and nervously examining his tires, stuck his head back in the driver's side window and barked at Lynette. "She was calling you. My father's mother. She just told you to do something."

Lynette's face, stained and swollen, bloomed over the wheel. She was a dirty blond, with little patches of hair that were bleached and torn. "Yes I heard," she hissed through the safety pins in her teeth. "You tell him."

Jerking the baby up, ankles pinned in the forks of her fingers, she repositioned the triangle of cloth under his bottom.

"Grandma told you to tell him." King leaned farther in. He had his mother's long slim legs, and I remembered all at once, seeing him bend all the way into the car, June bending that way, too. Me behind her. She had pushed a rowboat off the gravel beach of some lake we'd all gone to visit together. I had jumped into the rowboat with her. She had one son at the time and didn't think that she would ever have another child. So she spoiled me and told me everything, believing I did not understand. She told me things you'd only tell another woman, full grown, and I had adored her wildly for these adult confidences, for her wreaths of blue smoke, for the figure she cut. I had adored her into telling me everything she needed to tell, and it was true, I hadn't understood the words at the time. But she hadn't counted on my memory. Those words stayed with me.

And even now, King was saying something to Lynette that had such an odd dreaming ring to it I almost heard it spoken out in June's voice.

June had said, "He used the flat of his hand. He hit me good." And now I heard her son say, ". . . flat of my hand . . . but good . . ."

Lynette rolled out the door, shedding cloth and pins, packing the bare-bottomed child on her hip, and I couldn't tell what had happened.

Grandpa hadn't noticed, whatever it was. He turned to the open door and stared at his house.

"This reminds me of something," he said.

"Well, it should. It's your house!" Mama barreled out the door, grabbed both of his hands, and pulled him out of the little backseat.

"You have your granddaughter here, Daddy!" Zelda shrieked carefully into Grandpa's face. "Zelda's daughter. She came all the way up here to visit from school."

"Zelda . . . born September fourteenth, nineteen forty-one . . ."

"No, Daddy. This here is my daughter, Albertine. Your granddaughter."

I took his hand.

Dates, numbers, figures stuck with Grandpa since he strayed, and not the tiring collection of his spawn, proliferating beyond those numbers into nowhere. He took my hand and went along, trusting me whoever I was.

Whenever he came out to the home place now, Grandpa had to get reacquainted with the yard of stunted oaks, marigold beds, the rusted car that had been his children's playhouse and mine, the few hills of potatoes and stalks of rhubarb that Aurelia still grew. She worked nights, managing a bar, and couldn't keep the place as nicely as Grandpa always had. Walking him slowly across the lawn, I sidestepped prickers. The hollyhocks were choked with pigweed, and the stones that lined the driveway, always painted white or blue, were flaking back to gray. So was the flat boulder under the clothesline—once my favorite cool place to sit doing nothing while the clothes dried, hiding me.

This land had been allotted to Grandpa's mother, old Rushes Bear, who had married the original Kashpaw. When allotments were handed out all of her twelve children except the youngest—Nector and Eli—had been old enough to register for their own. But because there was no room for them in the North Dakota wheatlands, most were deeded parcels far off, in Montana, and had to move there or sell. The older children left, but the brothers still lived on opposite ends of Rushes Bear's land.

She had let the government put Nector in school, but hidden Eli, the one she couldn't part with, in the root cellar dug beneath her floor. In that way she gained a son on either side of the line. Nector came home from boarding school knowing white reading and writing, while Eli knew the woods. Now, these many years later, hard to tell why or how, my Great-Uncle Eli was still sharp, while

Grandpa's mind had left us, gone wary and wild. When I walked with him I could feel how strange it was. His thoughts swam between us, hidden under rocks, disappearing in weeds, and I was fishing for them, dangling my own words like baits and lures.

I wanted him to tell me about things that happened before my time, things I'd been too young to understand. The politics for instance. What had gone on? He'd been an astute political dealer, people said, horse-trading with the government for bits and shreds. Somehow he'd gotten a school built, a factory too, and he'd kept the land from losing its special Indian status under that policy called termination. I wanted to know it all. I kept asking questions as we walked along, as if he'd take the hook by miracle and blurt the memory out right there.

"Remember how you testified . . . ? What was it like . . . the old schools . . . Washington . . . ?"

Elusive, pregnant with history, his thoughts finned off and vanished. The same color as water. Grandpa shook his head, remembering dates with no events to go with them, names without faces, things that happened out of place and time. Or at least it seemed that way to me. Grandma and the others were always hushing up the wild things he said or talking loudly over them. Maybe they were bored with his craziness, and then again maybe his mind blurted secrets from the past. If the last was true, sometimes I thought I understood.

Perhaps his loss of memory was a protection from the past, absolving him of whatever had happened. He had lived hard in his time. But he smiled into the air and lived calmly now, without guilt or desolation. When he thought of June, for instance, she was a young girl who fed him black plums. That was the way she would always be for him. His great-grandson, King Junior, was happy because he hadn't yet acquired a memory, while perhaps Grandpa's happiness was in losing his.

We walked back down the driveway, along the flaking rocks. "He likes that busted lawn chair," Grandma hollered now, leaning out the door. "Set him there awhile."

"Want me to get you a plate from the kitchen?" I asked Grandpa. "Some bread and butter?"

But he was looking at the collapsed heap anxiously and did not answer.

I pulled the frayed, woven plastic and aluminum into the shape of a chair, he settled into it, and I left him counting something under his breath. Clouds. Trees. All the blades of grass.

I went inside. Grandma was unlocking her expensive canned ham. She patted it before putting it in the oven and closed the door carefully.

"She's not used to buying this much meat," Zelda said. "Remember we used to trade for it?"

"Or slaughter our own." Aurelia blew a round gray cloud of Winston smoke across the table.

"Pew," said Zelda. "Put the top on the butter." She flapped her hand in front of her nose. "You know, Mama, I bet this makes you wish it was like it used to be. All us kids in the kitchen again."

"Oh, I never had no trouble with kids," Grandma wiped each finger on a dishrag. "Except for once in a while."

"Except for when?" asked Aurelia.

"Well now . . ." Grandma lowered herself onto a long-legged stool, waving Zelda's more substantial chair away. Grandma liked to balance on that stool like an oracle on her tripod. "There was that time someone tried to hang their little cousin," she declared, and then stopped short.

The two aunts gave her quick, unbelieving looks. Then they were both uneasily silent, neither of them willing to take up the slack and tell the story I knew was about June. I'd heard Aurelia and my mother laughing and accusing each other of the hanging in times past, when it had been only a family story and not the private trigger of special guilts. They looked at me, wondering if I knew about the hanging, but neither would open her lips to ask. So I said I'd heard June herself tell it.

"That's right," Aurelia jumped in. "June told it herself. If she minded being hung, well she never let on!"

"Ha," Zelda said. "If she minded! You were playing cowboys.

You and Gordie had her up on a box, the rope looped over a branch, tied on her neck, very accurate. If she minded! I had to rescue her myself!"

"Oh, I know," Aurelia admitted. "But we saw it in the movies. Kids imitate them, you know. We got notorious after that, me and Gordie. Remember, Zelda? How you came screaming in the house for Mama?"

"Mama! Mama!" Grandma yodeled an imitation of her daughter. "They're hanging June!"

"You came running out there, Mama!" Zelda was swept into the story. "I didn't know you could run so fast."

"We had that rope around her neck and looped over the tree, and poor June was shaking, she was so scared. But we *never* would have done it."

"Yes!" asserted Zelda. "You meant to!"

"Oh, I licked you two good," Grandma remembered. "Aurelia, you and Gordie both."

"And then you took little June in the house. . . ." Zelda broke down suddenly.

Aurelia put her hands to her face. Then, behind her fingers, she made a harsh sound in her throat. "Oh Mama, we could have killed her. . . ."

Zelda crushed her mouth behind a fist.

"But then she came in the house. You wiped her face off," Aurelia remembered. "That June. She yelled at me. 'I wasn't scared! You damn chicken!'"

And then Aurelia started giggling behind her hands. Zelda put her fist down on the table with surprising force.

"Damn chicken!" said Zelda.

"You had to lick her too." Aurelia laughed, wiping her eyes.

"For saying hell and damn . . ." Grandma nearly lost her balance.

"Then she got madder yet . . . ," I said.

"That's right!" Now Grandma's chin was pulled up to hold her laughter back. "She called me a damn old chicken. Right there! A damn old hen!"

Then they were laughing out loud in brays and whoops, sopping tears in their aprons and sleeves, waving their hands helplessly.

Outside, King's engine revved grandly, and a trickle of music started up.

"He's got a tape deck in that car," Mama said, patting her heart, her hair, composing herself quickly. "I suppose that costed extra money."

The sisters sniffed, fished Kleenex from their sleeves, glanced pensively at one another, and put the story to rest.

"King wants to go off after they eat and find Gordie," Zelda thought out loud. "He at Eli's place? It's way out in the bush."

"They expect to get Uncle Eli to ride in that new car," said Grandma in strictly measured, knowing tones.

"Eli won't ride in it." Aurelia lighted a cigarette. Her head shook back and forth in scarves of smoke. And for once Zelda's head shook, too, in agreement, and then Grandma's as well. She rose, pushing her soft wide arms down on the table.

"Why not?" I had to know. "Why won't Eli ride in that car?"

"Albertine don't know about that insurance." Aurelia pointed at me with her chin. So Zelda turned to me and spoke in her low, prim, explaining voice.

"It was natural causes, see. They had a ruling which decided that. So June's insurance came through, and all of that money went to King because he's oldest, legal. He took some insurance and first bought her a big pink gravestone that they put up on the hill." She paused. "Mama, we going up there to visit? I didn't see that gravestone yet."

Grandma was at the stove, bending laboriously to check the roast ham, and she ignored us.

"Just recently he bought this new car," Zelda went on, "with the rest of that money. It has a tape deck and all the furnishings. Eli doesn't like it, or so I heard. That car reminds him of his girl. You know Eli raised June like his own daughter when her mother passed away and nobody else would take her."

"King got that damn old money," Grandma said loud and sudden, "not because he was oldest. June named him for the money because he took after her the most."

So the insurance explained the car. More than that it explained why everyone treated the car with special care. Because it was new, I had thought. Still, I had noticed all along that nobody seemed proud of it except for King and Lynette. Nobody leaned against the shiny blue fenders, rested elbows on the hood, or set paper plates there while they ate. Aurelia didn't even want to hear King's tapes. It was as if the car was wired up to something. As if it might give off a shock when touched. Later, when Gordie came, he brushed the glazed chrome and gently tapped the tires with his toes. He would not go riding in it, either, even though King urged his father to experience how smooth it ran.

We heard the car move off, wheels crackling in the gravel and cinders. Then it was quiet for a long time again.

Grandma was dozing in the next room, and I had taken the last pie from the oven. Aurelia's new green Sears dryer was still huffing away in the tacked-on addition that held toilet, laundry, kitchen sink. The plumbing, only two years old, was hooked up to one side of the house. The top of the washer and dryer were covered with clean towels, and all the pies had been set there to cool.

"Well, where *are* they?" wondered Zelda now. "Joyriding?"

I didn't answer.

"That white girl," Mama went on, "she's built like a truck-driver. She won't keep King long. Lucky you're slim, Albertine."

"*Jeez*, Zelda!" Aurelia came in from the next room. "Why can't you just leave it be? So she's white. What about the Swede? How do you think Albertine feels hearing you talk like this when her dad was white?"

"I feel fine," I said. "I never knew him."

I understood what Aurelia meant though—I was light, clearly a breed.

"My girl's an *Indian*," Zelda emphasized. "I raised her an Indian, and that's what she is."

"Never said no different." Aurelia grinned, not the least put out, hitting me with her elbow. "She's lots better looking than most Kashpaws."

By the time King and Lynette finally came home it was near dusk and we had already moved Grandpa into the house and laid his supper out.

Lynette sat down next to Grandpa, with King Junior in her lap. She began to feed her son ground liver from a little jar. The baby tried to slap his hands together on the spoon each time it was lowered to his mouth. Every time he managed to grasp the spoon, it jerked out of his hands and came down with more liver. Lynette was weary, eyes watery and red. Her tan hair, caught in a stiff club, looked as though it had been used to drag her here.

"You don't got any children, do you, Albertine," she said, holding the spoon away, licking it herself, making a disgusted face. "So you wouldn't know how they just can't leave anything alone!"

"She's not married yet," said Zelda, dangling a bright plastic bundle of keys down to the baby. "She thinks she'll wait for her baby until *after* she's married. Oochy koo," she crooned when King Junior focused and, in an effort of intense delight, pulled the keys down to himself.

Lynette bolted up, shook the keys roughly from his grasp, and snatched him into the next room. He gave a short outraged wail, then fell silent, and after a while Lynette emerged, pulling down her blouse. The cloth was a dark violet bruised color.

"Thought you wanted to see the gravestone," Aurelia quickly remembered, addressing Zelda. "You better get going before it's dark out. Tell King you want him to take you up there."

"I suppose," said Mama, turning to me, "Aurelia didn't see those two cases of stinking beer in their backseat. I'm not driving anywhere with a drunk."

"He's not a drunk!" Lynette wailed in sudden passion. "But I'd drink a few beers too if I had to be in this family."

Then she whirled and ran outside.

King was slumped morosely in the front seat of the car, a beer clenched between his thighs. He drummed his knuckles to the Oak Ridge Boys.

"I don't even let her drive it," he said when I asked. He nodded toward Lynette, who was strolling down the driveway ditch, adding to a straggly bunch of prairie roses. I saw her bend over, tearing at a tough branch.

"She's going to hurt her hands."

"Oh, she don't know nothing," said King. "She never been to school. I seen a little of the world when I was in the service. You get my picture?"

He'd sent a photo of himself in the uniform. I'd been surprised when I saw the picture because I'd realized then that my rough boy cousin had developed hard cheekbones and a movie-star gaze. Now, brooding under the bill of his blue hat, he turned that moody stare through the windshield and shook his head at his wife. "She don't fit in," he said.

"She's fine," I surprised myself by saying. "Just give her a chance."

"Chance." King tipped his beer up. "Chance. She took her chance when she married me. She knew which one I took after."

Then as if on cue, the one whom King did not take after drove into the yard with a squealing flourish, laying hard on his horn.

Uncle Gordie Kashpaw was considered good-looking, although not in the same way as his son King. Gordie had a dark, round, eager face, creased and puckered from being stitched up after an accident. There was always a compelling pleasantness about him. In some curious way all the stitches and folds had contributed to, rather than detracted from, his looks. His face was like something valuable that was broken and put carefully back together. And all the more lovable for the care taken. In the throes of drunken inspiration now, he drove twice around the yard before his old Chevy chugged to a halt. Uncle Eli got out.

"Well it's still standing up," Eli said to the house. "And so am I. But you," he addressed Gordie, "ain't."

It was true, Gordie's feet were giving him trouble. They caught on things as he groped on the hood and pulled himself out. The rubber foot mat, the fenders, then the little ruts and stones as he clambered toward the front steps.

"Zelda's in there," King shouted a warning, "and Grandma too!"

Gordie sat down on the steps to collect his wits before tangling with them.

Inside, Uncle Eli sat down next to his brother. They didn't look much alike anymore, for Eli had wizened and toughened while Grandpa was larger, softer, even paler. They happened to be dressed the same though, in work pants and jackets, except that Grandpa's outfit was navy blue and Eli's was olive green. Eli wore a stained, crumpled cap that seemed so much a part of his head not even Zelda thought of asking him to remove it. He nodded at Grandpa and grinned at the food; he had a huge smile that took up his entire face.

"Here's my Uncle Eli," Aurelia said, putting down the plate of food for him. "Here's my favorite uncle. See, Daddy? Uncle Eli's here. Your brother."

"Oh Eli," said Grandpa, extending his hand. Grandpa grinned and nodded at his brother, but said nothing more until Eli started to eat.

"I don't eat very much anymore. I'm getting so old," Eli was telling us.

"You're eating a lot," Grandpa pointed out. "Is there going to be anything left?"

"You ate already," said Grandma. "Now sit still and visit with your brother." She fussed a little over Eli. "Don't mind him. Eat enough. You're getting thin."

"It's too late," said Grandpa. "He's eating everything."

He closely watched each bite his brother took. Eli wasn't bothered in the least. Indeed, he openly enjoyed his food for Grandpa.

"Oh, for heavensake." Zelda sighed. "Are we ever getting out of here? Aurelia. Why don't you take separate cars and drive us in?

It's too late to see that gravestone now anyway, but I'm darned if I'm going to be here once they start on those cases in the back of June's car."

"Put the laundry out," said Grandma. "I'm ready enough. And you, Albertine"—she nodded at me as they walked out the door —"they can eat all they want. Just as long as they save the pies. Them pies are made special for tomorrow."

"Sure you don't want to come along with us now?" asked Mama. "We're bunking at Grandma's place."

"She's young," said Aurelia. "Besides, she's got to keep those drunken men from eating on those pies."

She bent close to me. Her breath was sweet with cake frosting, stale with cigarettes.

"I'll be back later on," she whispered. "I got to go see a friend."

Then she winked at me exactly the way June had winked about her secret friends. One eye shut, the lips pushed into a small self-deprecating question mark.

Grandpa eased himself into the backseat and sat as instructed, arms spread to either side, holding down the piles of folded laundry.

"They can eat!" Grandma yelled once more. "But save them pies!"

She bucked forward when Aurelia's car lurched over the hole in the drive, and then they shot over the hill.

3

"Say Albertine, did you know your Uncle Eli is the last man on the reservation that could snare himself a deer?"

Gordie unlatched a beer, pushed it across the kitchen table to me. We were still at that table, only now the plates, dishpans of salad, and pies were cleared away for ashtrays, beer, packs of cigarettes.

Although Aurelia kept the house now, it was like communal property for the Kashpaws. There was always someone camped out or sleeping on her fold-up cots.

One more of us had arrived by this time. That was Lipsha Morrissey, who had been taken in by Grandma and always lived with us. Lipsha sat down, with a beer in his hand like everyone, and looked at the floor. He was more a listener than a talker, a shy one with a wide, sweet, intelligent face. He had long eyelashes. "Girl-eyes," King used to tease him. King had beat up Lipsha so many times when we were young that Grandma wouldn't let them play on the same side of the yard. They still avoided each other. Even now, in the small kitchen, they never met each other's eyes or said hello.

I had to wonder, as I always did, how much they knew.

One secret I had learned from sitting quietly around the aunts, from gathering shreds of talk before they remembered me, was Lipsha's secret, or half of it at least. I knew who his mother was. And because I knew his mother I knew the reason he and King never got along. They were half brothers. Lipsha was June's boy, born in one of those years she left Gordie. Once you knew about her, and looked at him, it was easy to tell. He had her flat pretty features and slim grace, only on him these things had never even begun to harden.

Right now he looked anxious and bit his lips. The men were still talking about the animals they had killed.

"I had to save on my shells," said Eli thoughtfully; "they was dear."

"Only real old-time Indians know deer good enough to snare," Gordie said to us. "Your Uncle Eli's a real old-timer."

"You remember the first thing you ever got?" Eli asked King.

King looked down at his beer, then gave me a proud, sly, sideways glance. "A gook," he said. "I was in the marines."

Lipsha kicked the leg of my chair. King made much of having been in combat but was always vague on exactly where and when he had seen action.

"Skunk," Gordie raised his voice. "King got himself a skunk when he was ten."

"Did you ever eat a skunk?" Eli asked me.

"It's like a piece of cold chicken," I ventured. Eli and Gordie agreed with solemn grins.

"How do you skin your skunk?" Eli asked King.

King tipped his hat down, shading his eyes from the fluorescent kitchen ring. A blue-and-white patch had been stitched on the front of his hat. "World's Greatest Fisherman," it said. King put his hands up in winning ignorance.

"How do *you* skin your skunk?" he asked Eli.

"You got to take the glands off first," Eli explained carefully, pointing at different parts of his body. "Here, here, here. Then you skin it just like anything else. You have to boil it in three waters."

"Then you honestly *eat* it?" said Lynette. She had come into the room with a fresh beer and was now biting contentedly on a frayed endstring of hair fallen from her ponytail.

Eli sat up straight and tilted his little green hat back.

"You picky too? Like Zelda! One time she came over to visit me with her first husband, that Swede Johnson. It was around dinnertime. I had a skunk dressed out, and so I fed it to them. Ooooooh when she found out what she ate she was mad at me, boy. 'Skunk!' she says. 'How disgusting! You old guys will eat anything!' "

Lipsha laughed.

"I'd eat it," Lynette declared to him, flipping her hair back with a chopping motion of her hand. "I'd eat it just like that."

"You'd eat shit," said King.

I stared at his clean profile. He was staring across the table at Lipsha, who suddenly got up from his chair and walked out the door. The screen door slammed. King's lip curled down in some imitation of soap-opera bravado, but his chin trembled. I saw him clench his jaw and then felt a kind of wet blanket sadness coming down over us all. I wanted to follow Lipsha. I knew where he had gone. But I didn't leave. Lynette shrugged brightly and brushed away King's remark. But it stayed at the table, as if it had opened a door on something—some sad, ugly scene we could not help but enter. I took a long drink and leaned toward Uncle Eli.

"A fox sleeps hard, eh?" said Eli after a few moments.

King leaned forward and pulled his hat still lower so it seemed to rest on his nose.

"I've shot a fox sleeping before," he said. "You know that little black hole underneath a fox's tail? I shot right through there. I was using a bow and my arrow went right through that fox. It got stiff. It went straight through the air. Flattened out like a flash and was gone down its hole. I never did get it out."

"Never shot a bow either," said Gordie.

"Hah, you're right. I never shot a bow either," admitted King with a strange, snarling little laugh. "But I heard of this guy once who put his arrow through a fox then left it thrash around in the bush until he thought it was dead. He went in there after it. You know what he found? That fox had chewed the arrow off either side of its body and it was gone."

"They don't got that name for nothing," Eli said.

"Fox," said Gordie, peering closely at the keyhole in his beer.

"Can you gimme a cigarette, Eli?" King asked.

"When you ask for a cigarette around here," said Gordie, "you don't say can I have a cigarette. You say *ciga swa*?"

"Them Michifs ask like that," Eli said. "You got to ask a real old-time Indian like me for the right words."

"Tell 'em, Uncle Eli," Lynette said with a quick burst of drunken enthusiasm. "They've got to learn their own heritage! When you go it will all be gone!"

"What you saying there, woman. Hey!" King shouted, filling the kitchen with the jagged tear of his voice. "When you talk to my relatives have a little respect." He put his arms up and shoved at her breasts.

"You bet your life, Uncle Eli," he said more quietly, leaning back on the table. "You're the greatest hunter. But I'm the World's Greatest Fisherman."

"No you ain't," Eli said. His voice was effortless and happy. "I caught a fourteen-inch trout."

King looked at him carefully, focusing with difficulty. "You're the greatest then," he admitted. "Here."

He reached over and plucked away Eli's greasy olive-drab hat. Eli's head was brown, shiny through the white crew-cut stubble.

King took off his blue hat and pushed it down on Eli's head. The hat slipped over Eli's eyes.

"It's too big for him!" Lynette screamed in a tiny outraged voice.

King adjusted the hat's plastic tab.

"I gave you that hat, King! That's your best hat!" Her voice rose sharply in its trill. "You don't give that hat away!"

Eli sat calmly underneath the hat. It fit him perfectly. He seemed oblivious to King's sacrifice and just sat, his old cap perched on his knee, turning the can around and around in his hand without drinking.

King swayed to his feet, clutched the stuffed plastic backrest of the chair. His voice was ripped and swollen. "Uncle Eli." He bent over the old man. "Uncle Eli, you're my uncle."

"Damn right," Eli agreed.

"I always thought so much of you, my uncle!" cried King in a loud, unhappy wail.

"Damn right," said Eli. He turned to Gordie. "He's drunk on his behind. I got to agree with him."

"I think the fuckin' world of you, Uncle!"

"Damn right. I'm an old man," Eli said in a flat, soft voice. "*Ekewaynzee.*"

King suddenly put his hands up around his ears and stumbled out the door.

"Fresh air be good for him," said Gordie, relieved. "Say there, Albertine. You ever hear this one joke about the Indian, the Frenchman, and the Norwegian in the French Revolution?"

"Issat a Norwegian joke?" Lynette asked. "Hey. I'm full-blooded Norwegian. I don't know nothing about my family, but I know I'm full-blooded Norwegian."

"No, it's not about the Norwegians really," Gordie went on. "So anyway . . ."

Nevertheless she followed King out the door.

"There were these three. An Indian. A Frenchman. A Norwegian. They were all in the French Revolution. And they were all set for the guillotine, right? But when they put the Indian in there the blade just came halfway down and got stuck."

"Fuckin' bitch! Gimme the keys!" King screamed just outside the door. Gordie paused a moment. There was silence. He continued the joke.

"So they said it was the judgment of God. You can go, they said to the Indian. So the Indian got up and went. Then it was the Frenchman's turn. They put his neck in the vise and were all set to execute him! But it happened the same. The blade stuck."

"Fuckin' bitch! Fuckin' bitch!" King shrieked again.

The car door slammed. Gordie's eyes darted to the door, back to me with questions.

"Should we go out?" I said.

But he continued the story. "And so the Frenchman went off and he was saved. But when it came to the Norwegian, see, the Norwegian looks up at the guillotine and says: 'You guys are sure dumb. If you put a little grease on it that thing would work fine!' "

"Bitch! Bitch! I'll kill you! Gimme the keys!" We heard a quick shattering sound, glass breaking, and left Eli sitting at the table.

Lynette was locked in the Firebird, crouched on the passenger's side. King screamed at her and threw his whole body against the car, thudded on the hood with hollow booms, banged his way across the roof, ripped at antennae and side-view mirrors with his fists, kicked into the broken sockets of headlights. Finally he ripped a mirror off the driver's side and began to beat the car rhythmically, gasping. But though he swung the mirror time after time into the windshield and side windows he couldn't smash them.

"King, baby!" Gordie jumped off the steps and hugged King to the ground with the solid drop of his weight. "It's her car. You're June's boy, King. Don't cry." For as they lay there, welded in shock, King's face was grinding deep into the cinders and his shoulders shook with heavy sobs. He screamed up through dirt at his father.

"It's awful to be dead. Oh my God, she's so cold."

They were up on their feet suddenly. King twisted out of Gordie's arms and balanced in a wrestler's stance. "It's your fault and you wanna take the car," he said wildly. He sprang at his father but Gordie stepped back, bracing himself, and once again he folded King violently into his arms, and again King sobbed and sagged against his father. Gordie lowered him back into the cinders. While they were clenched, Lynette slipped from the car and ran into the house. I followed her. She rushed through the kitchen, checked the baby, and then she came back.

"Sit down," I said. I had taken a chair beside Eli.

"Uh, uh."

She walked over to Eli. She couldn't be still.

"You got troubles out there," he stated.

"Yeah," she said. "His mom gave him the money!" She sneaked a cigarette from Eli's pack, giving him a coy smirk in return. "Because she wanted him to have responsibility. He never had responsibility. She wanted him to take care of his family."

Eli nodded and pushed the whole pack toward her when she stubbed out the cigarette half smoked. She lit another.

"You know he really must love his uncle," she cried in a small, hard voice. She plumped down next to Eli and steadily smiled at the blue hat. "That fishing hat. It's his number-one hat. I got that patch for him. King. They think the world of him down in the Cities. Everybody knows him. They know him by that hat. It's his number one. You better never take it off."

Eli took the hat off and turned it around in his hands. He squinted at the patch and read it aloud. Then he nodded, as if it had finally dawned on him what she was talking about, and he turned it back around.

"Let me wear it for a while," Lynette cajoled. Then she took it. Put it on her head and adjusted the brim. "There it is."

Uncle Eli took his old cap off his knee and put it on his head.

"This one fits me," he said.

In the next room King Junior began to cry.

"Oh, my baby!" Lynette shrieked as if he were in danger and darted out. I heard her murmuring King's name when the father and the son walked back inside. King sat down at the table and put his head in his folded arms, breathing hoarsely. Gordie got the keys from Lynette and told Eli they were going home now.

"He's okay," Gordie said, nodding at King. "Just as long as you let him alone."

So they drove off on that clear blue night. I put a blanket around Lynette's shoulders, and she sank onto the couch. I walked out, past King. He was still breathing hopelessly into his crossed arms. I walked down to where I knew Lipsha was, at the bottom of the hill below the house. Sure enough, he was sitting there, back against a log from the woodpile. He passed me a bottle of sweet rosé, I drank. I tipped the bottle, looked up at the sky, and nearly fell over, in amazement and too much beer, at the drenching beauty.

Northern lights. Something in the cold, wet atmosphere brought them out. I grabbed Lipsha's arm. We floated into the field and sank down, crushing green wheat. We chewed the sweet grass tips and stared up and were lost. Everything seemed to be one piece. The air, our faces, all cool, moist, and dark, and the ghostly sky. Pale green licks of light pulsed and faded across it. Living lights. Their fires lobbed over, higher, higher, then died out in blackness. At times the whole sky was ringed in shooting points and puckers of light gathering and falling, pulsing, fading, rhythmical as breathing. All of a piece. As if the sky were a pattern of nerves and our thought and memories traveled across it. As if the sky were one gigantic memory for us all. Or a dance hall. And all the world's wandering souls were dancing there. I thought of June. She would be dancing if there was a dance hall in space. She would be dancing a two-step for wandering souls. Her long legs lifting and falling. Her laugh an ace. Her sweet perfume the way all grown-up women were supposed to smell. Her amusement at both the bad and the good. Her defeat. Her reckless victory. Her sons.

4

I had to close my eyes after a while. The mix of beer and rosé made my head whirl. The lights, shooting high, made the ground rock underneath me. I waved away the bottle when Lipsha touched my hand with the cold end of it.

"Don't want no more?"

"Later on," I said. "Keep talking."

Lipsha's voice was a steady bridge over a deep black space of sickness I was crossing. If I just kept listening I knew I'd get past all right. He was talking about King. His voice was slurred and dreamy.

"I'll admit that," he said, "I'm scared of his mind. You can't never predict when he'll turn. Once, a long time ago, we went out hunting gophers. I let him get behind me. You know what he did? He hid in the bushes and took a potshot."

"Lucky."

"That's right. I steer clear of King. I never turn my back on him, either."

"Don't be scared of him," I said. I was managing to keep a slim hold on the conversation. I could do this as long as I only moved my lips and not the rest of me.

"Sure. King never took a potshot at you."

"He's scared underneath."

"Of what?" said Lipsha.

But I really didn't know. "Those vets," I said, "are really nuts."

"He's no vet," Lipsha began. But then blackness swung too hard, tipping me. For a while I heard nothing, saw nothing, and did not even dare move my lips to speak. That didn't matter. Lipsha went on talking.

"Energy," he said, "electromagnetic waves. It's because of the temperature, the difference sets them off." He was talking about the northern lights. Although he never did well in school, Lipsha knew surprising things. He read books about computers and volcanoes and the life cycles of salamanders. Sometimes he used words I had to ask him the meaning of, and other times he didn't make even the simplest sense. I loved him for being both ways. A wash of love swept me over the sickness. I sat up.

"I am going to talk to you about something particular . . . ," I began. My voice was serious, all of a sudden, and it scared him. He moved away from me, suspicious. I was going to tell him what

I'd heard from hanging at the edge of the aunts' conversations. I was going to tell him that his mother was June. Since so many others knew, it was only right that he should, too.

"Your mother . . . ," I began.

"I can never forgive what she done to a little child," he said. "They had to rescue me out of her grip."

I tried again.

"I want to talk about your mother. . . ."

Lipsha nodded, cutting me off. "I consider Grandma Kashpaw my mother, even though she just took me in like any old stray."

"She didn't do that," I said. "She wanted you."

"No," said Lipsha. "Albertine, you don't know what you're talking about."

Now I was the one who felt ignorant, confused.

"As for my mother," he went on, "even if she came back right now, this minute, and got down on her knees and said 'Son, I am sorry for what I done to you,' I would not relent on her."

I didn't know how to rescue my intentions and go on. I thought for a while, or tried to, but sitting up and talking had been too much.

"What if your mother never meant to?" I lay down again, lowering myself carefully into the wheat. The dew was condensing. I was cold, damp, and sick. "What if it was just a kind of mistake?" I asked.

"It wasn't no mistake," said Lipsha firmly. "She would have drowned me."

Laying still, confused by my sickness and his certainty, I almost believed him. I thought he would hate June if he knew, and anyway it was too late. I justified my silence. I didn't tell him.

"What about your father?" I asked instead. "Do you wish you knew him?"

Lipsha was quiet, considering, before he answered.

"I wouldn't mind."

Then I was falling, and he was talking again. I hung on and listened.

"Did you ever dream you flew through the air?" he asked. "Did you ever dream you landed on a planet or star?"

"I dreamed I flew up there once," he said, going on. "It was all lighted up. Man, it was beautiful! I landed on the moon, but once I stood there at last, I didn't dare take a breath."

I moved closer. He had a light nylon jacket. He took it off and laid it over me. I was suddenly comfortable, very comfortable, and warm.

"No," he said. "No, I was scared to breathe."

I woke up. I had fallen asleep in the arms of Lipsha's jacket, in the cold wet wheat under the flashing sky. I heard the clanging sound of struck metal, pots tumbling in the house. Gordie was gone. Eli was gone. "Come on," I said, jumping straight up at the noise. "They're fighting." I ran up the hill, Lipsha pounding behind me. I stumbled straight into the lighted kitchen and saw at once that King was trying to drown Lynette. He was pushing her face in the sink of cold dishwater. Holding her by the nape and the ears. Her arms were whirling, knocking spoons and knives and bowls out of the drainer. She struggled powerfully, but he had her. I grabbed a block of birch out of the woodbox and hit King on the back of the neck. The wood bounced out of my fists. He pushed her lower, and her throat caught and gurgled.

I grabbed his shoulders. I expected that Lipsha was behind me. King hardly noticed my weight. He pushed her lower. So I had no choice then. I jumped on his back and bit his ear. My teeth met and blood filled my mouth. He reeled backward, bucking me off, and I flew across the room, hit the refrigerator solidly, and got back on my feet.

His hands were cocked in boxer's fists. He was deciding who to hit first, I thought, me or Lipsha. I glanced around. I was alone. I stared back at King, scared for the first time. Then the fear left and I was mad, just mad, at Lipsha, at King, at Lynette, at June. . . . I looked past King and I saw what they had done.

All the pies were smashed. Torn open. Black juice bleeding

through the crusts. Bits of jagged shells were stuck to the wall and some were turned completely upside down. Chunks of rhubarb were scraped across the floor. Meringue dripped from the towels.

"The pies!" I shrieked. "You goddamn sonofabitch, you broke the pies!"

His eyes widened. When he glanced around at the destruction, Lynette scuttled under the table. He took in what he could, and then his fists lowered and a look at least resembling shame, confusion, swept over his face, and he rushed past me. He stepped down flat on his fisherman hat as he ran, and after he was gone I picked it up.

I went into the next room and stuffed the hat under King Junior's mattress. Then I sat for a long time, listening to his light breathing. He was always a good baby, or more likely a wise soul. He slept through everything he could possibly sleep through.

Lynette had turned the lights out in the kitchen as she left the house, and now I heard her outside the window begging King to take her away in the car.

"Let's go off before they all get back," she said. "It's them. You always get so crazy when you're home. We'll get the baby. We'll go off. We'll go back to the Cities, go home."

And then she cried out once, but clearly it was a cry like pleasure. I thought I heard their bodies creak together, or perhaps it was just the wood steps beneath them, the old worn boards bearing their weight.

They got into the car soon after that. Doors slammed. But they traveled just a few yards and then stopped. The horn blared softly. I suppose they knocked against it in passion. The heater roared on from time to time. It was a cold, spare dawn.

Sometime that hour I got up, leaving the baby, and went into the kitchen. I spooned the fillings back into the crusts, married slabs of dough, smoothed over edges of crusts with a wetted finger, fit crimps to crimps and even fluff to fluff on top of berries or pudding. I worked carefully for over an hour. But once they smash there is no way to put them right.

Ofelia Zepeda

TOHONO O'ODHAM

I am the daughter of farm workers and grew up in the small cotton-growing town of Stanfield, Arizona. A lot of O'odham lived there and they were usually related. In that way it was sort of like an O'odham village. We were required to work on weekends and all through the summer to have money to buy our school clothes and stuff like that . . . I hated manual labor basically, because it's hard, hard work. I figured if I went to summer school I wouldn't have to work. It was sort of the lesser of two evils. For some crazy reason I enjoyed it. I enjoyed books and reading and pencils and all the accoutrements of school.

When I started to become more experienced in working with the language I used to get hired on various projects to work with teachers on the reservation to teach an O'odham language course. Our problem was always finding material. So some of my students and I had to create our own literature in order to promote our literacy. Some of my writing I used to transcribe from interviews with people or O'odham songs, just write them down so you can read them as poetry.

Traditional O'odham songs are very delicate, and in a way, very concise about how the singer viewed the environment, just for that split second. When they talk about the colors of the clouds, how they start getting closer to you, how they change dimension—it's a huge thing they're looking at, a very complex atmospheric change that they're observing. And they pack it all into a four-line poem.

Bury Me with a Band

My mother used to say "Bury me with a band."
And I'd say, "I don't think the grave will be big enough."
Instead, we buried her with creosote bushes,
and a few worldly belongings.
The creosote is for dusting her footprints away as she leaves.
It is for keeping the worldly earth away from her sacred remains.
It is for leaving the smell of the desert with her.
It is to remind her of home one last time.

Mary Tallmountain

ATHABASCAN

For the past twenty years, Mary had been active in the Native American literature renaissance. She contributed to numerous native publications and read at colleges and universities, at benefits and rallies, and at other events, especially in California and her homeland, Alaska. Her work is used in teaching Native American Studies at UC Berkeley, UCLA, UC Davis, and San Diego and San Francisco State Universities, and has recently been included in several textbooks for young adult readers.

In her work as an activist, she spoke out for native rights, for animals, women, the homeless, and others who are dispossessed in American society. She performed for inmates at San Quentin and other prisons and taught poetry and journal-writing to children and elders in Alaska and in the inner city of San Francisco.

[Editor's note: Mary Tallmountain passed on during the compilation of this anthology. She was a fine poet, a fine human being. We will miss her.]

The Last Wolf

The last wolf hurried toward me
through the ruined city
and I heard his baying echoes
down the steep smashed warrens
of Montgomery Street and past
the ruby-crowed highrises
left standing
their lighted elevators useless

Passing the flicking red and green
of traffic signals
baying his way eastward
in the mystery of his wild loping
gait
closer the sounds in the deadly
night
through clutter and rubble of quiet
blocks

I heard his voice ascending the
hill
and at last his low whine as he
came
floor by empty floor to the room
where I sat
in my narrow bed looking west,
waiting
I heard him snuffle at the door and
I watched

He trotted across the floor
he laid his long gray muzzle
on the spare white spread
and his eyes burned yellow
his small dotted eyebrows quivered

Yes, I said.
I know what they have done.

Linda Hogan

CHICKASAW

The Feathers

Our task is to enter into the dream
of Nature and interpret the symbols.
—E. L. GRANT WATSON
The Mystery of Physical Life

For years I prayed for an eagle feather. I wanted one from a bird still living. A killed eagle would offer me none of what I hoped for. A bird killed in the name of human power is in truth a loss of power from the world, not an addition to it.

My first eagle feather, one light and innocent, was given to me by a traditional healer I'd gone to see when I was sick. He told me a story about feathers. When he was a child his home had burned down. All that survived the fire were eagle feathers. They remained in the smoking ruins of their home, floating on top of black ash and water. The feather he gave me was one of those. I still keep it safe in a cedar box in my home.

Where I live is in a mountain canyon. It is not unusual to see golden eagles in the canyon, far above us. One morning, after all my years of praying for a feather, I dreamed I was inside a temple. It was a holy place. Other people were there, looking at the ornately decorated walls, the icons of gold, the dried and revered bodies of saints, but my attention was turned toward the ceiling. It was pink and domed, engraved with gold designs of leaves and branches. "Look up," I said to the others. "Look up." Still dreaming, I spoke these words out loud, and the sound of my own voice woke me. Waking, I obeyed my own words and looked up, seeing out the open window of my room. Just as I did, a large golden eagle flew toward the window, so close that I could see its dark eyes looking in at me for a moment before it lifted, caught a current of air, and flew over the roof of the house. I jumped up and ran barefoot outside to see where it was going.

If I told you the eagle was not in sight, and that there was a feather in the road when I reached it, you would probably not believe me. I, too, have seen how long it takes feathers to land, carried as they are by unseen currents of air. Once I waited for a hawk feather to fall. I covered distance, looking up, to follow it, but it never sat down. It merely drifted until it was no longer in sight. But on the day of my dream, a feather was there. On the ground had fallen the gift of an eagle, soft white with a darker, rounded tip.

I know there is a physics to this, a natural law about lightness and air. This even rubs the wrong way against logic. How do I explain the feather, the bird at my window, my own voice waking me, as another person lived in me, wiser and more alert. I can only think there is another force at work, deeper than physics and what we know of wind, something that comes from a world where lightning and thunder, sun and rain clouds live. Nor can I say why it is so many of us have forgotten the mystery of nature and spirit, while for tens of thousands of years such things have happened and been spoken by our elders and our ancestors.

When my granddaughter, Vivian, entered her life in the world of air, I was at her emergence to greet her and to cut her cord, the sustaining link between her and her mother, her origins. When the bronze-colored stem of the baby dried, we placed it in a tall black pot until I could make and bead an umbilical bag to contain that first point of connection to this life, to keep her with us, safe and well.

One day a few months later, my parents visited. As always my father's presence turned us toward our identity and origins, so we brought out the cradleboard. My daughter, Tanya, dressed in her traditional beadwork clothing. Then, suddenly, with a look of horror, she said, "It's gone!" and ran toward the black jar that contained the baby's cord. She was right, the cord, the most valuable thing in our home, was no longer there. Because of the height and shape of the pot, and because of its placement on the shelves, it was not possible that the wind might have carried it away. Nor could an animal have reached inside.

All that evening I searched, on hands and knees, under chairs, in corners, drawers, looking through entire house, under furniture, on shelves, until no place was left unseen.

Several times throughout the night of searching, I opened a cedar box that contained tobacco, cornmeal, sage, and my first eagle feather, the one that lived through fire. Again and again I returned to the box, puzzled by my own behavior. Each time, as I opened it, I wondered why I was so compelled, so drawn to the container. It is a small box, with no hidden place where the birth cord might have been unnoticed, yet I returned to it. Opening it, looking inside, closing it.

In the middle of all this searching, a Blackfeet friend called to invite us to an encampment in Montana. "I'm so glad you called," I said to him. "I've lost my granddaughter's umbilical cord." I told him how terrible I felt about losing it and that perhaps the cord wanted to be elsewhere, maybe on the South Dakota reservation of my daughter's origins. Or that it was a sign to me that I have neglected my spiritual life, which I often do when working and living and teaching in a world of different knowings.

He told me a ceremony that might work. I hung up the phone and went to prepare the rite. Soon I was walking uphill in the dark, moonlit night toward a cluster of trees where I made the offering. Around me was the song of insects, a nighthawk with its high-pitched call and clattering wings.

When I returned, I went once again to the cedar box. This time the feather, something else of value to me, was gone. I didn't know how this could be. Yes, I opened the box several times, but the feather never moved.

Getting down on hands and knees I looked under a chair, and I saw the eagle feather there, and the feather was pointing at the umbilical cord, so mysteriously now on the floor I had already searched.

It was the feather that took me to the baby's umbilical cord. The feather, that element of bird, so formed, so groomed to catch the wind and lift, that one-time part of a whole flying. It had once seen distances, had risen and fallen beneath the sun.

Perhaps there are events and things that work as a doorway into the mythical world, the world of first people, all the way back to the creation of the universe and the small quickenings of earth, the first stirrings of human beings at the beginning of time. Our elders believe this to be so, that is is possible to wind a way backward to the start of things, and in so doing find a form of sacred reason, different from ordinary reason, that is linked to the force of nature. In this kind of mind, like in the feather, is the power of sky and thunder and sun, and many have had alliances and partnerships with it, a way of thought older than measured time, less primitive than the rational present. Others have tried for centuries to understand the world by science and intellect but have not yet done so, not yet understood animals, finite earth, or even their own minds and behavior. The more they seek to learn the world, the closer they come to the spiritual, the magical origins of creation.

There is a still place, a gap between worlds, spoken by the tribal knowings of thousands of years. In it are silent flyings that stand aside from human struggles and the designs of our own makings. At times, when we are silent enough, still enough, we take a step into such mystery; the place of spirit, and mystery, we must remember, by its very nature does not wish to be known.

There is something alive in a feather. The power of it is perhaps in its dream of sky, currents of air, and the silence of its creation. It knows the insides of clouds. It carries our needs and desires, the stories of our brokenness. It rises and falls down elemental space, one part of the elaborate world of life where fish swim against gravity, where eels turn silver as moon to bread.

How did the feather arrive at the edge of the dirt road where I live? How did it fall across and through currents of air? How did the feathers survive fire? This I will never know. Nor will I know what voice spoke through my sleep. I know only that there are simple powers, strange and real.

Debra Earling

FLATHEAD

I write about the issues that trouble me, stories of my family and my people and myself that keep me awake at night, the stories that call me to drive dark roads at midnight, to return again to the small lakes and streams that are lit by moonlight. I write to find understanding, to find peace. I write in the hope that I will give voice to those who have never had an opportunity to tell their stories. I write to give voice to myself.

The Old Marriage

Louise's earliest memory of school was Clarence Yellow Knife. He used to follow her around, a beaver-dark boy with a stinking mouth full of rotting teeth. When they were very young he didn't bother her much. He was too shy and too stupid to actively do anything. But as they got older, it was all the things he did to show Louise he didn't like her that told Louise he liked her too much. He did things most other boys did, like lift her dress up at the drinking fountain or pull her hair. But most of the boys were happy to play kickball or look for snakes in the old graveyard. They grew tired of tormenting her. They learned fast she could plow a plumb-line punch to the belly or face when they least expected her to. Lester Blackroad even began asking her and Melveena Big Beaver to play Red Rover with the boys. But Clarence refused any friend-liness and skulked around the old nun graveyard alone, watching them all from an uncomfortable distance. Louise grew jumpy al-ways looking behind her to find Clarence hunkered in the stickery blue spruce or hugging the cold tether-ball pole, far enough away not to be spotted by simple glances, still close enough to hear all she said. And Clarence bothered Louise in and out of school. At powwows he liked to toss firecrackers through the knotholes in the lower half of the outhouse. He caught Louise once and startled her to standing. She looked down into the dim, stinking toilet hole, down to where she could see one eye framed by a knothole blinking back up at her. Louise ran to find Grandma at the stick-game grounds. She felt ashamed and dirty. When Louise told her grand-mother what Clarence had done the old woman reassured her it was nothing. "If you had pooped on him," she said, "he would have liked it. Nasty thing."

When Louise was eight Clarence began leaving notes in her desk that she stopped showing to others for fear of getting into trouble herself. The words were dark and funny. And when she was alone she said them to herself, sounding out each word carefully like a prayer. "Boner, trapcheeks, poontang, pecker." She told the words to Melveena and they laughed, not sure of the meaning of each word but knowing all the words together spelled out a terrible, grown-up shame. They whispered the words in each other's ears and drew pictures in the dust, feeling a strange and giddy new power.

In class Melveena shielded Louise's ear with her damp hands and spoke very fast. "These words are probably more bad than the blood rags my sister has to wash each month." Louise didn't understand what Melveena was talking about, but she nodded anyway. Melveena looked at Louise with a sudden serious face. "Whatever these words mean, Clarence wishes they mean you. My sister says these are the words for making babies and if we say them too much we're going to have one." So they said the words over and over again like a chant until the words became smooth and meaningless, no longer funny or bad, but loose and easy on their tongues like the sound of their own names.

When Louise was nine Clarence blew a fine powder in her face and told her she would disappear. She sneezed until her nose bled and Clarence gave her his handkerchief. She had to lie down on the school floor and tilt back her head and even then it wouldn't stop. She felt he had opened the river to her heart. The cloth he had given her was wet with her blood. She felt hot and sleepy. Sister Thomas Bernard pulled her up and told her to go to the bathroom and wash her face. Sister pinched the bridge of Louise's nose. Louise kept the handkershief pressed to her face, embarrassed by all the attention she was getting. She could feel her blood cool in slow streams between her fingers. The back of her head danced with silver stars and she fell back like a snagged fish released again to water.

She woke two days later in warm sunlight. Grandma squeezed her hand as she blinked awake. Louise's hands were cold. "We got this back," Grandma said. She held up the handkerchief that Clarence had given her. It was crumpled still and black with her blood. Louise didn't understand at first and then she remembered Clarence had been standing by as the school nurse lifted her into the car. He shyly asked the nurse for his handkerchief back. And as they pulled out of the schoolyard, Clarence smiled at Louise and lifted his bloody handkerchief up so she could see all he had taken from her. She remembered how Grandma had told her to stay away from him. He was the son of Dirty Swallow, the rattlesnake woman.

Louise asked her grandmother how she had gotten the handkerchief back. How did the old woman manage to snitch back her blood from Clarence Yellow Knife's tight fist, his ugly smile? Grandma didn't answer her. Louise imagined many things and settled on Sister Thomas and her hard thumping knuckles. She wouldn't let the boys play with dead rattlers or poke at the mouths of dead birds with sticks. And she wouldn't let Clarence keep a blood-soaked handkerchief.

Six days later Louise had a dream that followed her from a long night into morning. It was a familiar dream. She heard an Indian voice, neither a man's nor a woman's voice. The voice did not speak to her but to the dream she cupped in her small hands like a million water-colored glass beads.

It is cold. Snakes sleep in deep holes trapped by snow. We tell our stories now. Rattlers are quiet. It is so far back your blood smells like oil in the tongues of your grandmothers. The snow is frozen so hard it can bruise. The snowdrifts are razor-edged. Snow shines like a wet smile. We're locked here. Outside Grandma's house a naked man stands near a red fire. His face the face of a woman smooth and deep-planed. His back is lean with ribs. His hips are narrow.

Flames light high on the roof of Grandma's house. Base-blue tongues of flame burn buckskin tamarack. Black wood dust to white wood ash. The naked man blows through teeth, his cracked lips whistling to fire. His whistle calls a great wind up from snow. Firelight becomes one small candle. It flickers, then fails white, then fails, fails white to smoke. Steady wind scatters white ash to thin choking sheets of hot dust. Snow and timber powder, hot and cold. The man stands before the white stars, the endless snow. He is light left by fire. A blinding white wick neither fire nor snow. His white light is turning to morning.

Louise never asked her grandmother about the handkerchief again. She knew who had brought it back. She remembered stories of her great-grandfather: the secret training rituals of medicine people, sent to find a single pin in a night that pressed to forty below, one pin dropped deep in snow, miles from where they stood shivering and naked. Her grandfather had saved her. Somehow he had picked her blood from the dark hands of Dirty Swallow. And she knew it had been at a great price. She would never talk to Clarence Yellow Knife again.

When Louise was fourteen Clarence snuck up behind her and slipped a rattler's tail in her hand with the slick skill of a small wind passing. She wasn't sure what to do with it. She stared at it for a long while, then dropped it deep into her pocket hoping it would fall out of the hole she hadn't mended. But the tail became a power she was afraid of, a feeling she had never had before.

"Why didn't you just get rid of that when he gave it to you?" her grandma asked.

Louise didn't answer. She looked at her feet as Grandma was talking. She didn't know how to tell her grandma that once the rattle had gotten into her pocket, it began moving like the whole snake was still attached. She felt the rattle twitching on her leg, like a new muscle, and was afraid of it in a way that made her strong.

Grandma made Louise bury the rattle on the hill and mark the spot with three red-colored rocks. "That way we can avoid it," she said. Louise took her time burying the rattle. She found the nicest spot on the hill under the shade of a juniper tree. She dug a deep hole that was sweet with the smell of new roots. She carefully wrapped the rattle with a glove she had worn thin to fool it into feeling she was near. Then she covered the hole up as fast as she could with the sweep of her arms and the clawing cup of her hands. She walked away slowly from the small rock mound, pacing her steps, careful not to look back and reveal any desire to stay.

All that night dreams swallowed her. She was falling. Tall grass shot up around her and whispered with heat. Smooth flat rocks near Magpie Hill were shining with sun. She felt the warm breath of her mother and curled down into a dark sleep.

Louise found a power in ignoring Clarence Yellow Knife. He no longer existed for her. She did not hear or see him. He had less presence for her than the ghost of her sister's dead cat. When he came close behind her from any direction, she sidestepped him and talked as if he weren't there. Her memory of him was a nightmare forgotten in sunlight and denied from dusk to dawn. She stopped hearing the whisper of scales beneath the thin slat steps of Grandma's house. Sleep was good and she began to feel at ease.

She managed to keep distance between them for one year. And when she saw him again she was in the safety of Mulick's store, safe among rows of peanut butter and preserves, crates of fresh eggs. She walked down the main aisle passing him. He said her name as she was heading for the counter and she turned to him and smiled for the first time in years. She had no way of knowing the power she had given him again, not until she saw him from the smoke-stained window as she was leaving. He stood just outside the store, his arms were lank at his sides. Louise watched him for a time but he did not move from his place. He did not leave his long store vigil. Louise had only one nightmare in all the months she denied him. In her dream Clarence was an old man swimming against river water. His shoulders were harnessed, pulling something she could not see. He estimated each swell, each hesitant wave. Watching. She heard the slap of water against the pockets of his body, to rock. Up from a swell of water, silver as winter rain, he reached for her. He had not gotten her then and he would not get her now. Louise swallowed a deep breath of stale grocery air and stepped outside to face the hot sun and Clarence Yellow Knife.

There was something about his presence that made Louise think she should not ignore him this time. She felt his desire in the dense heat of her breasts, a thousand snelled hooks pulled by little sinkers weighed the tips of her nipples, the heavy lobes of her ears. A cold heaviness settled in her lungs like green water. She shifted her feet to brace herself against the son of Dirty Swallow. His presence was odd, like a pressing wind she had to lean into to gain strength.

"You don't talk to me," he said. "Do you hear me talking to you?"

Louise felt something was wrong. She felt heavy on the spot where she stood. She stamped her tongue hard against her front teeth and tried to think of Roger Mullan, his long yellow teeth. His own mother said he could eat apples through a picket fence. She strained to hold the image.

Clarence tugged at the swell in his crotch as he talked to her. She focused all of her attention on moving away from him. He struck a match to a yellow flame on the zipper of his pants, and like an old man, lit a pipe of kinnikinick leaves. His teeth were broken and stained and his breath was bitter. His voice was slow like water moving deep in the channel—pulling her. She knew he wasn't touching her, but the rasp of his swollen tongue pulled at her left breast. She turned to him and he was grinning. He knows what I am thinking. His watching was dark. Around the brown hub of his eyes the whites rimmed yellow as if they'd been boiled. She felt an urge to move closer to the bitter smell of him, a strange urge she didn't understand, like the feeling she had to look very close into the small dead mouths of animals. She knew she would cross the highway again for a closer look at a bone-broken deer, to see and smell the heavy bowels bubbling with maggots. And she knew she would have to move closer to Clarence.

"Louise," he whispered. Her name was thick on his tongue. She could feel a wet heat rising from his collar. Louise leaned forward and snaked her tongue out to touch the fat lobe of his ear. He tasted sour with old body salt. He pressed his cheek to hers leaving a damp imprint. Louise pulled back. She would not kiss him. He smelled different up close, like onions and warm earth and the sweet, burning lime that covered everything unclean. He crooked his head toward her, a fat robin listening for lunch.

The back of her head felt tight, as if every pore had shut down and closed. Louise tried not to look behind her. She breathed in slowly and listened. The wind was still. She imagined her head was smooth as the translucent round moon rising high above their heads.

And like the moon she sees all around them. The fields are brittle with weeds. Below her she sees Clarence Yellow Knife smaller than a hummingbird, his tiny heart beating down the thin, thin walls of her heart. One hundred yards from him, Mulick's store hides neatly stacked cans of soup, vegetables, baskets of penny candy. He can no longer touch her. The thought makes her breathless as clouds. She looks down over the sun-silver hills and begins to see something moving. She sucks her breath full of wind. She sees the root cellar of her great-grandmother, the hill mound of round rocks weathered smooth by rain, and deep inside the cellar, the fat rattler that has outsmarted her family for years is hiding behind fruit jars, and gunnysacks of jerky, leaving them the pale ghost peel of himself that grows longer and longer each year. She sees the hiding snakes in all their places.

In the damp shade of Grandma's woodpile, a slim rattler is sleeping. She sees the Ursuline school and all the snakes in the field close to the playground. Lorraine Small Salmon, just five years old, turning jump rope while close to the tips of her shoes a brown rattler is humming. She sees her sisters chasing each other toward and away from the bottomland where the tender-fanged mouths of one hundred snakes wait in the weeds. She sees a fisherman she doesn't know, vulnerable as his sunburned pate, at the Jocko surrounded on all sides by brown rocks and rattlesnakes thick as lichen. She sees the dead snake the boys have hung on the cross of the French nun's grave. She sees the milk-white eyes of a thousand August rattlers. She sees Dirty Swallow walking toward Grandma's rain-blistered door. Behind her, rattlesnakes trail like a wedding train.

From a great distance she heard Clarence Yellow Knife say, "Marry me." Louise stepped back from him to leave. The air was clean and hot. A sudden wind snapped her dress tight to the lean backs of her legs. She shielded her watering eyes from the grit of dust. He never stopped watching her, and for one small moment, she felt bad for him and bad for herself. She could hate him enough to pull him inside of her, to melt his bones to water. She turned from him and began to run. She dropped her small bag of groceries to run faster, to run home, more afraid of Dirty Swallow in her grandmother's house than any field or road rattler.

Her grandmother's place was closed up for the afternoon. The windows were glazed with white sun. The door was quiet. She could see the narrow shade line below the eyes, the twitching tails of swallows hiding from heat. She felt a dull-fisted warmth in her throat and she tried to swallow. She stepped carefully through the knee-deep sage, lifting her skirt up from the small snags of cheet grass. She could see the last edge of bush grass, the scuff-smooth cow trail that led around the pond toward home. There was a rhythm of water moving slowly around the creek. She thought of rainbow trout, their dense eyes watching, the scales ringing along their backs as they bit up toward the small white wings beyond water. There was a pause in the reed grass as a deep breeze pulled a small cloud of dust toward a higher place. The red-winged black-birds were quiet. She looked closer at the bloated cottonwood roots that stretched to the pond edge. A slow current writhed silver and then green in the sleeping shade. She threw a rock toward the pond, saw a sudden lap of water, then more waves, the smooth familiar wiggle parting grass, crackle of weeds, small hiss. She had come to know the language of August fields, the slow thin weave at the roots of grass. Snakes.

Louise remembered another time looking down on her grand-ma's small house in the huckleberry summer after her mother had died. She remembered listening outside the open kitchen window to her grandma talking about the choices of men, of bad medicine, and the power of the old marriage. And as a young girl standing barefoot to summer, she saw somewhere a skin bag, dark with the oil of many hands, curling round the singed tips of her hair, a heavy black smoke rising white from his teeth, Clarence, his heart drum leaving, his breath inhaling her blue, blue heart. And she thought, smiling, of how she had dreamt that night of running the

weed-tight ridge of their house with a braided whip of her dead
mother's hair, the small licks of dust turning to stars behind her.

Louise Erdrich

TURTLE MOUNTAIN CHIPPEWA

Fooling God

I must become small and hide where he cannot reach.
I must become dull and heavy as an iron pot.
I must be tireless as rust and bold as roots
growing through the locks on doors
and crumbling the cinderblocks
of the foundations of his everlasting throne.
I must be strange as pity so he'll believe me.
I must be terrible and brush my hair
so that he finds me attractive.
Perhaps if I invoke Clare, the patron saint of television.
Perhaps if I become the images
passing through the cells of a woman's brain.

I must become very large and block his sight.
I must be sharp and impetuous as knives.
I must insert myself into the bark of his apple trees,
and cleave the bones of his cows. I must be the marrow
that he drinks into his cloud-wet body.
I must be careful and laugh when he laughs.
I must turn down the covers and guide him in.
I must fashion his children out of Playdough, blue,

pink, green.
I must pull them from between my legs
and set them before the television.

I must hide my memory in a mustard grain
so that he'll search for it over time until time is gone.
I must lose myself in the world's regard and disparagement.
I must remain this person and be no trouble.
None at all. So he'll forget.
I'll collect dust out of reach,
a single dish from a set, a flower made of felt,
a tablet the wrong shape to choke on.

I must become essential and file everything
under my own system,
so we can lose him and his proofs and adherents.
I must be a doubter in a city of belief
that hails his signs (the great footprints
long as limousines, the rough print on the wall).
On the pavement where his house begins
fainting women kneel. I'm not among them
although they polish the brass tongues of his lions
with their own tongues
and taste the everlasting life.

IV.

DREAMWALKERS: THE RETURNING

Nora Naranjo-Morse

SANTA CLARA PUEBLO

I am continually enriched by
the specific worldview of Pueblo culture which I was born into.
Equally I am influenced by the modern world that dictates
many areas of contemporary native life . . . from these two
facets stream an endless supply of stories, incidents, and chal-
lenges which I use daily in my creative process.

Gia's Song

Thung joo Kwa yaa na povi sah
Thung joo Kwa yaa na povi sah
    Tsay ohi taa geh wo gi wa naa povi sah
    pin povi
    pin povi do mu u da kun
    ka nee na nun dun naa da si tah.
On top of Black Mesa there are flowers
On top of Black Mesa there are flowers
    dew on yellow flowers
    mountain flowers I see
    so far away that it makes me cry.
She opened her eyes slowly,
        to awaken from a trance
            caught by a song,
                transporting her to childhood,
    Back to the flowers
    growing atop Black Mesa,
    so far and yet clearly brilliant.
Awake from the song,
    Gia focused on her daughter,

anxiously awaiting
to be taught a new song.
The old woman chose to take her time,
she had learned from experience,
attention is better paid by children,
when there is a little pause,
and mystery
in storytelling.
Soon enough Gia spoke . . .
"When I was a young girl,
my family would camp
below Kwheng sa po,
during the farming months.
We spent most of our days
following my grandmother
through rows of corn
and playing in the streams below.
One day white men came in a wagon,
telling us about a school for Indians,
run by the government.
We were told this school would educate
and prepare us for jobs in the white man's world.
None of us knew what any of it meant,
but these men spoke sweetly
offering grandmother a roll of baling wire
for each child that went to school.
Before we knew what was happening,
we were sitting in the back of their wagon,
on our way to government school,
away from our families,
to another man's world.
Often we would cry,
out of loneliness,
but this song helped us
to remember our home."
Gia thoughtfully straightened

the pleats on her skirt,
swallowing the last of her coffee.
Smiling, she continued . . .

>"The government school taught sewing,
>I learned on an electric machine.
>By the time I returned to the village I could
>sew, but few of the people had heard of sewing machines,
>or even electricity.
>The machine I learned to operate as my trade
>could not be carried here and there,
>but this song you are learning,
>will always be carried in your heart,
>here and there."

Marilou Awiakta

CHEROKEE

I grew up in Oak Ridge, Tennessee—a reservation for atoms, not Indians—but I was centered and happy in my heritage until I went to college and began Western education in earnest. Everywhere I turned I found a "squared world," a society so compartmentalized that life, including my own, had no room to move around, to breathe. For twenty years I struggled against the Square World, but I unwittingly internalized it—tore my life-web and stuffed the broken strands into the "boxes"—until the day came when my spirit was so sick I couldn't function. My only hope was that the Creator/Provider would find me. A year dragged by. Then one day I wrote the poem "An Indian Walks in Me."

One quiet line marked the beginning of my healing: "No more will I follow any rule that splits my soul." Not for society or for government or for education or for any power whatsoever would I depart from the traditional teaching of my elders: "All of creation is one family, sacred." I also remembered that when I was young and said "I want to be a poet," Mother always said, "That's good. And what will you do for the people?" In my writing, I began to follow our mountain tradition of "take the materials at hand and make something comely and useful." Gradually, I saw how to take the positive aspects of my Cherokee/Appalachian heritage and of the high-tech world and weave them into a new harmony. I hope the poems and essays I've written since that time, 1978, have worked for the good of the people.

Amazons in Appalachia

The reader will not be a little surprised to find the story of the Amazons not so great a fable as we imagined, many of the Cherokee women being as famous in war as powerful in the council.

— HENRY TIMBERLAKE
Memoirs, 1765

Are the spirits of these women accessible to us today? Yes! According to Albert Einstein, there is a dimension beyond time/space where time stands still—past, present, and future are one. Native Americans have always known this dimension as "the time immemorial," a spiritual place we enter to commune intimately with all that is, a place abidingly real. Going there now, I return to my native mountains in east Tennessee and walk with the strong Cherokee grandmothers Timberlake met on his journey more than two centuries ago.

"Where are your women?"

The speaker is Attakullakulla, a Cherokee chief renowned for his shrewd and effective diplomacy. He has come to negotiate a treaty with the whites. Among his delegation are women "as famous in war as powerful in the council." Their presence also has ceremonial significance: it is meant to show honor to the other delegation. But that delegation is composed of males only; to them the absence of women is irrelevant, a trivial consideration.

To the Cherokee, however, reverence for women/Mother Earth/life/spirit is interconnected. Irreverence for one is likely to mean irreverence for all. Implicit in their chief's question "Where are your women?" the Cherokee hear "Where is your balance? What is your intent?" They see that balance is absent and are wary of the white men's motives. They intuit the mentality of destruction.

I turn to my own time (1989). I look at the Congress, the Joint Chiefs of Staff, the Nuclear Regulatory Commission . . . at the hierarchies of my church, my university, my city, my children's school. "Where are your women?" I ask.

Wary and fearful, I call aside one of Attakullakulla's delegation. I choose her for the gray streak of experience in her hair, for her staunch hips, and for the lively light in her eyes that indicates an alert, indomitable spirit. "Grandmother, I need your courage. Sing to me about your life."

Song of the Grandmothers

Her voice has the clear, honing timbre of the mountains.

I am Cherokee.
My people believe in the Spirit that unites all things.

I am woman. I am life force. My word has great value.
    The man reveres me
as he reveres Mother Earth and his own spirit.

The Beloved Woman is one of our principal chiefs.
Through her the Spirit often speaks to the people. In the Great
Council at the capital she is a powerful voice.
Concerning the fate of hostages, her word is absolute.

Women share in all of life. We lead sacred dances. In
the Council we debate freely with men until an
agreement is reached. When the nation considers war,
we have a say, for we bear the warriors.

Sometimes I go into battle. I also plant and harvest.

I carry my own name and the name of my clan. If I
accept a mate, he and our children take the name of my
clan. If there is deep trouble between us, I am as free to
tell him to go as he is to leave. Our children and our
dwelling stay with me. As long as I am treated with
dignity, I am steadfast.

I love and work and sing
I listen to the Spirit.
In all things I speak my mind.
I walk without fear.
I am Cherokee.

I feel the Grandmother's power. She sings of harmony, not
dominance. And her song rises from a culture that repeats the wise
balance of nature: the gender capable of bearing life is not separated
from the power to sustain it. A simple principle. Yet, in spite—or
perhaps because—of our vast progress in science and technology,
the American culture where I live has not grasped this principle.
In my county alone there are 2,600 men who refuse to pay child
support, leaving their women and children with a hollow name,
bereft of economic means and sometimes even of a safe dwelling.
On the national level, the U.S. Constitution still does not include
equal rights for women.

The Grandmother can see this dimension of time and space as
well as I—its imbalance, its irreverence, its sparse presence of
women in positions of influence. And she can hear the brave
women who sing for harmony and for transforming power. "My
own voice is small, Grandmother, and I'm afraid. You live in a

culture that believes in your song. How can you understand what women of time have to cope with?"

Grasping my chin gently, the Grandmother turns my face back toward the treaty council. "Listen to Attakullakulla's question again. When he says 'Where are your women,' look into the eyes of the white delegation and you will see what I saw."

On the surface, hardness—the hardness of mind split from spirit, the eyes of conquerors. Beyond the surface, stretching future decades deep, are crumpled treaties. Rich farms laid waste. And, finally, the Cherokee, goaded by soldiers along a snowbound trail toward Oklahoma—a seemingly endless line of women, men, and children, wrapped in coats and blankets, their backs bowed against the cold. In the only gesture of disdain left to them, they refuse to look their captors in the face.

Putting my arms around the Grandmother, I lay my head on her shoulder. Through touch we exchange sorrow, despair that anything really changes. I'm ashamed that I've shown so little courage. She is sympathetic. But from the pressure of her arms I also feel the stern, beautiful power that flows from all the Grandmothers, as it flows from our mountains themselves. It says, "Dry your tears. Get up. Do for yourself or do without. Work for the day to come. Be joyful."

"Joyful, Grandmother!" I draw away. "Sorrow, yes. Work, yes. We must work . . . up to the end. But such a hardness is bearing down on my people. Already soldiers are gathering. Snow has begun to fall. This time we will walk the Trail of Fire. With the power of the atom, they can make the world's people walk it. How can you speak of joy?"

"Because, for those who die, death is death. A Trail of Tears for the Cherokee, a Trail of Fire for all—it is the same. But without joy, there is no hope. Without hope, the People have no chance to survive. Women know how to keep hope alive . . . at least, *some* women do."

The reproach stings and angers me . . . because she is right. My joy, my hope *are* lost. I don't know how to find them again. Silently, my thoughts flow toward her. Hers flow back to me, strong, without anger.

"Come," she says.

"Where?"

"To Chota—the capital—to see the Beloved Woman."

I've heard of her—Nanyehi—"spirit person/immortal or 'the Path.'" Nanyehi, whom the whites call Nancy Ward and hold in great respect . . . the Beloved Woman whose advice and counsel are revered throughout the Cherokee Nation. She is said to have a "queenly and commanding presence," as well as remarkable beauty, with skin the color and texture of the wild rose.

Not ready . . . I'm not ready for this. Following the Grandmother along the forest trail, I sometimes walk close, sometimes lag behind. Puny—that's what I am. Puny, puny, puny—the worst charge that can be leveled at any mountain woman, red, white, or black. It carries pity, contempt, reproach. When we meet, the Beloved Woman will see straight into my spirit. I dread to feel the word in her look.

I know about her courage. She works ceaselessly for harmony with white settlers, interpreting the ways of each people to the other. From her uncle and mentor, Attakullakulla, she has learned diplomacy and the realities of power. She understands that the Cherokee ultimately will be outnumbered and that war will bring sure extinction. She counsels them to channel their energies from fighting into more effective government and better food production. To avoid bloodshed, she often risks censure and misunderstanding to warn either side of an impending attack, then urges resolution by arbitration. In the councils she speaks powerfully on two major themes: "Work for peace. Do not sell your land."

All the while, she knows the odds . . .

As the Grandmother and I pass through my hometown of Oak Ridge, I look at the nest of nuclear reactors there, and weight the odds of survival—for all people. The odds are small. But not impossible. My own song for harmony and reverence with the atom is a small breath. But it may combine with others to make a warm and mighty wind, powerful enough to transform the hardness and cold into life. It is not impossible.

I walk closer to the Grandmother. In this timeless dimension, we could move more rapidly, but she paces my spirit, holding it to a thoughtful rhythm as we cross several ridges and go down into the Tellico Valley. We walk beside the quiet, swift waters of the Little Tennessee River. Chota is not far off.

What time and space will the Grandmother choose for me to meet the Beloved Woman? I imagine a collage of possibilities:

1775 . . . Nanyehi fights beside her husband in a battle against the Creeks. When he is killed, she takes his rifle and leads the Cherokee to victory. Afterwards, warriors sing of her deeds at Chota and the women and men of the Great Council award her the high office she will hold for more than half a century. She is seventeen, the mother of a son and a daughter.

1776 . . . Having captured the white woman, Mrs. Lydia Bean, Cherokee warriors tie her to the stake. Just as they light the fire, Nanyehi arrives on the scene, crying, "No woman will be burned at the stake while I am Beloved Woman!" Her word is absolute. Mrs. Bean goes free. She teaches dairying to Nanyehi, who in turn teaches it to the Cherokee.

1781 . . . At the Long Island Treaty Council, Nanyehi is the featured speaker. "Our cry is for peace; let it continue . . . This peace must last forever. Let your women's sons be ours; our sons be yours. Let your women hear our words." (Note: no white women are present.) Colonel William Christian responds to her: "Mother, we have listened well to your talk . . . No man can hear it without being moved by it . . . Our women shall hear your words . . . We will not meddle with your people if they will be still and quiet at home and let us live in peace." Although the majority of Cherokee and whites hold the peace, violence and bloodshed continue among dissenting factions.

1785 . . . The Hopewell Treaty Council convenes in South Carolina. Attending the Council are four commissioners appointed by Congress, thirty-six chiefs, and about a thousand Cherokee delegates. Again, the Beloved Woman speaks eloquently. Knowing full well the pattern of strife that precedes this Council, she bases her talk on positive developments. "I take you by the hand in real friendship . . . I look on you and the red people as children. Your having determined on peace is most pleasant to me, for I have seen much trouble during the late war . . . We are now under the protection of Congress and shall have no more disturbance. The talk I have given you is from the young warriors I have raised in my town, as well as myself. They rejoice that we have peace, and hope the chain of friendship will never more be broken."

Hope—that quality so necessary for survival. The Beloved Woman never loses hope. Perhaps I will learn the source of her strength by sharing her private moments: I may see her bend in joy over her newborn second daughter (fathered by the white trader Bryant Ward, to whom she is briefly married in the late 1750s) or hear her laugh among her grandchildren and the many orphans to whom she gives a home. Or I may stand beside her in 1817 as she composes her last message to her people. Too ill at age seventy-nine to attend the Council, she sends the last message by her son. Twenty years before it begins, she sees the Trail of Tears loom ahead and her words have one theme: "My children, do not part with any more of your lands . . . it would be like destroying your mothers."

The Grandmother's hand on my arm halts my imaginings. We stand at the edge of a secluded clearing, rimmed with tall pines. In the center is a large log house and around it women—many women—move through sun and shadow. Some walk in the clearing. Others cluster on the porch, talking quietly, or sit at the edge of the forest in mediation. Not far from us, a woman who is combing another's hair leans forward to whisper and their laughter rises into the soughing pines.

A great weaving is going on here, a deep bonding . . .

"This is the menstrual lodge," says the Grandmother. "When our power sign is with us we come here. It is a sacred time—a time for rest and meditation. No one is allowed to disturb our harmony. No warrior may even cross our path. In the menstrual lodge many things are known, many plans are made . . ."

"And the Beloved Woman?"

"She is here."

"What year is this, Grandmother?"

"It is not a year, it is a *season*—you and the Beloved Woman are meeting when each of you is in her forty-seventh season." From the expression on my face the Grandmother knows I appreciate the wisdom of her choice: Four and seven are the sacred numbers of the Cherokee, four symbolizing the balance of the four directions. It is the season when no woman should or can afford to be puny. The Grandmother nods. Motioning me to wait, she goes toward the lodge, threading her way through the women with a smile of recognition here, the touch of outstretched fingers there.

With my hands behind my hips, I lean against the stout, wiry-haired trunk of a pine. Its resinous scent clears my mind. These women are not the Amazons of the Greek fable. While they are independent and self-defined, they do not hate men or use them only at random for procreation. They do not elevate their daughters, then kill, cripple, or make servants of their sons. But did the Greek patriarchs tell the truth? If Attakullakulla had asked them, "Where are your women?" they would have answered with a shrug. I'm wary of the Greeks bearing fables. Although there is little proof that they described the Amazons accurately, ample evidence suggests that they encountered—and resented—strong women like my Grandmothers and characterized them as heinous in order to justify destroying them (a strategy modern patriarchs still use).

In any case, why should I bother with distant Greeks and their nebulous fables when I have the spirits of the Grandmothers, whose roots are struck deep in my native soil and whose strength is as tangible and tenacious as the amber-pitched pine at my back?

Like the husk of a seed, my Western education/conditioning splits and my spirit sends up a green shoot. With it comes a long buried memory: I am twelve years old. Mother has told me that soon I will be capable of bearing life. "Think of it, Marilou. It's a sacred power, a great responsibility." I think . . . and wait for the power sign. It comes. Mother announces to my father, "Our little girl is a woman now . . ." He smiles. "Well . . . mighty fine." In the evening we have a dinner in my honor. Steam from corn on the cob, fried chicken, green beans, and cornbread mingles in my mind with the private odor, warm and pungent, that Mother describes as "fresh" (the rural term for mammals in season). I feel wholesome, proud, in harmony with the natural order.

I am ready now to meet the Beloved Woman . . .

"What was it like," you ask, "to be in her presence?"

"Come. I will show you." It is midnight, June, the full moon. Behind a farmhouse near the Kentucky border, you and I walk barefoot through the coarse grass. Crickets and treefrogs are drowsy. Birds are quiet. And we are enveloped in a powerful, sweet odor that transforms the night. Too pungent to be honeysuckle. Too fecund for roses. It recalls a baby's breath just after nursing, along with the memory of something warm and private that lingers at the edge of the mind . . .

Sniffing the air, we seek the source—and find it. The cornfield in bloom. Row on row of sturdy stalks, with their tassels held up to the moon. Silently, in slow rhythm, we make our way into the field. The faint rustle of growing plants flows around and through us; until we stop by a tall stalk, there seems no division between flesh and green. We rub the smooth, sinewy leaves on our cheeks and touch a nubile ear, where each grain of pollen that falls from the tassel will bake a kernel, strong and turgid with milk. Linking arms around the stalk, we lift our faces to the drifting pollen and breathe the spirit of the Corn Mother—the powerful, joyous, nurturing odor of one complete in herself.

"Where are your women?"

We are here.

Connie Fife

CREE

In the beginning, I wrote simply to break my own silence, to somehow find the words in which to respond to the voices I had grown up with that told me I had no voice of my own nor was I entitled to one. When I was young, poetry and the world of fiction, the tapestry of language itself was what saved my sanity. Still they were the words of Europeans. When black women's work came out in a big way, I gobbled up everything I could get my hands on . . . I remember when a good friend brought me home a copy of Gathering of Spirit (edited by Beth Brant). It was the greatest birthday gift I have ever received. I was not the only native woman writing poetry. Granted, it took me another three years before I showed anyone my stack of crumpled napkins, backs of envelopes, and scribbling on the borders of books.

Today I write because I believe there are so many of our stories (personal) that need to be told and celebrated. While I use the written word, I firmly believe that when spoken out loud words take on their own life and how we use them will be how they touch our hearts. Look at how devastating the language of Christianity has been . . . so I write using an outsider's tongue hoping that I can do honor to the words themselves, their value and meaning.

The act of writing itself is like the act of leaving my home each day. It is the act of having survived, the act of laughing in the face of the beast. It is deeply personal in that each poem demands that all of me is present on the journey.

Dear Webster

DEDICATED TO BETH BRANT

savage (sav'ij) adj. without civilization; primitive;
barbarous (a savage tribe) n. a member of a preliterate
society having a primitive way of life; a fierce, brutal
person.

i am the one who talks with the mountains
when i am not sliding down the stream of its face /
i am the one who walks the streets late at
night despite the danger
believing that this land is mine to roam freely /
i am the one who carved a mask from a thick tree
then wore it /
i am the one who raises her arms to the sun
then takes flight on winds from the east /
i am the one who says "no more"
then leaves the man whose fists have reconstructed
my bones /
i am the one who defies the narrow definition of love
and loves another woman
and heals a nation in doing so /
i am the one who meeting after meeting turns
away when men misconstrue my words
and goes on /
i am the one whose stories take our collective
pasts into the future
and guarantees that not one day is left behind /
i am the one sleeping on sidewalks
who speaks to all my relations as the masses
hear only their own silence /
i am the one who cradles close to her breasts
small children
and women who were old before they were young /
I am the one who shoots fire into the veins of those

who cannot re-ignite their own sparks
then gives them the responsibility of stocking
the wood /
i am the one who talks to herself and hears
others answer
then writes it down so that the words remain in
my throat /
i am the one who demonstrates against forced
relocation
and uses a shotgun to carry the message clean home /
i am the one who watched as my children's hair
was cut
and cried and wept then screamed "return them" /
i am the one struggling to find her way back
i am the one who uses brushes to paint my resistance
on a canvas
then hangs my tapestry across the horizon /
i am the one whose son died of AIDS while a piece
of myself died each day and couldn't halt either
then buried my child /
i am the one who was raped by my father then
my uncle
and spent years hiding then decided to change it all
and used all my rage to castrate my memory of them
and healed myself with love /
i am the one who late at night screams and howls
and hears voices answer /
i am the one whose death was intended
and didn't die

Mary Goose

MESQUAKIE CHIPPEWA

I wrote "Whale Song" because I felt a connection to a whale. It took me several years from the time I wrote my first version to the finished version of the poem. It came out of the anger I felt at seeing a beached whale on the East Coast in the news. I was angry because all the experts said they didn't know why a whale had beached itself. I knew it was because of what is happening to the earth . . . Everything is connected. Anything you do today will affect someone or something next to you or on the other side of the world—today, tomorrow, or years from now.

Whale Song

I always knew we would be in trouble
when whales leave prints on the ground
and the mud and sand on the beach
offer the last refuge, and sandcastles yield
as it sings its last song.

From miles away I drop Indian tobacco from my hand
and pray for all the water spirits and
my fellow water creatures.

As the Sun looks through salmon pink clouds
I hear two joggers clad in identical purple sweats
say how nice the Sun reflects
off the water like diamonds and gold.

I wonder why I can hear the whale sing
when I have never been close enough to look
into a whale's eyes, but have only seen
a mother Pacific gray whale and her baby near Long Beach.

The wind must be so powerful that it can
make the salty ocean waves sound like moans
as I clean the last remnants of the tobacco from my hand
each drop more valuable than diamonds and gold.

I know I will write a "whale song" poem
about how the whale's salty sweat and tears
from the act of dying have burned my paper-cut finger.

Leanne Howe

CHOCTAW

As a Choctaw I grew up in a house of women. From my single mother, the other women in my family, my mother's friends, I was influenced by the way they managed their lives. These very strong Indian women were providers: mother, friend, and sometimes enemy. I learned to be my own woman from watching them. I can't imagine a life any other way.

Indians Never Say Goodbye

There she was standing over me. She inched her face close to my face. She put her hands on my face. I remembered her immediately, but did not speak. My eyes blurred. They were hot and heavy. It hurt to look at Ain't Sally. It hurt to see. I closed my eyes. I felt her cool touch. She chanted. "You will be well. You will not die. Chim achukma taha che. You will be well. Chim peas taha che."

She sang to me. Then I heard her leave.

A woman, whose bed was surrounded by white partitions, moaned again. This was not a new sound. It was a constant. Her breath whistled irregularly. There was no escaping the whistle. The whistling sounds were everywhere in the white room. Then they stopped.

Another woman in another bed called out. No answer. She pushed the bell. Women wearing white dresses came into the room. They pushed the partitions back. They said the whistling woman was dead. I went back to sleep.

Before the hospital. Before the rheumatic fever. Before the dead woman. I had met Ain't Sally. I was seven years old.

Ain't Sally was an ancient Indian relative who lived in Hayrick, outside of Dublin. A place of Snakes. A place of memory.

Once a base camp for nomadic tribes following buffalo, once a county seat, Hayrick, Texas, took its name from a solitary mountain standing in the breadth of open grasslands. Only a state government road sign remains, marking the place of Hayrick. Marking the sing of the Snakes.

The only time we visited Ain't Sally, I rode in the back seat of our green 1950 Chevrolet, and listened to my Indian grandmother tell stories about our family.

Chapter went like this: Life in a Dugout, Making Lye Soap, How Grandfather got VD.

I don't remember much of the drive to Hayrick. We drove the rural roads of west Texas. There were two lanes of dust and dirt, stagnant, green-belted riverbeds, and one-lane bridges.

When we arrived at Ain't Sally's, the old woman ambled out of a rusted screen door of a paintless, wooden house. Breasts sagging, her thin body, lacking in strength, seemed unable to support her weight. She wore a sleeveless dress which revealed naked, brown skin, skin that was no more than a sheath for aging bones. Hairless underarms.

She fed us saltine crackers and cold squirrel dumplings. She asked me questions. She asked about my secrets. I don't remember having any to tell. She told me hers while I ate.

She said I reminded her of someone she's seen a long time ago. I remember dancing for her. I told her I was a bird. The man-bird. A hunter. I danced around the kitchen table and sang, and pretended to be a pow wow dancer. A bird of dance. A bird of rhythm.

When my mother and grandmother went to town, Ain't Sally took me for a walk around her place. The farm had belonged to her father and his father before him. We went down to the dry gorge and she pointed out all kinds of roots, and trees. She asked me if I knew about the plants of the pasture. I said yes. I thought I was lying.

As we walked farther from the house, I remember a hot gusty wind picked up her voice like dust tendrils on bedrock and blew it away from me. I ran to catch the sound. I found Ain't Sally sitting on a granite rock.

—Indian girl. Ala Teke.

—Come and see, on our land, the four winds of the old days will blow through our hair. Then she tugged at my black braids.

—Come and visit the Snakes, Ala Teke.

—When I was your age, they blew across this place like red dust devils on flat neutral plains.

—Do you hear the Snake People calling us?

—Yes. Yes. I can see them. I hear them. They are naked and wild. Their eyes, like black grapes, shining in the sun, stare back at me.

They're hungry.

I watch the Snake People eat the fleshy intestines of my uncle's butchered cow. I taste the hot blood, roll it around on my tongue and remember. It makes me sweat.

I watch the Snake People play games around the carcass. And before we walk back to the house, the old woman and me, she ran her crooked fingers across my eyes and said:

—Indian Girl. Ala Teke.

—The ghosts of your ancestors will visit you there.

The rest of the visit blurs. My last memories are of her waving to me from her front porch.

She never explained the Snakes. She only said, "Che pisa lauchi. I'll see you. Indians never say goodbye."

I never saw Ain't Sally again until the hospital. I thought she had died. I didn't know about the Snakes until some twenty-five years later. To make the sign of the Snake means: Comanches were here.

Leslie Marmon Silko

LAGUNA

When Sun Came to Riverwoman

that time
    in the sun
    beside the Rio Grande.

voice of the mourning dove
        calls
                long ago   long ago
        remembering the lost one
        remembering the love.

Out of the dense green
                eternity of springtime
        willows rustle in the blue wind
            timeless
                        the year unknown
                            unnamed.

The muddy fast water
      warm around my feet
      you move into the current slowly

          brown skin thighs
          deep intensity
          flowing water.

Your warmth penetrates
                yellow sand and sky.
Endless eyes shining always
        for green river moss
        for tiny water spiders.
Crying out   the dove
            will not let me forget

        It is ordained
        in the swirling brown water
                and it carries you away,
                my lost one
                my love,
                      the mountain.

man of sun
                came to riverwoman
                and in the sundown wind
        he left her
                to sing
                        for rainclouds swell in the northwest sky.
                        for rainsmell on pale blue winds
                                                from China.

Sonlatsa Jim-James

N A V A J O ▪ M O D O C

I am of the Sleeping Rock clan
and am born for the Mixed Breed clan. My grandparents, on
my mother's side, are of the Red Runs Into Water and Salt
clans. My home is Toh-la-kai, New Mexico. I am the daughter
of Elouise Johnson, full-blooded Navajo, a full-time mother
and constant victim of the U.S. policies on Indian lands. My
father, Sonny Jim, Modoc, is a part-time father and full-time
Indian rodeo cowboy.

"Diné Way" is dedicated to my grandmother, Sarah S.
Johnson. Shimá raised me and taught me the language and
cultural practices of my people, the Navajo. She embodies the
true spirit of life and struggle. She has labored long and hard
so that I might have the opportunity to read and write and
reinvent the enemy's language.

My life has been spent dealing with alcoholism, domestic
violence, poverty, and abuse. I realized that I could not talk to
anyone about my feelings or ideas because I would be too angry

or upset. So I began to write my feelings and ideas down in whatever I could get my hands on.

In the months following the murder of my aunt, Ella M. Johnson (1961–1991), murdered by her husband/police officer, my writing took a major turnaround. There was nobody to blame for the injustices except the "enemy" through whose language I learned to be uncaring and immoral. They talked about my aunt as if she were no one and her children were to be nothing more than problems for the system to handle.

From this experience, I have come to see that white America will not give me justice, will not give my family justice, and will not give my people, the American Indian, justice. I must command justice, my family must command justice, and my people must command justice.

Diné Way

I remember the days I spent with my grandmother on top of the mesa behind our home. In Toh-la-kai (which means White Water), New Mexico, the days are usually dry and hot during the summer. One thing that always amazed me is that my grandmother still had strength to climb the mesa in summers like these after a hard day's work. Her name is Sarah Johnson, and she is sixty-seven years old. I call her "Shimá," which means mother. Her clan is Tsénaabiłnii (Sleep Rock People) born for Táchiinii (Red Water People). During those days that I spent with her, I grew to love the land and all that it offered. When we picked different types of plants and made sure that our sheep were okay, she was happy. I knew my grandmother was happy when she softly sang a song.

As a child, a freshly dug carrot was not a source of survival to me, but a gift from the Holy People. Shimá told me to always fill up the holes so that the Holy People can make another carrot grow for me. Shimá would always tell me not to play with my food or the Holy People would starve my family. I was taught to respect animal skins, eagle feathers, holy plants, and corn pollen, as well as many other things. When they got older they learned all the "rules." For example, the young men would learn the procedure for hunting. The young women would learn the procedure for having a Puberty Ceremony. This is the way of the Diné, or the People. It is a part of Navajo life to know the culture and traditions and the land on which they are taught. It was very important to follow the "rules" in order to be happy. This idea is what the quote from *Between Sacred Mountains* represents: ". . . even when the game was very scarce, we always found one. Maybe it was because we did all the things we were told to do. We kept things holy. We spoke only the language that was used a long time ago. We followed the words that were spoken by the Holy People. We followed those. We used only those things. Maybe that is why we have always come home singing." Everything the Navajo learned related in some way back to the Holy People, the animals, and the land. When bad things happened to the environment, bad things happened to the Navajo. The Navajo's relationship to the environment has changed and will always change the physical world and be changed by it.

In the past, the Navajo used the land more than they do now for food, medicine, roaming, and ceremonies. My great-grandmother told me of the time the Diné were forced to go on the Long Walk. She was only a child, but she said that when they returned home, all the people started to settle down and make hogans. Clans joined together to survive and so there were many marriages. Even through these hard times, my great-grandmother says that the Diné still practiced the traditional ceremonies. These ceremonies always included a hataałii or medicine man. The medicine man had to be given food and gifts, and he would give healing, blessing, and holy plants, stones, or pollen. She said the Diné began planting corn and other plants in order to have food for everyone. The planting was holy and taken care of very well. The Holy People gave the Diné these plants and they were to follow the "rules" of planting. My great-grandmother says that all the clans had sheep. She said that every morning when the sun rose, she let the sheep out of the corral to graze. She herded them all day long and returned before the sun set. She liked to herd sheep because it was the only time she got to see all her friends from other clans. She said that everyone knew where everyone else was herding their sheep so that the stock would not get mixed up. Not only were plants important, but also animals. My grandfather told me the story of how the animal world existed before the human world. The animals had magical powers and each animal used his powers differently. For example, the coyote used his powers to play tricks on other animals, but always failed in the end. These animals spoke the holy words and knew all the traditional ceremonies. They are the brothers of the Diné.

Even in the modern world we live in today, these ceremonies, stories, and customs are still kept among the Navajo. Undoubtedly, they are not as strong as they were a long time ago, but they are not forgotten. The land is now distributed among the Navajo, and modern technology has taken its toll on the reservation. Food is produced faster, people can get to ceremonies faster, and the Diné get healing faster. This does not mean that the cultural identity of the Navajo is lost. It just means that the Diné are learning to function in two different worlds. They are getting the best of both worlds: the spiritual ways and the modern ways. Most non-Indians who go to a reservation and see Indians shopping at Safeway believe that the Indians have lost their cultural identity—just because they drive trucks and wear clothes made in Japan. If, however, a non-Indian went to a traditional ceremony, they would believe otherwise. All my uncles and aunts have jobs in a city and they dress up in nice clothes for work. But when the day of a ceremony comes, such as a Nid'áa' or Squaw Dance, they dress up in clothes that they can either work in or participate in. This ceremony is widely held on the reservation among the Navajo. It is a nine-day healing and blessing ceremony. The Nid'áa' is done by two different clans. The Nid'áa' also serves as a way for young men and women to find out who they are related to. This prevents any unholy marriages. Each clan travels to the other clan's home. A long time ago, people traveled in wagons or on horseback, but now they use trucks with campers and cars. The clans do have to have a few horseback riders to carry the Spirit Stick. There can be about five patients per clan and each patient's family prepares food for everyone who comes.

This is done in a very large and long shack made of green branches tied together with wire. Many families donate some of the corn from their fields or a sheep, and others donate store-bought things such as bread, vegetables, paper cups, bowls or plates, and sugar treats. The sugar treats are used to pass out to the other clans early in the morning while they sing. During this joyful family occasion in the shacks, things are very serious in the hogan. The hataałii is following all the rules, and so are his patients. When it is time to be serious and holy, all the families from both clans know. For instance, when the patients come out of the hogan and are painted all black, everyone must pay attention while they run. The men run toward the east a short distance, and the women wait for them as they wear yards of material, blankets, and skins. When the men return, they all run into the back of a shack and eat a big meal. They will eat out of bowls and plates also made somewhere in Japan, and they will eat Rainbo bread and drink Folgers coffee, but that would be besides the point to them and everyone else, because during the run they had the Holy People with them. They had the Diné's full attention, and they ran on the Holy Land, even if this meant running by my aunt's great big white satellite dish.

Sometimes I see Shimá with my six-year-old sister, telling her the same things she told me. They go to the mesa too. I even find myself telling my teenage sister and cousins the stories my grandfather told me. When I am with my mother, I ask her about my great-grandparents, who passed away before I knew them. All my friends that I grew up with are also doing the same thing. We go to college in hopes of learning the "white man's" way of thinking, and returning home to help our people. It is not because we have to, but because we were taught that this land is for us to take care of, that way it will take care of us. The future will be very tough for the following generations of Diné and the land they were raised on. This is a fact that nobody can deny. There are many programs being developed for the Navajo youth today, in hopes of teaching them the importance of their heritage and the land. Unfortunately, all Navajo children are not taught about the Holy People in the Diné way. These future generations will know, however, that they will have to follow the "rules" in order to be happy. They will remember that when bad things happen to the land, then bad things will happen to the Navajo. When I return home, I pray to the Holy People the way Shimá taught me: I climb the mesa with my Sony Walkman, and I look out to the dry horizon and wonder what is in store for the future of this Holy Land. The days I spent with Shimá on the mesa will never be forgotten because it is the Diné way.

Rosemary M. Huggins

T L I N G I T

I am a tribal member of the Teeth Dog Salmon clan, a member of the Raven Moiety, tribal member of the Thlawaa Kwaan, a Tlingit Nation of the region of Alaska.

I became interested in writing stories of my people when I realized that many of our young people were growing up with no knowledge of their heritage. I feel that by writing stories maybe these stories could be handed down to my grandchildren and great-grandchildren. By becoming assimilated into today's dominant society, we seem to have lost the ability to pass on the stories that were our history.

For Sean, Chris, and Caitlin, who made writing the stories necessary.

Grandma Weaver's Last Arrow

Grandma Weaver was 110 years old when the social scientists came to interview her. They came from the universities all over the United States—Yale, Harvard, Princeton, UCLA, and UW. There were thirty of them and they had come to southeast Alaska to help us find our lost Indian culture. Since we hadn't known it was lost we didn't know how to answer their questions, but we did tell them about the oldest member of the tribe. When they heard of Grandma Weaver they rushed to interview her with renewed hope and enthusiasm shining from their eyes, hopeful of capturing their elusive quarry.

All thirty of them trooped into her bedroom. Some of them immediately took out 35-mm cameras and started snapping away —all the flashbulbs flashing looked like a mini-thunderstorm occurring only in Grandma Weaver's room. The other social scientists gathered around her bed, pens and pads poised. They looked like giant birds of prey, dressed in three-piece suits, hovering over her as if to pluck morsels of knowledge from her mind. Grandma Weaver looked even more like an undernourished six-year-old as she sat huddled in the middle of her bed, frightened and alone. Were these strange noises caused by the *Kushtica*—evil spirits—come to take her away?

They took pictures of everything in her room—the dance masks sharply defined against the stark white walls, the reeds (soaking in the sink) needed for basket weaving, even her panties folded neatly in a drawer. Grandma Weaver ignored the cameras and notebooks and started weaving a new basket as she sat there, muttering away to herself in Tsimsian, the only language she spoke.

As each day passed the social scientists became more worried as if their last hope was disappearing. Wouldn't this old woman ever start speaking English?

Finally the social scientists held a whispered conference, packed up their 35-mm cameras, stuffed their pens and pads into bulging black briefcases, and left.

The next day they returned but this time armed with moving-picture cameras and tape recorders, the reels of which they could send to the experts at the University of Alaska's Indian Museum for translation. Moving swiftly they set all their modern equipment around her bed. Grandma Weaver, hearing all these strange new noises, sat up, her blind eyes darting from side to side as if she was trying to see what was going on around her. Muttering to herself in Tsimsian, she picked up her unfinished reed basket as if seeking comfort from the familiar act of weaving. Cameras and tape recorders clicked on and later it was said that the sound of the machines almost drowned out Grandma Weaver's voice.

When the social scientists got their films developed and the tapes translated, they invited some of the Indian community to share their triumph. Silently everyone waited with hushed expectancy; finally the movie started and there was Grandma Weaver on the screen, with a voice-over reading the translation of her Tsimsian. Except for the occasional muffled laughter of Indians, the group remained silent as the social scientists digested the translation. Interspersed with comments about walking across rivers on the backs of fish, about owning slaves and what tribes they were from, about which of her three or four husbands she had liked best, there were comments about these foreigners who came disrupting her peace. Would they like it if her grandsons went to their homes and disturbed their grandmothers? Why were these rude foreigners here, talking in a heathen tongue that no decent person would speak? Didn't these strange men know she was too old for all that? Maybe they were sent from the *Kushtica*—the evil spirits —to take her away.

After the show was over some of the social scientists packed up their equipment quietly, their faces red as if they knew they had failed and were embarrassed at their part in the fiasco. The others were jubilant, talking loudly about the great dissertations they could write about their important discoveries. They said the films could be put on our VCRs and the tapes on computers for future social scientists. As they filed out, one ran back to retrieve Grandma Weaver's unfinished reed basket—their proof that they had successfully captured the essence of an almost lost culture.

Grandma Weaver started murmuring to herself about these *cheechakos*—strangers—who didn't know that an unfinished basket had no value. Calmly she reached out for her reeds and began weaving a new basket.

Denise Sweet

ANISHNABE

I am Anishnabe (Ojibwe), enrolled at White Earth, and the mother of two fine sons, Damon and Vaughn.

Native people have always felt and respected the power of words, the beauty of great oratory, and the fierce pride of knowing that a language belongs to them and they to it. The language of poetry is no less sacred and, for me, holds that same power and beauty.

I pay homage to that gift every time I read or write a poem. Poetry is about the miracle of language. And miracles still happen all the time in this world.

My Mother and I Had a Discussion One Day

and she said I was quite fortunate
to have two sons
and I said how is that? and she said
with daughters you worry for them
birth control, child rearing,
you worry for them, the threat of rape,
and then there is the wedding expense.

I looked into her tired eyes
and clouded face and saw
that she was quite serious.
Yes, but, I said,
boys eat more.

and she said why do they call it
women's music?
and I said because they sing it,
take from it, feel good and strong
when they walk away from it
while we sit here this is going on.
Are you telling me, my mother said,
up until now, I have been listening
and no women have been singing?
and I said that is right
and she said that was ridiculous
and hummed a tune
of her own.

and she said why do you want to leave
this house, it is a fine house?
and I said I didn't think
there was much of a market
for a nose wiper, a kitchen keeper,
an under-the-bed sweeper
and she said my smart mouth
would get me in trouble one day
and I looked at her scarred knuckles
and quivering chin and realized
that I had spit in the face
of many women and I wept
with my mother

Jeannette Armstrong

O K A N A G A N

The major turning point in my life which involved my writing came as a result of returning to my community at the same time the chiefs of the Okanagan decided to make education a priority over everything else. I had just received a bachelor of fine arts degree. I had intended to work for a while before going on to a master's program. I was recruited to help organize an educational strategy to develop an Okanagan curriculum. My research and writing skills were a necessity, since I was a fluent speaker of Okanagan and English and had some background in the expressive arts.

The last twelve years, my life has been filled with writing and organizing to promote the discovery of my people's understanding of the world in the historical and contemporary contexts. I have always thought of my larger community as those who choose a way of life which protects and treasures the splendor of difference, as a way to carry health in a non-adversarial approach to being human. I hear in the voices of indigenous peoples, people of color, women, and those standing for a healthy earth a significant familiarity of purpose, which I have found here in my cherished Okanagan community.

The purpose of my writing has always been to tell a better story than is being told about us. To give that to the people and to the next generations. The voices of the grandmothers and grandfathers compel me to speak of the worth of our people and the beauty all around us, to banish the profaning of ourselves, and to ease the pain. I carry the language of the

*voice of the land and the valiance of the people and I will not
be silenced by a language of tyranny.*

I Study Rocks

I study rocks
strewn into the distance

I scan jagged faces of dark cliffs
for horses
with wings
examine underwater pebbles
rolling together
for signs
for a telling
of age old
crumblings
and majestic rises

I look long
at thunder eggs
lying silent unopened
wait ages
to discern the heart-shaped moment
frozen inside agate

I ponder bearstone glowing red
heaped in the center pit

I carry a round calm blue stone
secure inside a pouch
and lift tobacco
in a red smooth familiar shape
cupped in the palm

I strike rocks together
calling fishes upstream
watch pointed obsidian
arc upward
and trace ocher rock dust finger marks
on shadowy cave surfaces

I hold on to erect pestle contours
and move precise circles
against elegant curves
inside hollowed mortar

I release polar bears stealthy creeping
in midnight black slate

I observe rocks
placed shape to shape
become old sanctuaries
pounded
baked into brick
changed into garrisons
I weigh ores liquefied
forged into plows
into swords
poured into molds
polished into bullion
minted
into coins

I see boulders
move to roadsides
as solid bedrock blasted away
becomes tunnels
and mountains dissolve into gray slag piles
and coal black mounds
heaped on trains racing through the night

toward granite and glass wall towerings
in asphalt and concrete canyons
encasing marble stairways
burnished brass
and stainless steel
reflecting the cold lights
trapped in glitter rocks
set in gold
wrapped around fingers

I watched rocks
hurled and smashed
into cars of old Mohawk men
women and children
on a bridge
in Montreal
and the million-dollar
rock slide
blockages
on ten BC roads
after stones rained
down rock cliffs
on police lifting
human blockades
protecting the slow disintegration
of bones into sand
resting under headstones
on Liliwat land

In the foreground
rock-pillared bridges collapse
under the groan of earth's rock changed
into tunnelings
shiftings and spewings
as old stone-worked churches dissolve ever so minutely
in the sad rain

while in the distance
one tiny grain waits
to flower into blazing white

I study the rocks
I have set into a circle
opening to the east
on this mountaintop

Carolyn Brandy

CHEROKEE

I am a drummer, composer, performer, teacher, and mother. The writing of my story was a culmination of a whole lifetime of searching for myself and for my grandmothers. I feel completely blessed to be able to share this story . . . a particularly "American story" that many people share.

Heartbeat of the Ancestors

I knew her first in a dream. I'm six years old, I'm twelve, I'm twenty-seven or every age. She is the sound of the drum calling to me. I am the voice answering her. In my dream I'm being chased by a young soldier on horseback. I'm running, running, running up the sides of a dry riverbank. Long braids are tied behind my back, and as I look over my shoulder I see the man and horse coming faster and faster. I'm running for my life . . . the memory of this dream stays with me, always.

My mother was always prim and proper. She was born into a well-to-do San Franciscan family. Her father was a colonel in the army and her grandfather started one of the first newspapers in San Francisco. She tells stories of living on Nob Hill and going to parties and teas at the St. Francis Hotel. She often rode the ferry to the then country town of Berkeley to attend the University of California.

She met my Indian father at the NCO Club in Fresno, California. He was tall, dark, and handsome and he had a way with women. It was 1945 and he had just returned home wounded from the Second World War. He said my mother was the finest woman he had ever met, and that she had the most beautiful legs he had ever seen. He said he felt like a fish out of water with her and her society friends, but he loved every minute of it.

I was born right after the war, and since my father was still in the military, we moved around a lot from base to base. Sometimes he didn't come home for months at a time when he was overseas, but I always knew he was coming back. When he did come home, there started to be trouble between him and my mother. At that time, he drank a lot and my mother was always complaining about other women. They fought a lot. In 1955, my father became the proud owner of a brand-new cherry red and white DeSoto, which we drove across country. I was never happier. We ended up at Ft. Lewis, Washington. I was ten years old.

One day, my father didn't come home. But this time he never came back. My mother said he had shipped out. She never spoke about him again. It was as though he had disappeared into thin air. He became a taboo subject in our household. But that's how my mother dealt with everything that was hard. She just didn't talk about it anymore. Like her family. I never met any of them. She had been disowned when she married my father. And of course she didn't talk about my father's family. It was just all a big secret. I spent my childhood not really knowing who I was.

In the years after my father left, I fantasized about him. I wondered where he was in the world, and fantasized that he would be back at any moment. In fact, from the fourth grade through college,

I told all my friends that he was on maneuvers and that he would be back any day.

In school, I started playing classical violin, which helped me to survive those years. I could always escape into the music.

When I left my mother's house, I started an unconscious search for my father. The classical music I was playing was nothing like the feeling my father had left me, and I put the violin down and started playing the conga drums. When I played the drums, and the music got really good, I felt whole. I felt connected. I felt connected to my lost dad and to something bigger than him. I felt connected to the little girl in my dreams. I longed for those moments when the music put me back together, because the rest of the time I didn't know who I was.

One winter day not long ago the phone rang at my Berkeley house. The operator at the other end of the line was calling from a company in Chicago. She asked, "Is G. Brandy there?"

I said, "G. Brandy? G. W. Brandy?"

She said, "Yes."

I said, "That's my father, but I haven't seen him in thirty years. How did you get this number?"

"I called information and asked for G. Brandy."

"They gave you the number for C. Brandy."

"Well," she said, "he has a Berkeley address." She said she was not allowed to give me the address, but since she had found her own father only ten years before, she would give it to me.

It was eight blocks from my house.

I got in my car and circled his house all that evening. I was terrified. The next day I called my best friend and told her what had happened. She said, "Let's go see if it's him."

I said, "When do you want to go?"

She said, "Now."

We went to the house and knocked at the door. A little old man answered. Nothing like the man of my fantasy. My friend asked, "George Brandy?"

He replied, "Yes . . ."

I said, "George W. Brandy?"

He said, "Yes . . . who's asking?"

I said, "I'm looking for my father."

He looked straight at me with those steely black eyes and said, "Carolyn?"

"Yep, it's me. You found me. It's me alright."

He took us into his house and I saw pictures of myself as a baby all over his living room. He also showed me pictures of my family that I had never known. He told me stories about my grandmother Alpha and my great-grandmother Belle.

When Belle was a tiny girl, she and her family walked the Trail of Tears. They were long forced marches of the Cherokee from North Carolina into Texas and Oklahoma. They walked in the dead of winter with little food. Many people died.

My whole family died except Belle. The only reason she survived was that she was rescued by a young soldier, a Lieutenant Harrington. When he saw that she was still alive, he chased her and put her on his horse with him and took her to Texas, where he raised her with his family. When I heard this story, I knew immediately that the little girl in my recurring dream was Belle.

My dad says that Belle was psychic. She would put one hand on yours and the other on her forehead and tell you everything about yourself.

Belle married Ned Leach, a black Indian cowboy from Chickasha, Oklahoma. He played a mean violin. He put rattlesnake tails inside of it to make it buzz. Together they had twelve children in Anadarko, Oklahoma, a small Indian town. My grandmother Alpha was the youngest of the twelve and when she went to Pennsylvania to attend Carlisle Indian School, the family followed her.

It was here that my father was born. And here that he lied about his age, and enlisted in the army. When Alpha heard this she was furious. She said all soldiers are dogs, lower than the lowest in life. They were the same soldiers that had stolen our country and slaughtered our family. But for my dad, becoming a man meant being a soldier, and he was trained in the Special Forces of the U.S. Army. The elite of fighting men.

In the Second World War, he was one of Darby's Rangers in

the Anzio Campaign in Italy, one of nine men to survive. Then he went to Korea where he survived the Battle of Kundarit, one of nineteen to survive. After that, Germany, then Fort Lewis, the Berlin Wall '57, Gaza Strip '58. He trained troops in Thailand and did two tours in Vietnam, and was in Detroit during the riots of the sixties. Puerto Rico, Panama, Vacaville Penitentiary . . . post-traumatic stress syndrome . . . he had tried to kill three people in Oakland, California.

After I had seen the pictures, I felt like part of a family. We all look so much alike. Last summer I decided to go to Anadarko where my grandmother was born. I felt like I had gone to the center of the universe. I felt like I had gone home to my country.

When I got home and I was sitting on the stoop with my father, he said to me, "So you went to Anadarko and found out you look like those Indians down there, huh? Well, it's a shame it took you forty years to find out who you are."

I see my dad a lot now. He's very bitter, this man who was the recipient of a silver star, two bronze stars for valor, and a purple heart, this man who was called "Chief" and "Sitting Bull" by his army superiors. He tells me, "If the United States government were to give me a million dollars a day, it would never be enough to repay me for what I have given to this country." He says that every war he ever fought since World War II was to make the white man money. I asked him, "Dad, why did you do it?"

His reply? "The American Indian is the greatest fighter that ever walked the face of the earth."

I heard in his voice the determination of Belle and Alpha. I saw my own struggle—to become a woman drummer, and to raise my own mixed-blood son.

This is my story. It's my family's story. It is an American story about people intermixing and secrets, about soldiers and war and prisons and survival. It is the story of the Trail of Tears, a nightmare that will live forever in the dreams of our people.

Ofelia Zepeda

TOHONO O'ODHAM

Pulling Down the Clouds

N-ku'ipadkaj 'ant 'an o 'ols g cewagi.
With my harvesting stick I will hook the clouds.
Nt o 'i-wannio k o 'i-hudin g cewagi.
With my harvesting stick I will pull down the clouds.
N-ku'ipadkaj 'ant o 'i-siho g cewagi.
With my harvesting stick I will stir the clouds.

With dreams of a distant noise disturbing his sleep,
the smell of dirt, wet, for the first time in what seemed
like months.
The change in the molecules is sudden, they enter
the nasal cavity.
He contemplates the smell, what is that smell?
It is rain.
Rain somewhere out in the desert.
Comforted in this knowledge he turns over
and continues his sleep,
dreams of women with harvesting sticks
raised toward the sky.

Ramona Wilson

COLVILLE

I was born on the Colville Indian Reservation in Washington State. As a young person, the land that I could see was the whole world to me, and seemed eternal and unchanging. It had always been so.

But our house sat at the joining of the Okanogan and Columbia Rivers and I think long ago this point of land was formed from the continuous silting down of earth, the remembrances of where water once swirled and swelled with spring's heat. The land was not always there.

Then in the late sixties another dam was built on the Columbia and the water stilled and flowed backwards, covering again the land, and lapped at the foot of the trees that once surrounded our house, making a dark island. Years ago, we must have looked like an island then, too, only we were in an ocean of fields and pasture. I go back now and stand at the overlook and I can still, for all this destruction, recognize the remaining unflooded landmarks and trace with my eye where my child's body once ran and cast shadows on the ground.

In 1991, the house in Oakland where I had lived for seventeen years burned to nothing, except for stones and brick. This was where I watched my small daughter grow and enter school, where I brought my newborn son home from the hospital. This was the place of the fullness of being a young mother. I go back now and I still, more clearly than ever, see the lines of the earth, of the canyon and hill, the road we must *have traveled tens of thousands of times. When my son was a baby, I walked him there, under the tall pines and oak.*

What is left then? I can only answer: me, the children that are gifts to me, and their father. Also, the other gifts that have been given. I have been taught some of the things that are given to us, the Indian people. I have been privileged to see the land of my ancestors, to walk upon it, to receive its gifts of salmon and deer, berries and roots. I was privileged to have lived in our beautiful canyon for a while, to have seen the birds flash in and out of the shining leaves. My writing is a gift. If there is one person whose eyes are opened a different way upon reading something I have written, then I have been fortunate. The writing gives back to me a sense of completion, both of joy and of sadness. It helps me remember what was there and what will always remain.

Dry Rivers—Arizona

At Casa Grande, only the names
of stolen rivers
remain, echoes above the rock.
Yet everywhere
is the memory of water
that sweetened the mornings:
of birds, women dipping jars,
bathing, skin shining and soft.
The leaves of bean plants
stood stiff with water.
Blossoms of squash,
resilient and smooth.
Who would have thought,
standing by those rivers
older than stories,
as old as the beginning,
that they would someday vanish

and take with them
those who should have come after.
The memories of water
are the memories of ancestors.
They are everywhere,
the mark of feet and stream
clear to the eye.

We walk along arroyos.
We hear some singing
that sometimes sounds
like clear water
over rounded stones.

Elizabeth Woody

**WARM SPRINGS WASCO
NAVAJO**

By Our Hand, through the Memory,
the House Is More than Form

In contemplating the house of my childhood, the one that I grew up in, it is not the structure or the condition of the house I recall as much as the sentiments about dwelling and homeland that gave strength to its structure.

My childhood home was fourteen miles from the Warm Springs Reservation, in the town of Madras, Oregon. We were some 160 miles removed from the Columbia River and the pathways of the salmon that my mother's people cherished, celebrated, harvested, dried, and incorporated into their lifeways for over 14,000 years.

Few will understand how we came to be so far removed from our ancestral homeland of the Columbia River system, which carried large volumes of water inexorably to the Pacific Ocean. The geography of our landscape—the snowcapped Cascade range of volcanoes, surrounded by evergreen forests and high desert—is an integral element of the culture of the Plateau, as we are collectively called. I belong to a people who cherished the land.

My maternal grandparents were the first of several generations to be born within the reservation boundaries after the treaty of 1855 at Walla Walla, Washington, between "the Bostons" (as U.S. citizens were called by the Plateau people) and the political affiliation of people presently called "tribes." We had not called our people "tribes" prior to the treaty, as it is a term brought from feudal Europe. It is better to think of the basic component of Plateau society as having been set up for participants of shared political principles, living in villages governed by a leader who was not subject to outside authorities. Decisions were made by acclamation, and those who disagreed moved to another village.

The nature of our current regard for and belief in the inhabitants of the past is more than participation in the old coexistent economic system of task sharing and consensus. It is more than the ethno-racial identity of the citizens. It is the preexistent honoring and knowledge of the land that held the people together. Human beings flourish with a conscious regard for all beings, for the place that holds their lives, for the deceased, and for their stories of creation and creating. To speak of the spiritual in this context is too personal to present arbitrarily. That sense is a common bond we have with our bodies and share with one another, which I feel requires no explanation.

In the house of my childhood, my grandfather, Lewis Pitt, Sr., was a Wasco/Wishram/Watlala (Cascade/English) descendant of the ancient Fisher people, who made distinctive art objects of X-ray figures, male and female, of people, ancient sturgeon, condor, and deer. He spoke six dialects of Sahaptin and Chinookan Northwest indigenous languages as well as the intertribal trade language— Chinook Jargon. My grandmother, Elizabeth Thompson Pitt, a descendant of the Wyampum and a smaller Deschutes River band, was born and raised at the Hot Springs now known as Kah-nee-ta Resort. She was as settled on this land as the old junipers, the volcanic formations, and the hillsides that she loved to walk about on. She was an artisan and possibly, for a time, a healer. She made sure that we understood her reverence for the land and the traditional beliefs by taking us as children to the places where the people gathered for worship—places filled with symbolism and ceremony.

He was an "Agency" man, she a "Simnasho" woman. Two small gatherings of longhouses and houses, churches and tule shacks, and families—two distinctive cultural communities on the reservation. When they married, each planted a cedar tree, side by side. The trees intermingled their roots and boughs, symbolizing the tentative touchings of two separate beings. In the structures where these people gathered we heard all the many different languages spoken by both my grandparents and all the neighbors and visitors, but in their children they encouraged the use of English. They brought into it a passion for expression, and in that passion, a love for all things.

They moved off the reservation to be nearer to the schools for their three children. In this move, my grandmother was distanced from her immediate connections to her relatives and from the beading circles, healing gatherings, celebrations, winter dances, and the casual visiting at the general store/post office. She had to adjust to her new location. My uncle, Lewis Jr., recalls that she took refuge in her bedroom. Her room held the many bundles of the beaded objects, cornhusk bags, and Klickitat baskets inherited from our relatives. It seemed that to visit these things was to contact the thoughts of relatives who had passed on. The house brightened when she decided to make some leggings. For the first time alone, she drew her pattern and started beading. She asked Lewis Jr., "Do you like my leggings?" He was ecstatic, "Yes, they are beautiful." He knew at that moment, by the startling burst of her creativity, in her pleasant circle of light, that they would be all right in their new home.

It is this blessing of being able to make things that reconstructs my life, that gives me the knowledge to restore myself. The things I saw—the collaborative living structures, the places of worship and feasts, the outfits of antiquity, the buckskin garments, the beaded objects, the woven baskets for subsistence, the cradleboards for protection, the feathers of prayer, the couriers to a higher thought—are still magnificent. They were made, traded, and collected by great-grandparents and by living relatives, and I saw that they loved deeply. These messages—the beaded birds, horses, trees, stars, and geometric abstractions—are like prayer, a prayer for our present world to know again the root connection to our existence. The Earth provided for us, and through the Earth we prosper and absorb into ourselves the potency of life.*

To be a granddaughter was my privilege; to be a daughter, a niece, and sister, a cousin an honor. In this honor, this state of being respected, I thrived. To thrive is to learn how to respect others and how to act with courage, humility, generosity, and compassion. Although this is simple to say in English and is overused in daily language, it is complex to be an independent being, responsible to the nuances and dynamics of ancestral continuity. As a segment of the great weaving of cultures, which is continuous and as ancient as the mastodon and condor who have perished from this area, it is only ingenuity and the simple intention to live well that rendered the ability to endure. Our legacy is that we still live, in some manner, in congruence with the past, not in a linear fashion, as people tend to think of time, but cyclically, in accordance with the cycles that are as efficient as the spirals found in baskets and shells and petroglyphs.

After speaking about artistic collaboration at a recent conference, a Wasco "aunty" told me that "collaboration, in our language,

*All these objects were made from the Earth and did not disrupt its systems. The events and stories elaborated the cultural significance of place through the coupling of land and experience. The perspective and treatment of land, animals, and things to events during our tenure and to myth told in current life made the experience of telling and retelling a source of inspiration.

is also the word for science." I feel that this includes nature, which holds everything and which directs the patterned chaos and the tranquillity of being complete, even in its smallest form. Our language, now physically unspoken in my life but active in my brain, has a lucid regard for our environment.

I have heard from people who are native-language speakers that to use their language is to be more efficient in thinking. One Inupiaq man who had several advanced degrees said to a friend, "It's a shame you don't know your own language. The language holds all this knowledge by a greater conceptual capacity concerning the universe." It may make some people uncomfortable to see how eradication of the native languages through colonization has impacted massive stores of knowledge. Losing the indigenous language meant that I had to become proficient in a language entirely different from that of my Sahaptin-Wasco-Diné ancestors. I had to learn to speak well for myself, as speaking integrates and restores peace. The task of language wasn't taught; it was learned by example, by noticing what was happening around. Listening to the older aspects of myself initiated a life's work with words. Waking up to the aroma of coffee, listening to the Sahaptin words of Grandmother and Great Aunt Mary in the morning went beyond hearing the sounds to the softness of their walk and the song accompanying them from the birds in the junipers. Such simple pleasures elude me to this day, but the memory returns stronger as I age. I have been learning to weave root bags. It requires a thought process I've been in need of for a long time. It reclaimed me, coming from women on both sides of my family who are weavers. My teacher told me as we sat twining, "We are making beautiful houses for our little sisters."

I paused, then asked, "Who are our little sisters?"

"The roots—the *pia-xi, khoush, sowit-k, wak amu*," she answered. As we wove, I felt like a child again. Attempting to bead, I had shown my first rosettes to my grandmother and asked her to show me how to bead. She looked at them and said that I was an expert already. I threw the rosettes in the trash. I saw that she dug them out, sewed safety pins to the back, and wore them on her sweater. I worried that I could not accomplish these traditions, being too old to train myself away from the public school's demand to be like everyone else. My teacher said, "Don't worry—weave!" It seems that I grow stronger by learning this skill. My teacher said, "It is the spirit you feed when you work. When you bring out from the heart a wonderful being, it is all from the Earth—goes to the Earth. The spirit blooms and we must remember our source of nourishment, or we will starve."

The house comes again to my mind—the wild arrangements of the bundled "keepsakes" containing our heirlooms in my grand-mother's room, the photos of family, the roses bracing up the sides of the house. I see that as a person who rested there, as all the people who rested there, the sense of belonging grew inside. We fed ourselves with the work of stories told to one another, stories that explore how we live and the older past that we can know only through story. My grandparents built this creative place to nurture our physical and inner selves. Like them, we repair our culture and make it anew. The secret vitality of our imaginations presents itself all around us as this Earth, Homeland, and the House of Livelihood and Rest. All around this story, the eyes look into the sway of our industrious behavior, the hands move back to the beginning each time we work with material from the land. We listen, absorbed in the story by blood, by association, listening with the part that is internally one self and many selves. In the sound of water, the sheen of river stone, a song is pervasive and faithful to continuance, and the memory in its own language tells the story well.

Roberta Hill

O N E I D A

Waning August Moon

When the sun routinely sets
and words rest with the dust
falling thick on the dresser,
when the quarter moon dissolves
and cold rain comes early, five days
at a time, I think of your name,
breaking it over and over into syllables.
The full August moon rises over the dark thigh
of a mountain.   It hangs above the Gallatins
and answers an echo in the Pryors,
the light loved by thieves
that brought us to each other.

I shut the gauze curtain
and walk through moonlight to where you lay,
your left hand folded under your head.
You pull back the sheet and smile.
My fingers circle over your spine
like birds above the foothills of your home.
It's difficult to learn, this language of touch.
Ten miles up the mountain,
snow turns into water, two crystals at a time.
We looked and could not look completely,
fearing something may go wrong,
a trickster in the shadow.

Something will go wrong.   The moon wanes tomorrow.
You secure the jack, check the oil,
and mention your sick wife, eight adoring children.
What choices will I have?   Virgins never walk
toward men in the moonlight.   I'll admit
I've wrecked homes since sixty-eight.
Professionals give you one clean break.
The motto on my card: You won't miss them,
even once.   What choices?   Like water
down the long slide of a rapid
never leaps the same way twice,
so I want to dance and live, to move and breathe.
I rocked shut for years in a fog-bound country.

There on happy days, I waited for dinner
near humming fridge.   I hated the interior,
and stumbled through squalls on a concrete breakwater,
helping others home.   I lived a mute boulder,
facing a sea beyond boat and cable,
erased by the blind, indifferent sand.
One night I woke numb and heard my nakedness
say to the moonlight, Enough shame,
enough denial.   The dust blows away,
and this arm's an arm, not wing or spider leg.
The footprints we leave
only sometimes fill with rainbows.

You will never know I dared
to spring the tumblers in your glance.
It's difficult being real,
needing moons and names and people.
Needing to confide has kept me poor,
but I go on and risk without regret,
knowing I'll arrive in that rare country,
with its lonely cry infrequent in the dusk.
Something will go right.   In the west,

moving away from 'you', she is breaking the lock

a ray of light will move through grasses
all at once.   In the east,
with dark encouraging, the moon will wax again,
big and orange above October fields.

Gail Tremblay

ONONDAGA ▪ MICMAC

After the Invasion

On dark nights, the women cry together
washing their faces, the backs of their hands
with tears—talking to their grandmother, Moon,
about the way life got confused. Sorrow
comes through tunnels like the wind and wails
inside an empty womb. The need to be cherished,
to be touched by hands that hold sacred objects,
that play the drums and know the holy songs,
rises and moves as certain as the stars.
Women murmur about men who don't sing
when women grind the corn. There are too many
mysteries men learn to ignore; they drink together
and make lewd remarks—defeat makes them forget
to see the magic when women dance, the touch of foot
upon the Earth that mothers them and bears
their bodies across the wide universe of sky.
Men brag how many touch them, who they use,
forget to help women whose love must feed
children that speak of fathers harder to hold
than distant mountains, fathers as inconstant
as the movement of the air. Mothers cook corn
and beans and dream of meat and fish to fill

the storage baskets and the pots. On dark nights,
the women whisper how they love, whisper
how they gave and give until they have no more—
the guilt of being empty breaks their hearts.
They weep for sisters who have learned to hate,
who have gone crazy and learned to hurt
the fragile web that makes the people whole.
Together, women struggle to remember how to live,
nurture one another, and pray that life will fill
their wombs, that men and women will come
to Earth who know that breath is a sacred gift
before the rising sun and love can change
the world as sure as the magic in any steady song.

[handwritten margin note: community of women challenging the changing notions of unity]

[handwritten note: hopeful returning]

[handwritten note: Prayer involves something greater than ourselves]

Haunani-Kay Trask

NATIVE HAWAIIAN

From *Papahanaumoku (She Who Births Islands) and Wakea (Sky Father) came the islands of Hawai'i. From the islands came the taro plant, and from the taro came the Hawaiian people. We were born from the land, our grandmother, whom we must care for and respect.*

Since the coming of the foreigners to Hawai'i, our land has been ravaged, our people grown sick and small in number. Those of us who survive must protect our people and guide our nation. Our women are stronger than our men; we are able to carry more of the burden. Therefore, we have no choice but leadership.

Part of the leadership is to record our history. Tradition has bequeathed chant and dance, the poetry of song and movement. English came with colonialism, and now is used to resist it.

Like my ancestors, I write to tell a story. But my words do

*not recall our great chiefs and their chiefly deeds. Neither do
I write in Hawaiian, but the foreigners' language. I turn the
foreigners' words against them.*

*I write to resist, to tell my people how resistance feels, to
guide them through our pain to the triumph of our vision.
Every poem is an offering, sometimes in victory, often in sorrow. Words are spears, or storms of light, or the chattering
winds of hope. I live anew in every poem and my people live
through me.*

Sisters

FOR MILILANI

I.

doves in the rain
      mornings above
Kane'ohe bay   blue
sheen stillness
across long waters gliding

    remind me of us

II.

eight million
      for coconut island
five hundred thousand
for townhouses
on the hill   traffic
    and greedy foreigners
by the mile
rain pours
steady clouding
the light   dark
mornings   darker
    evenings   silted
in the night   smell of dead

fish dead
limu dead
reef

III.

haole world
    haole things
irretrievable
    loss
irredeemable
    fury

IV.

    in every native
place   a pair
of sisters
    driven by the sound
of doves
    the color of
    morning
defending life
with the spear
of memory

Josephine Huntington

ATHABASCAN

My desire to write has been with me for a very long time; however, it was not until two years ago that I decided to do something about it. The seed may have been planted when I was a child. Was it Mr. Kahl, *a World War II veteran who used his G.I. Bill to attend teachers' college and soon afterward made his way to a remote Indian village in Alaska? Mr. Kahl subscribed to dozens of magazines and set aside forty-five minutes each afternoon to read us stories. It was the highlight of my day. This introduction to fiction was supplemented by evenings in the presence of men who gathered at my father's store to "shoot the bull." Sitting on the floor in front of the potbellied stove surrounded by men drinking coffee, I would hear story after story of their adventures in the woods, in the city, and of their quest to become champion dog mushers.*

It was not until I left the village that I learned how different we were. There were places where the shopkeepers would barely hide their disdain for us. Native men were considered to be lazy and native women promiscuous. Over the years I noticed that practically every story written about Alaska natives included such characters and their association with alcohol. It was enough to send me into a rage! Why did writers apply these stereotypes to us when only a small, although highly visible, segment of the population was guilty? How could we hope to raise generations of healthy young adults if all they hear and read about themselves is trash?

It was in this frame of mind that I enrolled in a poetry class. My instructor's name was Cathy Calloway. After three months, I wrote four poems that were selected by Joseph Bruchac to be included in his anthology of North American native writers, titled Raven Tells Stories.

Aggi's Last Dance

It is late August when I decide to do a private performance for Madeline. Like me, Madeline has migrated from the old village, but she's quite a bit younger. She is my closest friend and someone whose opinion I trust. If she thinks something is not right, she will say so. One Sunday after church, as the congregation moves to the rectory for coffee, I see her waiting for me.

"Hi Jessie! Ah dee, I hardly see you this summer."

"Good morning, Madeline. Good to see you."

"Are you working today?"

"Eee. We sure work. Lotsa people this year."

"That's what I hear."

"Madeline, maybe you come have nikipaiq sometime?"

"Eee. Just this morning I was thinking about native food. Maybe tomorrow, eh?" Madeline works at the Native Hospital as a nurse's aid and sometimes drops in for lunch, especially when she craves our native food.

The next day when Madeline arrives I am busy in the kitchen cutting dried caribou meat and white fish into small pieces. We chat about who's in the hospital and how sick they are as Madeline peels and slices carrots for dipping in oil. I place a jar of seal oil and platter of boiled caribou meat on the table. Madeline carries the carrots to the table, easing her ample figure into a kitchen chair. She sits and stares at me for a minute before speaking.

"How you been? You look a little tired."

"I'm okay. Tourists almost gone. Goodness, listen to me, I sound like them young kids at the dance . . . only one more month . . . only ten more days . . . like it's hard work!"

Madeline laughs. "You work too hard, Jessie. Mmm . . . this is good seal oil!" Madeline is married to a white man and he doesn't care for native foods, so she eats them at the homes of her friends. I should wait until she's through eating, but I don't.

"Madeline, I made a little song."

"Oh, can I hear it sometime?"

"Eee . . . that's why I want you to come. After we eat I show you. Now eat. Ahdee! I almost forgot . . . I still got some white muktuk." I step into the front porch and return with a small bowl of white muktuk in whale oil and set it near Madeline's plate. She especially likes whale oil, because it's not as strong-tasting as seal oil, she says. The muktuk is from my nephew, Adolf. In June, he returned from his hunt with two good-sized white beluga. Madeline and I helped butcher and hang the meat and they gave me enough muktuk to fill a small barrel.

After we finish eating, Madeline clears off the remains of lunch and I prepare tea. After pouring Madeline a cup, I push the chairs out of the way. Madeline sits and watches as I move to the center of the cleared area. My voice quivers as I start to sing, but becomes stronger as I move in unison to the beat of invisible drums. When I am through, Madeline comes and wraps her heavy arms around my shoulders.

"Ah dee gaa! You should dance and sing that song at our next corporation meeting."

"You think so? People might not take it right. Women aren't supposed to dance lively like men. You think it's too lively?"

"It's not lively . . . it's graceful. And if they don't like it, what do they know. Times are changing."

"Eee. Times are changing."

After Madeline returns to work I continue to sit at the kitchen table. I feel worried. What if people think I am being disrespectful to the past? Am I? Just because I live a traditional lifestyle doesn't mean I'm not changing. If I break away from tradition what will it mean?

The tourist season comes to an end and everyone settles in for the winter. In early December a dim light filters through the white haze as I trudge along a narrow path. Hunched forward, I try to protect my face from the biting sting of drifting snow. It reminds me of when, as a child, my whole family walked through such storms to attend services held by a visiting priest. Now, at seventy-seven, I walk alone. An occasional snow machine traveling on the main road can be heard above the howling wind as it races across the tundra. I don't like to walk on the roads because drivers like to speed and in a storm anything can happen. As if by instinct, I lift my face and peer through narrowed eyes to locate the wooden building with its tall steeple. It's barely visible from where I stand.

When I reach the church my eyelashes are frozen and stuck together at the corners. Removing thick blue yarn gloves, I hold a hand over each eye to melt the ice. Then pulling open the heavy doors of the church, I step inside, hoping it will be warm this morning. Inside, the air feels cool. I decide to leave my parka on.

It's not quite eleven o'clock, but only a half-dozen people are seated in the long narrow pews. Three thin candles on each side of a plain wooden cross light up the altar. We are told the three candles stand for "trinity," but I don't remember what it means. Perhaps when service is over I'll ask Madeline. She's good with English. I see her seated in the front of the church with her two adopted daughters, Beth and Rose. The girls are wearing bright blue calico parkas with sunshine ruffs that frame their dark heads.

Father Daniel walks slowly to the altar and bows his head in silent prayer. Bowing my head, I start to recite the Lord's Prayer in English, but I am soon distracted. What I really want is for God to look into my troubled mind and clear a path. Father said God acts in mysterious ways, but I haven't noticed anything unusual happening to me. I resort to Inupiaq, my native tongue, to finish the Lord's Prayer before Father turns back to the congregation.

We sing a hymn in English and "Abide with Me" in Inupiaq. "Today's sermon is about burying your light under a bushel," Father Daniel announces. "By burying your light, you have not fulfilled God's promise . . ." Lifting my head I notice he is wearing only a wool sweater under his cassock and a slight shiver shakes his body. He paces back and forth before the pulpit with one bulky "moon boot" showing beneath the ripped hemline of his slightly yellow garment. It is then I see that even the seal-skin altar cover has lost its luster and turned from light gray to a dull gray-brown.

It's been thirty years since I left the old village and moved here. It was the year my husband and daughter died in the diphtheria epidemic. The following spring my brother took a small whaling crew to hunt for belugas on the southern coast and women followed. We were needed to help with the butchering. Many people were starting to migrate to the hunting camp from the surrounding villages and it seemed that a town sprung up almost overnight. I decided to stay. When I heard Wien Airlines needed Eskimo dancers for tourists, I rushed right over. Turned out I didn't have to hurry. Eskimo dancing was forbidden by the local churches and the company was having a terrible time finding dancers for their cultural program. They asked me if I could help recruit other dancers. I sought out the party of hunters from the old village and asked if they were interested. Hunting had been poor, so they accepted the offer and we formed the Midnight Sun Dancers. Now, most of the dancers are gone—died or moved back to the old village. I'm one of the few people left who know the old traditional songs and dances. These past few winters, I teach Eskimo dancing to the younger women. They are quick to pick up the movements, but only a few are able to sing the Inupiaq songs. People say the language is dying. The young native leaders express concern about preserving the culture. They want to get the elders involved. I am one of the elders. I even attend meetings of the Elders' Council. Two or three times a year we meet and listen to the young leaders talk about ways to preserve the culture. I enjoy listening to their ideas. Some ideas come from other native groups or from experts who write books about how to help people. Not like the old days. Aunt Grace used to say, "People were too busy just trying to stay alive back then." When we were growing up our lives centered around the church, working together for food, and gathering in the evenings to tell stories. I tell my nephews about how much fun it used to be when we did things together. They listen, but don't say anything. They are young and maybe I'm too old.

It all started happening last spring. In April, when the snow melted and the days grew longer and brighter, I went out for long walks. The bright sun reflecting off the snow hurt my eyes, but its warmth felt good on my exposed face. As summer neared, the frozen bay broke into a million pieces. People lined the gravel beach in evenings to watch the heavy chunks of ice heaving and grinding past our shores. I sat on a piece of driftwood in front of my house watching the seal hunters maneuver their boats through open leads. Spring is my favorite time of year.

A few days after breakup, the seagulls returned. They arrived in flocks, soaring and diving as they searched the shallow shores for food. I paid them no mind. They come every summer and blend in like fireweeds and wild cotton that blanket the tundra. A few days later, while cleaning the area of beach in front of my house, I saw one large seagull lagging behind as the others swiftly soared, twisted, and glided over the open water. It took him a little longer to gain height, but his drop was done with such ease and grace that he appeared to be dancing. How lovely! I thought. Sitting on an old weathered log I watched until my back started to ache. Finally, I stood up and slowly stretched out my stiff limbs. Returning to the house, I put a kettle of water on to boil and went to lie down on my narrow cot. Behind my closed eyes a large white seagull danced before me.

The whistling of the tea kettle jarred me awake. While preparing the tea I hummed an old song. It was a tune that often came to me, but not the words. Songs and dances are passed from generation to generation. I barely remember when we last had to learn a new song or dance. Setting my cup on the yellow Formica tabletop, my mind returned to the seagull.

The sun streaming through ruffled curtains turned to deep gold when I got up to reheat a pot of caribou stew. The bubbling stew filled the room with a delicious smell, but I hardly noticed. It's as if I were in a trance. Moving to the middle of the kitchen I took the position of a female dancer—standing with both feet together, knees slightly bent. With arms extended behind my back, I let them rise and fall . . . rise and fall . . . as if taking flight. Lowering my left arm, the right arm is stretched high above my head, first in one direction then another. I tried many different positions and changed the song a little each time. After almost stumbling into the table when leaning into a dive, I decided to stop. My legs were shaking and I was breathing hard. The last weak rays of the setting sun, which never quite drops behind the horizon, signaled the late hour. Resting my head against the wall, I closed my eyes, feeling tired, but excited.

All winter I think about what the young people are saying about Father Daniel. After church one Sunday we women decide to make a new altar cover. My eyes hurt when I sew, so I volunteered to help with the tanning. Father Daniel looked so pleased when we told him. Now, I sit at my kitchen table drinking tea, listening to the radio, and thinking. Except for occasional trips to the grocery store, church, or to attend evening classes on Thursday, I seldom leave the house.

Now it is February. Cold and windy. On the third Thursday of the month, I am plaiting my long silver hair into a single braid and listening to the radio when the announcer reports a chill factor of minus 60 degrees. I don't know what "chill factor" means, but can feel a cold draft creeping across the floor. Maybe only a few people will show up for the meeting this evening.

The annual village corporation meetings have become such big events they are now held in the school gymnasium. When I arrive the gymnasium is packed and noisy. Those who were unable to find a seat on the bleachers are sitting on the floor or standing along the wall. Old Abe, an Elder Representative who speaks both Inupiaq and English fluently, is asked to "open with prayer." First, he prays in Inupiaq and then in English. Reports and awards of community service follow. The Midnight Sun Dancers, billed as "entertainment," appear last on the agenda.

It is after nine o'clock and people are getting restless when the dancers come forward. The audience claps as each dancer files by wearing his or her finest native garments—women in parkas of bright fabric precede male dancers in white hunting jackets. Each wears knee-length mukluks and gloves trimmed in fancy beadwork with thick bands of wolf, fox, and wolverine. The drummers sit on the floor in front of the singers, who are seated on metal folding chairs. I am a singer, drummer, and dancer, so I enter last. I have chosen to wear a muskrat-skin parka trimmed with black-and-white reindeer strips and wolverine tassels. The parka is old, but still beautiful. My old friend Lillie made it for me when I was sent to Washington, D.C., to dance for the president of the United States many years ago.

When my turn comes, I see Madeline slip into one of the folding chairs. She has memorized the song in case the others might not have had time to learn it. Drumbeats fill the air as I struggle to my feet, pull on my gloves, and walk to the center of the stage. My own high voice starts the story. With subtle movements, I thrust my neck in and out and the wolverine tassels sway rhythmically. Arms gently flutter, then I thrust my chest forward and soar heavenward. I float on a breeze, then swoop, glide, and scan the shallow shores for signs of food. Search to the left, then to the right, flying until I spot a group of Real People butchering belugas and throwing the intestines into the water. With arms extended rearward, I proceed to descend. This is the most dangerous part for me—the seagull's dive—because of age my balance isn't what it once was. The flat-bottomed oogruk mukluks help, but if I should lean too far forward I fear falling in front of the whole village. When entering the dive, I concentrate on the drums, drawing my arms back as far as they will go, leaning forward, dropping lower and lower. As I near the floor I begin to beat my wings to propel myself upright, thrusting my chest forward. Slowly turning in a circle I repeat each motion. It is a few seconds before I become aware of the thunderous applause that fills the room. My face goes hot and I smile in happiness. The sound of my own people's applause fills my heart. Surprisingly, even people who supposedly don't approve of dancing are clapping.

Kim Caldwell

TSALAGI ∎ SHAWNEE

When the invaders came to this continent they did everything within their power to silence the voices of the indigenous women. They had already demanded the submission of the women of their own nations and the women of all the lands they subjugated and stole in their conquering and missionizing frenzy.

What they clearly did not consider was the incredible tenacity, intelligence, and adaptability of indigenous women in their relationship to the spirits and to all their relations. Contrary to popular belief, all was not lost in the process of forced assimilation. The women who came before us gifted us with a sacred endurance, carrying families, communities, and nations in their hearts and in the blood they passed on to us. They have kept our voices from eternal silence. They have given us the ability to speak now, in these times of such confusion and trouble on this continent, and throughout this world. To say what we see. To name it. To step outside our pre-programmed image of ourselves into the clarity of spirit and the strength of raising our voices into a diverse and richly textured song sung in present, past, and future tense.

It is now our responsibility to reach out to the young women and encourage them to not be afraid to lift their voices and be heard. They, in turn, will reach out to those who come after them. In this way we can guarantee the voices of future generations of indigenous women will not be silenced ever again.

Act of prayer
- entering a spiritual
alliance with creation - the moon

Moonlight

wander through the house in the wee hours
    like my aunties still do
        called awake by many dreams
            crowded together behind the eyelids
                forcing them open in startled flutter
                they are like sleeping birds
                    suddenly surprised into flight.

wander to the window
    looking for the moon
        tonight she waxes round and full
            lights the swirling water

the waves are pearly milk
       sloshing from the breasts
              of ancient grandmothers
                     made young again
                            dancing into winter.

the singing moon
     shoots light into the foaming waves
          calling granddaughters awake
               from restless sleep
                    pulling them to her
                         bringing needed nourishment.

thousands of miles away
     in another zone of time
          my aunties will wander
               in different houses
                    each at her window
                         looking for the moon.

no one talks about it much
     it is our natural rhythm
          and now, all past our years of knowing bleeding time,
               the stories of the moon have changed
                    revealing other secrets.

in the lonely time
     when the moon waxes full
          and pulls aside the blankets
               a family of women
                    stand in winter windows
                         purified in moonlight.

Anna Lee Walters

PAWNEE

Sometimes "writing" seems to be an inappropriate word for living. Writing is "vocational," or a "craft" or an "art," and while I am able to envision myself as a "writer," it is more difficult to make the leap to thinking of myself as that particular kind of "craftswoman" or "artist." My references—for how I am, who I am—are different from the references of other folk. I was born into two modern cultures of non-writers and these are the communities to which I best relate. In these communities, unwritten philosophies, ethics, values, and premises are at work for who I am, what I do. To know that these construct identity and being, and influence thought and action, no matter where—inside one's own community or out of it—is to accept the limitations of identifying oneself by occupation alone, particularly that of "writer." In my everyday life, I do a lot of unwriterly things. I care for little housebirds who know me quite well by now and our way of communicating does not depend upon writing either. I spend a lot of time walking in deep coppery canyons as a way of leaving writing behind and going forward into something else that is quite separate from everything as we know it in our modern everyday world. Writing is just a part of my lifestyle, a small aspect of how I am, who I am, in the three cultures in which I move.

Buffalo Wallow Woman

My name is Buffalo Wallow Woman. This is my real name. I
live on the sixth floor of the white man's hospital, in the mental
ward. This is not the first time I have been in a mental ward, I
know these places well. I wander through this one like a ghost in
my wrinkled gown. My feet barely brush over the white tile floor.
The long windows reflect the ghost that I have become: I am all
bones and long coarse white hair. Nevertheless, there are slender
black iron bars on the windows to prevent my shadow from leaving
here. Bars on sixth-story windows puzzle me. On the other side of
the bars, the city lays safely beyond my reach, the wrath of the
ghost of Buffalo Wallow Woman.

Bars or not, I plan to leave this ward tonight. I've already been
here too long. This place makes me ill, makes my heart pause and
flutter. Sometimes it makes me really crazy. I told that to those in
white, but they refused to listen, with the exception of one. I said,
"Hospitals make me sick! Here my strong heart is weak." In response, one of them shrugged, another frowned suspiciously. A
nurse replied, "Now, Mrs. Smith, you don't want to hurt our feelings, do you?"

Well, that made me grab her arm and dig my long fingernails
into it. I wanted to scream but I controlled this urge and said
calmly, "What's that you called me? My name is Buffalo Wallow
Woman." She and I stared each other in the eyes for five minutes
before we separated: she to her mindless patients, and me to my
room to locate the clothes I ought to wear when I escape from
here.

My clothes are missing. Why would someone take a ghost's
clothing? My possessions are so old. My moccasin soles consist only
of patches by now, but I don't care. They take me where I want to
go. I look at my feet stuffed into polyfoam and I hunger for beautiful things that are no more.

The closet is empty. Perhaps my clothes were never there. Perhaps
I really am a ghost now. Perhaps I did not live at all. I look in the

window to reassure myself—my spirit shimmers and fades, shimmers and fades. Am I deceased or alive? At this moment I really don't know.

I float down the hall, going from room to room. I search each one. Because I am a ghost, I go where I please. No one takes me seriously. Those who see me stare for a minute and decide to ignore the bag of bones and wild white hair that I have become. They underestimate me. They do not believe that I am really here. Down the hall and back again I haunt the ward. My clothes are not anywhere on this floor. I return to my room, climb upon the bed like a large clumsy child. I am waiting for nightfall, hours away, to make my departure. After all I've been through, this brief wait is nothing to *Buffalo Wallow Woman*, they whisper through the glass and the bars to remind me who the old bag of bones is and why I am here. I lift my head and square my sagging shoulders.

Far away, I hear a melody flow toward me. It is from my people's golden age and it has found me in this insane place where I am now held without respect or honor. A thousand years ago, or yesterday, in the seasons of my youth, my people danced and sang to the cloud beings in spectacular ceremony as the cloud beings gathered to shoot arrows of zigzag lightning and fiery thunderbolts across the sky. The cloud beings darkened to spirals of purple and dark red. They all twisted and turned in space like the mighty and powerful beings they truly were. And in the torrents of rain to fall later, slapping down upon the earth, filling the dry beds there to overflowing, my people lifted their heads and drank the rain thirstily. Afterward, with that taste still in their mouths, they sang in unison, "O you! That mystery in the sky!"

Miraculously, the words return to me in this alien room. I feel the wind of those clouds blow across my face, the raindrops splash the crown of my head one at a time. My face and hair feel soaked with rain. I lift my face and open my mouth. I sing, *"Hey yah hah!"*

My voice is as small as a red ant. It is swept away in the noises coming from the vents, crushed under the hospital sounds of announcements and rolling carts and beds going back and forth in the hallway. My room is suddenly quiet and dry. The clouds are disappearing in the sky, too. Bah! There is no magic in man-made places like this. This is why Buffalo Wallow Woman always brings it with her.

I look at my wrinkled hands. They are wide and large-boned. My nails are faded yellow and longer than they need to be. I wish I could hold a birchbark rattle with painted streaks of blue lightning on it in my idle fingers. I would shake it this way and that, in the manner of my people. They lifted their rattles to the cloud beings and shook them softly in that direction. To show the departing cloud beings that I remember who they are, their magnificent splendor and power, and also who I am, I stand on the step to my bed and face them. I lift the imaginary rattle and shake it just so. A soft hiss emanates from it.

Behind me, someone says, "Mrs. Smith."

I see part of him in the window. He is the doctor who arrives each day to study me, but now I am tired of him and I think he is tired of me as well. Nothing has been exchanged between us, and he always arrives at times like this. I look at the bars before I look at him.

I think of the animals my men have taken in communal hunts before there were grocery and convenience stores. The beautiful glassy eyes of a dozen soft-brown deer people stare at me from the walls of this room. They look me right in the eye, but I do not flinch. They say, *Buffalo Wallow Woman, here we are.* I see the trail of their last misty breaths arch up into the sky—rainbows they are. I hear a shaggy buffalo bull as he turns his great frame to face me. I see the dust rise in smoky spirals under his trotting hooves as he charges toward me. His breath is hot steam on my face.

Then come the human sounds, the footsteps, a pumping heart, blood rushing to the face, and the promised words of appeasement to the animals as they silently fall with a shattering thud, offering themselves to us. For this ultimate gift, we offered everything in return, our very lives were traded on the spot, and those animal people taught us thousands of prayers and songs to honor their spirits and souls from then on. In that way they permitted us to live, and they too lived with us. That is how we mutually survived all those years. The man behind me, the man who is here to help, doesn't know this.

He occupies the chair near the door.

"Do you come with prayers?" I ask. I turn to face him. The eyes of the deer and buffalo people surround us. They wait for his answer.

He is tall and angular with dark hair standing straight up. His eyes are foreign to me, colorless and jumpy, as if they must run somewhere. He glances behind him, over his shoulder. I am the one suspended here, but he acts trapped too. "If you come with prayers, I'll talk to you," I say, trying to figure out this odd creature whose habitat I do not know. Each day his behavior and appearance have become more unsettled. His presence disturbs the room.

He decides to speak. His voice booms at me. "Mrs. Smith, do you know how long you've been here? Do you understand that you have made no progress at all?" He is angry at me for being here.

I refuse to answer for this. I zip my lips together but I face him head-on. I have time, lots of time. I can outwait him. I become the ghost again. I start to disintegrate before him.

"Now don't do that!" he orders. He rubs his eyes and runs a hand through his wiry hair. His eyes dart everywhere. His breathing is rapid. He manages to hold his eyes in one place for a few seconds and he forcibly calms himself. He moves closer to me.

"All right, Buffalo Wallow Woman, if that's who you say you are, how did you get here? Do you know where you are?" He is still brusque and impatient, but he has called me by my real name and I must reply. My body becomes more solid and earthly again. I lean toward him.

"Do you come with prayers?" I venture again in my small voice.

"What kind of prayers?" he asks.

"Prayers to the spirits of those whose fate is in your hands." My voice is like the red ant again, crawling quietly across the room.

"What do you mean? I don't understand," he says while his eyes jump all over.

"You have no prayers then?" I persist.

"No!" he says.

"It is as I feared," I answer, turning away from him. "That is why I must leave here. Ghosts and spirits long for them. The hearts of human beings cannot beat steadily without them for long either. I know my own can't." I stand on the stepstool to move down to the floor.

"You aren't going anywhere. You don't know where you are, let alone who you are!"

We are almost the same height now. I stand before him, and he observes me from his throne.

"Where are my clothes?" I ask in my most rational voice. "I am going to leave here tonight."

He ignores me.

"You're very ill," he says with a frown. "You have no family, no one to take care of you. With your bad heart, you may not last long outside of here."

This time there is something in his voice I haven't heard before, but I want him to go. I seal my lips, and he sees immediately what I have done. He stands and goes. The room settles again.

For several weeks, there has been one in white here who is unlike this doctor and the others. Today she will appear when the sun reaches the third bar in the window. It will be soon now. In the meantime, I decide to haunt the hallway once more. I've covered its distance at least a dozen times each day for the last three months. It is the only exercise the patients have. I think of wolves in zoos, running in circles inside their cages, as I leave my room.

Today I look carefully at the occupants of each room and those people in the hallway. There are thin walls separating the two, skinny lines that distinguish the patients from the staff. I can't tell them apart except by their clothing. We patients just show our quirkiness.

In Room 612 sits a skeleton with frozen eyes. I am drawn to it, magnetized by its forceful pull. "I am a ghost," I confess to it. The skeleton does not move at all. Something whispers to me that its spirit is gone. I look around the room for it but I am the only ghost here. I leave 612 and go across the hall.

The man there is waiting for me. He embraces me tenderly and strokes my wild white hair. He calls me Grandmama and weeps on my gown. I sit down beside him, we stare into each other's souls while he holds my hand. He babbles at me, I nod. He weeps until his eyes are bright red. Then, exhausted, he lays down on his high bed. Asleep, he relaxes his grip on me and I move on.

Two nights ago, a hysterical young woman was brought into the next room. There she sits now, sullen and old before her time. Her wrists are wrapped in white bandages. I pause at the door. She raises a hand and a finger at me. "I am a ghost," I say. "That means nothing to me."

My words anger her. She rises abruptly to rush at me but hesitates after a step or two to clutch her belly and groan. It is then I notice the rise of it under her gown. I go to her rescue and she leans on me, breathing hard. Her eyes are scared.

"You would kill your child?" I ask as she bends into me. The moment passes, and she is able to stand on her own.

"Not my child," she said, "me!" Then she looks at me and adds, "I thought you were a ghost."

"I am," I repeat. This is our introduction to one another.

There is a loud disturbance in the hall, scuffling and a shouting exchange of words. One of the hospital staff is wrestling a middle-aged man. I and the young woman go to the door to watch. All the way down the hall, different-colored faces appear in the doorways of each room like wooden masks. The faces are expressionless and blank, like those on the street.

The patient is overpowered and wrestled to the floor before our eyes. A silver needle punctures his arm. After the initial outburst of anger, the whole scene takes place in silence. The patient is lifted up, whisked away. The staff quickly tidies the area as if nothing happened and the hall clears. Seconds later, no one remembers what just occurred.

Only the young woman and I remain. She asks if the incident

really took place. I say, "That's what will happen to all of us if we don't do what they say." The girl frowns at the bars on the window. She has just discovered them.

"When you leave here, you must live," I say. "If you don't see to your child, it could end up here."

The girl is confused. She looks at her bandaged wrists and again at the bars. She rubs her belly. I leave her there, alone and troubled. I make my way down the hall, looking in on each person in each room along the way.

Most everyone, patients and staff alike, look right through me. My presence is not acknowledged at all. Quite unexpectedly, from deep within me, I feel the wrath of Buffalo Wallow Woman for this indignity. My blood begins to boil. It is hot and dangerously close to making me explode! My heart flaps against my chest, voices caution me.

I pause and reflect on this feeling. That old fire still burns? Rage, this overpowering, is still a part of Buffalo Wallow Woman? How very strange, I thought that I had given up this human feeling years ago, the very first time I went into a mental hospital. I mutter my thoughts aloud and head toward my room.

Back there, Tina awaits. She is nervous, frantic, because of what I am about to do. Her voice is usually a coo. Now it is high and squeaky.

"Where were you?" she asks tensely. "For a minute I thought maybe you had already gone." She rushes toward me and embraces me.

I pat her tiny hand. "It's not time yet." I go to my bed, climb upon it, and say, "My clothes are gone, but where I am going, clothes don't matter I guess."

The first day Tina walked into my room I knew who she was. It was evident in her dark hair and high cheekbones, though her skin was more fair than mine. But where it really showed was in her behavior and her usually carefully chosen words. She was such a tiny thing. She carried bedpans past my door all day before she finally came in.

She read my name on the door and over the bed. "Mrs. Smith," she said, "I'm Tina. I'll be your evening nurse until you leave here, or until the shift changes in a few weeks, whichever comes first."

I stood at the door and watched her adjust my bed.

"It's Buffalo Wallow Woman, Tina, not Mrs. Smith," I responded, "and I am a ghost."

"I know," she replied seriously, "I've heard."

She gave me a red lollipop from a pocket and asked, "Why are you here, Buffalo Wallow Woman, if you don't mind me being so direct?"

I tore the shiny wrapper off the lollipop and stuck it in my mouth. I didn't answer. I sucked on the candy and counted the bars on the window, the way I did with the doctor when I wanted him to leave.

"Why are you here, Buffalo Wallow Woman?" she asked again.

I sucked the candy hard and motioned that my lips were sealed. I climbed on the bed, sure that she would leave.

Instead, she pulled out a wire hairbrush from the nightstand and answered with a mischievous smile, "If I ask you four times, and if you really are Buffalo Wallow Woman, then you will have to tell me, won't you?"

She began to comb my hair, pulling my head here and there. "Ghost hair is hard to comb," I said, as if this was our secret.

She replied, "You are not a ghost, Buffalo Wallow Woman. Do ghosts like lollipops?"

"Ghosts like a lot of earthly things," I said. "That's what often keeps us here."

"Why are you here, Buffalo Wallow Woman?" she asked a third time, and I knew then that I wanted someone like her, someone important, to know.

She braided my hair tightly around my head. Her fingers flew.

"I'm lost, Tina," I said. "I'm caught between two worlds, a living one and a dead one. This is the dead one," I motioned out in the hall, "right here. And this is the root of my illness. I have to return to the living one in order to be whole and well."

Tina's fingers stopped a second. She chuckled. "This is the dead one? How do you figure that?"

"Look around," I answered. "There is no magic here because everything is dead. I think that only ghosts are capable of surviving here."

Before I realized it, she asked me the fourth time. "Why are you here, Buffalo Wallow Woman?" She pulled a chair close to me as if she really planned to listen.

I decided to tell. I composed my thoughts for a moment and then began. "I am the ghost of Buffalo Wallow Woman. Do you know what a buffalo wallow is, my child?"

Tina nodded. "A watering hole, or something like that?" She reached over and held my hand as I spoke. Her hand was half the size of mine.

I asked, "Do you want to know about my name?" She nodded again.

"The name was taken about a hundred winters ago most recently, but I suppose it is older than that. It came out of a time when the animal people still had possession of the world. Then, they were the keepers of all sacred things.

"Wallows are shallow depressions in the earth that were made by most animals when they rolled around there and lay down. Several large ones are still visible today. They usually surround water holes or later become them because of the shallow bowls they eventually form. Today most of them, of course, are gone. They have either blown away, or towns or other things sit on top of them.

"The marshy areas that the wallows were, or became, often dried up as the summer days grew hot and long. Each, in turn, disappeared. Some time ago, there was one large wallow with water, a buffalo wallow, left. All the others had turned to dust. It was a precious thing to all life then, especially to a stranded or lost human being. One day, there appeared on the horizon of that sacred place a lost woman, on foot and traveling alone. The buffalo people stood up one by one when they saw her approach. They saw her stumble and fall from either weakness or illness, and the searing heat of the sun. Near the wallow, she collapsed and failed to rise again. One of the old buffalo bulls told two younger ones to go to her aid.

The young bulls trotted through the evaporating marsh to the ailing woman. Behind them, where their hooves sunk into the marsh, pools of water began to gurgle and bubble up. They trotted around the stranger in circles until she lay in a dirty pool of water, but she was cooled and revived. Afterward, she received more help from the buffalo people and then was able to travel on. She took the name Buffalo Wallow Woman out of humility to the buffalo people and the spirit of the wallow who gave her humility and gratitude, as well as her life. These were the lessons she had learned in the hands of the buffalo people."

Tina expected more. I promised, "Tomorrow I'll finish if you still want to know."

The next day she arrived in the afternoon and brought with her a dark green leaf of Indian tobacco and a small red tin ashtray. She lit the tobacco and burned it in the tray. The odor of that one small curled leaf filled the mental ward, but it was not enough to take away all the pain and fears contained on this floor. She hid the tray in the drawer just before another nurse popped in the room to ask what was burning.

Tina shrugged her shoulders and winked at me. "Would you mind if I called you something other than Mrs. Smith or Buffalo Wallow Woman? Where I come from we don't call each other by such names. One seems too formal and the other too sacred. Would I offend you if I called you Grandmother?" she asked politely.

I gazed at her with admiration and answered, "That would not offend me, my child. That would honor me. And if this is your plan and decision, then I must call you Grandchild, if that's the way it is to be."

Tina offered her hand to me and I took it. This is the way we joined forces. When her schedule permitted, I resumed my story.

"Buffalo Wallow Woman died in the year of the great smallpox epidemic, near the very place she had been saved as a younger woman. This time, she and others who were sick isolated themselves from the remainder of the people and, therefore, did not receive formal burials.

"As a young girl of perhaps eleven or twelve winters, I visited this place unexpectedly. At the time I didn't know who Buffalo Wallow Woman was or her story. I had been traveling by wagon with my family through an unfamiliar stretch of open plains country that was partly frozen but was beginning to thaw in a sudden burst of sunshine. When the wagon became bogged down in deep gray clay, the men got off to dig out the back wheels. I, too, climbed off and noticed a place to the side of the wagon trail that tugged at me. It was a very large shallow pool covered with ice. Its size was perhaps half a city block. Birds were soaring overhead and chirping at me. I watched them dip toward the frozen pool and fly away in flocks. Soon my family had dug out the wagon and were ready to leave. By evening we had reached our destination, and I thought that I had already put the shallow pool out of my mind.

"But that night I dreamed of it. I saw it in all the four seasons. There were buffalo at the pool's edges, and their reflections were in the water with the clouds and sky. Other animals were also there, such as bears, deer, and all species of birds.

"Every night I dreamed of the pool, and it seemed to be speaking to me. Then one night, Buffalo Wallow Woman visited me in my dreams and in a mysterious way told me who she was and what had happened there. She said that she had not died after all, and that in another world she had learned that she never would. She said this was all true and because it was, our people had never lied to us. They understood everything all along.

"She told me that it was an old spirit who had called me to the watering hole, the same spirit that guided her there each time she was close to death, and for this reason, she and I were tied together by it. The same spirit had called the buffalo people, the bird people, and all the others who came to drink, because that spirit made no distinction between the life of a buffalo, a cloud, a mountain, a stone, or a human being. It was the same indescribable force, no matter what form it took.

"At my tender age, it was truly remarkable that I actually understood what Buffalo Wallow Woman said. It was wonderful that I understood she had claimed some invisible part of me, and I claimed some part of her, and I accepted our relationship without question. I could not understand with my head, thought. I grasped it at the level of and at the center of my heart. I understood that I had been thirsty but didn't know it myself, and I had gone to the wallow so that my soul might drink. The spirit of the wallow knew me better than I knew myself."

Tina didn't press for more right then. She was quiet, staring outside at the evening sky. The room was quiet. We didn't speak about me again for several days. Then she came into the room and sat down without a word. She waited for me to continue.

"All my life, I have been told by the white man that I am crazy, my child," I picked up where I left off, "because I see things that other people do not. I hear voices that no one else does. But the craziest thing I do, they tell me, is take these visions and voices seriously. This is the way of all Buffalo Wallow Women, I suppose. I structure my life around the visions and voices because it pleases me to honor them this way. I am never alone because of this. It is my inheritance from Buffalo Wallow Woman, from my own flesh and blood, from the visions I have received, and from my identity as this kind of person.

"But each day the doctor asks me if I know who I am, and I have to bear this outrage. He also asks me if I know where I am. He talks about 'reality.' He tells me to face it, that this is, after all, a new time which has no room for Buffalo Wallow Woman. His questions, pretensions, and arrogance are ludicrous to me. I feel that he is more ill than I am. I am Buffalo Wallow Woman! Wherever I go, the spirits go with me.

"I am suspect and feared because I admit that I am a ghost. This is dangerous, I am told. It is the one thing the doctors have said that I know to be true. I *am* dangerous. I am dangerous because my craziness may spread from me to another and on and on. I am dangerous because I still have some rage left about what's happened to me over the years. It's not entirely squelched yet, although I've tried to empty it out of me. This surprises even me at the moment. And I am dangerous because I have great destructive powers within me that I haven't used yet.

"For instance, I can kill with my eyes if I so desire. I can shoot out poison and make my victims squirm with agony. There's all kinds of poisons for this, but most come from pure hate. I can use words in incantations that will steal the soul, the spirit, the will, and the mind away."

Tina looked at me mischievously. Before she could speak, I said, "Now don't say a word until you walk through this ward, look closely at every patient, and are able to explain how they became that way!"

We ended here, and Tina left. That night, lying in the dark, I decided to ask Tina to help me escape this unbearable indignity of forced confinement. A few days passed before I voiced my question.

I said, "Tina, my child, I am going to escape from here, I am going to fly away. When the time comes, I would like you to be there, to help me at the very last."

Tina replied, "If you're a ghost, why can't you just go?"

"It's not that easy. Some earthly person has to release me, you see."

She stood at the window staring at the iron bars. She turned around and asked, "You can really do it?"

I nodded.

She took a deep breath and crossed her heart like a small child. "Okay," was all she said.

Now that the time is here, Tina seems reluctant to have me leave. She's had weeks to prepare, but her eyes are actually moist and red.

"Tell me I am doing the right thing," she says. "I mean, you're my patient, what am I doing?"

She is panicky. She flutters all around.

"You and I, my child, are more than patient and nurse, much more than that. Don't make our kinship so small, so insignificant. This is the stuff that links the whole chain of life together, old to young, grandchild to grandmother, and on and on."

It is dark outside. Not even the bars on the window can be seen. I climb off the bed. My nightgown floats loosely around me.

Tina is watching me. She has a large brown sack with her. When she speaks, her voice is calm. "I brought everything you asked of me, and something that I thought of myself." She takes out a thin red flannel blanket from her package, folds it in half, and puts it at the foot of the bed. "This is for you," she says.

"Thank you, my child," I answer, touched by her thoughtfulness. I pick up the blanket and hold it to my heart.

"What do you want me to do?" she asks. I see her hesitate before she moves.

I lift the blanket and ask her to lay it on the floor.

"Sit here." I point to one end of the blanket. She takes her sack with her. I sit down at the other end.

"Now," I say, "I want to speak to you before I leave. Please, child, put those things between us."

Tina lays out a pouch of green tobacco and cigarette papers, and the red ashtray. She puts a beaded butane lighter inside the tray.

I ask her to turn out the fluorescent lights over us. Only a soft light comes from the bathroom. The door to it is half closed. Then I ask her to take my hair down and pull off my shoes.

We sit together in silence for a long time, gathering our thoughts together for the last thing we are about to do for one another.

Finally, I am ready. I say, "My child, you are the answer to a prayer, the prayer of Buffalo Wallow Woman. To find you in a place like this is very sweet to someone like me. I feel a stab of victory for Buffalo Wallow Woman, for though she is a ghost, you are alive and are as strong and thoughtful as she has ever been.

"You came to me with open arms and received a ghost in them, and you did not flinch at anything I said. All of it you took in, in your strong, gentle way. You have been taught well. I have told you everything—good things, ugly things, sacred things, and unholy things. We have even sung together. You have given me honor and respect in a way that only kin can pay. In exchange for that, kin to kin, grandmother to grandchild, I want to include you in my prayer tonight.

"Everything I have told you these last few weeks is the truth, you know. Sometimes we ghosts are full of rage and anger, such as I have been at certain times, but the ghost of Buffalo Wallow Woman can only speak the truth, even when it hurts, as it sometimes does.

"Anyway, I thank you, child, for the honor you have brought me, by listening to me, by singing with me, by calling me your grandmother, by praying for me tonight, and by setting me free.

"I have spent a lifetime in and out of this insane place that the doctors call reality, or the real world. I have spent a lifetime waiting to be set free, because no one else but you could do it for me. This is what we mean to each other. This is what life means.

"These are my parting words to you, my child. Do you wish to say anything?"

Tina nods her head. I can almost hear the movements. The spirit people have come into the room. They surround us.

"You don't understand," she says. "I'm not what you want me to be. I have flaws. I went to school. I can't speak my language because of this. I don't want to live in poverty the way my family does. I'm weak, and worst of all, I'm not very spiritual."

She pauses, threatening to break into tears.

"And I agreed to this because I thought you would change your mind. I didn't think you would really go through with it. I never thought I would actually be here right now."

"But you are here," I answer. "You are here with the ghost of Buffalo Wallow Woman. Most of us never know what we will do at a certain moment until that moment arrives. Then we know. Do you have doubts now?"

"Not doubts," she says, "but lots of sadness."

"This is not a bad thing, Tina," I say. "Soon you will feel like singing out, *Hey yah hah O!*" I say. "I promise you that you will feel it in you."

I pick up a cigarette paper and the Indian tobacco and begin to roll a smoke. I give it to Tina. I say, "When I have gone, you must light the smoke, then blow a puff to the earth and sky and then to the four directions. Then you must say in a clear voice, 'I offer this smoke for the spirit of my grandmother, Buffalo Wallow Woman. May she be forever at peace and may she forever live in nature all around me.' You must say this, Tina, not only think it."

The spirit people make noises all around me. Some of them are in the darkness, others are in the light.

Tina is flustered, but she acknowledges my directions.

I close my eyes and begin my prayer. "O Mystery of Life! The time has come for Buffalo Wallow Woman to depart," I say to the spirits in the room, the spirits that follow me everywhere. They agree with my words. Their voices answer *Yes* in chorus. I continue. "I want to leave this world without anger or hate, for in this final moment, I want none of that to remain. I leave this world to my grandchild sitting here. May she love it and care for it as much as her elders did. My final requests are that you spirits accept me and take me home, and that in my departure, you watch over my grandchild here."

My heart flaps against my breastbone. I feel it pause, flutter, and thump my breastbone again. I open my eyes. The room is cold. The spirits are everywhere. There are deer people, buffalo people, and cloud beings—so much life in one little room! They chant and sing.

I am strangely weightless and transparent. I feel myself break up into a fine, wet mist. Then, I am looking down from the ceiling. Tina sits alone. I see my body lying across the floor, a bag of old bones and long wild white hair.

Tina is holding the smoke. Her hand shakes violently. She looks up at the ceiling, takes a deep breath, and steadies herself. She picks up the beaded butane lighter and lights the sacred smoke. She tries to speak. Her words are timid and frightened. She clears her throat and starts again.

She says it all perfectly, word for word. The spirits answer joyfully, *Yes! Yes!* They turn to me and say, *Buffalo Wallow Woman, now you are free. No bars shall ever hold you again.*

The spirits guide me to the window, but now it is my turn to hesitate. I look back at Tina, my grandchild. She is sitting there all alone. She looks troubled and sad.

We'll always be here, the spirits say, and I nod. Then, as we begin to slip through the bars, I hear little Tina sing, *"Hey yah hah O!"*

Beth Cuthand

CREE

She Ties Her Bandanna

She ties her bandanna
swiftly, surely
tightly around her head
containing
all the images, thoughts
and doubts
assailing her.

Act of resistance

It is spring.
Soon the thunderers
will come
out of the west
they will come
      wrapped in their mysteries
      cloaked in mist.

Where are the others?
They
    who tie their bandannas
    tightly
Do their eyes

ache in the last light of the sun?
Do they fear their racing thoughts?
their memories, their dreams?

She remembers
    a blond-haired, blue-eyed suitor
    saying
"The prairies make mystics of us all."
    and his naive desire to impress her
    with his sensitivity
    and his innocent expectation
    that by loving her
    he too
    could become "Indian"

But that was long ago
so long ago
it feels like a dream
now
She is alone
and has been for some time
Sometimes she feels

like she has always been alone
and always will be.

Like all the widows
    of all the wars
like all the sisters
    and mothers and grandmothers
who have reason to grieve
    she keens; wildly tenderly

She remembers
    her sons' father
    dying of alcoholism

"I just got out of the psych ward.
I guess I went over the edge again.
I'm doing a lot of hunting
They say I don't drink so much
when I'm in the bush.
I'm saving money to come
and see my boys.
Please don't tell them.
I don't want them to get
disappointed."

She remembers
    the old man she met
    in old town
"You look just like my baby
    my baby   my baby
I didn't mean to hurt her
    I was drunk
    I was lonely.
    I didn't know what I was doing.

Will you forgive me?"

She remembers
    mothers in the bars and children
    eating pop and chips in the lobby.
"That's me, the little fat kid in ragged shoes.
That little one, beside me, under my arm
that's my deceased sister.
And that's my brother.
He's doing 5 to 10 in Walla Walla.
My sister? She o.d.'d in Van
She was seventeen.
Cops said she o.d.'d
I know her pimp did it.
He knows I'll get him.

Sometime   somewhere
I'll get him."

She remembers
    her cousin's blood
    dried on the door of his truck
    dried on the floor of her auntie's house
his blood
    melting the ground
    while three drug-crazed relatives
    danced wildly in the snow.

She remembers
    taking 24 tranquilizers
    singing her death song
    thinking her sons would
    be better off without her
    hearing her Grandfather Josie
    saying
    "Get up my girl.
    It's not your time to die."

So she lives
holding on to life; a newborn baby
feeding it, caring for it
tenaciously like a mother bear.

Like all widows before her
she grieves in order to live,
to live a life so full of life
that grief will not kill it.

Her head throbs rhythmically
under and around the tightness
of the bandanna.
She must remember the thunderers

They are awakening
They are coming
seeking the ones like her
who tie bandannas around their heads
and pray for strength
to birth the healing rain
so the people will live.

Hey yah ho
megwitche

Suzan Shown Harjo

CHEYENNE ▪ MUSCOGEE

My *Cheyenne mother and grandparents and my Muscogee father and grandparents all raised me to listen to others and to read for meaning, intent, and truth, to understand the difference, to trust only when I found no difference. They encouraged me to always be prepared to speak—which I thought was style and skill and later understood meant clarity of history, position, and belief.*

My father taught me how to hunt, swim, dance, and sing, and praised me when I excelled. My mother taught me how to write and, most important, listened to my work and told me when it touched her or taught her or made her stronger.

My parents also taught me to give the right answers in school, having learned themselves to be orderly and correct in government boarding schools. Early on, I insisted on the truth, rather than the right answer, and called my second-grade teacher a liar for his version of the Battle of Little Big Horn, where my great-great-great-grandfather was as both Cheyenne Peace and Dog Soldier Chief.

While I was right to set right our family history, I still got pushed out of a second-story window onto a rosebush (an accident, said the very white man teacher, who did not get fired until the next year when he dislocated the shoulder of a white boy).

That's how it was in the Oklahoma hills where I was born and raised. That and other abusive experiences were balanced on the side of sanity and safety by the strength of my relatives, the power of who our peoples were and would be, the magic of our medicines and ceremonies, and words that defied translation.

The Song Called "White Antelope's Chant"

White Antelope had a song
        it was a Tsistsistas song
        it was his song
        because he sang it

Clouding Woman had a song
        it was a Tsistsistas song
        it was her song
        because she sang it

Buffalo Walla had a song
        it was a Tsistsistas song
        it was her song
        because she sang it

Bull Bear had a song
        it was a Tsistsistas song
        it was his song
        because he sang it

The Song that sang itself
                had a Tsistsistas sound
                and a truth for all who heard it
                at the hour of the end

The Song that sang itself
                had no language
                it was a heartbeat that thundered
                through the canyons of time

The Song that sang itself
                had no chorus
                its voice was the Morning Star
                and the rain at the edge of time

The Song that sang itself
                had no time
                knew no season
                it sounded with the power of the end

The Song sang a Tsistsistas Man
                in the prayers in the sun
                in the sighs on the wind
                in the power of the end

The Song sang a Tsistsistas Woman
                in the offerings at dawn
                in the sighs of the wind
                in the power of the end

The Song sang a Tsistsistas Child
                in the cries in the night
                in the sighs in the wind
                in the power of the end

The Song sang a Tsistsistas sound
　　in the peace before dark
　　in the sighs on the wind
　　in the power of the end

Only Mother Earth endures
　　sang the man

Only Mother Earth endures
　　sang the woman

Only Mother Earth endures
　　sang the child

Only Mother Earth endures
　　sang the song

Only Mother Earth endures

Joy Harjo

MUSCOGEE

Perhaps the World Ends Here

The world begins at a kitchen table. No matter what,
we must eat to live.

The gifts of earth are brought and prepared, set on the
table. So it has been since creation, and it will go on.

We chase chickens or dogs away from it. Babies teethe
at the corners. They scrape their knees under it.

It is here that children are given instructions on what
it means to be human. We make men at it,
we make women.

At this table we gossip, recall enemies and the ghosts
of lovers.

Our dreams drink coffee with us as they put their arms
around our children. They laugh with us at our poor
falling-down selves and as we put ourselves back
together once again at the table.

This table has been a house in the rain, an umbrella
in the sun.

Wars have begun and ended at this table. It is a place
to hide in the shadow of terror. A place to celebrate
the terrible victory.

We have given birth on this table, and have prepared
our parents for burial here.

At this table we sing with joy, with sorrow.
We pray of suffering and remorse.
We give thanks.

Perhaps the world will end at the kitchen table,
while we are laughing and crying,
eating of the last sweet bite.

Contributors' Notes

PAULA GUNN ALLEN's most recent book of poetry is *Life Is a Fatal Disease, Collected Poems 1962–1995*. She has also recently published *Song of the Turtle, American Indian Literature 1974–1995* and *As Long as the River Shall Flow: Ten Indian Biographies*, with Patricia Clark Smith.

JEANNETTE ARMSTRONG resides on the Penticton Indian Reservation. A fluent speaker of the Okanagan language, she has studied under some of the most knowledgeable elders of the Okanagan. She has published a critically acclaimed novel, *Slash*, and a collection of poetry, *Breath Tracks*.

MARILOU AWIAKTA is the author of *Abiding Appalachia: Where Mountain and Atom Meet, Rising Fawn and the Fire Mystery*, and *Selu: Seeking the Corn-Mother's Wisdom*, which is also on audiocassette.

LUCI BEACH resides in Fairbanks, Alaska, with her son, Sean, and his father, Richard Seeganna. She works with single parents and displaced home-makers and is trying against many obstacles to finish her master's degree.

MARGARET BEHAN is known regionally in the Southwest as a storyteller doll maker. She graduated from the Institute of American Indian Arts in 1996, where she majored in creative writing. She lives in San Juan Pueblo, New Mexico. She is currently working on a documentary film, *Alcoholic Native American Women Bonding with Their Children*.

BETTY LOUISE BELL is an assistant professor of English, Women's Studies, and American Culture at the University of Michigan, where she also serves as the director of the Native American Studies Program. Her first novel,

Faces of the Moon, was published by the University of Oklahoma Press in 1994. Currently, she is working on a critical text on Native American women writers.

SALLI M. K. BENEDICT is the editor of *Akwesasne Notes* and is technician for the Mohawk land claims office at Akwesasne.

MARLA BIG BOY writes that "I Will Bring You Twin Grays" is dedicated to Native American women who seek the strength to overcome the obstacles that hold them down.

GLORIA BIRD is an enrolled member of the Spokane Tribe of Washington State. She is the author of *Full Moon on the Reservation*, winner of the Diane Decorah First Book Award, and a forthcoming chapbook, *The River of History* from Trask House Press. She is contributing editor of *Wicazo Sa Review* and lives in Spokane, Washington.

KIMBERLY BLAESER grew up on the White Earth Reservation. Currently an associate professor in the English and Comparative Literature Department at the University of Wisconsin–Milwaukee, she teaches twentieth-century American literature, including courses in Native American literature and American nature writing. Blaeser's publications include poetry, short fiction, personal essays, journalism, and scholarly articles. Her poetry collection, *Trailing You*, won the 1993 Native Writers' Circle of the Americas First Book Award, and her book *Gerald Vizenor: Writing in the Oral Tradition* is forthcoming from the University of Oklahoma Press.

GRACE BOYNE is completing her Ph.D. on intellectual/cultural property at the University of Arizona and working on publications dealing with narrative analysis and the use of sacred materials in literature.

CAROLYN BRANDY released a CD of original music in September 1995 called *Skin Talk*. It includes a passionate song, "Grandma's Voice," inspired by finding her father. Her story "Heartbeat of the Ancestors" was commissioned by Redwood Cultural Work.

BETH BRANT is the author of *Mohawk Trail*, *Food & Spirits*, and *Writing as Witness*. She is the editor of *A Gathering of Spirit* and *I'll Sing Till the Day I Die: Conversations with Tyendinaga Elders*.

MARY BRAVE BIRD lives with her family on the reservation in Rosebud, South Dakota. Her memoir *Lakota Woman* was made into a movie by Turner Productions.

HELEN CHALAKEE BURGESS saw one of her roles as an Indian journalist as interpreting national policy-making so that Creek people might understand and relate to policy consequences. She is thrilled now to be a part of the nationalistic effort to "reinvent the enemy's language."

KIM CALDWELL is a poet/writer/musician whose poetry and fiction have been anthologized in the United States and Canada, most recently in *For She Is the Tree of Life, Reclaiming the Vision,* and *Blue Dawn, Red Earth.* She is a regular contributor to *News from Indian Country.* Her work has been included in *Raven Chronicles, The Bloomsbury Review,* and *Indigenous Woman.* She serves on the National Advisory Caucus of the Wordcraft Circle of Native Writers and Storytellers. Her children's book, *Bear,* was published by Scholastic in 1996.

GLADYS CARDIFF, of the eastern band of Cherokee/English/Irish/Welsh descent, is an English doctoral student at Western Michigan University. Her poems have been published in numerous anthologies and textbooks, including *Harper's Anthology of 20th Century Native American Poetry.* She is currently poetry editor of *Third Coast,* a literary journal.

CHRYSTOS was born and raised off-reservation of a Menominee father and her mother's family from Alsace-Lorraine and Lithuania. Her books include *Not Vanishing, Dream On, In Her I Am, Fugitive Colors,* and *Fire Power.*

A. A. HEDGE COKE's collection of poetry, *Look at This Blue,* was published by Coffee House Press. Her poetry and prose have appeared in *13th Moon, Voices of Thunder, American Fiction, Caliban,* and many other magazines and journals.

KATSI COOK is a midwife and women's health specialist from the Mohawk Nation at Akwesasne. She is currently a Visiting Fellow at Cornell University.

ELIZABETH COOK-LYNN is professor emerita in the English and Native Studies Department at Eastern Washington University, Cheney. Her permanent home is in Rapid City, South Dakota. She is the founder and continuing editor of *The Wicazao Sa Review,* a native studies journal since 1985. Publications include a collection of essays titled *Why I Can't Read Wallace Stegner: A Tribal Voice, From The River's Edge, The Power of Horses, Then Badger Said This,* and *Seek the House of Relatives.* A nonfiction manuscript called *The Politics of Hallowed Ground,* a collaborative work with Oglala attorney Mario Gonzales, is forthcoming from the University of Illinois Press, and *I Remember the Fallen Trees* from Eastern Washington University Press. Her novel *Circle of Dancers,* a sequel, is still looking for a publisher.

BETH CUTHAND has earned a B.A. in sociology from the University of Saskatchewan and an M.F.A. in creative writing from the University of Arizona. Her most recent collection of poetry, *Voices in the Waterfall*, was published by Theytus Books.

NORA MARKS DAUENHAUER's first language is Tlingit. After raising four children, she received a B.A. degree in anthropology. She is Principal Researcher at Sealaska Heritage Foundation in Juneau, where she lives with her husband, Richard. She has twelve grandchildren and one great-grandson.

CAROLYN MARIE DUNN was born in Los Angeles in 1965. She has been a radio producer, television programmer, media adviser, production assistant, a university researcher and has taught Native American women's literature.

DEBRA EARLING is a member of the Confederated Salish and Kootenai Tribes of the Flathead Reservation in Montana. Her recent publications include *Ploughshares* and *The Best of Northern Lights*. She is forthcoming in *Song of the Turtle II*. She holds a joint appointment in Native American Studies and English at the University of Montana.

ANITA ENDREZZE's book of short stories, *The Humming of Stars and Bees and Waves*, will be published by Eastern Washington University Press.

LOUISE ERDRICH has written several acclaimed novels, including *Love Medicine*, winner of the National Book Critics Circle Award, *Tracks*, and her most recent, *Tales of Burning Love*.

JENNIFER PIERCE EYEN's poetry has appeared in magazines, tribal newspapers, and a special anthology, *The Cornfield Review*. She has published two children's books and is currently completing a collection of poems entitled *River Girl*, and is a local writer-in-residence for Thurber House in Columbus, Ohio.

CONNIE FIFE works at the Urban Native Youth Association in Vancouver, British Columbia, and is the author of *Beneath the Naked Sun* and editor of *The Color of Resistance*. Forthcoming is *Speaking through Jagged Rock*, a book of poetry.

ARLENE FIRE writes, "Being able to contribute to this anthology is my way of saying 'Thank you.'"

MARY GOOSE is currently living in Des Moines, Iowa, with her son, Lucas Wyatt Small Legs Goose.

JANICE GOULD is a member of the Maidu Tribe of northern California. She is working on a doctoral degree in English, with a focus on American Indian literature, at the University of New Mexico.

CATRON GRIEVES teaches ethnography, poetry, and creative writing in schools and communities in the American Midwest. Publications include two books of poetry, *Moon Rising* and *A Terrible Foe This Bear*. Individual poems have appeared in *New Plains Review* and *The Iowa Review*, and short fiction in *Aniyunwiya/Real Human Beings: An Anthology of Contemporary Cherokee Prose*.

JANET CAMPBELL HALE is a tribal member living on the reservation in De-Smet, Idaho. She is the author of *The Owl's Song*, *The Jailing of Cecelia Capture*, and *Odyssey of a Native Daughter*.

LOUISE BERNICE HALFE's first book of poetry is *Bear Bones and Feathers*. She has also appeared in *Writing the Circle: Native Women of Western Canada*. She was born and raised on the Saddle Lake Reserve in Alberta and lives in Saskatoon with her husband and two children.

DANA NAONE HALL lives on the island of Maui where she is actively involved in Native Hawaiian and public interest issues.

JOY HARJO's most recent book of poetry is *The Woman Who Fell from the Sky*. She has also released a CD with her band Poetic Justice, *Letter from the End of the Twentieth Century*, from Silver Wave Records.

SUZAN SHOWN HARJO, president of the Morning Star Institute in Washington, D.C., is a poet, writer, lecturer, and curator who has developed federal Indian policy in areas including religious/cultural rights, repatriation, land protection, and establishment of the national Museum of the American Indian, of which she is founding trustee. She is the mother of a grown daughter and son.

INÉS HERNÁNDEZ-ÁVILA is associate professor and chair of the Department of Native American Studies at the University of California, Davis. Her fields of interest include Native American "womanisms" and literary/cultural studies, from a Native American Studies and Chicana/o Studies disciplinary perspective. She is a poet, fiction writer, essayist, and scholar.

ROBERTA HILL's first collection of poetry, *Star Quilt*, and her second collection, *Philadelphia Flowers*, are available from Holy Cow! Press. Recent poems will appear in *Pemmican #5*. Her story "Summer Girl" is included in *Talking Leaves*, edited by Craig Lesley. She previously published as Roberta Hill Whiteman.

LINDA HOGAN's most recent books are *The Book of Medicines, Dwellings: A Spiritual History of the Living World*, and the novel *Solar Storms*.

LEANNE HOWE's *The Sewage of Foreigners*, a Choctaw women's history, was published by the University of Oklahoma Press in 1996. She is a writer, playwright, director, and producer of plays, films, and radio programs.

ROSEMARY M. HUGGINS is living in Hoquiam, Washington, and is working as a vocational rehabilitation counselor. She does volunteer work for various reservations for sexual abuse survivors.

NORA YAZZIE HUNTER lives in Albuquerque, New Mexico, with her family. She graduated from the creative writing program at the University of New Mexico and is working on a collection of poetry. She is also a maker of fine clay sculptures.

JOSEPHINE HUNTINGTON was born in Tanana, Alaska, in 1946. Her hometown was Huslia in interior Alaska. She was educated at the University of Hawaii and the University of Alaska.

JEANE JACOBS is a writer, speaker, teacher, and healer who has been involved with several indigenous groups as an organizer, activist, and leader. Her writing has been published in several magazines, anthologies, and newspapers, including the *Los Angeles Times* and *Indivisible*.

SONLATSA JIM-JAMES writes, "Currently I am doing grassroots activist work in my hometown communities of Toh-la-kai and Tohatchi, New Mexico. I develop and promote community-based projects to help empower Navajo children, youth, parents, and elders through the national Indian Youth Leadership Project. I am in the process of writing a life story of my childhood up to my college experiences and coming home. I will be submitting a short fictional piece called 'Coyote and Cougar' for publication in the near future which deals with domestic violence and a native family. I will be going to graduate school at the University of Denver in their master's degree program in American Indian Studies."

RITA JOE has four books currently on the market: *Poems of Rita Joe, Song of Eskasoni, Lnu,* and *Indians We're Called*. She has also written a textbook for women's studies entitled *Kelusultiek*, meaning "We Speak."

WINONA LADUKE is of the Bear Clan, Mississippi Band, Anishinabeg. She is living and working on the White Earth Reservation on land recovery and environmental restoration. She recently ran for vice president of the United States for the Green Party.

YVONNE LAMORE-CHOATE writes, "My story is only one of many stories Native Americans of my generation share, a special story about our beloved grandmothers and the experiences of growing up on the reservation."

EMMA LAROCQUE, a Plains Cree Metis, is originally from northeastern Alberta. She is a writer, poet, historian, social and literary critic, and a professor in the Department of Native Studies at the University of Manitoba. For more than two decades she has lectured both nationally and internationally on issues of human rights, focusing on native history, colonization, literature, education, and identity. She is the author of *Defeathering the Indian: Three Conventional Approaches to Native People in Society and in Literature* and numerous articles on colonization, Canadian historiography, native literature, racism, and violence against women. Her poetry has appeared in several national and international journals and anthologies.

ALICE LEE's work has been published in *New Bread* (Saskatchewan) and *Sanscrit* (University of Calgary literary magazine). Six of her poems and one short story will be featured in an upcoming anthology: *Writings of Western Canadian Native Women*. Her poetry has been broadcast on the CBS programs *Ambience* and *Homestretch*.

BERENICE LEVCHUK received Canadian and U.S. poetry awards for *Government Boarding School* and *Navaho Blessingway Wedding*. She has published work in *Fireweed* and other magazines.

WILMA MANKILLER served as Principal Chief of the Cherokee Nation in Oklahoma. She co-authored an autobiography with Michael Wallis, *Mankiller: A Chief and Her People*. She also co-edited with five other distinguished women *A Reader's Companion to the History of Women in the U.S.*

LEE MARACLE is the author of two novels, *Sundogs* and *Ravensong*, two nonfiction works, *Bobbi Lee* and *I Am Woman*, and a collection of short stories entitled *Sojourner's Truth*. She has published in over a dozen anthologies as well as numerous journals and magazines.

WILMA ELIZABETH MCDANIEL has lived away from Oklahoma for many years, but the origins of her poetry are beside Rock Bottom Creek.

JUNE MCGLASHAN is working on her first collection of poetry, to be called *The Snow That Melts The Snow*. Every year she teaches classes in poetry and Aleut history to students in Alaska.

BEATRICE MEDICINE is finishing up her book *An Ethnography of Drinking and Sobriety among the Lakota*, to be published by the University of Nebraska Press. She is collecting all her unpublished writings on women. She is also working on a book on contemporary Indian women's lives as well as a history of her own family.

TIFFANY MIDGE is the author of *Outlaws, Renegades and Saints*. She is also the author of a children's book titled *Animal Lore and Legend: Buffalo*. She currently lives in Seattle and is completing a novel.

DIAN MILLION is now living in Bellingham, Washington, working with Lummi, Nooksack, and Swinomish school districts on writing and history. She just finished an interdisciplinary-degree thesis at Western Washington University titled "Sovereignty."

SCOTT KAYLA MORRISON is an organizer of Indian communities on environmental issues. She graduated from the University of Iowa Law School and was the winner of the university's Phillip G. Hubbard Human Rights Award for her contributions to the Indian community. Her writing has been included in many anthologies and magazines.

NORA NARANJO-MORSE lives on the Santa Clara Pueblo Reservation. She has published a book of poetry, *Mud Woman: Poems from the Clay*. She is a renowned sculptor of clay and metal, and most recently has begun to work in video.

LINDA NOEL has published a chapbook entitled *Where You First Saw the Eyes of the Coyote*. Her work has appeared in the anthology *The Clouds Threw This Light* and in various small press publications.

NILA NORTHSUN has published many books of poetry, including her classic, *diet pepsi and nacho cheese* and a new book from West End Press, *a snake in her mouth*. She has stopped drinking and acting crazy, memoirs forthcoming.

ELISE PASCHEN's poems have appeared in *Poetry*, *The New Yorker*, *The New Republic*, and *The Nation*, as well as in the anthologies *A Formal Feeling Comes: Poems in Form by Contemporary Women* and *Unleashed*, among others. She is executive director of the Poetry Society of America and co-editor of *Poetry in Motion*. Her first book of poetry, *Infidelities*, received the 1996 Nicholas Roerich Poetry Prize and was published by Storyline in the fall of 1996.

INEZ PETERSEN writes, "Stories remind us of who we are and where we came from. They tell us how to be decent human beings in the world."

SUSAN POWER is an enrolled member of the Standing Rock Sioux Tribe and a native of Chicago. Her first novel, *The Grass Dancer*, was published in 1994 and is the winner of the 1995 PEN/Hemingway Award.

LOIS RED ELK is an award-winning actress (TNT's *Lakota Woman*, 1994), lives on the rez, does quillwork, and is a free-lance journalist.

MARCIE RENDON is a full-time mother, part-time writer of poetry, short stories, and plays, sometimes performance artist, and, recently, creator of art installation pieces.

ODILIA GALVÁN RODRÍGUEZ writes, "Words are powerful in any language. Learn yours and keep it alive; use it to unlock your ancestors' memories. Heal, thrive, be well and write!"

WENDY ROSE's most recent books are *Going to War with All My Relations*, *Bone Dance: New & Selected Poems*, and *Now Poof She Is Gone*. She is raising cacti and succulents, collecting dolls and figurines of female superheroes and villains, has been married twenty years to Arthur, and has a cat named "Nudge" who just moved in one day.

CAROL LEE SANCHEZ lives on a farm in rural Missouri and has recently published a chapbook of poems, *She Poems*, from Chicory Blue Press in Connecticut. She is teaching at State Fair Community College in Sedalia, Missouri.

LESLIE MARMON SILKO is the author of many novels, short stories, essays, poetry, articles, and filmstrips. Her works are classics in American literature. She also runs a publishing company, Flood Plain Press, and is a visionary painter. She lives in Tucson, Arizona.

DENISE SWEET is enrolled at White Earth and living in Green Bay. She teaches creative writing and American Indian studies at the University of Wisconsin–Green Bay. *Songs For Discharming*, her first book-length poetry manuscript, received the 1995 Diane Decorah Memorial Award from the Native Writer's Circle of the Americas.

MARY TALLMOUNTAIN published nine collections of stories and poems during her lifetime, including *Light on the Tent Wall*, *Quick Brush of Wings*, and *Listen to the Night*.

LUCI TAPAHANSO is an associate professor of English at the University of Kansas. She is the author of four books of poetry and two children's books.

DEBRA CALLING THUNDER is a journalist. She lives on the Wind River Indian Reservation in Wyoming. She has a son, Benjamin Noku.

LAURA TOHE is Tsenahabilnii (Sleepy Rock People clan) and born for the To'dich'iinii (Bitter Water clan). She is Diné (Navajo), was raised on the Diné Reservation, and currently teaches at Arizona State University.

DEBRA HAALAND TOYA is a member of the Pueblo of Laguna. She resides in Albuquerque, writes nonfiction, and nurtures her daughter Somah.

HAUNANI-KAY TRASK is the director of the Center for Hawaiian Studies at the University of Hawaii and a leader in the Native Hawaiian sovereignty struggle. Among her books are *Light in the Crevice Never Seen* and *Eros and Power: The Promise of Feminist Theory.*

GAIL TREMBLAY's last book of poems was *Indian Singing in 20th Century America* and she is widely anthologized. She is currently completing a new book of poems, exhibiting art nationally, and teaching at Evergreen State College in Olympia, Washington.

VELMA WALLIS is one of a family of thirteen children, all born in the vast fur-trapping country of Fort Yukon, Alaska, and raised with traditional Athabaskan values. A writer and avid reader, she continues to live outside Fort Yukon with her daughter.

ANNA LEE WALTERS lives and works on the Navajo Reservation. She is the author of *Talking Indian* and *The Sun Is Not Merciful.*

EMMA LEE WARRIOR lives in Calgary, Alberta. She is a counselor at the Calgary Women's Emergency Shelter and works at William Roper Hull Youth and Family Services. She is working on a novel.

RAMONA WILSON is very active in educational affairs in Oakland and the state of California. She is now assistant director for the Math, Engineering and Science Achievement-Success through Collaboration program in the state. She has also been working to help establish the American Indian Charter School in Oakland.

ELIZABETH WOODY lives in Portland, Oregon. She is the author of *Luminaries of the Humble: Seven Hands, Seven Hearts, Prose and Poetry.* She has been a professor of creative writing at the Institute of American Indian Arts in Santa Fe. She is currently writing essays, fiction, and new poems.

OFELIA ZEPEDA recently published a book of poetry, *Ocean Power*, from the Sun Tracks series of the University of Arizona Press. She also co-edited *Home Places: Contemporary Native American Writing* with Larry Evers, also from Sun Tracks.

Permissions

Index